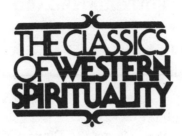

THE CLASSICS
OF WESTERN
SPIRITUALITY

THE CLASSICS OF WESTERN SPIRITUALITY
A Library of the Great Spiritual Masters

THE SHAKERS
TWO CENTURIES OF SPIRITUAL REFLECTION

EDITED, WITH AN INTRODUCTION BY
ROBLEY EDWARD WHITSON

PREFACE BY
GERTRUDE M. SOULE

PAULIST PRESS
NEW YORK ✦ RAMSEY ✦ TORONTO

Cover Art

An Emblem of the Heavenly Sphere. Hancock, 1854. Ink and water color. Courtesy of the Shaker Community, Inc., Hancock Shaker Village, Pittsfield, Mass.

9/0 2 gift

Library of Congress
Catalog Card Number: 83-80364

ISBN: 0-8091-2373-8 (paper)
      0-8091-0343-5 (cloth)

Published by Paulist Press
545 Island Road, Ramsey, N.J. 07446

Printed and bound in the
United States of America

Contents

Editor of this Volume

ROBLEY EDWARD WHITSON, after ordination and pastoral assignments in the New York Archdiocese, was Chairman of the Fordham University Theology Department. After appointment as Visiting Scholar at Princeton Theological Seminary and Advisory Board member for the Princeton world religions project, he was Professor of Theology and Anthropology at The Hartford Seminary Foundation. He is now President of The United Institute, an ecumenical body with special concern for the renewal of the Shaker tradition in the context of inter-Christian unity. He is the author of *Mysticism and Ecumenism, Shaker Theological Sources, The Coming Convergence of World Religions, The Center Scriptures: The Core Christian Experience,* and monographs on Shaker theology and spirituality.

Author of the Preface

After spending part of her childhood with the Shaker community at Sabbathday Lake, Maine, ELDRESS GERTRUDE SOULE entered the Society Covenant in 1915. She became community eldress in 1950, succeeding Eldress Prudence Stickney, with Elder Delmer Wilson as colleague. In 1955 she joined Eldress Emma King and Eldress Ida Cook in the Ministry (the Shaker collegial Episcopacy) governing the three remaining Societies of Canterbury, New Hampshire; Hancock, Massachusetts; and Sabbathday Lake, Maine. In 1965 she succeeded Eldress Emma King as Presiding Eldress of the United Society. She now resides at Canterbury with her colleague, Eldress Bertha Lindsay.

Acknowledgments

Over the years the libraries and archives of the United Societies at Canterbury and Sabbathday Lake have been made available for the textual research represented in the present work. Eldress Gertrude Soule of Sabbathday Lake and Eldress Bertha Lindsay of Canterbury have been most generous in opening these historic resources. I wish to acknowledge with gratitude this great sharing in the gifts from the past. I owe a special debt, happily paid, to Sister Mildred Barker for her many kindnesses and to all the Shaker Sisters of these latter days for their warmth and affection over the years.

In various ways the following institutions and members of their staffs have been helpful in locating sources: Case Memorial Library of Hartford Seminary Foundation, Western Reserve Historical Society, Connecticut Historical Society, New York Public Library, Philadelphia Museum of Fine Arts.

Two friends should be especially singled out for their contributions. Dr. John H. Morgan, former student and now colleague in The United Institute, has been a constant source of encouragement through his personal responsiveness to the potential of Shaker spirituality in the unfolding ecumenical context. Professor Ewert H. Cousins, so long a friend and academic colleague, has given most generously of his insight and time to the final shaping of the book, to assure both its continuity with the other volumes of the Classics of Western Spirituality series and its capacity to communicate something of the richness of the Shaker tradition.

For having given generously of their time and patience in helping to prepare this manuscript, I express my special gratitude to Sister Mary Elizabeth, SP, Grace Johnson and Kathryn Cousins.

The cover illustration has been made available by Hancock Shaker Community, Inc.; the kindness of John Ott, the executive director, and June Sprigg, curator, is gratefully acknowledged.

TO THE LATE SISTER AIDA ELAM who so kindly undertook to be my guide when I first "walked among Believers," sharing many hours as we searched the spirit of the past to understand the present and the possibilities for the future.

&

TO ELDRESS GERTRUDE SOULE AND ELDRESS BERTHA LINDSAY who have shared so much of themselves with me so simply, and who have had to bear the burdens of the Ministry at the closing of one season of gifts while trying to anticipate the next.

IN THE BLESSING SO OFTEN SHOUTED OUT BY
THE FIRST ELDERS:
Love! More Love!

FOREWORD

The Shakers is a theological presentation of Shaker spirituality. Only recently has there been any attempt to make Shaker writings and archives generally available through publication. This volume is the first instance of a substantive theological study of the sources. Since we are focusing specifically on spirituality, we cannot address the full range of religious concerns proper to Shakerism. But because the Shaker tradition is centered directly in religious experience (rather than on doctrine or practice—as we shall see, there is no Shaker *orthodoxy* or *orthopraxis*), concentration on spirituality is probably the most effective point of entry into the Shaker world.

Although the religious writings of many Shakers have been preserved in both published and manuscript form, it is not possible to look to any one writer to represent the tradition authoritatively. From the beginning Shakerism has excluded the possibility of any creed or confession as a test of faith, has never accepted the Scriptures or any other written formulation as a fixed source of revelation, and has not limited the revelatory process to any one era. Consequently no one individual or text can be proposed as the authentic Shaker statement. Therefore we must turn to a wide range of witnesses who speak to the ongoing development of Shaker insight if we are to arrive at a realistic vision of Shaker spirituality.

We shall draw texts from the several collections of personal testimonies by the original eye witnesses, which represent the oral tradition covering the foundational period 1747–1787. As compiled and published between ca. 1810 and 1850, these collections are inevitably quite uneven, portraying as they do the memories of many individuals attempting to reach back two and three generations to the original events. Between 1790 and 1856 a number of major theological works appeared. Especially noteworthy are Benjamin S. Youngs' *The Testimony of Christ's Second Appearing*, published in four editions (1808, 1810, 1823, 1856), and John Dunlavy's *The Manifesto, or A Declaration of the Doctrine and Practice of the Church of Christ*, published in two editions (1818, 1847). These are undoubtedly the most influential theological texts of the first half of the nineteenth century, and extended portions are treated throughout this study, together with a variety of other works of value in the sphere of spirituality.

In the second half of the nineteenth century the Shakers published a monthly journal, *The Shaker Manifesto*, which proves to be an extraordinarily rich resource, containing as it does hundreds of articles on religious themes by dozens of different writers over a period of thirty years. Many texts are drawn from this source. During the same period pamphlets, journals, and letters further augment the variety and number of witnesses. The last major Shaker publication, White and Taylor's *Shakerism: Its Meaning and Message*, appeared in 1905. In many ways it is a summary of the first century and a half. It also looks to the then uncertain future, during which the old Shaker communes have been forced to close one by one. Since White and Taylor, Shaker publications generally have been focused on the preservation of the historic culture of the passing communal villages. Religious publications, for the most part, have been confined to presentations of the communal period, in response to the interests of the visitors who come to Shaker villages as historic preservations.

As we shall see, especially in the concluding section of the book, Shakers have been looking beyond the experience of the past (however impressive that certainly has been) to a new unitive possibility of the future. It is to be hoped that this book can contribute to such a possibility, both by the openness of the approach to the values and dynamics of Shaker spirituality, and by the shared commitment to the ecumenical potential of the various Christian traditions together and to the encounter of Christianity with world religions.

PREFACE

The author of this inspired book has asked me to contribute a few words on behalf of all our beloved Shaker Brothers and Sisters. I feel honored to do so. As the last of the old communities become part of history it is important to look back upon the Gospel Path which so many have walked but even more important to look forward to the next opening of the Gospel.

In their everyday life Believers have labored with hands and hearts and minds in the glory of our Father Mother God by attending to every gift in its season and so enriching their own lives and those of countless others. Through their religious consecration they have always sought to share freely with all the spiritual tradition that is their heritage from Mother Ann and the Elders with her, and all the first Parents in the Gospel, and continuing down through the several thousand Believers over the last two hundred years. This Shaker heritage has its never-ceasing source in the true evangel which our beloved Jesus Christ taught, especially as witnessed in the Beatitudes: *Blessed are the poor in spirit, the meek, for theirs is heaven and earth.*

The sixteenth verse in the fifth chapter of St. Matthew's Gospel conveys the true meaning of the Shaker calling to witness the reality of the Christlife we all share: *Let your light so shine before men, that they will see your good works and glorify your Father which is in Heaven.* This light is the light of life, the life which is God, the God Who is Love: *to live in Love is to live in God.* This is the personal experience which makes each Shaker truly a Believer. We believe because we ourselves have seen. And we hope so to live that others will realize that they too

PREFACE

can see and so come to believe in the one and only Good News: *Christ in us, our hope of glory.*

We welcome this presentation of the Shaker Way with its hundreds of Shaker voices out of the past witnessing to the ever-unfolding meaning of travel in the Gospel. In these pages will be found the testimony of how Believers grew through the experience of Faith to seek and embrace all Truth as it is found. It is in this spirit that Shakers look to the future just now unfolding. Two hundred years ago Father James Whittaker preached the first public discourse which opened the Gospel in America. May this book of gifts help to open the Gospel in a new world committed to the unity of the Truth.

Gertrude M. Soule
Presiding Eldress, the Parent Ministry
Canterbury, New Hampshire
May 19, 1980

INTRODUCTION

The Shaker Way begins where other Christians expect the pilgrimage of Faith will one day end: the Second Coming of Christ in Glory. For the "people called Shakers" are those who themselves have experienced the fullness of Christ present once for all, come again in that inmost Glory of God which is the Power to transform those who see it into the very Reality they behold (2 Cor. 3:18). They experience and recognize the Mystery *Christ-in-us our hope of Glory* (Col. 1:27), a hope they are convinced is already fulfilled. And therefore their Way of Life in Christ is one which seeks to be a progressive unfoldment of the never to be withdrawn Presence as they *travel from gift to Gift and glory to Glory.*

The Shaker tradition is one of fully realized eschatology: the *parousia,* Christ's Second Appearing, is experienced not as an isolated historic event to take place "at the end of time," but as the ongoing reality of Christ in complete Union in-through-with all who receive him. This realization embodies implications for religious commitment and spirituality which Shakers have sought to flesh out in daily life for more than two centuries.

The Shaker Way is essentially a mystical tradition, for everyone who *believes* does so because each has personally *experienced* the unitive Christ Presence. It is a practical mysticism, for to accept the fact of true unity in Christ—*now the life you live is hidden with Christ within God* (Col. 3:3)—calls for a fundamental transformation: turn from the narrowness of individual self to the Union of all of us together in the

1

INTRODUCTION

One Christ in whom there is *neither Jew nor Greek, slave nor free, male nor female* (Gal. 3:28). And it is practical in being open to all, the young and the old, the inexperienced and the wise, those with many gifts and those with but few, for God-in-Christ comes to absolutely everyone, totally Self-given to be our One Life.

The Shaker Way is one of gift, *charism*, beginning and ending with what is ultimately the Only Gift, God Himself, but including all the myriads of great and small gifts which flow ceaselessly into lives lived in the Spirit. The process of learning to recognize gifts, relate them to one another, cultivate the more significant, and mature in living gifted lives underlies the essence of Shaker spirituality: simplicity. Many early Shakers literally *shook* with the excitement of the Gift of the Spirit welling up within them and overflowing in their wonder and delight; as they grew to maturity in this life of gifts they came to prefer those whose currents run deeper, within the great quiet of the Love Who is God.[1]

The Shaker Way is one of persons and communities of persons. The Christ Presence in the Spirit Life of gifts is actually experienced, and therefore experienced by actual persons. It is not an abstract doctrine or expectation for the future, and therefore the unique reality of each person is absolutely valuable. As each experiences Christ unitively, the presence of everyone else in Christ becomes inescapable. As it is the same Love which makes all One in Christ, each recognizes the call and desire to reach out and share life together. This life is, thus, an open-ended process constantly moving and growing through the enrichment of very differently gifted people. If those who live it are faithful to their sharing together, they will manifest what Shakers refer to as *eternal progression*.

The Shaker Way is personally historical, that is, always concretely embodied in the real people who are the *experiencers*. It is not a structure or a doctrine, but all its often complex structures and doctrines reflect the creative light of the persons experiencing—in the simplicity of an old Shaker saying: ideas don't have people, people have ideas. The Shaker tradition, therefore, is not static but dynamic. There is no normativeness in any established form or formulation, for all such merely bear witness to the level of development and insight

---

1. See Section Five, text 36, p. 302, Eldress Anna White's "Shakers are thinkers."

2

INTRODUCTION

reached at that moment.[2] The norm is to be found in the total living community-of-experience in its continuum of ongoing development. Or, more pointedly, the norm of Christianity is nothing other than the Living Christ who alone is the Word of God—and it must be the complete Living Christ *as he now is:* in–through–with all who member-for-member are the One Body of the Resurrection.

To travel this Shaker Way we must always keep in sight those who are the actual Shakers, to see what it is that they have experienced and how they live the experience. The earliest Shakers had been English Quakers who broke off from the Society of Friends in 1747. They established their own Meeting at Manchester, centered on the conviction that the Second Coming of Christ was about to occur. In 1758 the young Ann Lee (1736–1784) joined these "Shaking Quakers," seeking an interior enlightenment as the liberation from sin and as the power of the Spirit for growth into perfection. In 1770 she underwent a profound mystical experience in which she was overwhelmed with the Presence of Christ. She concluded, quite simply, that Christ had indeed come again since she had experienced Christ present, and if present he could not be any longer absent. When she spoke of this to her fellow Shakers they too suddenly experienced the same unitive Presence.

This is the central experience of the Shaker Way: the full reality of Christ recognized in–through–with all who are called into his unity. Shakers refer to themselves as Believers, but they *believe* because they themselves have *seen.* Ann Lee, thereafter spoken of as Mother Ann, is revered as the one through whom this unitive reality of Christ was first revealed among the community of Believers. She is a spiritual Mother because through her testimony of what began in her, others are brought into the life of the same experience. She herself is not seen as an individual embodiment of Christ come again; rather, she is the first one of the many *who together* are the Living Christ.

After suffering four years of persecution, Mother Ann and eight companions left England in 1774 for America, where, after several years of waiting, they began to make converts throughout the New York and central New England regions. In the years following Mother Ann's death in 1784, Shakers gathered into communal Societies, which

---

2. See *Millennial Praises,* Preface, Section Five, text 2, p. 269.

by 1820 numbered seventeen scattered throughout New York, New England, and the Midwest. These Societies together formed the Shaker Church, known as the United Society of Believers in Christ's Second Appearing.[3]

With the social and economic changes following the Civil War, the Shaker communes began to decline. By the end of the last century a number had closed, a trend which has continued to the present until there are now only two remnants left—at Canterbury, New Hampshire, and Sabbathday Lake, Maine—with a total of nine covenanted members.[4] But Believers have never identified essential Shakerism with the communally organized Societies. From the beginning they saw this form of their life as only one of many forms which would succeed each other as new eras called for new and different responses to concretize the Christlife.[5] From the 1880s on, they have had a growing sense of the principle guiding the new and different response which is called for: the quest for human unity. In the specific area of spirituality this principle has assumed a concrete meaning in the emergence of Christian ecumenism. It suggests that the gradual dissolution of the old separatistic way of life leads to a positive new opening: the gifts received by Believers in the first two centuries can now become a significant part of a new unitive Christian heritage—a heritage of heritages.

Theology and Spirituality

The present work is a theological study of Shaker spirituality. Historical, sociocultural, psychological, or other related explorations seek to study a religious tradition from the perspective of *outside*

---

3. The designation most commonly used is The United Society; also used: The United Society of Believers; The United Society of Believers in Christ's Second Appearing; The United Society of Alethians (briefly, in the late nineteenth century). The Society was referred to metaphorically as the Millennial Church and the Virgin Church.

4. "Covenanted members" are those who have formally entered a communitarian Society and have signed the legal covenant of that community, whereby they cease to possess private property and become the common possessors of all the property of the local Society. Not all Shakers have belonged to the communitarian Societies, and thus the designation "covenanted member" has not excluded as Shakers those who identify themselves as Believers by personal commitment.

5. See Father Joseph's vision of the seven travels, Section Three, text 19, p. 206.

INTRODUCTION

observers. As a theological exploration, on the other hand, this study is purposefully oriented *from within* the tradition as a participant observer, seeking to present and systematize the understanding of the tradition as seen by its own members in an ongoing community of experience. The differences in basic stance and methodology distinguishing theological and nontheological disciplines result in different kinds of study, and therefore it is important at the outset that we be aware of the theological character of the present undertaking. Further, as a theological study of Shaker *spirituality,* a special agenda is implied, concentrated first of all on the experiential, with the significance of other areas of interest viewed in relation to this center.

The fundamental constituents of Shaker spirituality are those rooted directly in the experience of individuals and communities, rather than in doctrinal formulations, social structures, and the like. All these latter are derivative of the directly experiential as its expressions. Shaker spirituality is essentially the mystical experience of personal Union in Christ, through the Gift that makes this possible— God–in–Christ–in–us—and hence the endless extension of the personal mysticism of Union interpersonally to embrace all those who share this same Gift. The many and diverse forms of historic Shakerism arise to communicate understanding and invite participation in this transforming consciousness.

The process of experience, then, takes place in the actual individuals who share life together in the community of Faith, which has continuity through them over time and space. The same individual is an experiencer spanning several decades, and the many individual spans overlap. Thus the process of change and development is an integrated continuum as perceived by the body of experiencers. They can recognize both differences over time and the identity of their past experience with their present. They are the same community and therefore they view the entire movement in themselves as integral. They thus evaluate the process of change as development, from the seminal to the mature, from less insightful to more insightful, from shallow to deep, and so on.

As the tendency in the experiencers over time is to integrate their essential experience with their total life context (which for Shakers includes expanding sociocultural horizons, especially in the nineteenth century), they gradually establish what is mainstream and what is variant—further developing and strengthening the former and abandoning, deemphasizing, or reinterpreting the latter.

INTRODUCTION

General Overview

Apocalyptic Expectations

The first English Shakers, who had gathered in 1747 under the ministry of James and Jane Wardley, were caught up in the expectation of the imminent Second Coming of Christ.[6] Apparently under the influence of the apocalyptic Camisards,[7] known in England as the French Prophets, the Wardleys and their followers were convinced that all was about to end as everything was made new. Drawing from their Quaker heritage, they undertook to prepare themselves by following the lead of the Spirit in an inward quest for greater light. Often gripped by the excitement of what shortly must happen, some spoke in tongues, sang wordless songs, and prophesied, while others danced in joy, trembled, or fell into ecstasy, while still others grew silent with a sense of the awesomeness of the Power of the Spirit clearly at work among them all.

Since the beginnings of Christianity every generation seems to have produced apocalyptic movements—the certainty of the end of the "old creation," to be overthrown by an imminent *parousia* of the final Coming of Christ in Glory. Apocalyptic expectations vary widely in theology, interpretations of history, and the agenda pursued in preparation. Their common elements are found in a threefold understanding of the Second Advent: the coming of a heretofore absent Christ, coming in Glory to establish the final Kingdom of God, and, most important of all, coming *shortly*.

The earliest representations of Christian apocalypticism, in the Pauline and Lucan documents of the New Testament, allow us to trace something of the usual process of development in communities with *parousia* presumptions. The oldest Pauline letters (ca. A.D. 50) present a vivid sense of Christ about to return at any moment (1 Thess. 4:13–18, 5:1–3) following upon the overthrow of the rule of the Enemy when the Lord comes in his glorious appearing (2 Thess. 2:1–12). About five or six years later, as Paul writes to the Corinthians, although he is

---

6. The general sequence of events and dates for the eighteenth century period follows the standard Shaker presentations, as in Giles Avery, ed., *Precepts*, and Benjamin Youngs, *Testimony*.

7. It is unlikely that there was any direct contact between the Wardley Quakers and the Camisards or their English followers; most probably it was a case of indirect influence exerted through the popular interest stirred up by the Prophets in London, an interest which spread quickly throughout the country.

INTRODUCTION

somewhat more cautious about the imminence of these events of the End, he thinks it will come in the lifetime of many of his hearers, and so, among other things, he advises the unmarried and widowed not to marry since the time might be too short to begin a new family life (1 Cor. 7:29–31). As he advised the Thessalonians, not all will die before the Second Coming (1 Cor. 15:51; 1 Thess. 4:15). At the end of the decade when Paul writes to the Romans he has rethought the Second Coming into a larger view of sacred history in which the End will not take place until all of Israel has accepted Christ, which itself will not occur until after all the world's peoples have accepted him (Rom. 11:25ff.). Clearly, as anyone could see, the End could not be soon since the evangelization of the peoples had only begun. The letter to the Philippians, written about the same time, speaks several times of an expected *Day of Christ*, but without any sense of immediacy; it is, rather, an expression of the culmination of each Christian's life-quest for the fulfillment of perfection in Christ.

The Lucan documents, the Gospel and Acts, reflect the next generation of communities. Because of Luke's vivid image of the Ascension (Lk. 24:50–53; Acts 1:9–11), the apocalyptic *need* for a Second Coming is firmly established: Christ has gone from the earth, is now absent, and so *this same Jesus will return in the same way as you have seen him go* (Acts 1:11). But Luke also indicates they expect him to return *soon*, as evidenced by the idealistic communal life depicted of the initial Jerusalem Church (Acts 2:44–47, 4:32–37). In the Gospel we find the promise that some of Jesus' hearers would not die before the Kingdom of God had come (Lk. 9:27), and the Kingdom coming can be presumed to be linked with Christ's coming.

Of course it is the Book of the Apocalypse itself which embedded apocalypticism so deeply in recurring expectations. Its complicated and obscure mystical symbolism provides almost limitless resources for reflection, calculation, and interpretation, enticing some in every generation to speculate *now is the hour*. Even more significant is its triumphalistic theology of history—the downtrodden and outcast arising in triumph overthrowing the powerful with irresistible Divine Might of Armies, angel destroyers unleashed against the unworthy, martyrdom transformed into glory, judgment and condemnation, and the establishment of a very tangible Kingdom. The mysterious Millennium, the battle to the death against the Beast, and the final triumph of Christ coming in Glory have provided the central focus for countless apocalyptic communities. When we step back for a moment we can

7

realize that the various patternings of all these elements can be in total conflict with another Christian vision: the ministering Christ of the Gospels, the one who came not to condemn but to bring life in its fullness, not to call the just but sinners, the one who in himself unveils the startling truth of God as Love, as Abba, as the limitless Giver, the One Who forgives all unconditionally and seeks only to save and bring back the lost. (We shall see how Shaker realized-eschatology took shape within the tension of this conflict, and eventually transformed the triumphalism of the Second Coming to conform to the Christ-who-serves.)

Preparation in the Spirit

In the nineteen centuries of Christianity there have been hundreds of apocalyptic-millennialist movements and sects. Though the early Shakers shared with them the basic expectation *now Christ is coming again,* there is a remarkable difference apparently separating Shakers from the others. In the movements and sects of which we have any knowledge, the expectation of the *parousia* always included some concrete plan, however general, about the Kingdom coming and this, in turn, suggested things to be done beforehand to prepare its inauguration. We remember the favor the mother of Zebedee's sons asks for them, that they be given first place, one on Jesus' right and the other on his left in the Kingdom. A Kingdom coming suggests a form of government, offices, patronage, and all the rest. In the Shakers' own immediate prehistory the Camisards organized into an actual army and began a violent apocalyptic war in the Dauphiné section of France in the reign of Louis XIV. But in what appears to be a feature truly unique to the Shaker experience, the Wardley community did not attempt to speculate at all about what would happen when Christ did come, and so had no preconceived plans for concrete preparations. This is all the more remarkable considering that their period of waiting stretched from at least 1747 until the summer of 1770, a full generation.

They took for granted that when at last he came all would be totally beyond present imagination and so speculation was useless. They were convinced they had to prepare, but the preparation could not directly reflect what was still beyond knowledge. But from their *present* experience they concluded that preparation would be in the Spirit and thus an inward work. It had a twofold character: the willingness to be led by the Spirit into a greater light than they had found previously as Quakers, and the presumption that this increase in inner light must entail a commitment to the pursuit of spiritual perfection. They thus embraced an open-ended and experiential agenda of preparation, which kept them free from any tendency to impose a narrowing imagination on the anticipated Coming and which also established firmly the most fundamental principle in the Shaker Way: unfolding experience as the dynamic norm of authenticity.

In the desire to be led by the Spirit, their worship began to develop directions ultimately leading away from both Quaker and contemporary English Protestant forms. The Friends had originally sought to worship without a form, and so be completely open to the Spirit's inspiration. They met in silence—the very positive silence of *waiting upon the Lord*[8]—with every expectation of being further enlightened with inner inspiration whereby the Spirit would lead the community; those so moved would give witness through spoken reflection, exhortation, and the like. However, with their new expectations and consequent experiences, the early Shakers found that, ironically, the Quaker "formless" mode of worship could be the most constraining form of all: sitting in silence unless moved to speak. For many Shakers were experiencing quite unexpected "movements of the inner Spirit," often overflowing into emotion-charged manifestations—songs without words, strange languages, prayer through bodily gesture such as kneeling, ecstatic spontaneous dancing, and disturbing bodily agitation and trembling. (It is from this last that their mocking neighbors called them "Shaking Quakers.") Many other Shakers remained outwardly calm in manner yet welcomed all these manifestations as the signs of a great inward work. They, in turn, moved away from a purely silent worship through the early development of worship songs and solemn discourses.

Although the nucleus of the Wardley gathering had been Quakers, new members came mostly from the Protestant Churches, primarily the Church of England, but probably Baptist and Methodist bodies as well. These Shakers tended to reject the worship and sacramental forms of traditional Protestantism for a variety of reasons. First, they had become disillusioned with the lack of vitality in the Established Church, which since the Puritan Commonwealth's overthrow was

---

8. This *waiting upon the Lord* does not indicate "expectation" for an absent Lord, but the courtly sense of attending to the desires of the ruler—"ladies and gentlemen in waiting."

INTRODUCTION

kept carefully under government control as a virtual branch of the Crown. They found the alternatives offered by the growing free-church tradition unsatisfying for reasons which struck at the heart of Protestantism. The gifts received in the Spirit leading them toward the *parousia* spoke to them of the ultimate radical perfectibility of human beings, and so they tended to reject the doctrines centered on the classic Reformers' sense of loss and guilt and the total corruption of human nature through sin. They therefore rejected forms of worship, prayer, and sacramental observance which reflected (as far as they were concerned) an endless congregational confession of sinfulness and failure which could not be removed but at best be "covered over" with the merits of Christ. Most important of all was the understanding of the sacramental Eucharist. Contemporary popular Protestantism saw the Eucharist as a *sign of absence:* it was a memorial of the past, reminding of Christ present once long ago with his disciples at the Last Supper and promising one day to return, and thus it was also a token of hope for the future when the now-absent Christ would return and the Messianic Banquet would be begun.[9] Convinced they were about to witness the Coming of the Lord in Glory, Shakers were uninterested in a form that signified absence, and so they did not practice a ritual Holy Communion.

Once again, the formative effect of this period of expectation was to establish a basic principle crucial to future development: worship as a response to and manifestation of the Spirit capable of taking on many very different forms. Quakers sought to worship "in spirit and truth" by having *no* form and succeeded in committing themselves to the most demanding form of all. Shakers responded to the truth of the Spirit with *any* form which would effectively give human shape to it. They freely rejected forms no matter how hallowed by tradition, even Biblical, which did not manifest their actual experience, and they adopted new and multiple forms which witnessed to the truth into which they were convinced they were growing.

The earliest continuing Shaker practice, beginning under the Wardleys' ministry, is the individual auricular confession of sin to elders as the witnesses of forgiveness and reconciliation in Christ. It

---

9. This commonly held understanding of the Eucharist did not necessarily reflect the official theology of all the Churches. Central to the Wesleys' teaching, for example, was a clear and vital doctrine of the Eucharist as Real Presence (yet, interestingly enough, even in the Wesleys' lifetimes Methodists quickly drifted away again into a Eucharistic sense of future hope, not presence).

rejects a traditional Protestant theology and practice regarding the guilt of sin. Shakers were certain they were being called to personal perfection, and so they sought to discern and bring to light every sin and imperfection. To confess each in a private "opening of the mind" to an elder was to identify and actively turn away from each obstacle to perfection. The intention was not merely to confess the guilt of the sin but to then *stop sinning*. The actual confession—the saying of it—was a psychological and spiritual crisis (turning point): acknowledging the concrete sources of what is wrong and thus being able to intend actively to change. In their quest for perfection—to live in all ways through the Spirit—they saw no value in the never-ending congregational confessings of guilt and unworthiness; individual confession with its effective repentance was the practical means to move away from real failures in life and so turn, *convert*, to Christ.

Ann Lee and Christ's Second Appearing

In 1758 the Wardley Shakers were joined by a young woman named Ann Lee. She had been born in 1736, one of the eight children of John Lee, a blacksmith. The poverty of the Lee family was typical of Manchester in this earliest phase of the Industrial Revolution. Like so many, the Lees had been forced from the land and small village life into the new slums of factory cities. None of John Lee's children received any formal education, since they were set to work before they had reached the age of ten. Ann was employed at a cotton mill when she was eight, and then as a cutter of hatter's fur. Later as a cook at the Manchester infirmary she witnessed the depths of despair among the sick poor who most often were sent to the infirmary to die. Under the persuasion of her parents she married a blacksmith, Abraham Standerin—and their still extant marriage record in the parish church signed with *X*s testifies to their illiteracy, the inheritance of poverty.

As a "Shaking Quaker" Ann was zealous in public witness and so was jailed several times for breaking Sabbath laws, culminating in imprisonment in a tiny cell in Manchester Gaol during the summer of 1770. Here, alone and hungry, she prayed for inner strength. Suddenly she was overwhelmed with the sense of Christ's Presence. The later written accounts of this experience vary greatly. Some speak of it as a vision in the sense of an apparition of Christ seen with her eyes, others as a series of such visions, including a variety of Biblical scenes such as the Creation and Fall of the first humans, but still others insist that it was not "seeing" in the external sense at all but rather a transforming consciousness of unitive presence.[10] But all accounts agree that this experience was the beginning of the long-awaited Second Appearing of Christ in Glory. Ann was released from prison shortly thereafter, and went immediately to the Shaker meeting. As she began to speak of her experience of Christ, all those at the meeting began to experience Christ themselves. They concluded that Christ indeed had come again, the *parousia* was now a fact *in them all.*

This is the turning point for the first Shakers, who now become *Believers* and henceforth call themselves the Believers in Christ's Second Appearing. We must be alert to several crucial aspects of the experience. First of all, it is *actual experience* which stands as the foundation of their "belief." For most Christians the sense of *belief* is often confused with *trust:* they "believe in Christ," meaning they "trust in someone else's experience of Christ." They trust that the original apostles actually saw and grasped a revelation of truths to be believed in and communicated to others on the authority of their word. Shakers *believe* because they themselves *experience.* The first Shakers did not merely accept Ann Lee's word for what she had experienced. Rather, as she spoke of her experience, those who listened experienced the same reality for themselves. Shakers are Believers, meaning Experiencers.

From this comes their understanding of the significance of Ann Lee and the meaning of Christ come again in Glory. In their historical experience, Ann was the first individual to experience Christ in Glory, and so they recognize her to be the unique person chosen to inaugurate the awareness of the *parousia.* But they did not think of her as a new incarnation of Christ or as a female Christ or anything similar (though as we shall see in the texts, some of the expressions of their belief can be misleading in this regard). Ann inaugurated the consciousness of the *parousia* as the first one among many to be drawn into the unifying experience of Christ alive and fully present in-through-with us all. She is the first one to awaken in experience to what ultimately all experience. And in Shaker experiential history she ministers this experience

---

10. The phrase "she saw Christ in open vision" is often used; *open vision* is a theological term taken over from Quaker usage, and means an inner transformation, a knowing not by the mind or a seeing not by the eyes but by a perception at depth from within; it reflects, for example, the "knowing that is beyond knowledge" of Eph. 3:19; the "vision" is "open" in the sense that the one who now *really sees* has been *opened* within.

to them by bearing witness to what had happened to her, thereby being the instrument of that same happening to them.

From this point on Shakers refer to her as Mother Ann: she has become their spiritual mother by being the one through whom they are reborn into Christlife. In the total experience of *Mother Ann and themselves all together* they locate the meaning of Christ come again in Glory: he is now fully One in the Union of Believers. They now see the apocalyptic image of Christ coming in Glory on the clouds as the coming in *clouds of witnesses* (as suggested in Heb. 12:1), the Body of Christ, the Body of Saints. They believe because Mother Ann ministered life to them by the living witness of her experience; they now experience for themselves and so in turn enter an ever-expanding ministry of living witness to others. This begins the essential *process of revelation* of the Shaker Way, spoken of as *progressive unfoldment.*

But Believers, as Experiencers of Christ alive in–through–with them, are experiencers of *a way of living* the Christlife. The Shaker vision is not a static *gnosis* or an inner–oriented mysticism. If Believers really do share the identity of Christ, it is the Christ living here and now in their tangible lives. The Shaker Way, therefore, involves a radical *metanoia,* a totally new consciousness, and hence a totally re-formed life. The first Believers saw this as the truly New Creation promised when Christ came again.

Central to this *metanoia* is celibacy, which has always been the most striking feature of Shaker spirituality. Although it will be explored at length, we should be aware that from the beginning celibacy was perceived as a positive commitment: to arise from limited, created nature into the very nature of the Godhead opened to us in Christ; to begin the Resurrection Life now in which there is neither marrying nor giving in marriage; to live fully the Christlife, meaning to live in a way capable of embracing all people, not being (properly) preoccupied with one's own spouse and family—to live as Jesus did, a ministering life open in the freedom to love all equally. This positive commitment can suggest a negative counterpart: to fail to accept this calling into the Resurrection can be seen as a sinful rejection, clinging to the limited in place of God. As we shall see, Believers had to work their way through many negative implications of celibacy, but the experience itself is the positive experience of identity in Christ and the inevitable call to others in sharing that identity. Similarly, Believers also recognized that in Christ they had to be committed to true peace toward all, a practical sharing of the things of life, and the realization of the equal dignity of women and men together as making up the Body of Christ in a complete humanity, male and female. These four principles—celibacy, peace, community, equality—flow naturally from the experience of Christ fully present in his Body, the Union of Believers. From their nature they are the dynamics of belief, carrying over the *metanoia* of the mind into the *metanoia* of action. It is a *metanoia* to be enacted in concrete experience, spoken of by Shakers from the beginning in terms of a regenerative Resurrection: rising out of the old nature into the new nature of the Christ Spirit. The *metanoia*, therefore, inevitably poses a tension to be experienced, a movement *from* one kind of human condition *into* another; in classical Pauline terms, from the *psychikon* to the *pneumatikon*, from the "physical" to the "spiritual" (1 Cor. 15:44).

The American Opening of the Gospel

Mother Ann became the leader of the Shakers, who, fired by their new vision of fulfillment, were soon bitterly persecuted by both the civil–religious authorities and sporadic mobs of neighbors. Attacks were often violent, including murderous attempts to stone Mother Ann to death as a witch. After four years she was convinced the Gospel would find no opening in England, and felt called by the Spirit to America. And so she and eight companions set sail on the ship *Mariah*, reaching New York on August 6, 1774, after a stormy crossing during which the ship nearly foundered. The Believers were penniless and so began two years of desperate poverty.[11] In the summer of 1776, they obtained the lease of a piece of land at Niskeyuna (Watervliet) near Albany, New York, and gathered there as a spiritual family to prepare for the opportunity to open the Gospel of Christ's Second Appearing in the New World.

In the winter of 1779–1780, a revival broke out in the churches of the Pittsfield, Massachusetts, area, characterized by an expectation of the *parousia*. As the winter wore on and nothing occurred, the members of the revival were on the point of dispersing when the little group of Shakers was discovered at Niskeyuna. Within a few weeks many embraced the Shaker Gospel, including the ministers. They committed themselves to the leadership of Mother Ann, who together with her brother William Lee and her adopted son James Whittaker formed the first Shaker Ministry. On May 19, 1780, a day so blanketed

---

11. It was during this time that Mother Ann's husband abandoned her, since he would no longer accept Shaker celibacy.

INTRODUCTION

with black storm clouds over the entire northeastern States that it was thereafter referred to as "the Dark Day," James Whittaker preached the first public *solemn discourse* and thus began what Shakers speak of as the Opening of the Gospel.

In the next few months many converts were made in the New York, Massachusetts, and Connecticut areas, often with entire families embracing the new celibate life of Christ come again. From 1780 through 1784 Mother Ann and the Elders made a number of journeys across the three States building up local centers of the faith, some of which eventually became the centers of the gathered communities. The spread of Shakerism brought an almost immediate reaction of persecution. The Revolution was at its height and suspicion immediately focused on these strange English enthusiasts who, among other things, preached Christian pacifism. Mother Ann and some companions were arrested as British agents by Revolutionary authorities at Albany and imprisoned until Governor Clinton intervened, realizing the honesty of their religious motives. In Massachusetts, however, persecution by local authorities and mobs was more serious. People were outraged by what they thought of as the popery of celibacy, which threatened to break up families. But they were even more incensed at the idea of full equality of women with men, which clearly struck at the roots of family and society, neither of which recognized anything approaching a legal autonomy of women. Mother Ann was accused of witchcraft, harlotry, drunkenness, and a host of related crimes. She and her followers were flogged, beaten, and driven out of their homes in a dozen towns. In the last violence against her, Mother Ann was tied by the heels behind a wagon and dragged over an icy road for several miles. A few months later (on September 8, 1784) she died at Niskeyuna, worn out by her labors and suffering the effects of these injuries.[12]

Father William Lee had died two months before his sister and so the leadership fell to the remaining member of the First Ministry, James Whittaker, who henceforth was recognized as spiritual Father. Realizing that they would not be left in peace, Father James called on Believers to gather together to form their own villages apart from their neighbors, thus beginning the development of the communitarian

---

12. Some years later when her grave was being moved to a new site her skull was found to have been fractured in three places, probably the result of this ordeal at Pittsfield.

form of Shaker life. The first gathering began in 1785–1786, about thirty miles east of Niskeyuna at New Lebanon, New York, centered around a meeting house built there by Father James. He died unexpectedly in 1787, after having made a visitation of the gathering Societies in New England. One of the leaders of the original Pittsfield revival who had assisted Father James in the initial New Lebanon gathering, Elder Joseph Meacham, was recognized as his successor and completed the formation of the new communities.

Communitarian Organization

Father Joseph led the Church from 1787 to 1797, and his ministry marks the transition from the first English leaders to their American followers. The new Societies took on a positive ideological significance under Father Joseph. Beyond its being a practical response to ongoing persecution, he saw the communal form of life as a positive manifestation of the full *metanoia* Believers sought to live. He conceived the call to perfection in Christlife as a call to separation: separate the regenerate-resurrectional way of life from that of the world. Henceforth he saw the ideal as Believers living completely apart from the "world's people" as Believers tangibly developed a perfect life in which the practical things of living would directly flesh out the inner Christ Spirit. The new communes would enable Shakers to practice celibacy without outside pressures; they could share the things of life in a complete religious communism; they could live at peace without violence or involvement with those who were violent; they could live totally equal in all things as men and women, brothers and sisters in Christ.

Father Joseph conceived of the communities as sanctuaries, using the imagery of the ancient Temple to symbolize the new relationships. Beyond the outer court was the realm of the world's people. The inmost court of the Holy Place was the community of Believers who had made a complete and irrevocable consecration of themselves and all their possessions to the common life. There were two other courts, one for gathering in new Believers, where those interested in the Shaker Way could come to see it for themselves and gain some experience of it, and the other for those who had been gathered but who were still gaining experience before being rightly able to make a final consecration (or who still had outside obligations). Father Joseph designated these three divisions of each Society the "gathering order," the "novitiate order," and the "church order"; contact with the outside world would henceforth be through the gathering order and the deacons and deaconesses designated to handle the community's affairs.

He established the Society at New Lebanon as the model for the other Societies as well as the center of leadership for the entire Church.[13] The community on the hillside of Mt. Lebanon was divided into several autonomous units, referred to as "families." Each family was led by two elders and two eldresses as a collegial pastor, while two deacons and two deaconesses administered the family's temporal affairs. The several families of Mt. Lebanon were presided over by the Ministry, again two elders and two eldresses together as the collegial bishop. The entire collection of families/communes was referred to as a "Society"; shortly after, the Society at Niskeyuna was formed, and both Mt. Lebanon and Niskeyuna were presided over by the one Ministry headed by Father Joseph and his colleague sister, Mother Lucy Wright, who had been one of Mother Ann's converts and companions. Other Societies in Massachusetts, Connecticut, New Hampshire, and Maine were gathered in similar fashion, and grouped in pairs presided over by local ministries who, in turn, recognized the ultimate authority of the Mt. Lebanon Ministry as the Lead in succession to the First Ministry of Mother Ann, Father William, and Father James.

Father Joseph was also responsible for instituting the progressive reform of the charismatic side of Shaker worship. An orderly man, he felt that totally unstructured worship in the more ecstatic gifts led to great disorder.[14] And so he devised the first "spiritual exercises," adaptations of simple folk-dance forms to give shape to ecstatic bodily operations and channel them into a harmony which would allow all to participate freely. For the next hundred years the sacred dance would be the most noted characteristic of Shaker worship, although by no means its only form.

While Father Joseph's genius for organization, both in social struc-

---

13. Earlier in the nineteenth century this first Society was referred to as the New Lebanon Society, from the local town's name; later it came to be known as the Mt. Lebanon Society, from its location on the hillside of Mt. Lebanon.

14. Referring to the Pauline experience of reconciliation in Christ (Eph. 2:19) in which we are no longer strangers or foreigners, Mother Ann had stated that *no strange feeling ever came from God*, that is, no feeling of estrangement. The idea of *no strange feeling* took another direction among the orderly (as opposed to the spontaneous and at times erratic ecstatics), and came to mean *nothing strange comes from God*. Finally this was transformed into a proverbial saying attributed to Father Joseph: *nothing odd comes from God*.

ture and the spirit of worship, was responsible for the consolidation and practical continuance of the Shaker Way after the First Ministry, he was also sensitive to the essential dynamism inherent in Shakerism. No form of society or worship could be allowed to be absolutized into a static tradition to be merely "preserved." The process of change must be built into the constitution of these inspired forms—or they would betray the commitment to follow whatever new light would come next in the Spirit. Father Joseph, therefore, refused to allow any printed publication of either the standing rules and regulations governing the Societies or the words of worship songs or other forms used in worship. He insisted that these be kept in handwritten manuscript so that they could always be changed, adapted to developing conditions, and ultimately, if need be, abolished altogether to be replaced by a new light. He would not even refer to the governing precepts as "rules" or "regulations"; he called them "Waymarks" such as a forester uses to mark out a path for the guidance of others if they walk the same way.

The pattern he set for the Mt. Lebanon Ministry reflects his and the other first Believers' experience of the Ministry of Mother Ann. Though clearly she was the one with the gift of ultimate responsibility, she always associated with herself her brother Father William Lee and her adopted son Father James Whittaker. Together they formed a collegial Ministry which combined a single ultimate authority with the *koinonia* of community, and hence the special gifts of supportive consensus, diversification of talents, distribution of leadership burdens, and, most important of all in an episcopacy, the nonisolation of the one charged with final responsibility. Father Joseph's design of the Second Ministry incorporated the experience of the First, with four bishops together constituting a ministry: a senior elder and a senior eldress each with an associated elder and eldress. At any one time either senior would be the first in the Ministry, with the other three as colleagues. Consequently, over the two centuries of this form of the Ministry about half of the leaders have been men and half women, as the first in the Ministry had tended to alternate by seniority between senior elders and senior eldresses.

Growth and Consolidation

Father Joseph's successor was Mother Lucy Wright, and under her a new group of Societies was established in the Ohio, Kentucky, and Indiana area, following mass conversions to Shakerism in the great Kentucky Revival of 1801–1805. By the time of her death in 1821, there

INTRODUCTION

were seventeen Societies in eight States with a total membership approaching five thousand; the period of physical persecutions had passed (though legal and social discrimination persisted) and the communal way of living had been consolidated. Pressure from both numbers and the geographic dispersal moved Mother Lucy to allow the printing of the first book of worship, *Millennial Praises*, in 1813, though she continued Father Joseph's policy of not printing any "Waymarks." But organizational pressures were such that her successors finally published the general regulations in 1821, under the title *Orders and Rules of the Church at New-Lebanon, August 7th 1821. Millennial Laws, or Gospel Statutes and Ordinances.*

From 1837 through 1847 (but continuing with declining impetus to about 1857) a remarkable period known as "Mother Ann's Work" dominated Shaker interest. It was a time of ecstatic gifts characterized by the inspiration of a broad spectrum of the membership who acted as *instruments* or *mediums* for messages, visions, and rituals thought of as portrayals of the spiritual realms into which mortals would ultimately progress in the completion of the Resurrection. Perhaps it is best thought of as a time of ritual mysticism in which words, songs, pictures, and ceremonies become *sacramental images* of the intangible reality of all that lies beyond tangible life. The period of Mother's Work caused Shakers to turn further from contact with the outside world. Forms of worship became so unusual that the leaders closed public worship for several years, fearing ridicule. The time suggested to Believers a call for an intense spiritual revival, which necessarily preoccupied their attention and energies. Some of the actions and ideas of the instruments tended toward extremes of subjectivist enthusiasm, but the supportive yet cautious guidance of the Ministry helped to moderate the overall impact and channel the effects to the spiritual upbuilding of the community as a whole.

For Believers all life and activity is supposed to be worship, not just the formal religious acts. A very positive effect of Mother's Work was to reinforce this, as many inspired admonitions called Shakers to renew their consecration of time and talents to the worshipful building up of the Body of Christ they shared. Some of the leading instruments, however, tended to be preoccupied with a drive toward an unrealistic perfectionism, insisting that all life and activity be structured in minute detail to guarantee its sacred character. This reached its most marked expression in the 1845 revision of the *Millennial Laws*. This new code, formulated under the inspiration of Elder Philemon Stewart of the Church Family at Mt. Lebanon, represents a total departure from the attitude embodied in Father Joseph's very flexible "Waymarks," or even the more formal *Millennial Laws of 1821.* In Stewart's code everything imaginable is regulated, and in the greatest detail. Communal life is made as uniformistic as possible (for example, all clothing the same color) and all activities are prescribed in such a way as to guarantee identical practice from one community to the next. The intent was to create a perfect reflection of the heavenly in the earthly. The effect was to constrain the experience of the freedom of response to ever new and diverse light in the Spirit. Happily, the formative experience of the first hundred years proved to have taken deep root, and the new *Millennial Laws* were simply not followed as enjoined, the various ministries and family elderships realizing the impossibility of relating this inflexible uniformity to the ultimate norm of authenticity, the unfolding experience of the Gospel life. The 1845 *Millennial Laws* were officially short-lived, being withdrawn by the Central Ministry of Mt. Lebanon after five years.[15]

The period of Mother's Work contributed in various ways to the transition then taking place. It helped a generation who never knew the first Believers personally to focus on some of the ongoing implications of Shaker spirituality. When the extreme expectations of the more enthusiastic instruments had ebbed, the Shaker Way had become stabilized in the path of *simple gifts,* henceforth moving methodically in the development of simple interiority, the spiritual subtlety of more quiet depth, and, hand in hand, a new openness to the "world" as sacred, not profane. For one implication of the luxuriant growth of ritual mysticism was the universal sacramentality of the world in which anything and everything was potentially capable of manifesting Divine Reality. The previous theological line of separation between the New Creation of the Shaker vision and the old creation of the world would be replaced by a call to recognize the possibility of consecrating the world, transforming it to share the New Creation.

---

15. It is unfortunate that most recent commentators on Shaker history are apparently unaware of the short life of the *Millennial Laws of 1845.* Andrews presumes they were the ongoing norms for Shaker communities throughout the nineteenth century, and almost all others have followed him in this, showing no awareness of the previous "Waymarks," the *Millennial Laws of 1821,* the revision and supplement of 1839, the reversion to the 1821/1839 standard after 1850, and the subsequent *Orders for the Church of Christ's Second Appearing* of 1878 and revised in 1887 (and which has stood in force since then with minor changes).

INTRODUCTION

Communitarian Decline

As the communitarian Societies reached their highest numbers and greatest economic and physical development in the 1850s, many leaders were alert to signs of change. The tragedy of the Civil War initiated these changes quickly. The emergence of widespread machine-tool industrialization seriously cut into Shaker hand manufacturing, which would diminish inexorably in economic effectiveness throughout the next fifty years. The shift in population from rural to urban and agricultural to manufacturing ended the unique ideal of the Shaker rural commune as a prosperous and pace-setting way of life. At their founding in the 1790s, Shaker communes represented to many American and European observers the vanguard of social development of agricultural-industrial communism. At the beginning of the nineteenth century, 90 percent of America's population was rural and agricultural; in the post–Civil War period this would decline to 60 percent; in the early twentieth century it would fall still more radically to about 30 percent. Shaker communes had been a practical response to persecution. In a predominantly nonindustrialized rural economy they had proved extraordinarily efficient with their concentration of labor and diversity of crafts. But in an increasingly urbanized-industrialized society their relative efficiency declined rapidly. Internally many Believers questioned the ultimate relevance of a way of life which did not significantly participate in the overall realities of the new kind of society evolving around them. At the beginning Shaker villages could supply for themselves virtually anything available in the outside world; a century later Shaker villages had to buy more and more of the diversified products they could not possibly duplicate.

Population was another focus in this crisis of change. From the first Pittsfield revival of 1779–1780, through the Kentucky revival of 1801–1805 and the Millerite revivals of the 1840s (and many smaller local revivals throughout the nineteenth century), Shaker growth was accounted for mostly by group conversions. Revivals oriented many people to search for a new path being opened by the Spirit, and many found the Shaker Way. Later nineteenth-century revivalism changed, however, becoming a means of reviving the flagging zeal of church members and reinvigorating them to become practicing Christians within their churches. Revivals tended less and less to send people out on the quest to discover a new path. Revivals ultimately became instruments for denominational renewal, effectively keeping most members within the existing folds.

INTRODUCTION

Shaker rural communes had depended on conversions from revivals, and now they were cut off without a broad population base. The policy of separation had discouraged them from methodically structured missionary activity, and also tended to limit any Society's influence and contacts to a small local area of near neighbors and towns. The Societies all had the practice of accepting orphans and unwanted children, raising them in the communities until legal age when they could decide whether to stay as brothers and sisters or go out into the world. Never more than one out of ten remained to become Shakers, and so all realized that this of itself could never be a sufficient source of converts. And, from the commitment to celibacy, there could be no "born Shakers." From 1871 until 1899 the Church published a monthly journal, *The Manifesto*, one of whose aims was to be a "quiet missionary" of Shaker ideas and ideals, and it certainly functioned as such and many came to the Shaker Way through it—but not enough.

The practical focus of the Shaker decline is the paradox of the communal form of life. Because it initially proved so effective, it tended to cut Believers off from the outside, preoccupying them with an enclosed form of life, locating virtually all leadership within the enclosure, and, most important of all, severely limiting the flexibility needed to meet the dramatic shifts in late nineteenth-century America.[16] Shaker communes created a beautiful and inspiring religious culture whose accomplishments are admired and prized by an ever-increasing audience. But in the process they became isolated. Many would locate the crisis of decline in the commitment to celibacy, which certainly requires continuing conversions to sustain membership. Celibate communities, Christian and non-Christian, have existed for centuries and millennia—Christian monastics, the Buddhist Sangha, and many others. But they continued to exist because they could draw from a larger population to whom they actively related. Believers had no larger hinterland.

Yet it is here that we encounter another paradox, for in the decades immediately following the Civil War Shakers developed a new light on their relationship with other Christians. In Mother Ann's time

---

16. Shakers have been self-critical of the economic "success" of their communities, especially with regard to the overextension of land holdings, which became a common pattern by the mid-nineteenth century. Societies acquired farm and timber land especially, at times far removed from the owning community and inevitably requiring hired labor. This preoccupation with expansion rendered many communities "land poor" and contributed significantly to the problems of the post–Civil War decline.

INTRODUCTION

Believers saw themselves as the first wave of a new and universal calling which soon would reach all people, the final opening of Christ's Gospel to humanity in this world.[17] The reaction of rejection and persecution drew the next generation to see themselves as something akin to the Biblical image of Israel as the pious remnant called out from a doomed world. Father Joseph's vision of the Society as a sanctuary of divine perfection was simultaneously the positive reality being experienced by Believers and a negative sign of witness against the "world." At the time of Mother's Work great expectations were generated of an approaching spiritual revolution which was beginning within the Shaker communities but would soon sweep the outside world as well. Most imagined this in very tangible terms, but many leaders saw a more far-reaching question: these were all signs of a great impending change *within the Church,* but what would the new gift be? Evidences of decline were already being noticed, but what was passing away and what would arise in its place?

New Vision of Unity

The new vision which took shape was both secular and religious. In the secular sphere Shakers saw their first hundred years of experience as a vital outward witness to new social, economic, and political values for the whole human family. Their communal form of economic life had experimented with many of the elements of practical communism, and they hoped these would be of positive influence in the abolition of economic slavery. Shaker communism had been studied by virtually all American and European social reformers, and through them Shakers saw their experience becoming a leaven in the larger world society.[18] Perhaps more important was the Shaker experience of the equality of men and women, with both sharing all forms of

---

17. They also saw this final Gospel call in terms of *eternal progression:* those who did not heed the call in this life would continue to have the opportunity to "travel into the regeneration" in the next. This final opening was "final" in the sense that no further Way would be revealed in a future period of history.

18. Shaker communistic forms and theory had direct influence on the mainstream of European socialistic thinking, including Marxism. For example, the Marxist formula "from each according to his ability, to each according to his need" seems to be an adaptation of the earlier Shaker formula "from each according to his ability to each according to his capacity" (note the striking difference, however, in the orientation to the collective implied in the Marxist "need" and the orientation to the individual person implied in the Shaker "capacity"). In his last message to the dying Marx, Engels tried to rekindle hope for the long-delayed social revolution with the exhortation "Remember the Shakers!" Correspondence such as that between Leo Tolstoy and Elder Frederick

INTRODUCTION

leadership responsibility, and this in an era in which women's legal and economic rights were still minimal. Women pastors and bishops were to be found in every Shaker Society as full colleagues with and often enough as seniors to men in the same offices—a scandal to some in the world, an inspiration to others. Shakers prior to the Civil War had been active opponents of chattel slavery, and they continued as opponents of economic slavery and sexist slavery.

In the religious sphere the new vision centered upon the conviction that the heretofore separate Christian churches were called to seek union together. Believers viewed separatistic churches as inauthentic responses to the Christ who could never be divided. This vision took concrete form in 1880 in an editorial by Elder George Lomas (of the Watervliet, N.Y., Society), "The Union of Churches," in *The Manifesto.*[19] He called for a meeting of all the churches to bring about the union of all into the one Universal Church, truly united and properly representing all authentic diversity of gifts. Shaker leaders recognized in this commitment to what later would be called ecumenism a demand placed on their own church: to grow into a new shape capable of unity with others and able to bring into this union the distinctive values of the Shaker heritage.

The new agenda of the post–Civil War era thus had to look for a reshaping of the Shaker Way to account for the larger socioeconomic pattern of urban industrialization, and it had to seek a new form responsive to future ecumenical unity. Both of these, however, contained what proved to be insurmountable difficulties. The extensive and successful rural-agricultural pattern could not be easily shifted without total dislocation. All their practical experience and tangible resources were based in their interlocking farm-craft factory system. Most significant, these were the roots of the leadership, who had no experience appropriate to a potential urban setting. Two urban Societies had existed in Philadelphia and, briefly, San Francisco, but the Ministry at Mt. Lebanon could not provide positive guidance beyond a readily given general encouragement. (The Philadelphia Shakers, under the leadership of Eldress Rebecca Cox Jackson, were an interracial black and white community of about two dozen members; after nearly

---

Evans of Mt. Lebanon, exchanges of literature, participation in conferences and countless visitations of Shaker communities, all testify to a continuing influence throughout the nineteenth century.

19. See Section Six, text 8, p. 312.

INTRODUCTION

forty years in the city, the last sisters withdrew and joined the Watervliet Society at the close of the nineteenth century. The San Francisco Shakers simply disappeared after the Great Fire of 1906.)

Ecumenically the situation was even more negative: to reshape themselves realistically for unity with other Christian bodies, Shakers would have to act in concert with some ecclesiastical partners. Unfortunately, apart from some pioneering individual theologians and churchmen, it would be another fifty years or more before ecumenism would take hold among the other churches. Believers were too early in their witness!

In addition, the vision of religious unity quickly extended to include the non-Christian Traditions, in which Shakers began to recognize a continuum of truth-in-the-Spirit with their experience of Christlife. As Christ could not be subdivided among Christians, so they began to realize that *somehow* a universality of Christ anointing/revealing through all Ways of Truth was a fact and commitment which had to be accounted for in unitive Christianity and therefore in a unitive Shakerism. By the 1890s, under the influence of Elder Alonzo Hollister, Eldress Anna White, and others such as Aurelia Mace of Sabbathday Lake, Shakers began to call themselves "Alethians," that is, "Truth-followers," identifying the ceaseless unfolding of the Gospel with Christ-the-living-Truth. They had reached a truly universal vision of "Alethian Ecumenism" and then had to face the frustration of that moment: they could find no companions among the other churches with whom to proceed into this unifying experience, and without whom they themselves could not proceed except by imagination. The overall effect of both the secular and religious impasses was an inability to take significant practical steps to give a new shape to Shakerism.

Thus began a long period of patient waiting, now stretching into a century—waiting for others to enter the unitive way, and in the meantime giving witness to the authenticity of the commitment by acknowledging the inability to give new unitive form to the Shaker Way alone.

The tangible decline among the Societies was heralded by the closing of the Tyringham (Massachusetts) Society in 1875. It had been the smallest and least viable of the original communities, and its passing was not a surprise. However the 1897 closing of the Canaan branch of the Mt. Lebanon Society came as a shock, since it clearly forecast a fast approaching future. Between 1897 and 1920 all the midwestern and half of the eastern Societies had closed, leaving six Societies with declining numbers. In 1938, the original settlement of Mother Ann at Niskeyuna in Watervliet, New York, closed and in 1947, just two hundred years after the first gathering of Shaking Quakers in Manchester, the Mother Church at Mt. Lebanon closed. By 1961, only two Societies, Canterbury and Sabbathday Lake, remained, with but two dozen members between them. During most of the twentieth century the leadership was moving to discourage potential new members for the old communes, culminating in a decision by the Ministry in 1958 to allow no one else to sign the communitarian covenant.

The Shaker Way, at least as it had been since the Second Ministry inaugurated by Father Joseph, was ending as had long been foreseen. But the question remained: how was the Shaker Way to continue in some other form? For Alethian Believers the century-long commitment to unitive Christianity still pointed to the future. If the communities as they had been were now a part of history, the tradition with all its gifts, values, and experience could still be a Way for Christians in the unitive heritage of an ecumenical Universal Church. In an old Shaker phrase, the issue was *how to send our gifts out into the world.*

Interpretive Issues and Problems

The presentation of the Shaker tradition in spirituality involves us in several levels of interpretation—the relative evaluation of texts and witnesses, the understanding of the developmental process in an evolving movement, the variety of changes which take place over two centuries, and the like. The most important question of interpretation, however, centers on the identification of the mainstream. We can pose the question simply enough: What constitutes authentic Shakerism? But we quickly discover it is possible to propose differing answers.

Our present theological exploration of Shakerism identifies as authentic the interpretation made by the ongoing community of Faith as constituted for the last hundred years or more and which has continued to the present. We seek to view the Shaker Way as these Shakers have seen and lived it.

Shakers look back to the eighteenth and early nineteenth century Believers and find direct continuity through a process of development which properly encompasses both stable principles and significant

26

evolution. As has already been noted, this understanding was shaped by the formative experiences of being led into ever greater light through the Spirit, of receiving an endless outpouring of gifts in the Spirit, and, most important of all, of actually living the Christlife in the experience of daily life with all its movement and change. This concrete process of progression and unfoldment implies both the gradual clarification of perduring principles and the open-ended further discovery of all that is new in the ever expanding horizons of the life of Spirit. Whatever case might be made for an interpretation that departs from the norms of authenticity proposed by ongoing Shakers, the particular value of this study rests in the commitment to represent Shaker spirituality as the living tradition which has actually come down to us.

The last full-length expositions of the Shaker tradition of doctrine, spirituality, and religious ideals appeared some seventy-five years ago at the beginning of this century: Anna White and Leila Taylor's *Shakerism: Its Meaning and Message* (1904) and the second edition of Henry C. Blinn's *The Life and Gospel Experience of Mother Ann Lee* (1901). A variety of short publications of the United Society have continued to be issued down to the present, mostly brief recapitulations drawn from older standard works. Thus, *The Shakers* seeks to fill a long-felt need of Shakers of this century—to present the religious tradition from the past to the present in its contemporary context and with the implications of its continuity into the future.

During the last thirty years a growing number of studies of various aspects of the Shaker tradition has addressed the history of Shaker social structure and theory, its local communitarian Societies with their industries, Shaker design in architecture, furniture, industry, and crafts, Shaker music and literary composition, and a host of other dimensions of Shaker daily life. These range from serious historical, sociological, and technical studies to more superficial presentations of Shaker artifacts as antiques and collectibles. All, however, have one element in common: the overall misunderstanding and consequent misrepresentation of the religious ideas and ideals that gave rise to the diverse works of Shaker hands. The misrepresentation of course, is not intentional, but the result of the attempt to understand the tradition as outside observers and a failure to study the abundant and complex primary sources. It is significant that of all that has been published on Shakerism during this century there is no major theological work on it as a religious tradition and no substantive commentary on the religious-theological source materials. The comment and summary which do occur in the historical and sociological studies are inevitably repetitions of misrepresentations of Shaker belief and practice which Shakers themselves have tried in vain to correct for two centuries.

As seen by the ongoing Shaker communities, perhaps the two most common misunderstandings center on Mother Ann Lee as the primary foundress, and the communitarian way of life imagined as the only authentic Shaker Way. Commentators almost always represent Shaker belief about Mother Ann quite simply: Shakers hold Mother Ann to be a female second incarnation of Christ, and it is in this female Christ that the Second Coming of Christ consists. In his unfortunate introduction to Edward Andrews' posthumous book *Religion in Wood*,[20] the late Thomas Merton epitomizes this error in his identification of Shaker belief as *the odd Shaker dogma of a female Christ*. The Shaker experience of the person and ministry of Ann Lee is far too crudely reduced by the phrase "female Christ," as will be seen in the section dealing with the male-female analogy in Shaker theology, God: Father and Mother.[21] The range of texts presented should persuade any reader that Shaker belief and experience were much more subtle.

The great majority of commentators have assumed a complete identity between the essential Shaker Way and the communitarian Societies of the nineteenth and twentieth centuries. They do not seem to be aware that the earliest Shakers, including Mother Ann, did not envision forming communes, that in fact these were founded as the immediate response to persecution, and finally that many Shakers always have lived outside the communal Societies and have enjoyed what Believers speak of as "full spiritual relationship" in the Church. As will be seen repeatedly throughout so many texts, Shakers of the last century looked forward to the emergence in the future of a new form of Shaker life which would not be communitarian, but appropriately complementary to the form of secular life of its time.

The identification of Shakerism with the communitarian form has led to serious misunderstandings. Most important is the false presumption that there is a "classic period" in Shaker history, thought to correspond to the 1840s, when the communitarian Societies reached their greatest numbers and prosperity. As the texts amply demon-

---

20. Edward D. Andrews and Faith Andrews, *Religion in Wood: A Book of Shaker Furniture* (Indiana University Press, 1966).
21. See Section One, text 19, p. 80.

INTRODUCTION

strate, essential Shakerism is conceived of as a nonstatic, open-ended *process* governed, in Shaker terms, by the principle of *eternal progression* in which there is an endlessly creative *unfoldment* manifested successively in potentially countless forms. This simply precludes any *classic period* or *normative form* as authentic to Shakerism, and thus a static reading of Shaker history must always be unrealistic.

The false identification of the tradition with the communes has led to two further popular misunderstandings. From already formed religious interests and expectations, some look to Shakers as representing a kind of "Protestant monasticism." (And another error emerges here, the presupposition that every Western movement not Catholic or Orthodox is therefore Protestant; there are in fact Western Christian traditions which are essentially autonomous, such as Quakers, Swedenborgians and Shakers.) The similarities between Shaker communes and monasteries are not substantively significant, representing nothing more than inevitable coincidences in structures and forms arising pragmatically from comparable organizational needs. Even as organized communally, Shaker Societies were always *full churches* encompassing the full range of ecclesial functions; monasteries are *specialized parts* of a larger church. Consequently the differences between Shakers and monastics are more notable than are the similarities. The second misunderstanding is the secular counterpart to the first: Shaker communes as exemplars of utopianism. Again upon close examination the similarities are ones of superficial organization. Presuming a technical rather than popular use of the term, utopias are conceived of in the vision of an overriding philosophical-sociological theory which dictates how the society is to be structured as the manifestation of a conceptual ideal. The people are to fit the ideologically dictated utopian social structure. This is virtually the opposite of the Shaker vision in which the form is shaped to meet human need and capacity; forms cannot ever be absolutized, as will be seen throughout the selections in Gifts and Orders.

The principle of *progression* which precludes any classic or static forms provides us with the basic organizational principle for the theological interpretation of Shakerism generally and Shaker spirituality as the focus of this study. As seen from within the tradition, the two century span of spirituality is an organically evolving process, a progression reaching maturity (rather than decline) in its latest understandings and emphases—in Shaker terms, its continuing unfoldment—which themselves can be found at least seminally in the earliest elements of the tradition. The theological analysis is systematized here as a process of progression and unfoldment. The mainstream of Shakerism is perceived in terms of what persists over time from the beginning, consolidates and ultimately prevails as the commitment of the participants. Such alternatives as have arisen from time to time (even elements originating with the founders) have ceased to exist or have been assimilated into the continuing mainstream.

Attention must be paid to the meanings of recurring theological terms and of vocabulary originally established in the context of the larger eighteenth century English-speaking culture. Earlier Shakers, for example, very often identify their experience as rejecting *lust* and all that is *carnal.* Both these words are rooted in the usage of the King James Version of the Bible. As a word, "lust" now tends to be focused on sexually oriented and usually sinful *desire,* but the word has had a much wider meaning (which we still use on occasion); "lust" refers to any emotionally dominated desire—a lust for food, a lust for fame, a lust for power, a lust for life. When Shakers reject lust (as the basis of all sin), they are rejecting *all enslaving desire for things* so as to be able to embrace the One Who alone transcends all things. Early Shakers so often accentuate the rejection of sexual lust in their rejection of all lust because the emotionally charged desire for other persons in possessing and being possessed—*eros*—was seen as the most entangling commitment preventing the transcendent commitment of men and women with God.[22]

The term "carnal" in the King James Version is the translation of the Pauline *psychikon,* which otherwise can be rendered "natural" or "creaturely" or "phenomenal," in contrast with *pneumatikon,* pertaining to "the spirit" or "the inner self" or ultimately "the Divine Spirit." *Carnal* as such does not mean *sexual* (although, of course, the sexual is included in the wide range of the phenomenal). The Shaker rejection of a "carnal life" is the turning from a *merely natural, creaturely life* to transformation into Divine Nature/Existence, the *Christlife,* the *Eternal Life* Who is God Self-given within us.[23]

While noting such terms and their historically changing meanings we must also be alert to evolving cultural contexts. Thus, virtually all Western Christians—Catholic, Protestant, and other—have felt the effects of the ancient Manichaean heresy which presumes that matter

---

22. See Dunlavy's treatment in Section Three, part 2, text 6, p. 189.
23. Ibid.

INTRODUCTION

is inherently evil and spirit (i.e., the immaterial) is inherently good. Prior to the present century Christians all too often presumed that human sexuality represented *material life* in this negative significance. If marriage was not actually evil, it at least embodied the unspiritual urges of "the flesh" and so was somehow *imperfect*. Christians generally spoke of the sacrament or ordinance of matrimony as "elevating" and "sanctifying" this otherwise base "animal" relationship; indeed, without such a blessing it must be judged sinful. The earliest Shakers, therefore, spoke of and felt about marriage from within this traditionally negative context. What is remarkable is how quickly they "progressed out of it" into positive insights allowing the relating of marriage and celibacy as stages in an unfolding transformation.

In moving through the two centuries of the *progressive unfoldment* of Shaker religious insight we can discern a succession of periods, each with its primary emphasis. In the foundational period the emphasis is on *transformation* as the Faith experience: a resurrection in the Christ Spirit out of the bounded realm of the natural human endowment and into the Christ-nature. This emphasis all too often is cast in negative terms of rising *out of* a fallen, sinful condition, of salvation/liberation *from* sin, of a separation *from* all that is "carnal." This is not to say that this initial period was essentially negative. On the contrary, one cannot but be impressed with the transforming vision of the glory of Christlife that Believers experienced as they came alive in Christ-come-again.

The tension between the negative and positive aspects of the fundamental experience was gradually resolved in favor of the positive—Shakers "progressed out of" these shadows into increasing light. By the mid–nineteenth century Believers were emphasizing their explorations of what they called "spiritualism" and "communism." The ecstatic gifts of the earliest Shakers and the mystical revival of 1837–1857 drew attention to the need to grasp the relation of the phenomenal world to further transcendent existence in terms of personal experience, not theological theory. By the close of the century we see the maturing insights of such leaders as Eldress Anna White, who distinguish the surface emotions and forms from the deeper participation in the ultimate Mystery. Shaker interest in social communism was the natural outgrowth of their experience with religious communism. The enthusiasm of the nineteenth century secular cult of progress gripped many of them, and they hoped to see the Shaker experience become the model for the general reshaping of economic society. The decline of

31

INTRODUCTION

their own communes and then the tragic betrayal of idealism in the First World War and its aftermath ended such hopes.

This shift coincided with the rise of a third period of emphasis centered on the commitment to unity: inter-Christian unity among the Churches, a secular unity among peoples, and an ultimate religious unity among all the great Traditions of the historic religions. This later nineteenth century development was identified as *Alethianism*, the commitment to *all Truth*. Alethian Shakers looked forward through this vision to the future and its eventual unfoldment of what Shakerism was to become next, beyond the ending of the communitarian Societies, led by the Spirit of Truth into all the Truth in union with others. Twentieth century Shakers continued to concentrate on this Alethian calling even while the preoccupation with "the closing of the season" for the old communes inevitably grew. The positive question for more than fifty years has been *how can we best send our gifts out to the world?*—a world no longer seen cut off in separation.

The Texts

Although there have been prominent and influential Shaker theological writers, the open-ended nature of the tradition militates against any one of them being regarded as ultimately authoritative. From the perspective of the twofold principle of progression and unfoldment, the role of authoritative witness is shared by the ongoing community as a whole, speaking through many individuals. The entire group of speakers would be regarded as inspired but in varying degrees and within the limitations of their time and place in the continuum of the revelatory process.[24] Therefore we shall explore the principal themes of spirituality through a variety of texts representing a wide spectrum of writers, eras, and insights.

The materials are gathered into six sections, each focused on a particular theme. In addition to the present general introduction, each section introduces the theme and texts with a commentary and brief notations about the texts, their authors, the positions they represent, dating, and the like. The texts are arranged in groups representing different aspects of the theme.

---

24. See Section Two, text 7, p. 114; Section Five, text 12, p. 278; Section Five, text 13, p. 279.

INTRODUCTION

In the first section, Christ Now Come Again (p. 43), we begin with the core of the Shaker experience: the realized eschatology of the Second Coming. The texts lead us through the unique witnessing ministry of Mother Ann to the central vision of Christ in the Union of Believers. The second section, Travel in the Gospel (p. 86), emphasizes the Shaker sense of Faith as a dynamic process rather than a static possession. The texts demonstrate the developmental character of this spirituality of movement through the application of the two principles of progression and unfoldment. The third section, Sharing the Christ-life (p. 156), identifies the four pillars of Shaker spirituality as these arise immediately from the experience of Christ in Union: if we together are truly member-for-member the living Christ of the Resurrection, than he/we live in *peace* with all others, he/we *share* the tangible and intangible gifts of life with all, he/we insist on the true *equality* of men and women together, and he/we embrace all in the open, nonexclusive relationship of *celibacy*. The texts concentrate primarily on the development of the understanding of community and celibacy both because they have such great importance in historic Shakerism and because Shakers have seen these two as fundamental to the implementation of universal peace and the equality of the sexes.

The fourth section, God: Father and Mother (p. 207), explores what is perhaps the most intriguing of Shaker theological insights: the extension of the human analogy for the Godhead to its fullest— male/female, father/mother, son/daughter. The texts enable us to see the variety of images developed and the awareness of the need to clarify and nuance this entire mode of attribution. The fifth section, Gifts and Orders (p. 258), is concerned with the acts of religion as such, both the forms (modes of worship, prayer, inner life) and the patterning of these into order. The texts include a sampling of forms employed at various times over two centuries, as well as theological and other reflections on communal worship and personal spirituality. Finally, the sixth section, In Spirit and Truth (p. 303), attempts to give a sense of the Shaker Travel as a movement always facing the future, including the future still to come. The texts portray especially those aspects of progression that by the end of the first hundred years of unfoldment brought Shaker expectations to universalism, and how this at least intimates what Shaker spirituality can signify in a future of Christian ecumenism.

Although all trends or positions of which we have record are presented, a discrimination is made on the stance we adopt as to what

33

constitutes the mainstream. Thus, mainstream materials are emphasized (especially through the introductory commentaries on the texts) in a way which shows their presence in every period. Those materials which over time prove not to be in the mainstream or are later modified as the nature of the mainstream is clarified are presented in that light. In passing it should be noted that some writers whose thought is later considerably modified (such as the very influential Benjamin Youngs) are represented by lengthy texts both because of the importance of the pieces at the time and because they provide us with excellent exemplars of the alternatives. In several instances they also contain significant elements of the mainstream position to which otherwise they are exceptions.

The commentary for each section of texts indicates what we might think of as the *density* of any theme in a given period, that is, the proportion of Shakers who at the time take the same position. This affects the number of writings which reiterate a given formulation, without necessarily adding substantively to it. In any given period certain ideas received great emphasis, and this is evident in extensive repetitions with but minor variations in the literature. But as we are orienting our study to see the tradition as an evolving whole, the developmental process of a new insight can be ultimately more important than whatever is momentarily prominent. Hence, the representation of the *range* of emerging thought is more crucial to our technical understanding than the configuration of thought arrested at any one point.

There are instances in which a text testifies to the conscious need on the part of Shakers to clarify or nuance a current mode of expression which, they feel, is otherwise open to misunderstanding. The recognition of the importance of such instances is crucial to our evaluation of what constitutes the mainstream. To turn to what is probably the most important illustration, Shakers in the first half of the nineteenth century very often referred to the Second Coming by such statements as "Christ made his Second Appearance in Mother Ann." As noted elsewhere, commentators have almost always taken such formulations to mean that Shakers believed (and apparently still believe, since the formulations are still used) that Ann Lee herself was a second, female incarnation of Christ in parallel to Jesus as the first, male incarnation. However, we find early Shaker texts which are purposefully designed to be statements of clarification, indicating that at least some Believers felt the formulations were open to misunderstanding. Even more important, we have instances where clarifying statements are by writers who enjoy high positions of authority in the Church. Here we have objective reason to evaluate the clarification or nuancing as the authentic representation of what has been established at that point and so what constitutes the then mainstream understanding. Thus, the citation from Elder Calvin Green (text 19, written in 1830, p. 80), who was one of the most prominent leaders of the Mt. Lebanon Society and who often spoke for the presiding Mt. Lebanon Ministry to the other Societies, demonstrates that the leadership in the 1820s and 1830s was attempting to correct what they held to be the misunderstanding of such phrases as "Christ *in* Ann Lee." We must be alert, therefore, to the sense of proportion involved in a set of texts. Put simply, to determine what is *received teaching* at any given point we must place more weight on a conscious clarification by an authoritative spokesman than we would on even quite numerous nonauthoritative statements.

Chronological sequence in arranging the texts is observed in those instances when it is essential to portray a stage-by-stage development over time. Otherwise texts are grouped thematically (but with each text identified as to date) as a constellation of different, significant expressions of the same element. The basis of the difference can be the liberal or conservative stance of the writer, the level of the writer's authority in the Church, or other similar factors. The commentaries preceding each section of texts together with the grouping of the texts within a section draw attention to the reason for the pattern in each instance.

The use of ellipsis in presenting some texts should be noted. In some of the longer selections from published theological works segments have been omitted simply because they digress into lengthy Biblical quotations or side issues not pertinent to the theme. There are instances of multiple ellipsis (especially in some of *The Manifesto* materials) because the item was chosen only for its particular mode of expression or emphasis of the theme; the omitted portions of the text are digressions into other unrelated areas, or complicated illustrations or analogies, or Biblical quotations, or the like. Ellipsis here is designed to highlight specific expressions of the designated theme in spirituality, which can occur in contexts not themselves addressing our interest, or which can include considerations not falling within the scope of

INTRODUCTION

the theme. In addition there are some instances of ellipsis supplemented with bracketed summaries of the omitted material for the sake of continuity within a passage.

Evident errors which could pose difficulties in interpretation are noted with the bracketed *sic;* purposeful variations in some spellings ("thro" for *through*, "brot" for *brought*, etc.) have been retained without note, reflecting Shaker experimentation with orthographic reforms. Manuscript copies present special problems since they were most often written by dictation. Hence there are inconsistencies in capitalization, punctuation, and paragraphing. Discretion has been exercised for the sake of clarity since, for example, capitalization is often used to signal technical theological terms.

The writers include leaders of the Church, theologians, members of the gathered communities as well as Shakers living outside the communities, and, in a few instances, non-Shakers whose statements either are of historical importance or are adopted by Shakers as properly representing their own views. The texts date from the late eighteenth century to the early twentieth century, covering the entire period of theological and related writings.

Texts fall into several classes. First, the oral tradition covering the foundation period of the First Ministry, 1747–1787, was gathered in several written forms from the original witnesses between 1800 and 1850 (with later redactions in 1888 and 1901).[25] Inevitably the materials

---

25. (1) Seth Y. Wells, ed., *Testimonies of the Life, Character, Revelations and Doctrines of Our Ever Blessed Mother Ann Lee And the Elders with Her,* Hancock, 1816. Collected by Elder Rufus Bishop in 1812, edited by Wells and issued in a limited edition. Later revised and reissued in 1888, as edited by Elder Giles Avery (this is usually referred to as the *Precepts* of Mother Ann and the Elders from the title on the binding, to distinguish it from the 1812/1816 version. (2) Seth Y. Wells, comp., *Testimonies Concerning the Character and Ministry of Mother Ann Lee and the First Witnesses of the Gospel of Christ's Second Appearing,* Albany, 1827. As the 1812/1816 *Testimonies* was not put into circulation, this compilation was the earliest generally available; unlike others (1812/1816), Grosvernor, 1888 *Precepts* or Blinn) this is a collection of independent testimonies identified simply by the names of the witnesses with no attempt made to interrelate them or work them into a running account. (3) Roxalana Grosvernor, comp., *Sayings of Mother Ann and the First Elders,* Ms., before 1845. The manuscript copies often represent differing versions or sequences of material. The two drawn upon here are the Sabbathday Lake manuscript (identified in references SDLms.), and that in the collection of the Philadelphia Museum of Fine Arts (identified in references Pms.); these two are readily available, more so than others perhaps; the variations in any of the several manuscript versions are not significant for our present purposes. A copy of the Philadelphia Manuscript has been made available through the courtesy of the Philadelphia Museum of Fine Arts. (4) Henry C. Blinn, *The Life and Gospel Experience of Mother Ann Lee,* East Canterbury, 1901, a

encompassed are very uneven, representing as they do the memories of dozens of different individuals, recorded from twenty to sixty years after the events and necessarily modified by the subtle shaping of subsequent experience. Often enough the speakers are quite conscious of the effects of hindsight, noting one or another element being recalled as a foreshadowing of a later development.[26] Further, the role of the compilers, redactors, and editors must be accounted for in any evaluation of materials. (To date the written sources themselves have not been subjected to textual analysis, which could be a very interesting study in itself since there is a partial analogy between this oral-to-written historical process and that of the New Testament Gospel documents: a long period of oral transmission; the formation of an early *logia* document—the lost Q source of the New Testament paralleling the Seth Wells *Testimonies* of 1827; the composition of at least two full Shaker episodic-narrative accounts, with variant manuscript versions and later formal editing and revision; a late narrative composition-compilation drawing variously from all the others.)

These written witnesses to the oral tradition are employed in several ways and for different purposes. First of all, of course, they testify to the original experience of the earliest Shakers, showing their several distinct perceptions of what the core of the Faith experience was, how they viewed the role of Ann Lee in the Second Coming, and the kinds of conscious distinctions they felt called on to make in expressing the essential experience. The texts provide us with a range of understandings as well as significant and clear instances of what eventually become the established interpretations. Selections represent all the principal views of these earliest witnesses while emphasizing the mainstream. The introductory commentaries draw attention in each section to important critical elements (the relative authority of a witness, nuanced vocabulary, technical terms, and the like) which enable us to recognize an emphasis as appropriately mainstream. The use of the oral tradition texts poses a special problem with regard to historic impact: an event or teaching originating in the eighteenth century might become important only in the nineteenth century as the result of written publication. (This is somewhat akin to the effect of the written New Testament Gospels influencing postapostolic Chris-

---

reworking of the previous materials into a running biographic narrative; no new items are introduced.

26. See Section Three, part 2, text 3, p. 185; Section Four, text 2, p. 213.

tians in ways at times very different from the initial oral teaching by
Jesus and the first disciples to their contemporaries.) Once again,
because of our interest in the ongoing tradition as a whole, the use of
texts most often will represent the developed perspective.

The next class of sources represents the major published theological works and related manuscripts issued between 1790 and 1904.
These involve three distinct but basically compatible modes of system-
atizing the Shaker experience of Christ in his Second Appearing: the
oldest, Christ in the Union of Believers, exemplified in Joseph Meacham's *Concise Statement* (1790) and John Dunlavy's *Manifesto* (1818);
next, the elaborated extension of the full human analogy of male-
female to the Godhead and Christology as Father and Mother and as
male and female, as developed in Benjamin Youngs' *Testimony*
(1808/1810/1823/1856); finally, the integration of these with an all-
inclusive quest for human and Christocentric unity of the Christian
and non-Christian traditions together, given statement in the works of
Alonzo Hollister, Anna White, and others from the 1870s through to
White and Taylor's *Shakerism: Its Meaning and Message* (1904).

Finally texts are drawn from pamphlets, addresses, biographical
notes, and the like, irregularly issued throughout the nineteenth century, and from the many articles and editorials appearing in the monthly
issues of *The Manifesto* between 1871 and 1899, when it ceased publication. *The Manifesto* materials are especially valuable since they represent dozens of different writers who themselves span the entire nineteenth century developmental experience and who witness to its
culmination.

With rare exceptions this copious body of resources has not been
the subject of theological study (apart from a few recent academic
dissertations[27]) or commentary. Virtually no secondary sources reflect
them substantively.[28]

---

27. See, e.g., John H. Morgan, *Communitarian Communism as a Religious Experience:
Exemplified in the Development of Shaker Theology* (Ph.D. diss., The Hartford Seminary
Foundation, 1972).

28. In 1969 the author published *Shaker Theological Sources* (The United Institute,
Bethlehem, Ct.), a sampling of theological texts, as an interim publication in monograph
form, to make some exemplars of Shaker theology available. The Sabbathday Lake
Society published *The Shaker Quarterly* from 1961 until its apparent suspension in 1973;
while emphasizing historical and related interests, the *Quarterly* has published or repub-
lished several articles reflecting upon the religious-theological sources, including the
author's "The Spirit of Shaker Christianity" (later issued by The United Society in
pamphlet form).

INTRODUCTION

*　　　*　　　*

An unidentified Shaker writing in *The Day-Star* in 1847, at the high point of the old communal Societies and in the midst of the excitement of the period of Mother's Work, sets out the interpretive issue boldly: progression and unfoldment dictate that normativeness rests with the dynamics of development rather than in an original static revelation. He replies to a letter from a J. B. Cook, who presumes that published theological books represent a Shaker creed.

> .... the *books* from which you undertake to condemn a *people*, if you had suffered them to speak for themselves, would have told you that they were neither the creed's [*sic*] nor "confession's [*sic*] of faith" of the Shakers, to which all else must bend. Those books claim that the work of God among his people, is an increasing work; and when you can set forth a better doctrine than is therein contained—demonstrated to be such from its practical effects—you will have written the Shaker's creed a little closer than you have found it.[29]

---

29. *The Day Star* XII, 6 and 7, p. 23 (March 4, 1847); in reply to a letter of J. B. Cook appearing on pp. 22–23.

THE SHAKERS

TWO CENTURIES OF SPIRITUAL REFLECTION

one

CHRIST NOW COME AGAIN

Introduction

Beginning about 1810 and continuing into the 1840s, a number of collections of the experiences of the earliest Believers were made for the sake of the generations who had never personally known Mother Ann and the first Elders. These testimonies are given quite self-consciously; they attempt to state exactly what was the experience of Christ in the Second Coming. Taken together the collections represent the remembrances of all the available witnesses, not just the selective memory of a few official representatives of the first generation.

A review of all the testimonies reveals a range of emphasis both in presenting and in interpreting each experience. For some the emphasis is on the community of Believers, the Church-who-are-Christ; for others, it is on the tension of conversion from a pervading sense of sin and unworthiness to the wonder of discovering a transforming perfection in Christ; for still others, the emphasis is on the person of Ann Lee and the recognition of Christ-come-again through her ministration. But whatever the emphasis in each instance, it is noteworthy that care is so often taken to make clear that Ann Lee herself is *not* an "incarnation" of Christ. The reality of Christ is indeed experienced in her, but also *equally* in each and every one united in Christ. She is a spiritual Mother because she ministered this indivisible Christlife given to her, giving Christlife to others (selections 1–11).

THE SHAKERS

Many Shakers of the next generation (especially in the period of the mystical revival, 1837–1857) came to think of Mother Ann as sharing complete equality with Jesus Christ—with such terms as "Jesus the Word, Ann the Word" and "Jesus the Father, Ann the Mother," and the like. Some spoke of Christ now *incarnate again in* a woman. But it is quite evident that such perceptions of Mother Ann do not conform to the original experience as represented by the first witnesses, who take pains to clarify modes of "incarnational" expression which might be misunderstood and so lead to such exaggerations. The period when the exaggerations occurred was very brief, a mere twenty years, and even then the extreme enthusiasts were actually few in number. It is unfortunate that this passing tendency to mythologize Mother Ann is most often portrayed by commentators as the authentic Faith-experience of Believers, ignoring both the nuancing of the original testimonies and the later explicit insistence by Believers that they did not at all share in the extreme fervor fostered by the zealots.

In 1790, Father Joseph Meacham as Presiding Elder of the Church published *A Concise Statement of the Principles of the Only True Church, &c.* (selection 12). It is designed to speak of Shaker belief to the "world" and is the first Shaker imprint. As an exposition of their belief it is notable in that there is no mention of Mother Ann at all. It centers, rather, on the essential *metanoia* experienced by Believers: the movement from imperfection to perfection in Christ. It is this experience which Father Joseph identifies unequivocally as the Second Coming in Power.

Elder John Dunlavy, one of the important leaders of the Ohio-Kentucky Societies, published his major work, *The Manifesto*, in 1818. A carefully reasoned and detailed theological analysis of Shaker belief, it is both a complement and a contrast to the *Testimony of Christ's Second Appearing* by Elder Benjamin Youngs of Watervliet (Niskeyuna), published in several editions between 1808 and 1856. Dunlavy's exposition of Shakerism is solely in terms of *Christ-come-again in the Union of Believers*, the Church as Christ. Youngs, in contrast, shifts the emphasis to a developing theology of *God as Father and Mother*, and hence *Fatherhood and Motherhood in the Divine Christ*, and this manifested through the male and female humanity of *Jesus and Ann as the First Agents of the New Creation*. Youngs does not at all dispute the Union of Believers experience; it certainly is the tangibly experienced reality of *Chirst-Come-Again*. But he is taken with the historical theological interpretation of the ministry of Mother Ann as unveiling the principle of

THE SHAKERS

Eternal Motherhood. As will be seen at length in the section God: Father and Mother, this occupies Shaker attention for much of the nineteenth century and includes a continuous movement toward realistic refinement and away from enthusiastic tendencies. But we must be aware of the fact that it never displaces the Union of Believers understanding of the *parousia* experience and its continuous unfoldment in the Church-as-Christ. Dunlavy's work remains the standard exposition to the present.[1]

The selections from Dunlavy (13–17) are representative of his emphasis on the direct experience of each Believer: salvation from sin and a sinful life, personal transformation, confession of sin as the entry into perfection in Christ, the Church-as-Christ, the ultimate universality of the Church as all who embrace Christ as he is. The selection from Youngs (18) is in complement to Dunlavy, concentrating on an understanding of the identity of Church and Christ—in the phrase of the closing paragraph, "the whole mystery of God . . . in and through the Church, revealed and progressively manifested."

Shakers have long been aware of the danger of misunderstandings or wrong emphases of their Faith-experience unless special care is taken with some easily misrepresented expressions of that experience. The selections from Elder Calvin Green (19) and Elder Richard McNemar (21, 22) are examples of early efforts at clarification during the period which includes some of the exaggerations mentioned above. The article of R. W. Pelham (20) is an excellent example of developmental understanding of the difference between *what* the Coming consists in and the historic person(s) *through whom* the experience takes place.

The final selections (23–27) are examples of the universalized understanding of the Christ-experience characteristic of the last hundred years of Shaker reflection. This will be pursued in detail in the final section, Spirit of Truth, but it is crucial to this initial representation of Shaker realized-eschatology if its essential dynamism is to be recognized. In the Shaker vision, a universality in the Christ-experience is inherent in the logic of Christianity, creating an inevitable tension between the gathered community of self-conscious Christians and their awareness (or lack of it) of a Christ not confineable within

---

1. It is unfortunate that non-Shaker commentators ignore this fact; they are more attracted to Youngs' Father–Mother Christology, usually representing it as an exotic outgrowth of a Shaker preoccupation with Mother Ann as a "female Christ."

the organizational or social limits of "Church." The Shaker experience begins historically with narrower expectations of Church but inevitably reaches an opening into universalism/ecumenism (not only inter-Christian but also Christian/non-Christian), and this from the dynamic of *progressive revelation,* that is, the progressive unfolding of their experience, rooted in the initial "seed experience" of the first community gathered through Mother Ann, then the exclusive perfectionist communities of Father Joseph's design, and finally the growing awareness of the *total giving* of God in Christ to all, and the manifestation everywhere of the evidences of this universalism of the "Christ of the Ages."

I

Jesus Christ, when speaking to his disciples of his second coming, was asked, "Where Lord?" He did not point out any particular place, but said, "Wheresoever the body is, thither will the eagles be gathered together." (Luke, xvii. 37.) By this he plainly intimated that his presence, and his work would be in his body; that is, *"the church,* which is his body, the fulness of him that filleth all in all. And he is the head of the body, the church." (Eph. i. 23. & Col. i. 13.) By the gathering of eagles, he shows, in a striking figure, that the evidence of his coming, and the nature of his work, will be seen and understood by the spiritual discernment of those who, like watchful, keen-eyed eagles, in quest of food, will be able to discriminate between a living and a dead body, and gather to that which affords spiritual life and nourishment, and let the dead alone. Thus, in his true and living body will Christ be found, "in the dispensation of the fulness of times." (Eph. i. 10.) There will those truly honest and faithful souls, "who hunger and thirst after righteousness," be gathered; and there "they shall be filled;" while the lifeless church of Antichrist, like so many dead carcasses, which have long been sinking in their own corruptions, are cautiously avoided.

(Calvin Green, *Summary View,* p. 202) [1823]

2

15. While Mother Ann and the Elders were at Asa Bacon's, in Ashfield, a number of the Believers were there one evening, and there

appeared very extraordinary Northern Lights. One said, "It is the sign of the coming of the Son of Man in the clouds of heaven." Mother replied, "Those signs which appear in the sky are *not* the sign of his coming; but the Second Appearing of Christ is in his Church; and Christ is come to put away sin from his people, and this is the Cloud [of witnesses] alluded to."

Anna Mathewson
(Giles Avery, ed., *Precepts*, p. 179) [1816/1888]

3

5. After this Elder James came forward, and said, "My name is James Whittaker; I have prayed to God for you, as earnestly as I ever prayed for my own soul." He then spoke of the great loss and fallen state of man; and of the necessity of a restoration through Christ, in order to find salvation and redemption now offered through the medium of the gospel. "The time is fully come," said he, "according to ancient prophecy, for Christ to make his second appearing, for the redemption of lost man. This is the Second Appearance of Christ, and we are God's true witnesses, through whom Christ has manifested himself, in this day of his second appearing; and the only means of salvation that will ever be offered to a lost world, is to confess and forsake their sins, take up their cross, and follow Christ in the regeneration."

(Giles Avery, ed., *Precepts*, p. 136) [1816/1888]

4

I have been with Mother day and night, at times when she was under great and most severe sufferings I ever saw endured by a mortal, and also in seasons of joy; and in all this she was ever the same, a perfect pattern of godliness, showing forth in every word and action that pure, Christ-like spirit, which I never saw in any other person save Father William and Father James. I know she was the Lord's Anointed, the Bride, the Lamb's Wife, spoken of in ancient days by holy inspiration; for she did the same work and performed miracles in the same spirit that Christ did when on earth. I now stand a living witness of the great work of God and the marvellous displays of His power thru Mother and the Elders for the salvation of souls. As soon as would I dispute that Christ made his first appearance in the person of Jesus of Nazareth as I would that he had made his second appearance in the person of Ann Lee; for whosoever denieth Mother denieth Christ in works, if not in words, for no soul will ever have power to do the works of Christ in this day, but by and thru the testimony brought to light by Mother Ann and her witnesses.

Father William and Father James were in possession of the same gifts and power, according to their measure, that was so wonderfully displayed in Mother. Many gifts and manifestations of the Spirit were revealed thru them for the confirmation of their testimony, and to strengthen the faith of young Beleevers.

Mother Sarah Kendall

(Roxalana Grosvernor, ed., *Sayings* [Pms.] pp. 10–11) [1845]

5

I can say, for one, that I have not been led blindfold by a vain imagination these forty-five years past. I know by the revelation of God in my own soul, that Mother was the Lord's anointed, and that Christ really began his second appearance in her, and dwelt in her, and that her body was a temple for the Holy Spirit. (See 1 Cor. vi. 19.) However incredible this may appear to an unbelieving world, we know that we are not left in darkness and doubt concerning these things; they are as clear and certain to us as the light of the sun in a clear day. Here we find the promise of Christ verified: "He that followeth me shall not walk in darkness." (John viii. 12.)

I know of a certainty, that Mother Ann had the gift of prophecy and the revelation of God, by which she was able to search the hearts of those who came to see her; for I have myself been an eye and ear witness of it. I have known some to come to her under a cloak of deception, thinking to conceal their sins in her presence; and I have seen her expose them by the searching power of truth, and set their sins before them, so that they have been constrained to confess, with guilt and shame, that she had told them the truth, and to acknowledge that the light and revelation of God was in her. I am not insensible of the spirit of unbelief which prevails in the world against the spirit of truth, and especially against testimonies of this kind; but I can say with the apostle Paul, "I speak forth the words of truth and soberness;" my eyes have seen and my ears have heard what I have stated; it is no vain imagination.

By obedience to the testimony of the gospel, which I received from Mother Ann and the Elders who stood with her, I have found salvation from sin; and this, I can truly say, feels more precious to me than all created things. Why then should I hold my peace? I regard not the sneers of an unbelieving world. I am not ashamed to acknowledge Mother Ann as my mother in Christ. I know she lived a pure and sinless life; and I know that she was not guilty of any of those shameful crimes which the wicked have laid to her charge.[2] I know that she loved righteousness and hated iniquity; and I can bear witness that her soul abounded in goodness and love; and that she was able to administer the same to others; I have seen and felt it in numberless instances. I know that the spirit of Christ was formed in her; and I have ever found the same spirit in all her faithful followers. I have been well acquainted with all her successors in the Ministry, and I have always found in them the same godly example, and the same Christ-like spirit; and I feel a firm and unshaken confidence that, in obedience to her precepts, they follow her as she followed Christ. Under their ministration, and in obedience to this gospel, I feel my faith established and my soul resting on a sure foundation, against which the tongue of slander and the gates of hell can never prevail. . . .

HANNAH COGSWELL
New-Lebanon, June 6th, 1826
(Seth Wells, ed., *Testimonies*, pp. 30–32) [1827]

6

My native place was Durham, in Connecticut. My parents were members of the Presbyterian church, in good standing, and respectable in the world. I was brought up strictly, and carefully instructed in the principles of their religion. From a child, I was the subject of religious impressions, and had strong convictions of sin.[3] When I was about six years of age, I well remember, while walking in the garden one day, my mind was turned to a serious consideration, that death was the

---

2. Accusations of drunkenness, debauchery, and witchcraft were the common excuses for the mob persecutions.
3. "Conviction of sin and conversion to Christ" principle of Calvinism.

common lot of all, and I knew not how soon it would be mine. These thoughts filled my mind with great concern about what would become of me if that should soon take place. I saw at that early period, that my nature was lost from God, and prone to evil. After this, I used to retire alone and pray to God the best way I was able, and sought religion according to the best of my understanding. I spent much time in secret prayer, when I was alone and exposed to danger or temptation; and was careful to kneel and pray to God for protection, before I went to sleep. I believed that if I indulged myself in any wickedness, I should never see God in peace, but should be banished from his presence, and sent to hell at last; the thoughts of which I could not endure. Still I could not subdue the carnal propensities of an inbred nature; and therefore I could not feel a justified conscience, not find power over sin. On the contrary, I found my evil propensities grew stronger as I grew older; so that after all my labor, I found myself still lost from God, and destitute of the power of salvation.

But after coming to the age of maturity, my religious experience was considered sufficient to entitle me to membership in the Presbyterian church. And being strongly solicited, I became a member of that church, and made a public profession of that religion, and was instructed in their doctrines of election, decrees of God, imputed righteousness, the resurrection of the natural body, and other doctrines maintained by that sect; and, like other professors, I endeavored to conform myself to all their rules of discipline, and, under the influence of those principles, for a time, thought myself a good christian.

In 1764, being about twenty-one years of age, I entered Yale College, where I pursued my studies with assiduity, and was zealous to bend the course of my literary attainments to theology, having a view to the ministry, according to the custom of the times. After spending one year in college, I was sent on a school mission, to teach the Indians of the Five Nations.[4] Here I had many opportunities to learn the artless simplicity of unsophisticated nature, in these poor natives of the wilderness; and to contrast it with the sophistry, superficial pomp and artful dissimulation, so common in countries and among nations claiming the exalted benefits of civilization. This increased my views of the

---

4. I.e., the Iroquois of western New York State. The affinity expressed here for the Indians was characteristic of Shaker interest throughout the nineteenth century, as was their positive concern for blacks (which included having black members integrated in many Societies from the beginning).

lost state of the world, where the displays of genius and the artful refinements of civilized man, in many cases, only tends to add corruption to a fallen nature.

After spending one year among the Indians, I retured to college; where I continued my studies three years longer, and was graduated in 1769, and two years after, received the degree of A.M. During my residence in college, my mind was greatly exercised respecting the Christian world, so called. It appeared to me that they were all far short of the order and power of the primitive Church. I enquired of the most learned and able divines, particularly of the celebrated Dr. Goodrich, of Durham, whether there was any regular succession of the order and power of the Divine Spirit, from the apostles to the ministry of the present day. I was informed that there was not; but as we had their example and precepts in the letter of the scriptures, we could do no better than to follow them. This put me in a great labor. I could not see how those who had not the Spirit of Christ, could be true ministers of the gospel. Nor could I see how there could be a Church of Christ without a transmission of the same power, in regular succession, down to it; because the churches, so called, must, in that case, be off from the primitive ground of the Church established by the apostles; and therefore could not be the true churches of Christ. Nor could I see any way for them to find the true ground on which the primitive Church was built, without a second manifestation of the same Spirit through some medium or other; since, according to the confessions of the most learned divines, Christ must be absent from the churches which went by his name.

From this time, my mind was directed to look for the second coming of Christ. I enquired of the most eminent divines around, how long it would be, according to their calculations, before Christ would make his second appearance. They informed me that it was near at hand, and according to the best calculations that had been made, it would be about twenty years. I have since observed that this calculation brought the period very near to the time when the Church of the United Society began to gather into order. About this time, in passing through the burying ground at New–Haven, I felt my whole soul absorbed in prayer to God, that I might live to see the second appearing of Christ.

After I left college, I still felt strong religious impressions; but as I could not find any who could show, to my satisfaction, any greater light than that of the church to which I belonged, I concluded to continue my connection with it, and seek religion according to that system. And being fervent in spirit, I soon felt as tho I had a call to preach the gospel. After passing through a course of preparatory studies, under the instruction of Dr. Goodrich and others, the call was approved, and I was licensed to preach, by an association of ministers at Pittsfield, Massachusetts. For a time, I preached where opportunity offered. At length I received a call, and was ordained pastor of the Presbyterian Church in New-Lebanon, November, 1772. This was the first congregation ever formed in this town. I continued in this charge about three years and a half, and endeavored to discharge my duty according to the best of my understanding and abilities. But I could not find that spiritual substance which my soul craved, altho I felt a measure of justification in doing the best I could do in my situation. I still felt a great lack of the spirit and power of salvation, and could say, in the language of St. Paul, when speaking in the character of the natural man seeking after spiritual life, "With the mind I served the law of God; but with the flesh the law of sin." As I knew of no way out of the flesh, I conformed to the customs of the world, was married and had a family.

At the commencement of the revolutionary war, I was inspired with an ardent zeal in the cause of liberty; and in the station I held, contributed my best efforts to my country's cause. The disorganized state of the society where I was settled, occasioned by the war, induced me to seek a dismission from my congregation; and I obtained an honorable discharge, with a recommendatory certificate from the association. Soon after this, I had another advantageous call; but I did not feel myself at liberty to comply with it; because my mind had begun to be awakened concerning that system of religion which I had hitherto professed and preached. I saw that it was on a false foundation, and that it did not and could not administer the power of salvation. This filled my soul with inexpressible tribulation.

I labored and cried earnestly to God that I might find something better, and more substantial than I had hitherto found in any scheme of religion, or among any of the professors of religion I had ever met with, I saw that they were all, or nearly all, more or less guilty of biting and devouring one another, and shedding each other's blood. I was led to see, and was fully convinced, that the spirit of war, according to the apostle's doctrine, proceeded from lust; and that people could not be the followers of Christ, and live in wars and fightings; because we were required, by the very spirit of christianity, to put

away all contention and strife, and to "follow peace with all men."
Hence I saw that war and bloodshed could not belong to the Kingdom
of Christ; and that they who pursued this course of life, could not be
led by his Spirit.

Some of the most eminent among the *Reverend Doctors* labored
hard to bring me back to the old foundation, and to the traditions of
our forefathers; but all to no purpose. I told them we were all lost and
blinded by these things, and that the true nature and spirit of christianity was not among us. The labor and tribulation of my mind increased,
till I was driven to the borders of despair; nor could I find any thing to
afford consolation to my spirit, or alleviate the anguish of my soul; and
I was only saved from distraction by the hope that I should live to see
the second coming of Christ; without which I could see no way of
restoration from the corruptions of a fallen nature, nor any deliverance
from the shackles of a false religion. I fasted and prayed to God, night
and day, for a long time.

At length it pleased God to give an answer by his mighty power,
which descended in divine operations, and struck a death blow upon
all my natural powers, and paralized every propensity of my nature. It
was then clearly manifested to me, by the visions of God and the spirit
of prophecy, that the coming of Christ and his Kingdom were at hand,
even at the door. These gifts of the Divine Spirit, I considered as the
fruits of my being baptized into the spirit of that remarkable revival
which took place in New-Lebanon, and the adjacent towns.

After despairing of ever finding the real work of salvation, upon
the old ecclesiastical foundation, and hearing of this revival, I went to
see whether I could find the work of God among them. I first attended
a meeting in Hancock, among the subjects of this revival; I went,
praying to God that I might know the truth, and be kept from error. I
was soon convinced that the Divine Power attended this meeting; and
here I first received it. I then requested the brethren "to come over and
help us." They accordingly came to Strockbridge, where I then lived;
and many there caught the spirit of this revival, and received the like
spiritual gifts. The substance of all those gifts evidently tended to show
that the second appearing of Christ was at hand; that a complete
separation from all the creeds and systems of religion known among
professors would then take place; and that the way of salvation from
sin would then be made manifest to the people.

Altho the spirit of that revival soon ceased, I still maintained my
confidence in the promises of God then given, and firmly believed I

should soon see them fulfilled, and that the second coming of Christ would shortly be ushered in, by a clear and evident manifestation of his Divine Spirit. Nor was I disappointed in my expectations of this great event; tho the manner of it was beyond all human calculation. Its commencement was, indeed, "as a light shining in a dark place;" and the messengers who first proclaimed the glad tidings, were people "wondered at."

The first direct intelligence I had of them, was from Tallmadge Bishop, about the beginning of June, 1780. He was one of the first who had visited them from these parts. He came to see me at my house, in West-Stockbridge, and informed me that he had seen a people who had all the gifts of the apostolic church, and gave me a particular relation concerning them, which need not be here repeated. As I knew the man well, and had knowledge of his former labors in the revival, I fully believed his report, and he was indeed a welcome messenger to me. The next Sabbath I attended a meeting at New-Lebanon, where I saw Samuel Fitch, who had also been to see these strangers, and had united with them.—He had the power of God upon him, and was exercised in divers operations. I felt an evidence in my soul, by the sensible operations of Divine Power, that this was the fulfillment of my former prophecy, and was fully convinced that it was the beginning of the second appearing of Christ, and the setting up of his Kingdom on earth. Some years before this, I had been afflicted with a long course of the fever and ague, which finally settled in my legs, and produced a lameness that prevented me from walking much on foot. But when I received this confirmation of the glad tidings of the gospel, and saw and felt these wonderful operations of Divine Power, it produced such a miraculous effect upon my bodily powers, that I was enabled to set out immediately on foot, to go and visit these strange people. And tho I travelled about thirty miles the next day, I felt no inconvenience from it.

When I arrived at Watervliet, where they lived, I was received with great kindness. The leader of this people was *Ann Lee*, whom they called *Mother*; and truly she seemed like a mother. Her countenance, and the countenances of those who stood as witnesses with her, shone with brightness and glory, as evidently as the shining of the sun upon clear water. This confirmed me that the glory of God was upon them. The first words I recollect hearing from Mother Ann was, "James, take this man and let him open his mind." This was just what I desired; and by this I perceived that she knew the state of my mind. I opened my

THE SHAKERS

mind and confessed my sins, freely and honestly, before Elder James, as a witness of God.

I had frequently confessed my sins to God in secret, as many others do; and in conformity to the practice of public preachers in Antichrist's kingdom, I had frequently, in public, confessed myself and the congregation to be great sinners. But in all this I brought nothing to light, nor did I find any abiding releasement of soul. The burden of my sins returned upon me, and the condemnation still continued. I was therefore convinced that I did not confess to God's acceptance: for I read, "If we confess our sins, he is faithful and just to forgive us our sins, and to cleanse us from all unrighteousness." (1 John i. 10.) This promise I had never before found verified. But now, by bringing my deeds to the light, I found the promise of God fulfilled: for I felt entirely released from the burden of sin. All condemnation and despair were entirely taken away, and my soul was filled with heavenly peace and comfort, accompanied with a godly sorrow and repentance for sin.

I tarried about a week, and witnessed many beautiful displays of divine power and goodness, and heard many precious instructions and exhortations. Here my soul received the precious "unction of the Holy One," which is the baptism of the Spirit, and by which I knew the spiritual things of God, which cannot be understood nor discerned by the natural man. This produced in me many heavenly gifts, and many operations of Divine Power. Here I obtained the full answer of my former prayers; for I had now lived to see the second coming of Christ, and the commencement of his Kingdom on earth. In this I was confirmed beyond a doubt.

I left them with great reluctance; and nothing but my duty to my family, enjoined by Mother Ann's counsel, could have reconciled my feelings, to retire from a place and a people so evidently filled with the Spirit of Christ, and so blessed with the Divine presence. I returned to my family, and felt myself blessed in my obedience to Mother Ann's testimony, and daily enjoyed the presence of God, and felt the powerful influences of his Spirit. And I have reason to bless God that my wife and children all embraced the same testimony of the gospel, and, with the exception of one daughter, who died firm in the faith, they are all now living in the Society, and continue in faithful obedience to the gospel. . . .

SAMUEL JOHNSON
New-Lebanon, Jan. 19th, 1827
(Seth Wells, ed., *Testimonies*, pp. 104–111) [1827]

THE SHAKERS

7

Having been blessed with forty-four years experience in the important work of salvation and redemption, and feeling myself near the close of my earthly existence, I consider it my duty and privilege to give a short statement of that important work, which God has wrought in these last days, for the restoration of fallen man, and the effect which this work has produced on myself and others. This work I have seen, felt and experienced, and can testify that it is truly of God; and that it has been wrought by virtue of the testimony received through Mother Ann Lee, and the Elders with her. This I received, not as the word of man or woman, but as the truth of God, revealed from Heaven, which is a searcher of the heart and a trier of the reins: for such it has proved to me. And I can say of them, in truth, as the woman of Samaria said of Jesus; "they told me all things that ever I did;" and I can put the same question; "Is not this the Christ?" or in other words, is not this the work of his Spirit revealed through them?...

...

This experience, (if I had no other evidence,) I find fully sufficient to confirm my faith and confidence in the present work of God, beyond the shadow of a doubt. Those truths which have been confirmed by a long experience of actual obedience, and the constant testimony of a living witness within, can never be doubted. This testimony assures me that Jesus Christ, that despised Nazarene, who was accused by the rebellious Jews, and haughty scribes and Pharisees, as the wine-bibber, and a friend of publicans and sinners, was the first pillar in the regeneration, to call souls from darkness to light, and from the power of Satan unto God. And this same testimony equally assures me that Ann Lee, that despised female, who is equally accused by rebellious sinners, and modern scribes and Pharisees, of intoxication and lewdness, was anointed of God as the second heir in the all-important work of redemption, as all can bear witness who, from the heart, have obeyed her heavenly precepts, and followed her Christ-like example....

JOHN WARNER
Harvard, [Massachusetts,] July 7th, 1826.
(Seth Wells, ed., *Testimonies,* pp. 134–135) [1827]

8

... However incredible or unaccountable these things may appear to those who are without Christ and without God in the world, I am fully established in this truth, and can confidently testify to all men, without the least doubt or hesitation, that Christ did indeed commence his second appearance, by his Spirit, in Mother Ann, to complete the work of salvation and redemption, according to his promise;—that she was a chosen vessel, anointed and commissioned of God, to reveal to fallen man the seat of human depravity, and to preach the gospel of salvation to a lost world;—and that she and the first witnesses did actually administer the only way of life and salvation, to all who believed and obeyed her testimony.

These things are well known to me, and to hundreds of others, not merely because of the visible and miraculous operations of the power of God which wrought in us; but because, through obedience to their testimony, during a period of more than forty years, we have found that full salvation and deliverance from the law of sin and death, which we had long sought in vain among other professors of Christianity. This saving grace of God, and these gifts of the Holy Spirit, have not been exclusively confined to Mother Ann, and the first witnesses with her; but the same anointing Spirit and power have been transmitted, through them, to their faithful successors in the ministry, who have continued to bear the same testimony, and to bring forth the same fruits of holiness, righteousness and peace, to this day; and which, according to promise, will abide in the true Church of Christ forever.

BENJAMIN WHITCHER
Canterbury, [*New Hampshire,*] *July 23rd, 1826.*
(Seth Wells, ed., *Testimonies,* p. 155) [1827]

9

Elijah Wilds—autobiographic sketch. I.

. . .

... My mind continued anxious to find the way of God, and so intense was my thought of God's work in the days of the apostles, that I often wept, hoping and praying that I might live to see the glorious day of Christ's Second Coming.

THE SHAKERS

. . .

In the summer of 1781 I heard of a new sect of people who were at the Square House, so called in Harvard. I went to see them, and they taught that the gospel of Christ required us to confess and forsake all sin, and to bear a daily cross. They testified that in order to obtain salvation from sin, God required the self–denial of every impure act, word and thought. They also testified that Christ had commenced his second appearance, without sin, unto salvation, to all who were willing to believe and obey. And truly, salvation was the object of my desires. The power of their testimony, and the spirit of godliness, which I felt from them convinced me that Mother Ann was a person sent to administer eternal life, to the children of this world.

On my second visit they presented a further degree of light, to my mind, than before. The trumpet gave a certain sound, and I felt it my duty to prepare for battle. They said, we must overcome sin before we could sit down with the Lamb of God in the Kingdom of Heaven. That we must overcome, even as Jesus overcame. The evidences of the testimony, and the manifestations of the power of God, were so powerful and convincing, that I could not resist them. I therefore confessed my sins, to God, in the presence of his witnesses and found that assurance and releasement which I had never found before.

They taught me the necessity of righting all my wrongs, by making restitution where I had done injury to any one, and of living a pure and holy life. They also taught me that the only repentance that was acceptable to God, was to cease from sin: and that there could be no real repentance of sin without forsaking it.

This was now the work before me, and in faithfulness I should certainly find the blessing of God. I soon began to see clearly the difference between traveling into sin, and traveling out of it: as the one was directly contrary to the other. . . .

(*The Shaker Manifesto* XII, 8, pp. 178–179) [1882]

10

16. One evening, afterward, two men came to dispute with Mother, one of whom was called Colonel Smith. They went into the room where Mother Ann and the Elders were, with a number of Believers, but did not know Mother. Smith asked, "Is there not a woman here that is the head of the Church?" "Nay, Christ is the head of the

Church," replied Mother. Elder William Lee said, "We do not allow *man* nor *woman* to be the head of the Church, for *Christ* is the head of the Church." "But," said Smith, "there is a woman here that teaches, is there not?" "We must not suffer a woman to teach." Father William Lee replied, "We do not suffer man nor woman to teach except they have the spirit of Christ in them, and Christ teaches through them, and then either man or woman may teach." This answer so confounded the Colonel that he had no more to say, but soon went away.

. . .

13. . . . To prove the charge of blasphemy, it was testified that Samuel Fitch had declared that "in Mother Ann, dwells the fullness of the Godhead, bodily." To this charge, Samuel, by Elder James' direction, replied, in his own defense, "We read, in the scriptures, that the fullness of the Godhead dwelt in the Lord Jesus Christ, bodily." And again, "except Christ be in you, ye are reprobates." The inference was at once perceived, by the Judges, who found themselves unable to proceed with a charge which must, in the issue, prove themselves reprobates.

14. But Samuel, feeling great boldness, stood up and warned the Judges in these words, "Take heed what you do to these people—Mother Ann and the Elders—for they are God's Anointed Ones whom he hath sent to America."

(Giles Avery, ed., *Precepts*, pp. 105–106; 130) [1816/1888]

20. Samuel Fitch was among the first who visited Mother Ann and the Elders at Watervliet. He arrived in the evening, and tarried over night. In the morning Mother came into the room and sat down with him, and related to him the manner in which the spirit of God wrought upon her, in the first of her faith. She continued her discourse several hours and related many remarkable dealings and manifestations of God to her from time to time.

21. Among many other visions which she related, she said, "I saw, by revelation, the loss of all mankind, not only the present generation, but the generations of past ages; and I saw them, as it were, clothed with blackness and darkness, many of whom I knew. I saw my own natural mother in the same condition, and when I saw her, I cried to God; for I had thought that my mother was a good woman, if there were any good upon earth.

22. She also said, "I have seen souls in the world of spirits who had wandered in the regions of darkness, in such agony and distress,

that, to my vision, they had worn gutters in their cheeks with their tears in mourning and weeping; and when the gospel was offered to them they were so hungry for it, they came, as it were, with wide-open mouths to receive it. I have seen vast numbers of the dead rise and come to judgment, and receive the gospel, and begin their travel in the regeneration."

23. She mentioned the names of some whom she had seen rise from the dead, and among others, a number of Samuel's relations and acquaintances, who had been dead, some of them, many years. She further said, "I have seen the poor negroes, who are so much despised, redeemed from their loss, with crowns on their heads."

(Giles Avery, ed., *Precepts*, p. 33) [1816/1888]

I I

Every true believer is led and governed by the same Spirit, which is the Spirit of Christ; and thus we become one with Christ, as he is one with the Father. As the blood, which is the life of the body, circulates through every member of the body; so the Spirit of Christ (which in the scriptures is sometimes called the blood of Christ) circulates through every member of the body of Christ, and is *the life of his body*, which is the *Church*. Every true and faithful believer is a member of that body, and receives strength and nourishment from it.

Joseph Main
(Seth Wells, ed., *Testimonies*, p. 103) [1827]

*   *   *

Father Joseph Meacham:

A
CONCISE STATEMENT
OF THE
PRINCIPLES
OF THE
ONLY TRUE CHURCH
ACCORDING TO
THE GOSPEL
OF THE
PRESENT APPEARANCE
OF
CHRIST.
As held to and practised upon by the true
followers of the LIVING SAVIOUR,
at NEWLEBANON, &c.

. . . .

A SHORT INFORMATION of what we believe of the dispensations of GOD'S GRACE TO FALLEN MAN: And in what manner
they have found acceptance with GOD, and salvation from sin in
former dispensations: with particular reference to the present display
of GOD'S grace unto us: And in what manner we find acceptance with
God, and hope of ETERNAL LIFE thro' our LORD JESUS CHRIST
in obedience to the gospel of his PRESENT APPEARANCE.

A
CONCISE STATEMENT

We believe that the first light of salvation was given or made
known to the patriarchs by promise; and that they believed in the
promise of Christ, and were obedient to the command of God made
known unto them, were the people of God and were accepted of God
as righteous, or perfect in their generations; according to the measure
of light and truth manifested unto them; which was as waters to the
ancles [sic] signified by Ezekiel's vision of the holy waters (chapter 47).

61

THE SHAKERS

And altho' they could not receive regeneration or the fulness of salvation, from the fleshly or fallen nature in this life; because the fulness of time was not yet come, that they should receive the baptism of the Holy Ghost and fire; for the destruction of the body of sin, and purification of the soul; but Abram being called, and chosen of God as the father of the faithful; was received into covenant relation with God by promise; that in him (and his seed which was Christ) all the families of the earth should be blessed, and these earthly blessings, which were promised to Abram, were a shadow of gospel or spiritual blessings to come: and circumcision, though it was a seal of Abram's faith, yet it was but a sign of the mortification and destruction of the flesh by the gospel in a future day. Observe, circumcision, or outward cutting of the foreskin of the flesh, did not cleanse the man from sin; but was a sign of the baptism of the Holy Ghost and fire: which is by the power of God manifested in divers operations and gifts of the spirit, as in the days of the apostles; which does indeed destroy the body of sin, or fleshly nature, and purify the man from all sin both soul and body. So that Abram, though in the full faith of the promise; yet, as he did not receive the substance of the thing promised, his hope of eternal salvation was in Christ, by the Gospel to be attained in the resurrection from the dead.

The second dispensation was the law that was given of God to Israel, by the hand of Moses; which was a further manifestation of that salvation which was promised through Christ by the gospel, both in the order and ordinances which was [sic] instituted and given to Israel, as the church and people of God according to that dispensation; which was as waters to the ancles [sic], Ezekiel XLVII. by which they were distinguished from all the families of the earth. For, while they were strictly obedient to all the commands, ordinances, and statutes, that God gave them, they were approbated of God according to the promise for life; and blessing was promised unto them in the line of obedience: Cursing and death, in disobedience: for God, who is forever jealous for the honor and glory of his own great name, always dealt with them according to his word; for while they were obedient to the command of God, and purged out sin from amongst them, God was with them, according to his promise. But when they disobeyed the command of God, and committed sin, and became like other people, the hand of the Lord was turned against them; and those evils came upon them which God had threatened; so we see that they were wholly obedient to the will of God made known in that dispensation, were accepted as just, or righteous: yet, as the dispensation was short, they did not attain that salvation which was promised in the gospel; so that as it respected the new–birth, or real purification of the man from all sin; the law made nothing perfect, but was a shadow of good things to come; their only hope of eternal redemption was in the promise of Christ, by the gospel to be attained in the resurrection from the dead. Acts of the Apostles XXVI. 6, 7.

The third dispensation was the gospel of Christ's first appearance, in the flesh: and that salvation which took place in consequence of his life, death, resurrection, and ascension at the right hand of the father being accepted in his obedience, as the first born among many brethren; he received power and authority to administer the power of the resurrection and eternal judgment to all the children of men: so that he has become the author of eternal salvation to all that obey him; and as Christ has this power in himself, he did administer power and authority to his church at the day of Pentecost, as his body: with all the gifts that he had promised them, which was the first gift of the Holy Ghost, as an in-dwelling comforter to abide with them forever: and by which they were baptised into Christ's death; death to all sin; and were in the hope of the resurrection from the dead, through the operation of the power of God, which wrought in them. And as they had received the substance of the promise of Christ come in the flesh, by the gift and power of the Holy Ghost; they had power to preach the gospel in Christ's name to every creature;—and to administer the power of God to as many as believed, and were obedient to the gospel which they preached; and also to remit and retain sin in the name and authority of Christ on earth: so that they that believe in the gospel, and were obedient to that form of doctrine which was taught them; by denying all ungodliness and worldly lusts; and became entirely dead to the law by the body of Christ, or power of the Holy Ghost, were in the travel of the resurrection from the dead; or the redemption of the body. So that they who took up a full cross against the world, flesh, and devil; and who forsook all for Christ's sake; and followed him in the regeneration, by perservering in that line of obedience to the end; found the resurrection from the dead, and eternal salvation in that dispensation was only as water to the loins; the mystery of God was not finished; but there was another day prophesied of, called the second appearance of Christ, or the final and last display of God's grace to a lost world; in which the mystery of God should be finished as he has spoken by his prophets since the world began: which day could not come, except there was a falling away from that faith and power that the church then stood in; in which time anti–christ was to have his reign, whom Christ should destroy with the spirit of his mouth and brightness of his appearance: which falling away began soon after the apostles, and gradually increased in the church, until about four hundred and fifty seven years from Christ's birth (or thereabouts) at which time the power of the Holy People, or church of Christ, was scattered or lost by reason of transgression: and anti–christ, or false religion, got to be established. Since that time the witnesses of Christ have prophesied in sackcloth or under darkness: and altho' many have been faithful to testify against sin; even to the laying down of their lives for the testimony which they held; so that God accepted them in their obedience; while they were faithful and just to live or walk up to the measure of light and truth of God, revealed or made known unto them, but as it is written, that all they that will live godly in Christ Jesus, shall suffer persecution; and so it has been, and those faithful witnesses lost their lives, by those falsely called the church of Christ: which is anti–christ; for the true church of Christ never persecuted any; but were inoffensive, harmless, separate from sin, living in obedience to God they earnestly contend for the fame. Therefore it may be plainly seen and known, where the true church of Christ is: but as it is written anti–christ or false churches should prevail against the saints and overcome them, before Christ's second appearance, 2 Thess. II. 3. Let no man deceive you by any means for that day shall not come except there come a falling away first; and that man of sin be revealed, the son of perdition, Rev. XIII. 7. And it was given unto him to overcome them, and power was given him over all kindreds, tongues, and nations; and this is the state Christ prophesied the world of mankind should be in, at his second appearance, Luke XVII. 26. And as it was in the day of Noe, so shall it be in the days of the son of man, verse 30. Even so shall it be in the day when the son of man is revealed; plainly referring to his second appearance to consume or destroy anti–christ, and make a final end of sin; and establish his kingdom upon earth: but as the revelation of Christ must be in his people, whom he has chosen to be his body, to give testimony of him and to preach his gospel to a lost world.

The fourth dispensation or day is the second appearance of Christ, or final, or last display of God's grace to a lost world, in which the mystery of God will be finished and a decisive work, to the final salvation, or damnation of all the children of man. (Which according to the prophecies rightly calculated, and truly understood, began in the year of our Saviour Jesus Christ, 1747.) See Daniel and Revelations. In the manner following, 1st. To a number,[5] in the manifestation of great light—and mighty trembling by the invisible power of God, and visions, and revelations, and prophecies; which has progressively increased, with administration of all those spiritual gifts, that was administered to the apostles at the day of Pentecost: which is the comforter that has led us into all truth: which was promised to abide with the true church of Christ unto the end of the world, and by which we find baptism into Christ's death; death to all sin, become alive to God, by the power of Christ's resurrection, which worketh in us mightily; by which a dispensation of the gospel is committed unto us; and woe be unto us if we preach not the gospel of Christ. (For in finding so great a salvation and deliverance from the law of sin and death in believing and obeying this gospel which is the gospel of Christ, in confessing and forsaking all sin, and denying ourselves and bearing the cross of Christ, against the world, flesh, and devil.) We have found repentance of all our sins; and are made partakers of the grace of God wherein we now stand: which all others in believing and obeying, have acceptance with God, and find salvation from their sins as well as we; God being no respecter of persons but willing that all should come to the knowlddge of the truth, and be saved. Thus we have given a short information of what we believe of the dispensation of God's grace to mankind, both past and present: and in what manner the people of God have found justification, or acceptance of God, which was and is still in believing and obeying the light and truth of God, revealed or made known, in the day or dispensation in which it was revealed: for as the wrath of God is revealed from heaven against all ungodliness, and unrighteousness of men, who hold the truth in unrighteousness or live in any known sin against him; so his mercy and grace is towards all them that truly fear him, and turn from all their sins, by confessing, and forsaking, and repenting, which is the way and manner in which all must find the forgiveness of their sins, and acceptance with God through our Lord Jesus Christ, or finally fail of the grace of God; and that salvation which is brought to light by the gospel. But to conclude, in short, as we believe, and do testify, that the present gospel of God's grace unto us is the day which in the scripture, is spoken or prophesied

---

5. Note the emphasis on community "To a number" rather than the single person Ann Lee.

of, as the second appearing of Christ to consume or destroy anti–christ, or false religion, and to make an end of the reigning power of sin (for he that committeth sin is the servant of sin and satan) over the children of men: and to establish his kingdom, and that righteousness that will stand forever: and that the present display of the work and power of God, will increase until it is manifest to all; which it must be in due time: for every eye shall see him; and he will reward every man according to his deeds: and none can stand in sin or unrighteousness; but in that righteousness which is pure and holy: even without fault before the throne of God which is obtained by grace, through faith in obedience to the truth of the everlasting gospel of our Lord Jesus Christ, in denying all ungodliness and worldly lusts; by confessing all sin, and taking up the cross of Christ, against the world, flesh, and devil: we desire therefore, that the children of men would believe the testimony of truth, and turn from their sins by repentance, that they might obtain the mercy of God, and salvation from sin before it is too late.

(Joseph Meacham, *A Concise Statement, &c.*, pp. 1–17) [1790]

*   *   *

13

For what purpose then did Christ come into the world, and do and suffer all that he did? This is an important question and worthy of a sober reply. It comprehends the whole of that relation which Christ bears to God and to men as Mediator between them both. The following particulars are proposed to give satisfactory information on this subject.

He came to reveal the Father to men. "No man hath seen God at any time; the only begotten Son, who is in the bosom of the Father, he hath revealed Him." (Jno. i. 18.) "He that hath seen me hath seen the Father." (xiv. 9.) The true knowledge of God was not with men, but he is revealed in Christ, Who is *the brightness of his glory and the character* (the express image) *of his existence.* (Heb. i. 3.) By this revelation men are taught what God is, and how far they are fallen from their original rectitude; for as man was created in the image of God and to be the glory of God, and had fallen by sin, God sent another, a second or a new man, in his own image *more deeply expressed,* to be the beginning of a new creation, in whom to recover man in his fall and restore him to favor and fellowship in a more happy condition than at the first.

He came to open *the new and living way;* a way before unknown, and containing in it true and eternal life, being infinitely preferable to the ministration of death and condemnation which was before. "But if the ministration of death, written and engraven in stones, was glorious, so that the children of Israel could not steadfastly behold the face of Moses for the glory of his countenance, which glory was to be done away; how shall not the ministration of the Spirit be rather glorious? for if the ministration of condemnation be glory, much more doth the ministration of righteousness exceed in glory." (2 Cor. iii, 7, 8, 9.) "Having therefore, brethren, boldness to enter into the holiest by the blood of Jesus, *by a new and living way,* which he hath consecrated for us through the vail, that is to say, his flesh, and having an high priest over the house of God, let us draw near with a true heart, in full assurance of faith." (Heb. x. 19, &c.)

And as he came to open the new and living way, he also came to be our example, that we should walk in his steps. "But if, when ye do well, and suffer for it, ye take it patiently, this is acceptable with God. For even hereunto were ye called: because Christ also suffered for us, leaving us an example that ye should follow his steps." (1 Pet. ii. 20, 21.) "If any man will come after me, let him deny himself, and take up his cross daily, and follow me." "And he that doth not take up his cross and follow after me, is not worthy of me." (Luke. ix. 23; Matt. x. 38.) Thus he is our forerunner, the author and finisher of our faith, the first who introduced it to the world, and the first who perfected it by obedience. For as the faith of Abraham was made perfect by works, so is also the faith of Jesus Christ made perfect in obedience; as well as that of all Christians, who are called to "lay aside every weight, and the sin which doth so easily beset us, and run with patience the race which is set before us, looking to Jesus the author and finisher of faith; who for the joy that was set before him, endured the cross, despising the shame, and is set down at the right hand of the throne of God." (Heb. xii. 1, 2.) Thus for our benefit he came to set us the example of denying self and doing the will of God. "Him that cometh to me I will in no wise cast out. For I came down from heaven, not to do mine own will, but the will of him that sent me." (Jno. vi. 37, 38.)

He came into the world that men might be saved and have eternal life through him. "For the Son of man is come to seek and to save that which is lost." "For God so loved the world, that he gave his only begotten Son, that whosoever believeth in him should not perish, but have everlasting life. For God sent not his Son into the world to condemn the world; but that the world through him might be saved." (Luke xix. 10; Jno. iii. 16, 17.)

He came to reconcile the world to God, by revealing God to men and showing them the terms of reconciliation, to wit, "That God was in Christ reconciling the world to himself, not imputing their trespasses unto them." (2 Cor. v. 19.) This is the subject in relation to which there has been so much darkness in the world of professors,[6] so much error, and much contention, supposing that God in Christ, or through him, was reconciled to the world, contrary to the language of Scripture, instead of the world being reconciled to him; which would mean, if anything, either that God had through Christ become an approver of man's ways, corrupt and sinful as they are, or else, that God had been so angry at sin and sinners as to put him out of his proper element, and make him unwilling to receive the returning sinner until he had spent his vengeance on the sinner or his substitute; which having done on Jesus Christ, he becomes calm and can be approached by a returning penitent, whom he now receives with the utmost complacency. But these things are incompatible with the perfections of God, and not worthy to be imputed to him. The Scripture is plain enough that men through Christ are reconciled to God, and are then at peace with him; and that establishes peace between the God of peace and men of peace.

The same is true of the word *atonement,* which has commonly been understood, as applied to God, the effect of a pacifying satisfaction, to appease his anger, when the Scripture so expressly declares that *we have received it,* and also shows that atonement is the same as reconciliation. "For if, when we were enemies, we were *reconciled,* we shall be saved by his life. And not only so, but we also joy in God through our Lord Jesus Christ, by whom *we have now received the atonement* or *reconciliation.*" (Rom. v. 10, 11.) This connection is a testimony for the English reader, that *the atonement* here said to be received is the same as *reconciliation,* that is, the effect or fruit of the death of Christ, or being reconciled to God, as mentioned in the former clauses. The Greek

---

6. "Professors," a common eighteenth century term for those professing a creedal faith.

word also here rendered *atonement* is properly rendered by *reconciliation*. And by whichever word it be rendered, it is evidently that which must take place in the creature, for God is unchangeably the same. And that change, or reconciliation, must also be in reality; not by imputing the righteousness of another; the Scripture makes no mention of any such thing in the case. (See B. W. Stone's Letters on Atonement.)[7]

He came to be the end of the law for righteousness to those who believe in him. That is, to put an end to the Mosaic law, by fulfilling it in himself and showing the people how to be righteous without it, by believing in him, confessing him, and doing the will of God as he did, and thus becoming their sacrifice and their righteousness. . . . And that he is the end of the law for righteousness to those who believe, not merely by offering himself a sacrifice or sin-offering to God in their room, but by doing the will of God as it ought to be done, and so becoming an example and establishing that which should supersede the law, is evident from the very pointed language of the Apostle [in Heb. x. 4–10.] . . . Thus expressly it is stated what he established as the second, to succeed the law of sacrifices which was first, that is, doing the will of God. . . . Let these things suffice at present, to show how Christ is the end of the law to believers; not by offering up himself a sacrifice as our surety or substitute, but by consecrating *for us*, through his flesh and by his own example, a new and living way, *to do the will of God* as the *second, the substance*, to supersede the first, the unprofitable shadows of the law. . . .

Other particulars might be named, as his taking away, or bearing the sin of the world, but all these are either included in those already stated, or will be in those subjects yet to be considered in connection with this. But in all these things, which comprehend the purposes of his coming into the world, there is not a word of his righteousness, or what he has done or suffered, being imputed to believers for their justification. Neither is there any prospect of any man's being a partaker with Christ in his salvation and glory, unless he first partake with him in his sufferings and death, unless he embrace the same faith of Christ, to do the will of God, walking as he walked. "For in that he died, he died unto sin once; but in that he liveth, he liveth unto God.

---

7. Barton W. Stone, a leader in the Kentucky Revival, was at first attracted to Shakerism but subsequently became a bitter enemy; cf. Part IV of Dunlavy's *The Manifesto*.

Likewise reckon ye also yourselves to be dead indeed to sin, but alive to God through Jesus Christ our Lord." "For if we be dead with him, we shall also live with him: If we suffer we shall also reign with him: if we deny him, he will also deny us." (Rom. vi. 10, 11; 2 Tim. ii. 11, 12.)

(John Dunlavy, *The Manifesto*, pp. 72–77) [1818/1847]

14

Christ redeems from vain conversation, or an unprofitable manner of living.[8] "Knowing that ye were not redeemed with corruptible things, as silver and gold, from your vain conversation received by tradition from your fathers; but with the precious blood of Christ." (1 Pet. i. 18, 19.) This vain conversation doth not relate merely to useless discourse, of which no doubt they, as well as people in these days, had a great deal; old wive's fables and endless genealogies, which are unprofitable and vain; but to the whole circle of active life, and with the utmost propriety, to the vain forms and ceremonies of religious worship, which they had received of their fathers by tradition, in which there was nothing saving, nothing of that godly edifying which is in the faith of Christ. The Greek word ἀναστροφῆς (anastrophees) in the connection in which it stands, fully justifies an acceptation thus extensive, and its common use in the Scriptures is not contrary thereto. From this vain circle of life and religion then, in which is no true foundation of hope, Christians are redeemed by Christ through his blood, or life, who set them a better example, to teach them and lead them to God in the new and living way, which he hath consecrated, at the expense of his life and blood, through the vail, that is to say, his flesh.

Christ having redeemed his people from this vain conversation, it follows as a necessary consequence that they are redeemed from the carnal mind, or fleshly principle, which rules in men and holds them in bondage; for that is the very core and foundation of the vain conversation of the world, as it is before written, "And you hath he quickened, who were dead in trespasses and in sins; wherein in time past ye also walked according to the course of this world, according to

---

8. "Vain conversation"—conversation in the ancient sense of *conversatio*, the conversion or change of *metanoia*, as in the *conversatio morum*, "change in the ways of living," of the monastic tradition.

the prince of the power of the air, the spirit that now worketh in the children of disobedience: among whom also we all had our conversation, ἀναστροφῆν, in times past, in the lusts of our flesh, fulfilling the desires of the flesh and of the mind; and were by nature the children of wrath even as others." Out of the wretched state, therefore, of death and carnality, Christ redeems his people, or which is the same, God in Christ, and quickeneth them together with him. "But God, who is rich in mercy, for (or through) his great love wherewith he loved us, even when we were dead in sins, hath quickened us together with Christ; (by grace ye are saved;) and hath raised us up together, and made us sit together in heavenly places in Christ Jesus." (Eph. ii. 1–6.)

(John Dunlavy, *The Manifesto*, p. 113) [1818/1847]

15

He who confesses his sins in secret is not certainly conscious that any being hears or regards him, or if he believes he is heard, he has no idea, that any thing more is known after his confession than before. He may say it is his choice to confess to God whom he fears and regards more than man. But that he has more fear toward a man like himself than towards God is evident; because when he is confessing his sins to God in secret without dread, were he conscious that a man of like passions with himself, especially a hater of sin, were in hearing, he would be alarmed, or filled with consternation. And why so; only because the fear of man is deeper in his heart than the fear of God out of man? It is infinitely more mortifying for a man to confess his sins in faith and honesty, in the hearing and presence of God's witnesses, than to confess to God, as they say, abstractedly from men; which conclusively proves that to confess to God in men, is the deepest work, and the nearest possible approach to God. It fills up what is written: "He that covereth his sins shall not prosper: but whoso confesseth and forsaketh them shall have mercy." "For every one that doeth evil hateth the light, neither cometh to the light, lest his deeds should be reproved," (Discovered, or convicted, in the Greek, that is, lest he should be convicted of them, they being laid open in their true colours to his conscience,) "There is nothing covered that shall not be revealed; neither hid that shall not be known." But to confess secretly brings nothing to light; it makes nothing known. These hate the light, and come not to the light; they seek deep to hide counsel from the LORD;

for no man will imagine he can hide from God absolutely, or attempt to do it; but many seek with profound subtlety to hide from him in his witnesses. And, Wo to them, saith the LORD. But he who confesses to God in the true and established order, knows and sensibly feels, that he is heard and understood; that what he hath done is made known. This is coming to the light and uncovering; it is coming to truth and honesty; it is contrary to the spirit, or principle, which inclines men to commit sin; for that spirit can never lead a man to confess and expose his sins in so open a method, in so near an approach to God, until Satan can be divided against Satan. By thus confessing in the light, the spirit of sin and of darkness which rules in the corrupt and deceitful heart, is sensibly detected and exposed; this is coming to a light and a judgment of which the sinner is sensible; and this shows the necessity and propriety of God's having a witness. This is coming to the living God, on his living throne and in his living temple. As it is written: "Ye are the temple of the living God," and again: "The place of my throne; and the place of the soles of my feet; where I will dwell in the midst of the children of Israel for ever." And again: "To whom coming as unto a living stone disallowed indeed of men, but chosen of God, and precious, ye also, as living stones, are built up a spiritual house, an holy priesthood to offer up spiritual sacrifices (not legal types, but sacrifices in the spirit, or of a spiritual nature,) acceptable to God by Jesus Christ." (Ezek. xliii. 7; 1 Pet. ii. 4, 5.) Now we have already shown that the priesthood were God's ministers to the people, and the people's ministers to God; that the people presented to the priesthood what they offered to God, and confessed to God in them, or to them in God's stead, the sins which they had committed against him. Thus believers in Christ are (not now a legal or cermonial, but) a holy priesthood. Not that each one of them is an appointed ministering priest; but the true priests of God are all among them, Jesus Christ being the high priest: and separately from them, there is no access to God for salvation.

(John Dunlavy, *The Manifesto*, pp. 213–214) [1818/1847]

16

As the priesthood, under the law of Moses, included both the high priest and the second order, so in the Gospel of Christ, the Church, or body of Christ, is composed of the head and the members, and there is no true church, or body, without both. But, as under the law, when Aaron was anointed, he was the priest, and the only anointed one on earth, though incapable of serving at the altar, until he had offered a sacrifice, and then his sons were anointed with the same oil; and yet the service could not be all performed in order, in behalf of the people, until the high priest went into the Most Holy place and returned. So when Jesus was anointed with the Spirit, he alone was the only anointed priest of the Gospel; the only true habitation of God on earth, the true tabernacle, which the Lord pitched and not man, until he had made his sacrifice, and then his disciples were anointed with the same Spirit and became one with him; for he breathed on them, and said, Receive ye the Holy Ghost. Howbeit they were not fully commissioned nor qualified to minister the Gospel to the people, until he had ascended to the Father and returned in the gift of the Holy Ghost, on the day of Pentecost. They were then fully empowered, according to the work of that day, to preach repentance and the remission of sins in his name, and to do all that work in the spiritual house, which was set forth in a shadow, by the service of the tabernacle. They were then one with Christ and with the Father, according to the work of that day; and these in their proper order and power are the true body of Christ, and the true Christ, having received the same anointing of the Father, as Jesus himself, while he stood alone, and of the people there was none with him. Accordingly, it is written, "He that hath seen me hath seen the Father." And again: "At that day ye shall know that I am in my Father, and ye in me, and I in you." (Jno. xiv. 9, 20.) And again; "But ye have an unction from the Holy One, and ye know all things—But the anointing which ye have received of him abideth in you; and ye need not that any man teach you: but as the same anointing teacheth you of all things, and is truth, and is no lie." Further,

To prove that the Church is one with Christ, they being one body and constituting the true seed and true Christ, to whom the promise was made, the words of the apostle Paul may be introduced: "Now to Abraham and to his seed were the promises made. He saith not, And to seeds, as of many: but as of one, And to thy seed, which is Christ." (Gal. iii. 16.) Now, all of the faithful are the seed; not seeds, for they are one, as it is again written: "The children of the promise are counted for the seed." (Rom. ix. 8.) And, as it were, to put the question beyond a doubt, the following words are to the point: "For as the body is one, and hath many members, and all the members of that one body, being many, are one body: *so also is Christ.* For by one Spirit are we all baptized into one body: whether Jews or Greeks, bond or free; and have been all made to drink into one Spirit. For the body is not one member but many." (1 Cor. xii. 12–14. See the chapter throughout. . . .) The Apostle calls the Church, CHRIST, by name. So, then, wherever the true Church of Christ is, there is the true Christ of God, the light of the world, the light of men, and the salt of the earth; as said Jesus to his disciples, "Ye are the salt of the earth;" "Ye are the light of the world." (Matt. v. 13, 14.) And wherever a true Church of Christ is found, having regained the communion and unity of the Spirit, after the falling away by Antichrist, there is Christ in his second appearing without sin to salvation. Such was the light into which honest believers brought their deeds, by confessing them, in the apostolic dispensation, according to the work of that day; and such is the light to which all souls, who esteem Christ and his salvation above all inferior enjoyments, bring their deeds and expose them in the judgment, in his second appearing for a last and finishing work of salvation.

As it was the anointing of the Holy Ghost that constituted Jesus the Anointed, or the Christ, which is the same; so, the Church being anointed with the same, they were constituted the Anointed, the Christ. And the same authority, power, and office, ascribed to and possessed by Jesus, the CHRIST, as such was also ascribable to and possessed by the Church, as will be seen by and by. But to Jesus were given other names or titles besides *Christ,* or in addition to that, as, "The mighty God, the everlasting Father," which are not ascribable to the Church. Nor is it to be understood that any one member of the Church received that anointing in its fullness which constituted Jesus the Christ, but the Church collectively. "The glory which thou gavest me, I have given them; that they may be one even as we are one; I in them, and thou in me." (Jno. xvii. 22, 23.) "To one is given by the Spirit, the word of wisdom; to another, the word of knowledge by the same Spirit; to another, faith by the same Spirit; to another, the working of miracles; to another, prophecy; to another, discerning of spirits; to another, divers kinds of tongues; to another, the interpretation of tongues: but all these worketh that one and the self-same Spirit, dividing to every man severally as he will. For as the body is one and hath many members, and all the members of that one body, being many, are one body." "For we are members of his body, of his flesh, and of his bones." "Know ye not that your bodies are the members of

Christ?" "Touch not mine anointed, מְשִׁיחִי,[9] my christs, and do my prophets no harm."

(John Dunlavy, The Manifesto, pp. 218–220) [1818/1847]

17

The body of Christ does not depend on any name which its members may bear, or by which they may be called; for many have a name to live and are dead; and it is no uncommon thing for the enemies of the cross to fix terms of reproach on those who live nearest to God—*They shall revile you, and shall cast out your name as evil.*

In describing the body of Christ, we would not be understood as rejecting any real light from God, which any people may have received, because it has been at first short of full measure, but as acknowledging every degree of the light and power of God to its full extent. But, at the same time, we cannot consider any measure of light and power sufficient to characterize the Church, which comes short of that character which Christ has given. It is not by any means intended to cramp or restrain the spirits of men from improving every degree of light to the best advantage, to increase in the knowledge of God and the true Christian life, but we are perfectly willing to own the work of God wherever it appears, and to acknowledge the members of Christ wherever they are found, and under whatever name, provided they are furnished with that evidence which is indispensably necessary to constitute their real character. The object of our labour is not to create parties and divisions in the body of Christ, but to be in the number of his real followers, and to use our faithful endeavours, as far as our knowledge and duty extend, that others also may partake of the same blessedness. But it cannot be uncharitable to require, in every man, the genuine evidences of Christianity before he be encouraged to consider himself one of the body; for evidently, it can do no man any good to be seated in the guest-chamber without the wedding-garment, much less can it avail to any good effect, to betray mankind with the notion of having already obtained it, until the time is past; but in these cases it is by all means best, to honestly point out the way, as opportunity may serve, faithfully maintaining what is the real character of the Chris-

---

9. Sp.: מְשִׁיחִים

tian, and what the genuine marks of the body of Christ, and leave all men under the most forcible impression possible, as to these points— *who are the body of Christ, what the true marks,* and *not to stop short of an inheritance with them:* for, that these are attainable and free to all, is just as certain as that they exist. *Whosoever will let him take the water of life freely.*

(John Dunlavy, *The Manifesto,* pp. 237–238) [1818/1847]

18

1. The Church of Christ is composed of such as are called and chosen of God out of the spirit and practice of the world. And in obedience to that call, they are separated from all the rest of mankind, and united in one body, constituted a holy and peculiar people, actuated by one holy Spirit, and are devoted to the cause of truth and virtue.

2. The Church of Christ is called the kingdom of heaven, because it is under the government of heaven, and is a state, habitation, or society, necessary to prepare mankind for the happiness of heaven itself; and such is that line of order and disposition of things in the spiritual world, extending from the source of true happiness, to this world, that no soul can enter heaven, but through that kingdom, or Church of Christ.

3. Hence, the Church is called the *light of the world,* (Mat. v. 13, 14.) inasmuch as the men of the world can receive no true saving light, but in and through the Church. It is also the *salt of the earth,* (See Mat. v. 13.) as none upon earth can be saved but by the Church: It is therefore plainly, *the saviour of all who are truly united with that body.*

4. The Church is properly the house or habitation of God on earth, which signifies that God is not to be found any where else on earth. [God may be seen in the order and works of his creation and providence; yet he can be found for the salvation and redemption of mankind, only where he has revealed himself for that purpose, and that is in his Church.] As it is written: *Son of man, the place of my throne, and the place of the soles of my feet, where I will dwell in the midst of the children of Israel forever.* (Ezek. xliii. 7; 1 Tim. iii. 16.) Great is the mystery of godliness: *God manifested in the flesh.*

5. The essential properties of the Church of Christ are *purity and unity.* The Church is *one* in faith and practice; *one* in doctrine, disci-

pline, and government; and *one* in the mutual and equal enjoyment of all things, both spiritual and temporal. And where this *oneness* doth not exist, there is neither fruit nor evidence of the true Church of Christ; for *Christ is not*, nor can he be *divided*.[10]

6. The Church has but *one* faith, and that is *the faith of Christ, the faith of the Son of God*, which overcomes the nature and spirit of the world, enlightens the understanding, influences the will, and purifies the heart. It is *one* in doctrine, which is, according to godliness, sound, pure, wholesome, and free from error; inasmuch as it makes no provision for the flesh or any evil, or any sin great or small, and leads only to the practice of true godliness, unspotted piety, and sound virtue. *There shall, in no wise, enter into it, anything that defileth.* (Rev. xxi. 27.)

7. The Church has but *one* government, because all the members are governed and influenced by *one* Spirit, which is the Spirit of Christ, who is the Head of the body, and the centre of influence to the members. *They shall lift up their voices together—they shall see eye to eye.* (Isa. lii. 8; ix. 21.) It is *one* in practice, which is righteousness and peace. *Thy people also, shall be all righteous. He that doeth righteousness, is righteous.* (1 John iii. 7.) It is therefore by doing right, that the Church is righteous: and of the Church all must learn righteousness, who will be righteous. *Let your light so shine before men.*

8. The Church is of *one united interest*, as the children of *one family*, enjoying equal rights and privileges in things spiritual and temporal, because they are influenced and led by *one Spirit* and love is the only bond of their union. *All that believed were together, and had all things common—and were of one heart, and of one soul.* (Acts ii. 44; iv. 32.)

9. And therefore, in the sense of an aspiring and selfish nature, there is neither Jew nor Greek, high or low, rich nor poor, bond nor free, male nor female; for they are *all one in Christ Jesus.* (Gal. iii. 28.) But the Church claims no relation to that which is most highly esteemed, as the common interest and principle, and common enjoyment to the children of this world; namely, to the works of the flesh.

10. In this respect, the Church is perfectly united—they have one common cross, which is the cross of Christ Jesus—they crucify one root of evil, which is the flesh with all its affections and lusts; and hence they possess one common salvation from all sin. Where there is not a common salvation from all sin, there is neither Christ nor his

---

10. This principle eventually becomes the basis for Shaker ecumenism/universalism; cf. Section Six, In Spirit and Truth.

Church; for his name was called *Jesus,* i.e., *a Saviour,* because he saves his people from their sins. (Mat. i. 21.)

11. As all have sinned, and none can be fully saved from their sins out of the Church; so all that come to the Church must needs come in their sins; and by bringing their deeds to the *light,* that is, by confessing and forsaking all their sins, they may find their relation to the Church, according to the degree of their faith and obedience to the light which they receive.

12. But they cannot hold that relation, nor become as "pillars, in the temple of God, to go no more out," in any other way, than by receiving a ministration of that gift and power of God, which abides in the Church, and in obedience thereto, resisting and overcoming evil, and growing up in all things into Christ, who is the Head. Therefore, all are not the Church, who at first find their relation to the Church, until their souls become purified in obeying the truth. *For the temple of God is holy.*

13. But persons may, for a time, receive faith and light, and the gifts of God through the Church, and by being unfaithful and disobedient, may fall away; but the Church itself can never fall, nor be shaken; because the foundation thereof is everlasting, being laid by the revelation of God, in the unchangeable nature and order of his own eternal power and Divine majesty; and the building itself has been raised according to the unchangeable purpose of God, which he purposed in wisdom, to accomplish in the fulness of times.

14. And although there was a true Church, according to the light in the days of the Apostles, yet it was supplanted and trodden under foot; because the order in the foundation of the building, was not completed, according to the purpose of God in the fulness of times, nor could it be, until Christ made his second appearing.

15. And if there were in the succeeding ages, after the Apostles, false and divided churches, it was because they sprang from false-hearted and divided men. And if there is one church now on earth, faithful, holy, and righteous, it is most certainly the offspring of a faithful, holy, and righteous God, who created the Church and all things therein, both visible and invisible, by Jesus Christ. (Eph. iii. 9, 10; Col. i. 16.)

16. And as certain as the only true God did promise to establish a holy Church, in the latter day, in which He would dwell, so certain that Church is brought forth, and contains the principles of all that

was promised, as pertaining to the Church, temple, tabernacle, house or habitation of God, in the latter day.

17. A house or habitation is built to contain the property and furniture, as well as the person of the builder; so the Church of God contains all the unsearchable riches, and treasures of wisdom and knowledge, pertaining to the redemption of man, which God hath treasured up in Christ, who is the head of the Church, and who is before all things therein, and by whom all things therein consist. (Col. i. 17, 18.)

18. The Holy Spirit was promised, and dwells in the Church, with all her gifts, powers, and diversities of operations. The gifts of faith, wisdom, knowledge, discerning of spirits, gifts of healing, miracles, prophecy, tongues, and so on. All which gifts of the Holy Spirit are given to the Church, for the manifestation of the spirit—for the perfecting of the saints—for the work of the ministry—and edifying the body of Christ, till they all come into the unity of the faith—unto the measure of the stature of the fulness of Christ. (Eph. iv. 11, 12, 13.)

19. Thus by his Holy Spirit, God sanctified and cleansed his Church, *that he might present it to himself a glorious Church, not having spot, or wrinkle, or any such thing; but that it should be holy, and without blemish.* (Chap. v. 27.)

20. The law and the covenant were promised, and are in the Church. *The law shall go forth out of Zion.* (Isa. ii. 3.) Christ is the head of his body, the Church, which is the light of the world. *I will give him for a covenant of the people, for a light of the Gentiles.* (Chap. xlii. 6.) The word of God was promised and is in the Church—that word *which is quick and powerful, a discerner of the thoughts and intents of the heart—and liveth and abideth forever.* (Heb. iv. 12.)

21. Repentance and remission of sins were promised, and are in the Church. Him hath God exalted—a Prince and Saviour, for *to give repentance to Israel, and forgiveness of sins. The son of man hath power on earth to forgive sins.* (Acts, v. 31.) This power is given to the Church: *Whose soever sins ye remit, they are remitted unto them; and whose soever sins ye retain, they are retained.* (John, xx. 23.)

22. Salvation and redemption are in the Church, and no where else. *I will place salvation in Zion for Israel, my glory. The Redeemer shall come to Zion, and unto them that turn from transgression in Jacob.* (Isa. xlvi. 13; lix. 20.)

23. In a word, *the* whole *mystery of God,* and of the Father, and of

Christ, and all that pertains to eternal life and godliness, are, in and through the Church, revealed and progressively manifested, and according to the order of God in the fulness of times, are to be received and acknowledged for the purposes of Redemption, and the perfection of the dispensation of the fulness of the times. (Eph. i. 10.)[11]

(Benjamin Youngs, *Testimony*, pp. 375–379) [1808/1810/1823/1856]

*   *   *

19

. . . But when He [Jesus] had chosen the twelve apostles and sent out the seventy disciples to preach, he by this means formed a Church, which was his spiritual and visible boddy [sic], in which the heavenly elements operated and in its influence had the dominion; which never was before manifested on earth. Then the kingdom of God was revealed on earth in visible bodies. Here Christ had the lead and was their King; and chosen instruments were thus brought forward, in and through which, the will of God was made manifest; and visibly seen by its fruits, and conciquently [sic] the kingdom of God was *among* them.

. . .

[Ann Lee] did not pretend that she was Christ; but only that through his spirit, the same divine anointing was revealed in her. We do not profess that Christ has made his second appearing in Ann Lee only. But as every new dispensation must have an agent, that first receives the spirit and revelation of the work to be performed thereby, and through the first agent, it must be transmitted to others, and none can be benefited by it but such as receive the same spirit by receiving their testimony; So Ann Lee, was the first chosen vessel, or agent to receive the true spirit of Christ, in his second coming; but a portion of the same spirit, must be in every member of the Church, or they

---

11. By this theological position Shakerism stands completely apart from the Protestant traditions which look to the Scriptures as the normative witness to the revelation of the *whole mystery of God*, not the Church; to Luther's *sola Scriptura* Shakers counter with *sola Ecclesia*. In this they also stand apart from Catholic and Orthodox traditions, which look to Scripture, Tradition, Conciliar Canons, and Magisterium for the norm.

cannot be his boddy [*sic*]; "for if any man have not the spirit of Christ, he is none of his" and thus it is propagated from soul to soul.

... She declared that God and Christ are one in nature; and that he and his Father are one; so his people must become one in the same spirit and life ... and this forms the true body of Christ; "for there is one Lord, one faith and one baptism, one body and one bread."

(Calvin Green, *Atheism, Deism, &c.*, n.p.) [1830]

20

Second Revelation of the Gospel *vice* Christ's Second Appearing. *R. W. Pelham*

... the statement that *Christ*, or Jesus Christ, had made HIS second appearing in a WOMAN.... This phraseology was in full use then (i.e., c. 1817), and probably had been from the beginning of the institution, and is continued to the present day. After becoming a member of the Society, I set about probing the meaning of this mode of expression, and trying to deduce the radical idea, and to set it forth in rational and intelligible language.... Jesus the Messiah was the first man in and through whom the way of salvation from sin was *revealed*. This revelation was called in Greek, *Evanggelion*, "Gospel" ... its true principles ... first practically carried into effect on the day of Pentecost, when the community of goods was fully established at Jerusalem.... That true church ... was ultimately [destroyed] ... and that ... REVELATION was banished ... and became extinct among men.... As this Gospel was not a human invention, it could only be restored by a SECOND REVELATION. When, therefore, the Shakers tell you that Christ has made His second appearance *in a Woman*, they mean that the Gospel which was revealed in and by Jesus, the Christ, after having been lost, has been revealed a second time through a woman. Thus, we do not pretend that Jesus Christ has made his second appearing in a woman, or in any other way *literally*, nor do we believe he ever will; but we testify that there has been—not a second appearing of Christ, but a SECOND REVELATION of the Gospel first revealed by Jesus, the Christ; and that revelation was made through a woman. ... for one, I should like to have our testimony presented to mankind on this subject in this way. But if it be generally

preferred to continue the old mystical method, I am well aware that in Paul's writings there are abundant examples to support the practice.
. . .

. . . So we point to Ann, or Ann The Christess, by and through whom a SECOND REVELATION of the *same Gospel,* with an increase, is made; and testify that "this is the Jesus, or Jesus the Christ, that was for to come." And she, also, came forth in the same power of the Spirit, was inspired from the same eternal source, and qualified of God to initiate and establish the SECOND REVELATION of the Gospel, and she did it! . . . as it was the special mission of Jesus to reveal the *Fatherhood* in God, so it was the special mission of Ann to reveal the *Motherhood* in God. . . .

(*The Shaker* II, 9, pp. 66–67) [1872]

2 1

. . . what other resurrection is there to life, but to come out of that state of sin into which the *first Adam* fell, and come into Christ the *second Adam,* who is *the resurrection and the life?* The matter we now animate and which is constantly upon the change, we are not to expect after its dissolution, to be again subtracted from the elements of this globe and re–possessed in its primitive form, at the expense of every other body with which it may have been incorporated. And what other final judgment are we to expect, but simply and honestly, in the presence of God, and Christ, and before the saints who are appointed to judge the world, confess all that we have ever done amiss—repair our wrongs—set out to forsake every evil, and grow up into Christ, as the infant grows into a man? *There is a natural body, and there is a spiritual body;* the former belongs to the fall, the latter to the resurrection. Therefore it is not old skulls and rotten flesh that are to be raised up in glory, but that spiritual body of which we are called to be members; which is already raised up by the power of God, and ascending into the heaven of heavens, far out of sight from this lost world.

(Richard McNemar, *The Kentucky Revival,* pp. 96–97) [1807]

Their testimony principally respected the character of the true Church of Christ;—that it was one & not many;—the body of Christ, consequently pure; that Christ is in his Church, and to be found there and no where else for salvation;—that the meaning of salvation is, to be saved from sin;—that it is found by believing on Christ where he is manifested, confessing and forsaking all sin in our knowledge and taking up a full cross against the world, flesh & devil;—that Christ had actually made his second appearance;—that his Church is already established on earth possessing every gift of God necessary to the regeneration and redemption of souls, &c. . . .

(Richard McNemar, *Important Events*, p. 5) [1831]

22

Christian Distinction—No. 2.   *"W. H. B."*   [*Wm. H. Bussell*]

There is hardly anything in the Apostolic writings more evident than the fact of the intimate connection between the Body of Christ on the earth, and his body or church in the heavenly world. They are represented as being risen with Christ, sitting together in heavenly places in Christ, and as having Christ formed within them the hope of glory. God's fullness, or complete spiritual possession, was said to be in Christ; the same term was applied to his Church. There was a oneness between him and them as between him and the Father.

. . .

Salvation from sin, or from the tendency to trangress God's law of love, was the characteristic work of Christ's first manifestation; complete deliverance from the nature that is subject to trials, and liable to fall into sin, is the glorious and crowning work of the second.

(*The Shaker* I, 3, p. 21) [1871]

23

The Church of Christ.   *Wm. H. Bussell*

The church of Christ, then, consists of those persons, wherever they may be, who are so united to him that his life, which is the highest element of life in the universe—divine love—pervades their being and has a controlling influence upon their entire conduct. In this sense the oft-repeated expression, "There is no salvation out of the Church," is true. There is nothing else that will save one, in the broadest and highest signification of salvation, but that which unites him to the divine life, and when he possesses this within himself, he is an integral part of that body in which is the *divine completeness.*

... But the figure of the family admits, if not as great a variety and splendor as that of the kingdom, yet more naturalness, more attractiveness to the soul in its gentler and kindlier moods, and is really more in accordance with the spirit of divine love and tenderness that dwelt in Christ....

(*The Shaker* I, 4, p. 31) [1871]

24

Ann Lee

... While lying in the Manchester jail ... she saw, and experienced the manifestation of the baptism of the Christ Spirit—the same that made Jesus, the Christ; and the same that will make every man and woman Christ, when prepared; and the manifestation of this Christ through her, taught many strange things....

(*The Shaker* I, 2, p. 11) [1871]

25

Religion and Spiritualism   *F. W. Evans*

... Jesus appeared to her in person, and baptized her into and with The Christ Spirit, as John had baptized *him.* By his ministration, the eyes of her understanding "were opened" to discover the "foundations of the world," and to see plainly that they were "out of course."

Evidently, the way to redeem humanity, as a whole, was thus to begin with one, *human* being, as a nucleus, for Christians to gather to.... This was religion—cease to *do* evil; learn to *do well*—distinct from mere theology. Religion in this illiterate woman, and in her followers, would create its own theology, as the soul creates and shapes its own body.

(*The Shaker* I, 3, p. 18) [1871]

26

Testimony of Prudence Hammond

. . .

. . . I know of a truth that Christ was manifested in her; because I know that I received the spirit of Christ through her ministration. I have obeyed her testimony and I have ever found the same spirit in all her successors, down to the present day.

(*The Manifesto* XVII, 2, pp. 33–35) [1887]

27

We have taught thru the years that the manifesting spirit of God—the Christ of the Ages—incarnates wherever man or woman with sincere purpose, honest effort and faithful obedience lives a pure life, and in self–denial and devotion to others becomes by self-effort and spiritual baptism at one with God.

(Anna White, *The Motherhood of God*, p. 10) [1903]

two

TRAVEL IN THE GOSPEL

Introduction

The *Opening of the Gospel* began with a public discourse given by Father James Whittaker on May 19, 1780. It was a dramatic occasion, with the first converts from the Pittsfield–New Lebanon revival gathered around Mother Ann on a day so overcast with storm clouds that the sun never seemed to have risen—the day ever after called the Dark Day. The first Believers saw this as the meaning of the Opening of the Good News publicly to all: the Light shining in the darkness.

The word "Opening" is a characteristic term in Shakerism. An opening is made, a doorway allowing one to move *from* one place *into* another. It is expressive of the dynamics of *metanoia* in which the Believer is called into a way of life in the light and out of a way of death in the dark. *Opening* necessarily implies that the ones called *must themselves move* into the opportunity standing before them. For Shakers an Opening of the Good News is the freely bestowed gift, the realm of light which can be entered, and to move into it we *Travel in the Gospel*.

As has been noted elsewhere, in the eighteenth century the word "travel" was still linked with "travail" and Shakers often used both forms interchangeably. To travel in the Gospel, thus, embraced three levels of meaning: movement from one locus to another, arduous and sometimes painful labor, and the labor of childbirth. Going to the "new place" and bringing forth "new life" meant a commitment to hard work.

Travel implies both the individual person and the community of persons. Each one labors to progress into the fullness of the gifts of life in Christ, and so all together are committed to progression. The selection of texts presented here makes it clear that the authentic norm of "orthodoxy" in the Shaker Way is the *progressive unfoldment* which takes place in the growing experience of *travel*. The founders, however venerated and loved they always would be, are no criterion in themselves for authenticity. Believers unhesitatingly depart from even the most authoritative teachings of the founders—of Mother Ann herself— if the growth in the experience in living the Christlife leads them into further light. And such departure is in no way felt as an embarrassment: the commitment is not to *what* the founders taught, but to the *Christlife* into which the founders begot and bore them as true Parents in the Gospel. We must be aware of an all-important implication from this: there is no "classic form" for Shakerism, whether thought of in religious-spiritual terms or in terms of the socio-economic cultural shaping of the common life. As there are no creeds or dogmas in the sense of fixed normative doctrines, so there is no abstract authenticity in the nearly two centuries of Shaker communitarian social structure.

The initial selections (1–3) present a range of clear statements of the commitment to the normative principle of progression. Next (4) is the entire text of a major theological treatise by Elder John Lyon of Enfield, New Hampshire, illustrating the self-conscious movement away from basic ideas held and taught by the founders towards new perceptions experienced in the travel of the community of faith. The open-ended nature of this travel is made explicit in Lyon's closing paragraphs.

The following four selections (5–8) speak to the principle of progression as essential to the Church in its witnessing function: the sanctioning of all new light as it comes to be understood, the progressive reformability of the Church regardless of past positions or the ignorance or errors of previous generations, and all this assuming the possibility of the quest for true perfection, which must be seen as attainable at any one limited moment and yet as always unfolding.

The next series of selections (9–20) reflects upon the principle of progression as arising from God and extending through nature as it comes from God; and thus progression is Divine, spiritual, and evolutional. Beginning with two formal treatments by Dunlavy and Youngs, seven selections (21–27) apply progression to the place of Scripture in the process of belief: the sacred writings are witnesses to the state of belief in their day and can guide later Believers in the light of that earlier phase of *travel*, but cannot be a static norm for belief. Shakers welcomed the growing body of critical study of the Scriptures and assimilated positively the developing insight into the writings as relative to their place in history, culture, and language, and also to Christianity as a dynamic tradition not governed by the past merely because of the authority of "the beginnings."

Taking up some of the same lines of development as illustrated earlier are responses (28–32) to the ongoing process of reshaping the understanding of the Shaker Tradition, in conscious contrast to formulations of earlier generations. The final selections (33–46) provide us with concrete instances of attempts to rethink the theological conceptualization of God and Christ (and of course these themselves cannot be "final statements" and indeed may be nothing more than further probings). The two concluding groups allow us to see something of the actual community process at work in the evolving of new insight. In the case of the dialog initiated between Elder Frederick Evans and Elder Hervey Eades (41–46), at issue is the very basis of Shaker Christology and ecclesiology: the recognition of God-in-Christ and how Christ is in us—and how, therefore, Shakers would view Mother Ann and her ministry of witness in the Second Coming. The last group (47–49) is a small part of an interchange that spanned twenty years or more, reexamining the idea of separation from the world. Shakers found it harder and harder to exclude anything on the grounds of its being secular and not religious. If all life and activity animated by the Christ Spirit was worship,[1] could not everything be taken as a true gift if properly received and integrated into Christlife? Shakers predictably answered affirmatively as called for in the spirit of progression. This in turn led them ultimately to the issue of the future unfoldment of Shakerism beyond the communitarian experience. If a line of separation should not be drawn, what would be the proper form for a nonseparatistic Shaker Way? Although this will be explored elsewhere, the root of the question is properly located here in the commitment to progression in the Travel in the Gospel.

---

1. Cf. Section Five, text 1, p. 268.

THE SHAKERS

I

The writer is what may be justly called an old, or rather ancient fashioned *Shaker*. This term has been objected to, as tho it meant what is stationary and precluded increase. But far from this: it signifies that primary Shakerism which is founded upon the Revelation of the Eternal principles of Godliness, that looks for and requires an endless increase, right forward into higher and higher degrees of that which is heavenly—that which is taught by the Wisdom of the Holy Spirit, coming down from above, from a Divine Source, and not from the natural wisdom of the world, and keeps it in its proper Order.

(Calvin Green, *Biographic Memoir,* pp. 130–131) [ca. 1850]

2

Christian Communism. No. 3. *Theo. Kaiandri* (Cincinnati Post)
[Interview with Elder Leopold Goepper, Union Village]

... The chief defects that our community is laboring under—and now I am only giving you my opinion—are relics of its theology, that were brought in with it in its formation, with regard to certain forms of worship; but these do not, however, hinder an individual from living here his highest and most perfect conception of goodness.

These forms may even have their uses for some, and no doubt, do. But I have small use for the forms of religion. I consider all formal religion fetichism. My life, my everyday acts and thoughts are my religion.

(*The Manifesto* XVII, 6, pp. 138–140) [1887]

3

[Editorial Item]

... THE SHAKER, abjuring creeds, relies upon "the Spirit" to finally lead it into all truth; therefore, each contributor is measurably responsible for his or her utterances—*opinions* only, being growing truths—knowledge in the process of formation.

(*The Shaker* II, 5, p. 40) [1872]

4

Certain Important Points of Religious Doctrine
Considered and Investigated.

Elder John Lyon

Section I.[2]

For what purpose was man created? In viewing the work of
creation, not only as we have it from the Holy Scriptures, but from the
common observation of all ages, we find that before man was made
there was a gradation of animals created, from the greatest and most
noble species of the brutal creation down to the least insect, as recorded in the 25 ver. of the I Chap. of Genesis. And these constituted the
order of the terrestrial or natural world. We also have abundant proof
in the Sacred Scriptures that there was a spiritual or Celestial Empire
whose inhabitants were a gradation of spiritual beings, from Michael
the arch Angel down to the least of those ministering spirits sent forth
to minister to those that should be heirs of salvation. But in all the
orders of beings that existed prior to the sixth day of the Creation there
was no order of beings that could join the natural and spiritual worlds
together. Until man was made there was no habitable part or place on
the earth in which the eternal creative Powers could take up Their
abode and place Their Law for the Rule and government of this power
world. It would be highly derogatory to the honor and glory of
Almighty Power and Infinite Wisdom[3] for us to suppose They had
Their abode in the brute creation, even though the most noble, or to
think They were dependent on animal sagacity, through which to
show forth Their power and glory. But Wisdom declared that Her
rejoicing was in the habitable part of His[4] earth, and that Her delights
were with the Sons of man. Thus we see that man was made a link in
the vast chain of creation to join the natural to the spiritual world, who
as an animal was endowed with all the five animal senses and all the
propensities of animal nature which constitute him an animal in the
chain of the animal creation subject to all the feelings and frailties of

---

2. In this transcription of the treatise from a manuscript copy, the copyist's
inconsistencies and minor errors have been corrected.
3. I.e., God Father and Mother.
4. Virtually interchangeable pronouns He/She are characteristic of some Shaker
writers in the light of the Father–Mother God image.

animal nature, and in this part of His creation he had nothing to distinguish himself from the rest of the animal world, except he was deficient in having no instinct to govern and regulate his senses and propensities like the other part of the animal world. This was left to be supplied in the other moiety of his constitution. Thus the animal part of man being destitute of any principle by which to govern and direct his inclinations and propensities, was created of two parts, the one rational and the other irrational. That part which constitutes the soul of man is both spiritual and rational, and this distinguishes this animal, the creature man, from all the rest of animal creation. It is this that gives him his superiority and dignity above all the terrestrial creation, and constitutes him the Lord of the earth;—but not Lord of Heaven. Yet as this spiritual part of man was taken from and created of the elements of the spiritual and Heavenly world, the same as the body was taken and created from the elements of the earth; consequently he holds a legitimate relationship to the Heavenly world as well as to the earthly. And by this means he is constituted the only link in the vast chain of creation which joins the two worlds together. Thus being placed where the two worlds approximate, and being the only medium by which they could be united: man was endowed with powers and rational faculties capable of knowing and receiving the Will of God, and performing his agency according to it. And while he performed this union with his Creator, there was no power capable of interrupting the free exercise of those powers which were delegated to him. And in order for him to keep the station assigned him, he was placed under the strictest obligations of faithful obedience, and to perform this agency in perfect subserviency to the Divine Law as it would, from time to time, be communicated to his living soul, which was designed for the habitation of God on earth. This man having been created to fill the important station as above stated could not act as agent without being placed in a situation wherein he might have been tempted; for he could not have been man, without being made a creature of choice, and he could not be a creature of choice without having two things placed before him, for there can be no choice where there is but one thing to fix the choice upon. But man was not left without the privilege and means of choosing—obedience and disobedience having been placed before him. In obedience to the Law of God was the source of his protection, and in disobedience the source of misery, it having been left freely to his own option, after having been warned of consequences. Now it is evident that the very fact that God required obedience of man, and that a fulness of his happiness depended upon it, precludes the idea of man's being tempted out of fatal necessity to his happiness; yet as choice was of fatal necessity to his happiness, it presupposes at once that he must have been placed in a situation wherein he *might* have been tempted. For no one can possibly be happy without the freedom of choice; thus he was left in a situation wherein he might or might not have been tempted. But not at his own option; but his option or choice was called into requisition after the temptation should be offered, whether to choose or refuse it.

Section II.

The next consideration is, of what does the soul of man consist in distinction from the body, and subsequently of the agency of man, and whether free.

Firstly of the soul of man. The soul is a spiritual substance, composed of seven distinct intellectual substances, through which there is a communication of spiritual things from the spiritual world. These seven intellectual senses may be denominated as follows: Seeing, Hearing, Feeling, Tasting, Smelling, Intellectual Speech and Cogitation. These seven constitute the soul, in which there is [*sic*] placed seven intellectual powers, arranged as follows: 1st Principle, 2nd Comparison, 3rd Judgement, 4th Determination, 5th Memory, 6th Choice, and 7th Affection, and these seven rational powers constitute the rational tribunal in the soul of man. And it is by this Court or tribunal that all things, as it respects good and evil, are examined and tried, either according to the Divine Law of Heaven, the order originally placed in the soul, or by the cravings of the animal propensities, which since the fall have been the guide of the fallen race. Thus there is a medium of communication of spiritual things from the spiritual world; the same as there is a medium of communication of natural things from the natural world. The former medium is the seven intellectual senses, while that of the latter is composed of the five animal senses. As the soul of man was created of the Divine elements of the spiritual world, it was designed for the habitation on earth of the Creative Powers— The Eternal Two; where They could deposit Their Holy and Righteous Law from time to time, for the government of this lower world, over which man was appointed ruler. And for this purpose God breathed into him the spirit of life (not the air into his nostrils as some suppose) and he became a living soul. Then his soul became a tabernacle for the angels of his power and goodness. And from whence the seven spirits of God were sent forth into all the earth. Thus man being qualified, was constituted the agent to govern and rule this lower world, according to the will and appointment of God. For it is evident that these seven intellectual senses which constitute the soul of man are the recipients of seven angels or spirits, who continually were before the Throne of God, and in His presence, agreeably with the words of Christ, Mat. XVIII Chap. 10 ver., "For their angels do always behold the face of my Father which is in Heaven." This placed man continually under the means of inspiration; so that at any time when the mind and will of God was to be made known the means were at hand to communicate it to the soul of man. Thus it is easily seen that man was not made to be his own God, nor principal in the order of the government of the lower world, but an agent acting under the authority of his Creator. And that he might hold his union to Heaven, and rule the earth according to his agency, he was placed under the strictest obligations of obedience to the Will of God, as it should be made known from time to time through those ministering spirits to whose charge he was committed. This placed him in a situation to act freely according to the instructions he should receive. It has been above stated that man was an agent acting under the authority of his Creator; and to prove that this agency was free, is only to prove that he was appointed an agent to act for God, under His direction in the government of this lower world. If God appointed man His agent, it necessarily follows that he was free to act to the extent of the instructions which constituted his agency.

Now to prove that God appointed man His agent see the following scriptures to the point—Gen. I Chap. 28 ver. Ps. VIII. 4, 5, 6, 7, 8, 9 verses, and many other passages which might be quoted to the same effect, but I think this point will not be disputed. I think it clearly proved from the foregoing quotations, that man was made an agent to rule for the Creator over all the works He had made, by the authority and dominion He had given him over all cattle, creeping things and over all the earth. This power and dominion was not given him without instructions, as will be seen by the quotation just made from I Chap. of Gen., 28 verse: "And God said unto them be fruitful and multiply and replenish the earth and subdue it and have dominion over the fish of the sea, and over the fowl of the air, and over every living thing that moveth upon the earth." These were his first instructions; and was he not left free to add according to them? It is plain that he was to the extent of his agency, hence he was of course a *free* agent; but not left free to add his own will as principal. It is not to be understood that these instructions were all that he was to receive but he was endowed with full power to act under the instructions which he had and should afterwards receive from time to time from those angelic spirits who were appointed agents to protect and direct him in his agency. Thus we see man made free, and endowed with power to act in union with his Creator, being placed under the direction of these angelic spirits, who were constituted the medium of communication from the Throne of God to his living soul, and having *all* terrestrial things put under his dominion. In this we see him made a little lower than the angels crowned with glory and honor, being the habitation of God on the earth, made lord of the natural creation, endowed with power to subdue the earth, which is to bring every earthly propensity into subjection to the superior dignity of his living soul. Hence it appears that man being thus organized, and endowed with sufficient powers, was capable of fulfilling the object and design of his Creator in thus creating and endowing him. It then follows as matter of course that man being placed in this free situation and being capable to act according to the instructions given him, had the responsibility wholly upon him, and made every act his own—whether good or evil—in obedience or disobedience to the instructions given him. Hence it is made clearly evident that in obedience he would stand, and in rebellion he would fall, as will be illustrated in the next section.

Section III.
How Man Fell into the Deplorable Situation as
Exhibited in the Present Day.

It has been before stated for what man was created and how he was endowed. The subject now before us is how man fell, and what constituted his fall. It has been shown in the previous sections that man was made a creature of choice and left in that situation, having two things placed before him, one of which to choose, Viz. to be directed by the Divine Will of his Creator who placed him in his agency, or to throw off his allegiance, and yield obedience to the source of all evil—denominated the Serpent or Devil. And having these two sources open before him it made the act by which he fell, an act of his own freedom and choice. It will readily be granted that the crime which constituted man a fallen creature consisted in his compliance with the temptation of the Serpent. And it will also be granted that it was the design of the Serpent to hold forth something alluring in order to draw them into compliance with his will. The first enquiry then is, what was the temptation presented? to be as Gods knowing good and evil. See Gen. III Ch. 4 & 5 verses: "The serpent said unto the woman, thou shall not surely die, for God doth know that in the day ye eat thereof your eyes shall be opened and ye shall be as Gods knowing good & evil." Thus it is evident and plain that it was only necessary for him to rise in positive rebellion against God his Creator, throw off his allegiance to Him, and trample upon His Divine Law. This opened the way that he might stand as God to himself, and be his own Lead— subject to no law but his own. This was evidently the nature of the temptation; and as it was the design of the serpent to separate man from God. When this was consummated man was emphatically a fallen creature, had he never afterwards committed another act. This makes it appear plain that the fall of man consists simply and solely in his open and wilfull rebellion against God, by setting himself up as God to be his own Lead and to act according to his own will, regardless of the Will of God. Thus when man had fallen in with the temptation of the serpent, his design was accomplished. But as man and all the rest of the creation were pronounced by God to be very good, it may be asked what was there desireable or alluring to man in this temptation "to be as gods knowing good and evil?" Answer: It originated from one of the noblest dispositions or propensities ever placed in man or angels, which was simply an inclination to rise above that which was low and mean to that which is great and noble in his sphere. And here the serpent took advantage of this noble disposition placed in man for a good and wise purpose, and prevailed upon him to transcend his own sphere to that of a God. This being perhaps the only pregnable point in the nature of man through which the serpent could find access to him, it could have been nothing short of a temptation to be independent of any higher power. And nothing could so effectually accomplish that deplorable situation so appropriately denominated Fall, and alienate man from the care and protection of his Creator, as this one single act of rebellion and treason, in withdrawing himself from the protection of God and aspiring to be independent of Him. But man was not intended for a Deity to know and determine what was good and what was evil, but to rely wholly upon what was commanded by his God and Creator. And that certainly was the intent of God in His creation and endowment. From the foregoing, it follows that the fall of man consisted simply in this one single act of rebellion and treason.

We will now proceed to notice the effects. Firstly. Man having been overcome by the serpent, and alienated from God, received that penalty which God had denounced upon him. Viz. "In the day thou eateth thereof thou shalt surely die." This he received in being cut off from that heavenly and divine element which he had enjoyed, but to which he had now become dead. And instead of retaining the Divine spirit of his Creator, he received the foul spirit of the serpent and thereby became earthly, sensual and devilish. And being thus separated from God and being cut off from his union to the Heavenly world, he was left in a situation to be led and dictated by the serpent through his animal propensities. Then as the propensity for sexual intercourse was the predominant animal propensity of course as he had now nothing else to lead him but the serpent through these animal propensities, this one claimed the highest seat in his soul. And having become fallen creatures they were now prepared for fallen actions, and perhaps among their first acts they perpetrated the act of sexual intercourse, regardless of the Will of God,[5] but in obedience to their own lust, dictated by their new established lead. It ought to be here understood that this act was not the Fall nor the cause of it, but the effect, and not only this act but all other evils that have since existed in the world have resulted from the same cause as effects and consequences inevitably.[6] So altho it is evident that sexual intercourse was not the fall of man as a cause, yet it is most certainly evident that he did fall into it as an effect. And after enumerating the long catalogue of crimes that have been committed on the earth as effects resulting from this woeful alienation from God, and all the error and false conceptions of things, all the superstitions and false traditions, we have still remaining that same tenacious and almost unconquerable disposition in man universally at the present day, to have his own will and way in all things, discarding every thing that does not coincide with his conception whether it comes from God or not. But there may a query arise with some. —If the act of the Fall consisted in rebellion against God, and setting themselves up as God according to the instigation of the serpent, Why was the forbidden fruit called the Tree of the Knowledge

---

5. Note: the evil is not sexual intercourse as such, but insofar as it is dictated by lust rather than right order; this is true of everything else not done in right order, as indicated in the next sentence.

6. Lyon's identification of the act of the Fall as an attempted usurpation of Divinity, rather than as sexual intercourse, represents a movement away from the majority attitude of the first Believers, and thus is an important instance of "travelling into progression."

of Good and Evil? In answer. There is not, nor was there ever, but one tree whose fruit or product was Knowledge. Viz. *Experience.*[7] Of this tree, man was imperatively commanded, upon the penalty of death, to not partake, for he was not created at the beginning and left at random to experience this or that, to find out what was good or what was evil. But was placed in a situation to be wholly dependent upon what he should from time to time receive from his Divine Law Giver, from whence no evil could ensue. But had man kept his union to God and his dependence upon His Law, there had been *no fall.* Thus when the fall is rightly considered and understood, the necessity will clearly appear that one should come capable of laying a foundation for a work which would effectually supplant and overthrow this system of the Serpent.

Section IV.
Of the necessity of Christ's coming into the world
and introducing the Order of Grace.

There can be nothing more important to the welfare of each and every soul, than for them to understand the true nature and cause of the Fall, and wherein it consisted, and also the means provided to raise them out of it. For if he does not know what the fall was, he certainly does not know what to reject in order to rise out of it. Hence it is necessary that he should know what the fall consisted in, and that it is the cause of all the effects that have followed, and where the means have been made known, he can then set himself to remove the cause that the effects may cease. It is preposterous in the extreme to think of removing the effects so long as the cause should remain undisturbed. And as man had lost the knowledge of the cause of his separation from God and knew not the means by which he could rise out of it; it became necessary that Christ should come into the world to make known the cause of his separation and the means by which he could be restored. And this he accomplished when he commenced the work of regeneration in this short declaration "I came not to do my own will but the will of Him that sent me" (See John VI Ch. 38 ver.). Here we plainly see that he not only made known the cause of this great

---

7. "Experience" here is conceived of as haphazard acting by whim and must be distinguished from the process of experiencing as integral to life in which experience takes place as the response to what is objectively unfolding as the gifts of God. (See below, Section Five, Gifts and Orders.)

separation, Viz. "To do my own will" but he also made known the way of restoration Viz. "To do the will of Him that sent me"—or the Will of God. Here we see that this great stroke was aimed directly against the root and foundation cause of all evil, as was declared by John the Baptist, "Now is the axe laid at the root of the tree," (See Mat. III Ch. 10 ver.). This is further made evident by his own declaration (See Matt. XVI Ch. 24 ver.) "Then Jesus said unto his disciples, if any man will come after me, let him deny himself and take up his cross and follow me." Herein we see the cross required, Viz. To reject his own will and do the will of Christ, even as Christ rejected his, and did the will of God who sent him. And this is made plainer, if possible, by a parallel text, (See Mat. X Ch. 40.) "He that receiveth you receiveth me, and he that receiveth me receiveth Him that sent me." Everyone will grant that it was the mission of Christ into the world to lay the foundation of a work which would supplant the system of the serpent and destroy the works of the devil. Hence it is evident that it was his work through his whole ministration to lay his own foundation and expose that foundation on which Satan's kingdom was built. This is easily seen by a recourse to his testimony throughout, by which is seen in every point of his doctrine he struck at the foundation of the system of the serpent, as first set up in man. Herein we see the foundation of Christ's work, to restore man from his fall, by his establishing the Mediatorial office in man on the earth: See Luke X Ch. 16 ver. "He that heareth you, heareth me, and he that despiseth you despiseth me; and he that despiseth me despiseth him that sent me." Also John XX Ch. 21, 22 & 23 verses, "Then said Jesus unto them again peace be unto you, as my Father sent me, so send I you." "And when he had said this he breathed on them and said unto them receive ye the Holy Ghost. Whosoever sins ye remit they are remitted unto them, and whosoever sins ye retain, they are retained." Thus he accomplished his mission. So that when he had done his work on the earth and left the world, man was not left under the necessity of consulting his own understanding to find out what was good or what was evil, for it was left in the Mediatorial office he had established on the earth to decide. For although Jesus had departed, yet Christ or the anointing power remained. Thus far upon the foundation of the work of regeneration as established and made known on the earth in Christ's First Appearing. I will now proceed with a few remarks upon the progress of his work in his Second Appearing, built upon the same foundation.

The first thing acquired, and one absolutely necessary for a soul when called to come into the order of grace, is to place his confidence in the Lead established by the Order of God, and feel his dependence and submission, so that he can there confess his sins believing it to be the true established Order of God, and there be taught how to subdue his own will, and give himself up to the Will of God, manifested in the Mediatorial Order. And as we do positively know that this is the only door of admission into the order of grace in Christ's Second Appearing, it is strikingly manifest that the work progresses upon the same foundation that was laid in his First. "For other foundation can no man lay." Thus it is that all the actual self denial dictated by any system of morality or philosophy, tho ever so rigidly practiced, cannot touch the root, nor in any way or manner effect the cause. And tho it may be the means of lopping off ever so many of the branches, it will never kill the root of the Tree. And this is the reason that many have been known among Believers since the work of Christ's Second Appearing commenced, who have received faith in the cross, so far as external self denial, and have strenuously lived it; Yet at the same time being in positive opposition to the established Mediatorial Order of Christ placed in a visible Lead, and being dictated [to] by the lead established in themselves, have never progressed one single step in the work of regeneration. But after continuing in external self denial for months and even years, have finally apostasized and lost their Day. And why? Because the axe *was not* laid at the root of the Tree.

But on the other hand, Who ever knew of a soul to fall or to be unfruitful who at the same time stood in union and felt his dependence and submission to the Lead established in Zion? And why? Because "the axe *was* laid to the Root of the Tree." But it may be asked, If this was the case, why was it not more emphatically taught by Mother and the First Elders, instead of an incessant warfare against the Lust of the Flesh?[8] The answer is plain. The time had not come for the true order of Zion to be established. But as the lust of the flesh had become a second cause, or the cause from which proceeded all other evil actions, hence it was that their attention was so strenuously drawn to this to prevent any further faults or effects, until the true Mediatorial Order of Christ was established and perfected, which was accomplished when

---

8. Note the self-conscious shift of understanding from the primary emphasis in the witness of Mother Ann, Father William, and Father James; as usual, the authenticity of teaching is not located in past tradition, even that which clearly goes back to the founders, but in the experience of unfolding revelation.

the Church was established in its present Order. And however profi-
cient souls may be in their travel in the work of regeneration on the
earth, and however Holy the Congregation may arrive to be, it should
ever be remembered and borne in mind that this true subordinate
dependence and submission to the visible Lead will never be supersed-
ed by the doctrine circulated by the serpent at the beginning, Viz. "To
be as Gods" themselves or to be their own lead. Altho in the foregoing
I have contended that the lust of the flesh was not the fall of man nor
the cause of it, but that it was his rebellion against God, and his setting
himself up as God, to be his own lead, which constituted him a fallen
creature,—yet I do acknowledge that the lust of the flesh was a woeful
pit into which man fell when he lost his hold on the Heavenly World.
Then should man undertake to rise out of it, or after he had been
helped out, to try to stand, without first finding his union to God in
His established Order, he would find it as utterly impossible as it was
for Adam after he had lost his union, for the like cause now would
produce the like effect. Then as it is clearly established that no soul can
stand without first finding his union to God in the Order He has
established, and cannot possibly fall while he keeps it, would it not be
far better to direct souls to this great separating cause, as that upon
which their life or death depends, than it would be to hold up the lust
of the flesh, or all of the numerous effects of this cause as being the all
important object of their warfare, thereby keeping their minds continually engrossed in it and about it, while from the fact of the root or
cause not being destroyed, it must continue to live? For without this
fundamental principle which Christ first fully taught as the foundation upon which his work was to be established being first planted in
the soul, it would be in vain to teach such souls the necessity of
destroying any of the effects originating from the original cause, as
they have not the power to do it—and even worse than vain, for by
teaching them to keep a continual warfare against the flesh would be
only keeping their minds continually in it, which would inevitably
torment the soul by suggesting fleshly thoughts and ideas otherwise
avoided. But on the other hand let the soul be impressed with this
important truth that the great cause of their separation from God and
their liability to fall into the lust of the flesh is their insubordination to
the Will of God, and their setting themselves up as their own lead, and
disregarding His Order. This will correspond with the numerous gifts
and manifestations from the Spiritual World to the inhabitants of
Zion. Viz. "To come low and keep low and feel dependent." Thus

when this principle is fully established in the soul, the warfare against the flesh has already commenced, and, so long as it is adhered to the warfare, will be victoriously maintained.

Section V.
Of the Wisdom of God in creating man subject to
Divine Revelation and Inspiration, which is
often manifested in Signs and figures.

It will be readily seen that man was created of two parts—soul and body. He was made superior to all the rest of the animal creation in that he possessed a rational soul, to which was delegated natural wisdom and discretion by which he could conceive ideas of natural things, such as the nature and causes of such things as belonged to the natural world. (See Isaiah XXVIII Ch. 26 & 29 verses.) This endowment qualified him to be the natural lord of the terrestrial world, so that the rule and government of the earth might have gone on harmoniously had man but retained his first rectitude. But far different was it with man in relation to spiritual things. He never was designed to be a Lord of the Celestial World. Hence it is, that it was not given to man to know good and evil. But all the knowledge he was to receive of spiritual things he was under the necessity of receiving by inspiration from the Almighty in His own Order. Which Order consisted in God's placing seven Spirits or angels in the seven intellectual senses which constitute the soul of man. These seven spirits were appointed the agency which existed between God and the soul of man. Thus the means by which he could obtain the will of God were continually within him, these heavenly messengers always having access to the Throne of God, according to the Savior's own declaration, "Their angels do always behold the face of my Father which is in Heaven," (See Matt. XVIII Ch. 10 ver.). Thus he was not taught good and evil, but what *to do* and what *not to do*. And here let it be considered that there was but one tree placed in the garden, or literally the situation of man, of which he might not freely eat, and this was the tree of knowledge of good and evil. As there is no tree in the natural world which produces this fruit it must be sought for in a metaphorical sense, where we can find but one existing and this is *experience*. For without experience there can be no knowledge either of things spiritual or temporal. Hence it is plain that man was not left at random to experience this or that to find out what was good or what was evil, but was dependent upon the Heavenly agency aforementioned for his knowledge of spiritual things, which he could only obtain by inspiration. In this situation he could keep his union to the Spiritual World and govern the earth. But being incited by the adversary to throw off his allegiance to God and rebel against His Law and Order, communicated to him by his Heavenly protectors, he lost the Wisdom which is from above and became a stranger to inspiration, the only access he could have to the Spiritual World. Altho by this alienation from God and his heavenly state he became earthly, sensual and devilish, Yet that natural wisdom and sagacity with which he was qualified to constitute him the lord of this lower world was not taken from him in consequence thereof. But as his soul had become degraded and made servile to his earthly propensities, he could no longer direct and govern the earth according to the Divine Law of the Creator. But that wisdom, not being directed by the Divine Law of Heaven, became foolishness, being directed by the most sordid passions and propensities of a fallen nature.

Nevertheless God in Wisdom and Goodness provided a way by which to restore man from his fallen state and place him in a situation to gain his union and relation to the Spiritual World. This restoration God promised from time to time to certain individuals whom he raised up as His witnesses, inspiring them by His angels to reveal His Will to the children of man. Yet the testimony of these witnesses was rejected. And why? It is plain: because the generality of mankind had become total strangers to the spirit of inspiration, being cut off from the elements of the Spiritual World, consequently could receive nothing but what they could comprehend thru their corrupted natural wisdom. But God was determined that all flesh should see and know His requirements, and appear either justified or condemned according to their works in receiving this His means of communication with them. Therefore in order to bring about His purposes, God adapted the means appropriately to the consummation of the work He had designed. Altho He often visited the earth with judgments for their reformation, yet fallen man by his natural wisdom readily ascribed them to natural causes, thereby hardening his heart against God and Divine Revelation. Thus when God sent forth His inspired servants with His Testimony He endowed them with power to work myracles and exhibit signs before them, thru which many were reclaimed having their senses aroused by the power of the Testimony and these evidences set before their eyes. But altho a greater part of mankind rejected the inspired messengers of the Almighty, it never altered His purpose, but they stood justly condemned according as they had slighted His warning and testimony. Thus it is evident that God has from the beginning visited the earth with His Testimony accompanied by miracles, signs and wonders by which to arouse the senses of mankind to a belief in the Revelation of His Will thru His inspired servants.

It was thus with the Patriarch and Prophet Noah. God sent him to preach repentance to the ante–deluvian world and to teach them His Will in righteousness, and to warn them of the judgment then pending in consequence of their refusal to harken to His warning voice. But this He did not do without first exhibiting a sign to their natural senses of the impending danger of which they had been warned. For He built the Ark which kept the warning constantly before their eyes for the space of 120 years. So that when the judgment came upon them they stood guilty before God and their condemnation was just. Next Moses, when he was called of God to deliver His chosen people from their bondage under the Egyptians, was first aroused to a sense of his call by a sign or manifestation unaccountable to his natural senses. And when he was expostulating with the Lord he said, "They will not believe me nor harken unto my voice for they will say, The Lord hath not appeared unto thee. Then the Lord provided him with two signs; firstly, that of his rod turning into a serpent, and 2ndly, that of his hand becoming leprous as snow." Then the Lord said, "If they will not believe thee nor harken to the voice of the first sign, that they may believe the voice of the latter sign." And in case there should still be unbelief prevailing, the Lord provided him with another sign, saying, "If they will not believe also these two signs neither harken to thy voice, that thou shalt take of the water of the river and pour it upon the dry land, and the water which thou takest out of the river shall become blood upon the dry land. (See Exod. IV Ch. from 1 to 9 vers.) Hence it is evident that altho Moses was a chosen and inspired instrument to commence a new dispensation, yet he first had to be addressed thru his natural senses before he could gain a full confidence in the mission to which he was called. And how much more necessary was it, to those to whom he was sent to have their natural senses and earthly wisdom arrested and confounded by miracles, signs and wonders before they could believe that he was a chosen instrument sent of God to be their Savior and Protector from their temporal bondage.

Moses was inspired but they were not. Therefore as matter of course, they had nothing in them to direct but that natural wisdom which was left in man after the fall, as before stated, and this under the control of their animal and fallen propensities. It is evident that man never would, after the fall, submit himself to God and His requirements until he was confounded in his own wisdom by signs and judgments. Numerous instances of the Divine manifestation of the Will of God to His creatures, thru signs or miracles, are recorded in the Scriptures, of which it will only be necessary to notice a few, as the Scriptures can be consulted. In the case of Gideon it may be plainly seen how prone fallen creatures are to confide in their own natural senses. Altho he had been visited by an angel and commissioned by him to deliver his people from their enemies, yet he could not confide in the authenticity of his mission until he had been confirmed by at least four signs presented to his natural senses. We might appeal to various circumstances related by the Prophets Isaiah, Jeremiah, Ezekiel, Daniel, Hosea and many others. But suffice it to say that these dispensations were upheld by these and many other manifestations until Christ made his appearance on the earth, at which time he began that work which had been promised, to purify the soul of man from the inspirations of unclean spirits, and to make it a fit receptacle for the seven spirits of God. And now began the true inspiration of the spirit of God as it was first placed in man while he stood in union to the Spiritual World—progressing in such souls as were willing to be cleansed from the seven devils who inhabit the souls of the whole fallen race.

When Christ came, he came to a Nation who had been blessed with a manifestation of the power and goodness of God made known through the ministration of angels to those whom God had raised up as witnesses of His Testimony accompanied by miracles, signs and wonderful works, and these were called the oracles of God. But when the Son of God had declared the purpose of His Divine Wisdom and made it plain before their eyes by his wonderful works, they shut their eyes, stopped their ears and hardened their hearts, not only against his testimony but against the oracles of God which had been given to them in former dispensations. So there remained but one more manifestation for them, this was judgment with vengeance, which is sure to follow deliberate and willful rebellion. Hence it was that our Savior declared, "This is an evil and adulterous generation that seeketh after a sign, but there shall no sign be given it." But when Christ commissioned his disciples to preach the gospel to the nations of the earth, He said, "These signs shall follow those that believe." And it is evident they did and wrought wonderfully, being accompanied by the inspiration of the Spirit, they did arrest the natural senses wherever they went. And all such as desired to find their relation to the Spiritual World received the testimony to their justification and happiness, while those who rejected the Testimony of God and the evidences attending it stood justly condemned, fitted for wrath, and obnoxious to vengeance.

It is therefore plain to the understanding that in all the past dispensations God always accompanied His Testimony and work with evidences adapted to the external senses of the natural man. And why not so in this dispensation as well as in the former? Perhaps some may object and appeal to the Apostle Paul to the Corinthians where he says, "Whether there be prophecies they shall fail, whether there be tongues they shall cease, whether there be knowledge it shall vanish away." (See I Cor. XIII Ch. 8 ver.) Paul had a very good reason for this declaration, knowing there was to be a falling away, and that antichrist was to have his reign and trample the gospel under foot, with all its power and gifts, which was to continue until Christ should make his Second Appearance without sin unto salvation, when he would restore these gifts according to promise. "That of all which the Father hath given me I shall loose nothing, but should raise it up again at the Last day." (See John VI Ch. 39 ver.) And it is evident that the Father gave him all the gifts and power manifested in the gospel. The greatest obstruction to faith in Divine Revelation at the present day is the fact that the same adversary, who incited man at the beginning to rise above God and all that is called God, has invented the universal and popular doctrine that it is altogether unnecessary and unexpected that there should be inspiration, revelation, signs or any spiritual manifestations. This doctrine was obviously invented for the purpose of preventing mankind from believing any thing that would arrest the progress of fallen man in pursuing the course of his own natural wisdom. But why is it not as necessary now as it was in any former dispensation for God to apply His convincing power? Does he not value himself as highly upon his earthly wisdom as in former dispensations? If so, then there is as much need now of revelation and signs as there ever was, and much more if we but consider the importance of the work of the day which is to bring every soul to judgment after which they will receive their destiny before the close of the day. Thus natural man cannot stand obnoxious to the temporal judgment of God until after he is arrested by the Testimony of God and the evidences accompanying it. Hence it is evident that God ever had and has now the means of arresting the senses of mankind whenever He has a manifestation or a requirement for them. So that if they reject His Testimony they are left without excuse, and stand the object of His vengeance.

But perhaps some may urge as an objection against the necessity of the present revelation of God that there is more light and knowledge in the present age than there was in any of those that have preceded it, as we have all the benefit derived from the experience of past ages as well as our own. This objection leads many to suppose that there is wisdom and knowledge enough at the present day to supercede the Revelation of God in his own way as formerly given. This argument and supposition places mankind in precisely the same situation that the serpent placed him at the beginning, when he hurled him from his happy situation, saying, "Ye shall be as Gods knowing good and evil." We are willing to acknowledge that there does exist much knowledge in the world, both natural wisdom, and that knowledge of evil which is the fruit of that forbidden tree *Experience.* And thus it is that the wisdom of this world and the knowledge of evil so mightily prevail among the children of man. And these are displayed in the arts and sciences being supported and carried on by the philosophy of nature. Hence it is made plain that this is not the wisdom that is from above, for by it no one is able to discern the things of the Spirit of God, for they are spiritually discerned. And if the things of God are spiritually discerned, why then try to substitute the wisdom of this world instead of the Revelation of God by the inspiration of His Spirit made known by the various means adapted to the various situations of those to whom it is sent? And as it is well known that the religion of anti–christ was established and has ever been supported by the studied wisdom of this world and vain philosophy, therefore all religion supported by these means must be anti–christ. But the "pure and undefiled religion before God the Father" was not established by and does not need the wisdom of this world nor any system of vain philosophy to support it, but the revelation of God by inspiration, manifested by the various means of His own choosing. Then let us take a view of the effects of this earthly wisdom operating upon the various systems of religion at the present day.

It is plainly evident that mankind in general are more alienated from the true Order of God, as it was revealed by His Spirit in the gospel both in the First and Second Appearing of Christ. They are more independent of Divine Revelation to direct them in obedience to the immutable Will of God. But what has all this worldly wisdom with all the religion attached to it accomplished towards effecting the great and grand object for which the gospel was sent into the world? Nothing, but they have rather created a labyrinth of darkness from which no one can be extricated without revelations and manifestations of the Spirit of God with power. Altho it cannot be but admitted that the wisdom of the world distinct from the systems of anti–christ has done much toward ameliorating the condition of the political wellbeing invisibly directed by the Almighty, yet it has done nothing towards directing the soul how to find its relation to the Heavenly World; but has left the whole world under the control of the corrupt systems of anti–christ for direction, which like a dark fog does envelope the whole of Christendom, except the little spot, Zion, where the Revelation of God is made known. One more evidence may suffice in proof of the foregoing section. It is and has been known among those who have received the Revelation of God, thru the first witnesses of Christ's Second Appearing, for the last sixty years, that many who have had the privilege of hearing the true Testimony revealed in its purity with the evidences attending it, instead of receiving it as the true Revelation of God given by the inspiration of the Spirit, have applied their own natural wisdom to comprehend that which nothing but a true spiritual sense can reconcile, and therefore excluded the true inspiration of the Spirit from their souls and lost their day. According to the above view of the present state of mankind there never was a day or dispensation of God's work upon the earth, when there was so much need of the powerful display of the manifestation of the power of God in Testimony, signs and Revelations. For there never was a time when the senses of the children of men were so deeply enveloped in darkness, as at the present day—occasioned by confounding religion and spiritual things with the false philosophy and wisdom of this world.

Section VI.
A brief illustration of the true Resurrection
as it is maintained in the Scriptures.

It will be easily seen and perhaps readily granted that there is no subject in theology treated of in the Scriptures so obscure to the senses of the natural man as the doctrine of the Resurrection. But this is in consequence of the ambiguity of the scriptural words and phrases employed in treating upon it. Even while the Savior was on the earth, and after all he had said upon the subject, his Apostles themselves who had the best chance of any on earth to hear his declarations concerning it, knew not what the rising from the dead should mean. But why should they not know if it meant the reanimation of the animal body? for they had already seen at least three such bodies reanimated, and yet they knew not the true Resurrection. The truth is they were natural men and could not discern the things of the Spirit, and as such they remained until they were endowed with power from on High, which took place at the day of Pentecost; after which they knew what the rising from the dead meant and felt the power of it. Not that they had already attained it. But the work then began by which it was to be effected, when the Seventh Angel should sound to usher in Christ at his Second Coming to establish a pure and perfect work without sin unto salvation. Altho many were awakened in the day of his First Appearing, yet they could not come forth in the true Resurrection, for the time had not then arrived for the Resurrection Trump to sound. This is plain from the declaration of the Apostles where they have treated upon this subject. (See Acts XVII Ch. 31 ver. also Phil. III Ch. 11 & 12 verses, also I Thes. IV Ch. from 14 to 17 ver., I Epistle John III Ch. 2 ver.) These and many more might be quoted, but these are sufficient to show that the true Resurrection had not then arrived.

But the idea that there is to be a rising from the dead is founded upon the word Resurrection in the Scriptures, and this word is rendered from the Greek word, *anastasis*. This word is compounded of two Greek words, the preposition, *ana*, which signifies the same as the Latin or English, *re*, and *histemi* (Greek) which signifies to raise, to establish, or to stand again. Thus the compound word *anastasis* signifies to raise up again, to reestablish or to stand up again. Hence it is evident that the true idea of the Resurrection must be predicated upon the consideration that all mankind have become fallen creatures and must be restored or reestablished in their primeval state of happiness and innocence, or never attain to happiness in this present time nor in eternity. And hence it is that an *anastasis* or raising up again from the low and depraved state of the fall was promised. And without its accomplishment there can be no salvation. This clearly shows the reason that the Apostle puts such stress upon the importance of the *anastasis* or reestablishing of man in his primeval state, in the XV Ch. of the I Cor. from the 13 to the 22 ver. And here it is important to observe that the Apostle had three different positions to establish in his remarks here upon the subject of the Resurrection. First, In what true Resurrection consisted. Secondly, To maintain the doctrine in opposition to that of the Sadducees. And Thirdly, To show that, altho the Church and order of that day must fall, yet it should be raised up again. In ver. 13 he says, "If there be no Resurrection—*anastasis*—of the dead then is not Christ arisen." The true sense of what is contained in this verse is simply this: that if there is no *anastasis*, reestablishing of man in his primeval state, then is not Christ raised out of that low and fallen state of fallen man into which he descended to open the way for their recovery. He then declares that if Christ is not raised, their preaching was in vain, and their faith was also vain. But why was their preaching and faith vain? Answer. Because their preaching consisted in opening a way and means to them by which (as they declared) Christ arose out of the state of fallen man to happiness and glory, and that they might obtain the same by obeying his precepts and following his example. It is plain that this was their faith, and who would not at once see, that it were all in vain if there existed no *anastasis*, or Resurrection from the Fall, or any prospect of their being reinstated in their original state of innocence and happiness? And the promises of God from the beginning wholly consisted in man's Resurrection from the Fall, altho the word Resurrection was not used. All will admit that He promised to restore and reinstate man in his primeval state of innocence and happiness; and the means and way by which these promises were to be fulfilled were manifested and made known in the promises themselves, Viz. to cleanse them from all their unrighteousness. He then promised, "I will live in them and walk in them and I will be their God and they shall be My people." (See II Cor. VI Chapter 16 verse.) These promises of the restoration were the foundations of all the hope of all who received and believed in them, from the time of the Fall down to the time in which Paul wrote.

Altho the principal object of the Apostle's argument in the Chapter was to establish the true Resurrection or *anastasis* as above stated, yet he employs a part of it to controvert the doctrine of the Sadducees. The doctrine which they taught was that there was one God, which was Spirit, and that all, when they died, were resolved into this one fountain of Spirit which they called God. And this position was controverted by the Apostle in his argument that the soul did exist in a future state individually, and was a subject of the true Resurrection or *anastasis* without the reanimation of the animal body. See 18, 19 and 32 verses.—18, "Then they which are fallen asleep in Christ are perished"—19, "If only in this life we have hope in Christ, we are of all men the most miserable."—32, "If after the manner of men I fought with beasts at Ephesus, what advantageth me if the dead rise not. Let us eat and drink for tomorrow we die." From the above quotations it is clearly evident that it was the intention to show that the soul of man had spiritual future existence, and should have a part in the true Resurrection or *anastasis*, when the day appointed for the Resurrection should arrive. In the next 17 verses he proceeds to show them how natural they were. Beginning at the 33 ver. he says, "Be not deceived; evil communications corrupt good manners. Awake to righteousness and sin not, for some have not the knowledge of God. I speak this to your shame. But some will say, how are the dead raised up and with what body will they come." Here it seems they were so natural that they thought the old animal body was the subject of the *anastasis* or Resurrection. And no wonder he breaks out in the next verse with "Fool, that which thou sowest is not quickened except it die." It must be plain to every one that every thing sown must have the principle of life in it, or it cannot germinate and produce its likeness; then, who will be so natural, as Paul's fool, as to suppose that the dead body of a man will germinate and produce a living body in its own likeness? See 38 ver. "But God giveth it a body that hath pleased Him and to every seed his own body." Here it is evident that he is laboring to show them that there is a natural body, and a spiritual body, or two orders, one of the first Adam who is natural, and the other of Christ who is spiritual; then as the seed or germ of the Resurrection was sown in the natural body or Adamic order, so when the day shall arrive for the Resurrection or *anastasis* to take place, then will it come forth spiritual in its own order; for every seed must have its own body.

He then proceeds to show that the seed of the *anastasis* or rising again was sown in the natural or carnal state of that dispensation. It was evidently a carnal state for the order of the first Adam was in part admitted in that day. This is clearly the Apostle's understanding of the subject, for he says, "It is sown a natural body but it is raised a spiritual body." Here it should be observed that the Greek word *psuchikon*, here rendered "natural", would be more properly rendered "carnal", or something animated with sensuality, as expressing passionate, or indulging the inclinations or appetites. Such was the order of the work of that dispensation under its indulgences. Thus we see that the body established in that day was a carnal body with the seed of the Resurrection sown in it. And this body being planted or established in this natural state, it was said with propriety that it was sown a natural or carnal body, because it was established in a situation to admit of the indulgences of the passions, inclinations and appetites of the carnal mind. But the Apostle, knowing that the Church or order of that day must be supplanted and die, made this declaration, "That which thou sowest cannot be quickened except it die." "Thou sowest not that body which *shall be*, but God giveth it a body as it pleaseth Him." And here he shows what kind of a body pleased Him. "It is raised a spiritual body." But the order then existing bore the image of the first Adam, who was of the earth, earthly; as the Apostle says, "As we have borne the image of the earthly, so shall we also bear the image of the Heavenly." The Apostle does not say that they bore the image of the Heavenly, but should bear it in a future day.

It is plainly seen from all the Apostle's writings that he well knew that the order of that dispensation would be supplanted, and that the Church then existing would die and be dissolved. Therefore he calls it a mortal body, as will be seen, as we pursue the subject. As the term *anastasis* implies a reestablishing of any thing that has fallen, or any thing to be raised again, it is applied to the raising up of the Church of Christ in the Last Day. It ought to be borne in mind that he kept up a distinction between those who believed in Christ in that day and those who did not, and held up as a consolation to the Believers that when the *anastasis* or reestablishing of the Church in the order of grace should take place, "the dead in Christ should rise first." See I Thes. IV Ch. 16 ver. But he told them that they would be changed from that mortal, carnal or sensual body they then were. This will readily appear from his following declarations, where he closes up the subject and comes directly to a point, See 50th ver. "Now this I say, brethren, that flesh and blood cannot inherit the Kingdom of God." "Neither doth corruption inherit incorruption." But after closing his argument in general, he favors them with further information concerning the *anastasis* or reestablishing of the Church, which he told them was a mystery. 51 ver. "Behold I shew you a mystery: we shall not all sleep, but we shall all be changed, in a moment, in the twinkling of an eye, at the Last Trump. For the trumpet shall sound and the dead shall be raised incorruptible and we shall be changed. For this corruptible must put on incorruption, and this mortal must put on immortality." From the above quotations it is evident that Paul acknowledges that the Church of that day stood in a mortal or corruptible state; but he declared that they should be changed from that state of corruption to a state of incorruptibility. Thus it manifestly appears that altho the Church stood in that corruptible or mortal state, yet there were many among them who lived in that measure of spirituality that when they left the world they did not fall asleep, but remained awake waiting for the Coming of Christ with the voice of the Seventh Trump. But the generality of them did not rise to that degree of spirit and life that kept them alive, but fell asleep and were to be waked at the sounding of the Last Trumpet. But altho some were asleep and others alive yet they all had to be quickly changed, as represented by that metaphorical expression "in the twinkling of an eye," which signified that when this dispensation commenced, they should all be quickly changed from the order of that dispensation to the order of this. Then that corruptible put on incorruption and that mortal put on immortality. It is not to be understood that the immortality here spoken of refers to individuals, but to the immortality attached to the order and work as it is established in the Church of the present Day. Thus when Christ made his Second Appearing with the sound of the Seventh and last Trumpet, then was the way made manifest by which souls could rise from their fall. And then the true *anastasis* or Resurrection began to take place, and as fast as souls heard the sound of the last Trump and arose out of the order of the earthly Adam so fast they became participaters of the *anastasis.*

In the foregoing pages I have written an epitome of my views of the subjects therein contained. But not as dogmas but to be submitted, examined, and tried at the centre of Zion.

It will be observed that the subject contained in the fifth Section, on the Wisdom of God in creating man subject to Divine Revelation, &c., is the same that Brother Philemon[9] received last summer, and the reason why it is here inserted is because I had it partly written when he made the application, and I wanted it to occupy its place in connection with the rest in this manuscript.

In the sixth Section, on the Resurrection, It will be seen that it has been my object to show forth what the true *anastasis* or Resurrection of man consists in, and that these ideas are consistent with Scripture; rather than to confront the Resurrection of the animal body.

Leaving to the abettors of that doctrine to prove that it was the animal body that was the subject of the *anastasis,* which word may be properly applied to any other fallen body as to the fallen dead body of

---

9. Elder Philemon Stewart, of the Church Family of Mt. Lebanon, one of the primary leaders in the ritual-mystical revival of Mother's Work, especially active in the 1840's.

man, unless they can first prove that the animal body of Jesus was actually raised, and that it was that body which ascended to Heaven. And this will be their task to prove but not mine to disprove, at least until after they prove it—which they cannot do. The best means which I have ever found to confound these *natural* reasoners on this *spiritual* subject is to require proof positive that the animal body of Christ was actually raised, and on my part to prove the true Resurrection as it actually exists.

Enfield NH 1844   Written by Elder John Lyon. [1844]

*   *   *

5

... The principal concern of the church–lead has been to see that no ray of new–light should be sanctioned, that did not consist with the simple faith of the Church. ... the Church ... may support or reject any such new–light or old–light according as its good or evil effects appear.

... doctrines have circulated in every society with a general aim at uniformity, yet an open door for consistent improvements on any point.

(Richard McNemar, *Important Events*, pp. 39, 40) [1831]

6

To have found the everlasting Gospel, the perfect work of God, is one thing, and to be perfected in the knowledge and experience of the same is another. Of the first we speak confidently, having no remaining doubt. But as to the second, our proficiency is only according to our time and travel. The everlasting Gospel is only in its increase on the earth, as yet far short of its meridian; and my experience only in minority. If therefore a much clearer elucidation of many subjects in the following work should hereafter appear, it will be no disgrace to the Gospel, in the one faith, one cross, one self–denial, and one Christ. And my junior age and short experience in the Gospel is a sufficient apology for the imperfection which in time may appear in the following work; or rather which appears already; for were the whole work to be reprinted immediately, I can see many places which could be stated in much greater perfection. And it is our privilege to grow in the knowledge of God. Or should any calculation of time which depends on the letter, and not clearly expressed, hereafter be more correctly and satisfactorily opened as the light increases, it will not be inconsistent with our present faith. Had the work been inspected by those who are farthest travelled in the faith, it would no doubt have been much more perfect: but they were at too great a distance.

(John Dunlavy, *The Manifesto*, p. vi) [1818/1847]

7

Benjamin Youngs: to Thos. Brown

We know there has [*sic*] been many things done and said by the people, for want of a better understanding; and we believe several have lost their faith and left us, who, if they had been wisely dealt by, would have continued. Admitting it to be true, that the first or any of the present leaders in the church, or any of the old believers, have done wrong, you should not let that hurt your faith, and destroy your own soul; but you should still travail[10] on with the people, (as they profess to be in a travail,) for as soon as they feel they have erred, or done wrong, they will put their errors away and mend; and you know they are daily endeavoring to learn and improve—and that they have travailed into a farther increase of wisdom, understanding, and purity of conduct, is clearly manifested when we have compared the church and the order therein with what it was in first Mother's day. There were many things done then, that the church has no union with now. It was sometime after the opening of the gospel before the church was brought into order; and previous to that time there was much confusion.

The people or church of God, may properly be compared to natural creation, which is believed to have been from a chaotic state; and God is represented as having been six days in creating and bring-

---

10. Note the interchangeable *travel* and *travail:* to travel or progress in Faith involves a constant travail or labor.

114

ing all things into order;[11] it is also the same in creation, for nothing grows to perfection in a moment; and it is also the same in building a house, or constructing any machine, each part naturally lies in apparent confusion till the artist brings them together, and puts each one in its proper place; then the beauty of the machinery and the wisdom of the artist are apparent. Therefore, the church is fitly compared to Solomon's temple: God is the great artist and master builder, the gospel is the means, the ministration are his labourers, and are instruments under his direction, and we must labour in union with them to cast away all rubbish out of, and from around the building; and to labour to bring every thing, both outward and inward, more and more into order. Therefore, if a true written description had been given of this building, i.e. the church, and faith and practice of the people, twenty years ago, it would not be, in every respect, a true description in the present day. Also, if a correct description of the present standing of the church was now written, it would not be, in all respects, applicable to it twenty years to come, on account, as I said, of the church continually increasing in wisdom, upright conduct, and order.—Therefore, it is not wisdom in you to condemn the church, and cast yourself off, for wrongs that have been, or that you see now, in individuals, (or indeed in the whole body) proceeding from a want of wisdom; when, at the same time, it is their intention, after they have attained more wisdom or a better understanding, to see wherein they have erred, or done wrong, to renounce the error and put away all wrong, and labour to do better for the time to come. Which you must acknowledge is truly commendable and praiseworthy; for creatures cannot travail out of errors and wrong practices faster than God pleases to enlighten them. Again, that may not be error or wrong practice in us at one time, which may become so at another time, when we have attained to more light and understanding. The increase of light makes objects to be more clearly seen; and this travail, of which I have been speaking, will last eternally; for to suppose a creature ever to arrive at a state in which he will not err, would be to suppose him

11. Unlike the older but then current Western interpretation of the Genesis creation account as a *creatio ex nihilo*, Shakers saw it as an account of a progression from disorganization toward ever greater organization (a process not completed "in the beginning"); late-nineteenth-century Shakers would find the new empirical theories of cosmic origins, the development of energy-matter, human evolution, etc., completely in harmony with their progressive vision of Faith. As Elder Frederick Evans observed, they were the only Church to welcome Darwin as a revelator!

perfect, or infinite in wisdom, and therefore equal with God; which state of equality no creature can ever attain.

(Thomas Brown: *An Account of the People Called Shakers &c.*, pp. 293–294) [1812]

8

Many controversies have been excited and maintained among the professors of christianity, concerning the doctrine of christian perfection; and modern professors of religion have most generally rejected the doctrine as unreasonable and unscriptural. Hence nothing seems to excite contempt and opposition sooner than to talk of attaining to a state of perfection in this life. This opposition evidently proceeds from two causes; first, a wrong conception of the true nature of perfection; and second, the impossibility of attaining to it while living in any known sin, as has been fully proved by the general experience of professed christians.

But those who profess to believe the Bible to be the word of God, ought to acknowledge the testimony of Jesus Christ which is contained in the Bible; for surely *that* cannot be *unscriptural*. "Be ye therefore perfect, even as your Father which is in Heaven is perfect." (Mat. v. 48.) Would Christ require any thing impossible or unreasonable of his people? Certainly not. Then perfection must be attainable; for Christ does positively require it.

The doctrine so frequently taught, and so extensively believed among mankind; "That no one can be perfect in this life," originated in the dark kingdom of Antichrist, and is admirably calculated to ease the conscience, and encourage slothfulness and indifference in the duties of religion: for who will seek after that which he believes to be unattainable? But a little attention to this subject will show the inconsistency of such a belief.

1. God who is infinite in righteousness and goodness, can never require impossibilities of any of his creatures. If then, perfection were not attainable in this life, God never would require it. Yet he does require it. He required it of Abraham: "Walk before me, and be thou perfect." (Gen. xvii. 1.) He required it of the Israelites under the law: "Ye shall be holy; for I am holy." (Lev. xi. 44 and xix. 1.) Perfection is therefore attainable.

2. It has been attained. God declared Job to be "*a perfect and upright man.*" (Job, i. 8; ii. 3.) Noah was also declared to be "a just man,

and *perfect* in his generations." (Gen. vi. 9.) The apostle Paul saith, "We speak wisdom to them that are *perfect*." And again; "Let as many as be *perfect*, be thus minded." (1 Cor. ii. 6; Phil. iii. 15.) Hence it is evident that there were those in his day, who were perfect, according to the work of that day. Perfection has therefore been attained in this life.

3. Anything may, with strict propriety, be called *perfect*, which perfectly answers the purpose for which it was designed.[12] A circle may be called *a perfect circle*, when it is perfectly round; an apple may be called *perfect*, when it is perfectly sound, having no defect in it; and so of a thousand other things. A child who is perfectly obedient to all the requirements of its parents, is, in that respect, a truly perfect child: for what more can justly be required of it? Yet that same child, when grown to manhood, would be capable of doing much more than he could do in his childhood; and of course, more would be required of him. So when a man comes up to all the requirements of God, he then stands perfectly justified in the sight of God, and is, in that sense, *a perfect man*, and walks before God with a perfect heart. Hence we may see that perfection, in this sense, (which is all that can be required,) instead of being unattainable, is perfectly easy.

The idea which most people have of perfection, is a state in which there can be no increase for the better. This is a mistaken idea; such a state never will be attained, neither in time nor eternity: for the very life of all things which have life, whether vegetable, animal or spiritual, consists in an increasing growth of some kind or other. Stop that increase or growth in any thing, and its life will immediately begin to decay, and it must at length die. So it is with the soul of every true christian; if the increase and growth of the soul in the knowledge and nature of Godliness, ceases, its spiritual life must begin to decrease and die. Therefore, tho a soul in the progress of faithful obedience to the increasing light and work of God, may become divested of all sinful desires and propensities; yet his life and happiness must and will consist in a further and progressive growth in the knowledge and nature of God, to the endless ages of eternity. And yet a soul who is perfectly obedient to the revealed will of God, is equally perfect before God, in every step of his travel, according to his capacity and God's requirement.

Thus the real nature of perfection, when applied to a christian life,

---

12. This sense of the *perfect* reflects the Shaker meaning of *simplicity*: functional, unembellished by useless ornamentation, appearing to be what it actually is.

consists in nothing more nor less than in doing what God requires of us, which is to improve all our faculties in doing good, according to the best of our understanding and capacity: and in so doing every person who sincerely desires and rightly pursues it, *may attain to perfection.*

(Calvin Green, *Summary View,* pp. 319–320) [1823]

*　　　*　　　*

9

... the conjoined interior Spheres, constitute the Spirit world, which, tho invisible, yet fills every part of the exterior, visible world, and is the source of its living properties, powers and operations. Hence, it is the real, enduring world, its subsistence being Eternal. But it is evident that this interior world is an emanation from the subsistent principles of the Eternal and Divine Spheres and Worlds above, which is abstractly distinct from it. The Natural Interior world originated in an infant condition, and hence it has been progressively improving and rising into higher degrees of developed increase from its beginning. All the increase and improvements that have ever been manifested on Earth or in the visible world have originated through this medium. For the exterior and visible is an outgrowth of the Interior and invisible. The Source of the improving increase in the Interior, or Spirit part of the world, lies in the diffusion of the heavenly elements which come down from the Divine Orders above, and have their first existence in the Eternal Creator. (James, i. 12)

All the works and manifestations of God, both in the natural and Spiritual Orders, are continually moving forward. None "turn back;" tho the outward body of man is shed off, the soul enters a superior subsistent state, and so with all the things of Creation. But we see that all on Earth, do not improve at once. An improvement rises up in one part, and then in another, both in the natural and spiritual economy, and these become centers of emanation by which their influence extends in the world. This shows that the advance into superior degrees is by a similar process in the Spirit world, since the exterior is but an emanation therefrom. All the improvements of man begin small, and are adapted to that circle of beings in which they arise; and so it is with every degree of the work of God, which brings forth a superior Order of Goodness, as has been fully demonstrated in all ages.

(Calvin Green, *Biographic Memoir*, pp. 64–66) [ca. 1850]

10

Christian Progress. *Marcia M. Bullard*

. . .

One star differs from another in glory, yet all shine; so one organization comprehends more of the Divine than another; yet all truths are of God. The agitation of thought develops mind. A rap on the head set Newton to thinking. So prone is the human mind to the narrowness of educational prejudices that it often requires severe raps to break the old shell of conservatism and let in the new light of progressive truths.

It is a wise provision of nature that we differ, and a revelation of truth that we agree to differ peacefully. Here is the patience of the saints, and herein is the wisdom of the saints, that difference of opinion does not hinder conformity to the good, the pure and the true. Neither will it impede the flow of those Divine influences that fill the soul with wisdom and love—God.

When revelation ceaseth, the people perish, starve, spiritually. "A famine, not of bread and water, but of hearing the word of God." . . .

But how shall Christians progress? Shall they be wafted about by every wind of doctrine, or stand stiff in conservatism? Shall they run after the fashions, follies and gaieties of the children of this world, or shall they attire themselves in plain, neat apparel, corresponding with their profession, becoming a living testimony of the Christ-life, and a swift witness against the vanities of worldliness?

It is often remarked that among an array of ideas, which ones shall be adopted? But here is a criterion by which to try the spirits. Every spirit that sayeth come up higher,[13] bear more cross, practice more self-denial, live more separate from worldly influences, is safe to follow. . . . In former times Wisdom required the whole heart. How can

---

13. This is often referred to as a come-up-higher gift; cf. Section Five, Gifts and Orders, introduction, p. 261.

THE SHAKERS

Christians devote the whole heart to God and godliness when so much of it is given to the unnecessary things of this life? For artificial wants far exceed the real needs in the earth–life.

(*The Shaker Manifesto* XI, 9, pp. 195–196) [1881]

I I

The Silent Forces. *Hamilton DeGraw*

Of the manifestations of life in its varied forms, the most powerful and far-reaching in their results are the forces that to the materialistic mind are void, because in their operation they are removed from the glamor that surrounds and seems necessary to impress the undevelopt spirit. When the Divine teacher announced the importance of retiring into the closet and in silent devotion sending forth the prayer, he announced one of the grandest truths that was ever presented for human acceptance.

In the movements of life upward it is from the silent, the powerful forces from which is evolved the strength that is lifting toward the higher. When before the prophet's vision there past in review the noisy demonstrations of life in the earthquake, thunder and tempest, but not to them was the highest manifestations of Divine life, but in the voice of silence there was demonstrated the highest embodiment of truth. That the external may be necessary to attract and center the life on the reality is admissible. As toys in the hands of childhood, so the powers that appeal most strongly to the material sense are a proof that there are yet unfolded forces hid under their noisy demonstrations.

Evolution is not a backward movement, for on it is written the law of eternal progression. The life history of our planet, written on its rock strata, and read by the clear eye and unclouded intellect of the true scientist gives proof of the convulsive periods in the remote past when the forms of life then existing were destroyed, and as the creative forces replaced the old with new and better conditions the primitive forms of life could not retain their position, for onward must be the eternal watchword.

In the realm of mechanics the nearer that ideal is attained which is seeking to grasp and control the forces operating in the material world the less demonstrative to the extreme sense are their manifestations.

120

THE SHAKERS

Simplicity is the close companion of perfection and the nearer its realization the less complicated are its forces. The mysterious only remains so until it is understood.

Like the pent up forces in the material world which result in explosions and upheavals have been the political and religious convulsions which have destroyed nations and overthrown civilizations. Neither one in the highest sense had within them the elements of progress, but were a means used to remove the debris that had collected preventing further growth. The powers which to–day are the most potent factors in the advancement of life move so silently that those who are looking for a great sign in the heavens which is to usher in a new and improved order of life, feel that nothing is being done because it is not heralded with the blast of trumpets and immediate destruction of all opposing elements.

"The kingdom of heaven is within." From the internal to the external is the true order of development. The source from which the soul draws its inspirations makes it either an obstruction or a builder who is helping to shape and expand the temple of universal life.

The intuitive faculty that enables us spiritually to feel the condition of surrounding life is closely allied to the prophetic gift, and while in that illuminated state are [sic] enabled to predict future events. This power "cometh not with observation," the method by which unilluminated minds arrive at results. It is felt and thereby the evidence which is given is known to be real. It is the silent voice speaking to the soul that has been prepared to receive those heavenly ministrations.

In the interior life even if clouded by externalities or obstructed in its expansion by false theological teaching is that "temple not made with hands." How to attain the knowledge that will open it to the divine Spirit is a problem that perplexes the soul living in the externalities of life because it does not understand the things of the Spirit.

Many ways are devised by which admittance may be gained, but whosoever cometh not through the gate the same is a thief and a robber. Those who have been admitted to communion in that temple, are the ones who have given all they possest to advance the truth in a manner that the left hand knoweth not what the right hand doeth. Like the dew, as it is silently distilled, so are the forces that have in them the greatest power to build a truer and better life in the individual or the state.

(*The Manifesto* XXVII, 11, pp. 168–169) [1897]

THE SHAKERS

12

Invitation. *Oliver C. Hampton.*

. . .

We know whereof we affirm, by practical experience, and we know we live the life which Jesus Christ lived and taught, because we constantly experience the fruitions and beatitudes which he declared to be the inevitable result of such a life. Would you not be glad to be ushered into a society of practical christians ignoring all private, selfish habits and indulgences, and living for the good of each other? Whose Comfort and blessing were augmented exactly in proportion to their interest and zeal in promoting the comfort and blessing of others? . . .

Now we testify to you sincerely, joyfully; we are living in just such a Christian Church as is able to afford you immunity from actual sin, and open to you the gates of a sinless Paradise which no man shall be able to shut, so long as you adhere to its holy ordinances and are willing to be guided by its love and disciplined into the saving efficacy of its wisdom.

Once legitimately joined in spirit to this Christian Church of Believers, by a sincere confession and repentance of every recollected sin and dereliction from right, you need go no more out forever or be left to stumble and fall among the gloomy crypts of sin and despair. . . .

We are well persuaded that could mankind see these things as they really are, great numbers would choose this life and its purity, unselfishness, and felicity—and so we continually and lovingly hold out the hand of invitation, to all who feel ready for something better than the pleasures of a rudimental plane of existence, and a fugitive, perishing world; in the same spirit and words of Jesus which begins [*sic*] this article [i.e., Matt. xi: 28].

(*The Shaker Manifesto* XIII, 2, pp. 26–27) [1883]

13

Let Us Reason Together. *Antoinette Doolittle*

. . .

At one time when speaking to certain of his disciples concerning the order of his spiritual kingdom, of its faith and principles, he [Jesus] gave them to understand that there would be no limit to its growth and increase, and no diminution of power when he had finished the work that was given him to do, and he had passed from their visible presence into interior spheres. And while he gave pledges that he would be with them in *spirit* to assist them in their ministrations after his departure and that they should be blest with still greater spiritual power than he himself had possessed while in mortal form, he also laid them under great responsibilities concerning the use they should make of delegated powers conferred upon them as leaders and directors, and in regard to the faithful performance of duties which would bring them to occupy the position of servants as well as rulers. The greatest must also be least. . . .

We reason that man is a duplex being in his nature and in his desires and attainments. It is requisite while we are in a rudimental state of existence; and are dependent upon the material products of the earth for subsistence, that we etter into rapport, and form a union with material substances, and seek to discover and develop the hidden sources of supplies which have been held in reserve for ages, by a wise and beneficent father and mother, for the benefit of their children; and in so doing, if we would cooperate with the divine will respecting us— we should be very careful to maintain moral integrity, and learn to commune with God's creation, as revealed in the exterior, visible world of matter, and strive lawfully and earnestly through that medium, to comprehend something of the interior world toward which we are all journeying of which it is said by many who claim to be spiritually illumined that the visible world is but a reflex.

What benefit might accrue to each and all, if, while we are placed upon middle ground, and have it within our power to honor the creative power that spake all worlds of mind and matter into being, if we would maintain our rectitude; by holding each and all in their proper sphere; use them as needful for our own subsistence and the good of humanity. By so doing, we might hold unbroken communion with the angel world, through pure ministering spirits, who would grasp, and hold us in their loving embraces, and guide us in safety to our heavenly home, where all our needs will be supplied without the aid of material substances. By maintaining just and proper relations with the two worlds, we might unfold and perfect our duplex natures, the natural and spiritual, the earthly and heavenly—. . . . And we should learn to comprehend more fully that "the earth is the Lord's, and the fullness thereof;" that the gold and the silver and the cattle upon a thousand hills belong to Him; and are ours in usufruct only.

We can develop the godlike attributes of our being the most

effectually by being in strict and harmonious accord with the well-devised and executed laws, placed to guide intelligent manhood from rudimental, earthly conditions to higher destinies in the great beyond. Thus we shall be able to see God in the tiny leaf, in the unfolding fragrant flower, in the towering oak; also in the little streamlet which courses its way through meadows and valleys onward to mingle with the waters of the great ocean; and in all we shall recognize the impress of the Divine originator and dispenser of blessings for humanity's weal.

"God is not slack concerning his promises, as some men count slackness;" neither is He angry or impatient, because the race makes slow progress. He awaits the growth and advancement of sentient beings, and the fulfillment of times and seasons; knowing that in the sequel, *justice* will prevail: TRUTH will be victorious. His work will be accomplished, and wisdom will be justified of her children!

(*The Shaker Manifesto* XI, 4, pp. 79–80) [1881]

14

Discord–Concord. No. 2. *Wm. H. Bussell*

. . .

"God is Love," is the fundamental doctrine of Christianity. Love is harmony; Infinite Love is therefore Infinite Harmony.... but the geologist and the historian speak of earth's upheavals, of the clashing of elements, of continual conflicts.... How is this to be reconciled with the idea of Infinite Harmony? ... [with] the idea of progress from original, lowest to the highest conditions both in the physical and in the mental worlds.... by gradual changes it [the world and human race] has become what we now behold it.... The Christian believer who rejects what has been styled orthodox Christianity, finds nothing in this [evolutional] view inconsistent with the teachings of Jesus....

But, to turn from theory to practice, how is one to assure himself that *God is love,* and that the discordant feelings, appetites and passions inherent in human nature may be removed, and something infinitely better take their place? Let him test it for himself, just as he would test the value of anything that has been recommended to his attention.

... One has the proof within himself of the harmony of the Divine Nature, when he has asked and received the inspirations of Divine Love.

THE SHAKERS

The tendency of these inspirations is to harmonize all within him. His warring passions cease their conflict, at least for the time being; his peace is like a river, gentle in its flow, whose sediment is not so mixed with it as to prevent clear seeing. He is satisfied of its divine origin, just as he is satisfied with the proofs of any truth presented to his understanding. He need then only to apply to the same source of inspiration until he has satisfied himself that all within is harmony, peace and love. When all persons shall have done thus, each for each, we shall have a harmonious world. Earth will then have become heaven.

(*The Shaker Manifesto* XI, 4, pp. 76–77) [1881]

15

Principles do not change, but to the advancing pilgrim they present various aspects of mutually sustaining relationships. Utterances of people may vary in dealing with the same, or with different aspects, without necessarily involving a conflict of ideas. Our system is in its infancy, but its principles attribute unlimited advance to mind in the discovery and practice of truth. Mother Ann taught, "You should make the way of God your occupation. The way of God is to be learned as much as any trade. You learn to have faith, learn to believe. A man that has a trade, is industrious to work at it to get a living. You ought to be as industrious, and as much engaged in the way of God."

(Alonzo G. Hollister, *Synopsis of Doctrine Taught*, pp. 3–4) [1893–1902]

16

[Untitled] *Andrew Barrett.*

If we wish to make a renewal of spirit power, a thing to be prized, valued and truthful among the people,—make it so by bestowing confidence and love upon those who are and will be, targets for the scorn of the infidel and unbeliever.

Accepting new truths honestly and candidly given is the path to true progression.

Truth is eternal. God's truths are forever the same, but the modes of presenting them may vary somewhat with each age. Languages change, human condition changes, and while meeting these changes, the true, the pure, the good will never surrender any part of the principles of truth.

(The Shaker Manifesto XIII, 12, p. 276) [1883]

17

Stability of Principles. *Alonzo Hollister*
. . .
The principles of eternal life revealed in Christ, are unchangeable, remaining the same to every individual that receives them, now and ages hence. . . . the revelation upon which we claim to be founded being a new revelation, not of essentially different truths, but of the same truths, by the same spirit, to every soul that receives that Spirit; and a revelation of further truths in the same line, as the increase and growth of souls in these, and the general progress of the work of God demands them.

(The Shaker II, 9, p. 67) [1872]

18

Shirley Village. *Wm. H. Wetherbee.*
. . .
While toiling to accumulate a substance of the needful things of this life, they were not unmindful of the spiritual welfare, both of themselves and of the generations to come after them. Uppermost in their pursuits was a practical illustration of the principles of purity, honesty and righteousness. The Christ life and salvation from sin, being their motto. These principles, have been handed down and kept intact, while some errors, and some superstitions and prejudicial customs are giving way, and the watch–word now is, Progression, holding first to the truth, and to fundamental principles.

The present number of able and devoted workers, is small, and they are watching, working, waiting.

(The Shaker Manifesto XIII, 2, p. 28) [1883]

THE SHAKERS

19

Christian Culture. No. 8.   *Wm. H. Bussell*

Activity. Life is action; death, the cessation of action. But, in its strictest sense, there is no cessation of action, hence, no death. Every particle of matter in the universe is instinct with activity. . . . Change, or progress from lower to higher forms of life, is incessantly going on.

Action is an essential attribute of beauty. . . .

The life of the christian in its highest stage corresponds to the life of God, which is action in its supremest sense. The Divine action evolves worlds and systems of worlds and sends them forth on their never-ending journies. It develops therefore the various grades of life, both mankind and spiritual, and carries them forward in their continually ascending course. . . .

(*The Shaker Manifesto* VIII, 1, p. 2) [1878]

20

Science and Religion. *Oliver C. Hampton.*

There never was, is not now; and never will be any antagonism or conflict between Science and Religion. Nothing but sheer ignorance in any man could suggest such a possibility. . . . all truth is of, and from God and God cannot antagonize Himself. If this is not so, there is no truth, no reason, no sense, no anything.

. . .

All truth as comprehended by finite man, must necessarily be more or less tainted with the feculence of error and the beautiful progress of Evolution will be necessary to gradually fan away this feculence throughout all time and through the interminable cycles of Eternity. . . .

The best mode of development we can adopt is to become if possible equally perfect, physically, scientifically, spiritually. An excess of life–intellect–or emotion is sure to be disastrous sooner or later. . . .

(*The Manifesto* XVI, 6, pp. 127–128) [1886]

*   *   *

21

Now, it is very exceptionable for those who believe the Scriptures, to teach that the Church is built on the Scriptures; for, according to the Scriptures, the house of God, or Church of the living God, is the ground and pillar (base, or foundation and style) of the truth; and the law goeth forth from Zion and the Word of the Lord from Jerusalem, and not Zion from the law, or Jerusalem from the Scriptures; neither are the Scriptures ever said to be the foundation on which the Church is built. The saying of the Apostle to the Ephesians, (ii. 20) "And are built on the foundations of the apostles and prophets, Jesus Christ himself being the chief corner–stone," hath been alleged as a proof that the Church is built on the Scriptures. But the argument is foreign and inconclusive; for the foundation of the apostles and prophets is evidently the foundation on which they were built, or to which they bore witness, which could not be the Scriptures, for they were built before the Scriptures were written, and stood firm while they were writing them, each one according to his day; and the foundation to which they bore witness was Christ. *To him gave all the prophets witness,* as well as the apostles, saying, *Other foundation can no man lay than that is laid, which is Christ.* Or the foundation of the apostles and prophets is the revelation of the truth of God, which centers altogether in Christ, who is the chief corner–stone. Some professors may object, that this is Popish doctrine. And what then? It is the truth of God; and is any truth objectionable because a people accounted corrupt believe it? The revelation of God is in the true Church of Christ, in every place where that Church is, and is its foundation and support, as well as its cement and Spirit of union.

There are serious disadvantages attending the opinion that the Scriptures are the foundation of the Church, which show themselves in the fruits of those churches or societies who believe so, none of them being able to exhibit the genuine fruits of the Gospel, the unity of the Spirit in the bond of peace, love, which is the bond of perfectness, and the like. And it is natural that this should be the case; for it is understandable that the Scriptures have suffered by the hand of time, through transcribings and translations, and have lost, especially to the English reader and others who have them by translation only, much of that perfection which they at first had, consequently the building which is built on them, or even squared by them alone, must be proportionably imperfect and uncertain. But this is not all; The Scriptures in no case represent themselves as the foundation of the Church, but the revelation of God, or Christ himself; it is therefore subverting the Scriptures, and as they are true, subverting the truth, to make them the foundation. "For other foundation can no man lay than that is laid, which is Christ." (1 Cor. iii. 11)

But in the progress of the work of God and in the increase of the Church in the second appearing of Christ, matters will have a different train, and the truth of the Scriptures be confirmed, while they serve their own proper use in the hands of the people of God. "All (holy) Scripture is given by inspiration of God, and is profitable for doctrine, for reproof, for correction, for instruction in righteousness; that the man of God may be perfect, thoroughly furnished to all good works." (2 Tim. iii. 16) In the true Church of Christ the genuine fruits of the Gospel may be found in such a manner as eventually to confound all scruples as to the truth of revelation; for in its progress, which hath already begun to appear, may be found—peace, for its members do not go to war against men's lives, or property, or rights—safety, for its members shed no human blood—union, or the unity of the Spirit in the bond of peace, for there is one body and one Spirit, one faith, one baptism, being all baptized by one Spirit into one body; one Lord, Jesus Christ, one God and Father of all, who is above all, through all, and in them all. No place is found for selfishness, covetousness, or partiality; *for they have all things common and no man calleth any thing which he possesseth his own.* No room is left for even a plausible suspicion of worldly or sinister views in their possessions; for they gain their living by their own industry, and their preachers receive not a cent of pay in money or other value of earthly goods as a compensation for preaching. And the testimony which they bear against sin in nature and works, including the visible and manifest order of their lives, cuts off all room for sensual indulgences.

(John Dunlavy, *The Manifesto*, pp. 21–22) [1818/1847]

22

1. Those books which have been collected into one, under the title of Holy Scripture, are so called from their being written by holy men, who were moved by the Holy Spirit. And, as far as they have been

preserved entire, in their original sense, free from the errors of translators and transcribers, they are justly denominated "The Scriptures of truth."

2. They contain a true account of the will and purposes of God, revealed to man in the different ages of the world, and of the operations of his power, from the beginning of the world, relative to the salvation of souls, until the real work of redemption began: and they contain also the true predictions of all the principal events that were to take place in the earth, until the work of redemption should be finally accomplished.

3. But, as the Scriptures are composed of letters, and letters are no more than signs, marks, or shadows of things, and not the very substance of the things which they signify; therefore it is contrary to the dictates of reason and common sense to suppose that any of those real things are in the Scriptures, of which they contain a written account.

4. They contain an account of the Spirit by which the writers thereof were inspired, but they do not contain that Spirit itself: They contain a true record of the promise of eternal life; but that *eternal life* is not in the Scriptures, but in the Son of God, according to the record of truth. "Search the Scriptures, (said Jesus Christ to the Pharisees,) for in them *ye think* ye have eternal life; and they are they which testify *of me.*" (John, v. 39.)

5. The Scriptures contain a true account of the law of God, but Scripture is not that law. "I will put my law *in their inward parts,* and write it *in their hearts.*" (Jer. xxxi. 33.) They also contain an account of the Gospel of Christ, but they are not the Gospel itself.

6. The beginning of the Gospel is not the beginning of the Bible, but the beginning of *the power of God unto salvation;* (Rom. i. 16.) for the Gospel itself is the power of God unto salvation to every one that believeth in the power of God, wherever it is made manifest by living and chosen witnesses of God, who have it in possession.

7. The Scriptures also contain a true account of the Word in different ages, according as it was delivered, at sundry times, and in divers manners; but the Scriptures themselves are not that *Word,* but a *record* of the operation of that *Word* in different ages.

. . .

9. The word of God is incorruptible, and *liveth and abideth forever;* (i Pet. i. 23.) but the Bible is not incorruptible, nor doth it abide forever. And if all the Scriptures and books on earth were consumed, the Word of God would still be the same quickening *sword of the Spirit.*

(Eph. vi. 17.) Therefore they are greatly deceived, who imagine that the Scriptures are the Word of God; there is no such idea communicated, in any part of the Scriptures, from beginning to end.

. . .

16. From all which there appears a manifest distinction between the Word of God and the Scriptures; and notwithstanding those who receive the Word of God as their guide, are led according to the Scriptures; yet it is not in word only, but in power, such as the Scriptures never could communicate. It must be granted by all, that the Spirit which inspired the matter of the sacred writings, is greater than those writings, and is therefore the living and true guide into *all* truth, which was but in part written.

. . .

27. In confirmation of this truth, we need but look to the numerous divided sectaries now upon earth, who, for ages, have been contending about the sense of the Scriptures, and shedding each other's blood in defence of their respective opinions. This is an incontestable evidence, that the Scriptures are not a sufficient guide without a present inspiration of the true Spirit.

28. By establishing the Scriptures as the word of God, for all future ages, the most inconsistent ideas have been formed of the Divine goodness; while the comments and precepts of men have prevailed, instead of the *living Word;* and a total ignorance of the spiritual world, instead of the knowledge of the true and quickening Spirit of revelation; which is particularly manifest in that horrid and blasphemous doctrine of *"eternal and unconditional decrees."*

. . .

(Benjamin Youngs, *Testimony*, pp. 588–590, 592) [1808/1810/1823/1856]

23

Teachings of False Theology, Infidelity, and True Religion. *G. B. Avery.*

. . .

True religion: A recognition of a portion of the Bible as a *record* of God's truth; a revelation from God, and a necessary guide to life; but many instructions and tolerations of the Bible adapted to one age of humanity, *not* adapted to succeeding ages of progress. Portions of the biblical record, a history of human weakness, wickedness and depravity much to be deplored. . . .

(*The Shaker Manifesto* X, 3, p. 51) [1880]

24

[Letter: *F. W. Evans.*]

. . .

As to the "Sacred Roll" and "Wisdom's Book,"[14] some believers had as good a right to make fools of themselves, about *two* books, as the whole of Christendom had, to do so, for centuries, about *one* book which they had made. . . . After worshiping Jesus so long, what if we did worship Ann Lee for a season? And after bowing down, for ages, to the idol King James set up—The Bible—what if we did bow down, for a few years, to two books, that ourselves had made? They contain almost as much good as the Protestant *male* book, and a great deal less evil. At least, they did represent *duality*.

(*The Shaker & Shakeress* IV, 10, p. 75) [1874]

25

Inspiration. *Wm. H. Bussell*

. . . He in whom God breathes the divine life, may impart that life to others, and even his writings, though subject to numerous copyings and translations, will have an influence for good on all after generations, so that the apostle has justly styled such, "God–breathed scripture." This inspiring influence is not confined to the books of the Bible, whether Catholic or Protestant, but is discovered, also, in the writings of many others, by those whom the Divine Spirit illuminates. . . .[15]

(*The Shaker* I, 10, p. 76) [1871]

---

14. Two elaborate books of inspirational-prophetic witness (mostly exhortations to reform and warnings against the unrepentant) by Philemon Stewart and Paulina Bates—two of the most exotic products of the mystical revival of 1837–1847.

15. John Wesley and others are cited.

26

... What is needful to use the Scripture profitably as a testimony to the work of Christ's Second Appearing, is to take it according to the Order in which it was given, as a witness of the superior Order and work that follows, but not as a rule, binding to any inferior degree.

... For the real Spirit and Life of Faith which produces corresponding Works, and makes them useful to the upbuilding of Christ's everlasting Kingdom, must flow from vessel to vessel thro living channels.... The Oral Word, spoken by those whose lives have become identified with the Spirit of Christ, possess the same virtue to us that the Savior's words did to the Disciples of his time. [Transcriber's Note]

(Calvin Green, *Biographic Memoir*, Ms. pp. 150, 157) [ca. 1850]

27

[Shakers hold what is now called] Higher Criticism. Shakers have always distinguished between the Bible and the Word of God. To them, the Word of God is not a book, but the Christ–Spirit, ever revealing God, the Infinite, the Unknown; and to the finite being, the Unknowable save as revealed by the Christ Spirit.

(Anna White [?], *Present Day Shakerism*, p. 8) [ca. 1890]

*   *   *

28

Oneness of Faith. *Giles B. Avery.*

Christ's Church is a school; the spirit of Christ the authorized and inspired teacher, and believers are the pupils. Perpetual revelation of truths, new to the pupils, is the law of eternal progression, the guiding star of destiny for the School of Christ....

[Oneness from:] ... *First,* to the Divine character of the School, and the authority of the Master....

Second. To the harmonious union of the scholars. . . .

Third. To the travel or *progression* of the pupils in the perception and reception of truth and knowledge of godliness. . . .

Thus, oneness of faith refers prominently to the principle of an ever increasing revelation of the truths of God in Christ's Church, manifest through the quickening spirit—Christ. And as truth is eternal, there will be a oneness of faith in all souls who have traveled, or progressed to the same degree of light and Christian baptism . . . those who have learned the same lessons in Christ's School . . . practical life lessons, taught by facts. . . .

. . . "What is the essential principle of unity of faith?" is to *live wholly to God;* . . . If, then, the souls of the children of God, all led and governed by the spirit of Christ, flow together to partake of, and disseminate the feast of His great salvation and redemption to humanity, it is well and it is enough!

(*The Shaker* II, 4, pp. 26–27) [1872]

29

Truth, vs. Speculation, vs. Transition. *Giles B. Avery.*

. . .

The sources of truth's manifestations or discoveries are twofold— revelation, through inspired media, and the researches of human reason. . . .

Inspired media, —ascetics and recluses, have existed in all ages . . . these, prompted by the inspirations and illuminations of truth to them vouchsafed, as a fruit of their separation from the herd of humanity, and honest devotional seeking to God; for truth and wisdom, have been in varied degrees, shining lights and conservators of truth and wisdom, and dispensers of the same to the human family; and the truths they enunciated have been blessings to our race, and they are eternal as God is true. . . .

. . . many have been teachers of righteousness whose enunciations of truth, in measures adapted to the day and times in which they lived, are links in the vast chain of truth's revelations that shall embelt the world; and their revelations of truth can never be ignored, justly, because they are steps in the march of human progress.

. . . The Christian dispensation is a school, and of its scholars some are constitutionally organized with capacities as teachers; others as scholars and learners of them, while, in turn, they are also learners of teachers in advance of them; thus, on in gradations, up to the Eternal Throne. The Christ Spirit and baptism is the master in the Christian School! This Jesus beautifully taught as a government of God, through a viceregency,—*A Theocracy*. (Jn. vi: 38; v: 30, 37; Mtt. xxiii: 8, 10)

This same government of God through mediation of the *Christ Spirit* was also beautifully taught as a theocracy by the Ministers of the testimony of Christ's Second Appearing, Ann and William Lee, as manifest on the following occasion. One Col. Smith came to see the Elders at David Meacham's, in Enfield, Ct. He asked, "Is there not a woman here that is the head of the Church?" Mother Ann replied, "Nay, *Christ* is the head of the Church." Elder William Lee also said, "We do not allow *man* nor *woman* to be the head of the Church." "But" (said Smith,) "there is a woman here that teaches, is there not?" Elder William replied, "We must not suffer *man nor woman* to teach, except they have the spirit of Christ in them, and then either man or woman may teach."

But, while Christ's Church is in the state and capacity of the Church militant . . . there will be in it some who do not have the Spirit of Christ in them; and of course, could not, with propriety, be authorized to teach, nor exercise government in a democratic sense.

And, when *all* the members of the Church of Christ are fully redeemed from all that is not of the Christ spirit, the baptism of the Father and Mother,—God, they will then be in the Father and the Father in them; and not be "many masters" but their united ministrations will be a full and complete government of God, as the Church triumphant over all the powers and passions that work divisions among men. This will be a perfect Theocracy,—A Church *not* ruled of *man* nor *woman*, but by the Christ Spirit—The Viceregency of God!

(*The Shaker Manifesto* XIV, 7, pp. 147–150) [1884]

30

What Shakerism Teaches. *F. W. Evans*

. . .

All existing forms of Christianity, whether Catholic, Greek, or Protestant, are, in their essence, Church and State organizations. Collectively they are the Church in the Wilderness state—1260 years. This Church in the Wilderness claims authority, in the name of God, as against the right of private judgment in matters of faith and conscience. It assumes to regulate the human understanding.

The subordinate Protestant sects—little images—protest against this claim to authority and infallibility on the part of the Greek and Catholic churches, while they, each in its sphere, exercise the same power as those churches, so far as they can control the State. They send heretics to prison in this world, and to an eternal hell in the next.

. . .

What are the claims and principles of the new order in earth and heaven? 1. God is dual—Father and Mother. 2. Christ is not Jesus, but a Spirit that may be in each human soul as really, practically, as it was in Jesus. 3. No man or woman is a sinner until he or she willfully commit sin, nor any longer than the sin is persisted in. Total depravity does not exist. 4. Repentance goes with existence, and the mercy of God endureth forever in all worlds. 5. There are many heavens and hells. Those in the heavens and hells of our dispensation or degree may be gathered into the heavens of the succeeding dispensation or degree, as scholars may leave the ignorance, errors, and faults of one class, or school, by going up. 6. The Church, Christianity, when first seen was pure and holy, like a woman clothed with the sun, standing upon the moon, and crowned with twelve stars. When she formed improper connections, she was called hard names. . . .

(*The Shaker Manifesto* XII, 3, pp. 49–50) [1882]

31

The Christ Ideal in Shakerism. *Paul Tyner*

. . .

II. In the year 1770, while Ann Lee was imprisoned in Manchester on account of her preaching of repentance and righteousness, she believed that Jesus came to her, as He had come to the disciples after his Resurrection, to Paul on the road to Damascus, to Swedenborg when his spiritual vision was opened concurrently with his attainment of "a new manner of breathing." Jesus the undying Man, came to Ann Lee, as He has come and will hereafter come to every man or woman whose consciousness is prepared to receive, assimilate and transmit even the smallest further comprehension of that grand mystery by which the Oneness of Father and Son, of God and Man, was made manifest in the flesh, and every enemy, even Death, that last and most terrible, was vanquished. Jesus, who had never been very far away from her and who,—flesh of our flesh and bone of our bone, One with the Father only through His Oneness with us,—has never been really absent from any of us, however much our eyes may be blinded to His presence,—this same Jesus visited Mother Ann in prison. He conveyed to her mind with clearness and conviction that measure of Divine Truth embodied in the Christ Ideal which her consciousness,—developed as it had been by sin, suffering and aspiration,—was enabled to grasp and pass on to her fellows. She was permitted to see in clear and open vision,[16] she tells us, the root and foundation of human depravity, "the very act of transgression committed by Adam and Eve in the Garden of Eden,"—which we may, in the light of later development, take to mean that her mind was opened to the fact that all the ills that flesh is heir to, all the vices and crimes that affect humanity, disease and death itself, may be traced to selfishness, and mostly to that form of selfishness called lust; to the man's subjection to his will and pleasure, by brute force and not by love, of the woman on whose perfect purity, through perfect freedom, the very life of the race depends.

Ann saw and understood this plainly, since it was through this subjection that her own womanhood had been despoiled and defiled,—and, seeing this, it is not to be wondered at surely that she saw nothing more. To her literal mind, what more there was to be shown—the more known to Shelley and Godwin, and Mary Wolstoncraft—would have been incomprehensible and confusing. It was essential to the success of her great mission to humanity that she should not see all, as that she should see and feel what she did with all her heart and all her mind and all her soul. To her this was the basis of the existing social system; it was what her husband called *love*, what her father and mother and brothers and sisters upheld, what the law allowed and the Church sanctioned. She had never known any other sort of love—never known real love!

Ann Lee went forth from prison filled with the godlike resolution to give her life, at any and all costs, to the one glorious cause of man's redemption. Thenceforth she lived only to bring sinners to a realization of their sins and to lead them through the gate of repentance into the regenerated life of the purified and the free. . . .

---

16. See Introduction, note 10, p. 12.

THE SHAKERS

. . .

III. It should be kept in mind that acceptance of Ann Lee's revelation implies belief in continuous and progressive revelation, and so in perpetual advance. It would be a grave mistake to suppose that the Shakers regard the measure of Truth revealed through Ann Lee or through any of her successors, as final and irrevocable. On the contrary, it is recognized that the Christ Spirit, lives in every one of us. It awaits only clear recognition to spring into conscious manifestation and is exercised in some measure by every believer who preserves a pure soul in a pure body, and faithfully follows Mother Ann's favorite injunction: "Give your hands to work and your hearts to God." To quote from the preface to Ann Lee's "Biography" signed by Elders Frederick Evans, Giles B. Avery and Calvin Green—"The records of past dispensations are interpreted aright only by means of a present living revelation; we therefore hold ourselves untrammelled by the better of yesterday, expressing our views and living in accordance with the increasing light of to–day."

. . .

The Shakers have held—still hold in large degree—that the peace, plenty and purity of their common life would be impossible at any less cost than the absolute cutting off of all these things which in any way pertain to what they call "the carnal, generative life."

So far, I am afraid, it must be admitted that no other community in Christendom has proved them to be wrong by successfully combining purity of social life and sexual love.

And yet the fuller solution of our social problems which the future holds, must assuredly rest in such a combination as the Shakers say is impossible, and of which non-Shakers have yet to furnish a successful instance, in a society exhibiting all the strength and beauty and truth flowing from love in its purest expression, and none of the evils flowing from love that is defiled and impure.

. . .

Shakerism, as has already been said, being based on continuous revelation is in its very nature progressive.

. . .

[*Note.*—A few lines near the close of this article have been omitted as they were peculiarly local and had reference only to the domestic relations of one family. We appreciate the kindly and considerate spirit in which the article has been written, and republish it for a more extended circulation among those who are interested to be properly informed. *H. C. Blinn.*]

(*The Manifesto* I. XXVI, 6, pp. 95–97; II. XXVI, 7, pp. 108–112; III. XXVI, 8, pp. 124–127)

[Republished from the *Humanitarian*, January 1896] [1896]

32

Christ Not Divided. *Alonzo G. Hollister*

. . .

But although a continued revelation was always necessary, by which to know the present will of God (to the living,) yet an all important principle has ever been paramount to all others, in every age of the world. And that is, *an unerring rule*, by which to judge, distinguish and know divinely inspired revelations from those which are spurious and fake. . . .

An unerring test being an acknowledged necessity in a church which is continually advancing into the ever increasing light of truth, where can we find it more surely than in the lives and testimony of its founders and perpetuators?

A pure stream never came from a corrupt fountain, neither a pure stock from hybrid seed. The first, universally recognized criterion of truth, is its perfect oneness, from whence arises harmony, consistency and agreement. . . . The gospel itself must agree with certain concepts of truth in the mind to which it is addressed, or it will not be received. It was the work of . . . Christ in his first appearing to form a foundation . . . [Originating] in revelation. . . . It is the work of Christ's second appearing to build upon and increase those concepts.

Hence we cannot ignore the past altogether, without severing the trunk from the roots which nourish and keep it alive, without ignoring the wisdom, strength, and growth of the past, so far as that was growth in light and right, it forms the basis of present attainments.

May those who view the past, as a limit to all increase, or as sanctioning acknowledged error, reject with discrimination lest their light become extinguished. Increase, on a true foundation, will not conflict with, but confirm and strengthen the foundation. . . .

The church or congregation of Christ, is his visible body, which, as it is raised up and sustained by Divine Power and Wisdom, can never have but one head, and is therefore indivisible. As it embraces all the interests of man in his redeemed and complete state, including all truth necessary to raise, endow, and perfect mankind in that state, it is not, and never can be a sect [i.e., a party or division, implicitly disunified from that "cut off"]. For as the Apostle declares, Eph. i: 10. It is the Divine purpose in the fullness of times, to gather all things into one Christ, both the things in heaven and the things on earth, it must draw all that is salvable from every sect, being as superior to all sects, as the heavens are superior to earth.

Some twelve years ago, E. Amos Parkhurst, queried in himself: What is the body of Christ? There opened to his view, a great multitude of Shakers, disciples, perhaps a million of them together, and all were actuated and moved by the one spirit of Christ. That was the body of Christ. Well, how do they get this one spirit? How does it operate? It seemed to operate through the nerve fluid, or nerve spirit, so that what one knows, they all know.

Again, electricity was presented as another medium of operation, for the influence proceeding from the fountain head, which must be an individual intelligence of course. This spirit began to be manifested in Jesus Christ, and can ever come only through him. The work has been increasing since, and when it is perfected, such will be the body of Christ. "For though it is one body, it hath many members." This view was not to represent what is now, but what is to be when the church is perfected.

(*The Shaker Manifesto* XIV, 12, pp. 268–270) [1884]

*　　*　　*

33

Revelation. *Elijah Myrick*

All discoveries, inventions, improvements in the arts and sciences, are so many revelations emanating from the same source as the spiritual. . . .

. . . people of sincere motives, in all ages, through a false punctuation, have put a period or an exclamation in place of an interrogation

or comma, or where the subject indicated no pause; and . . . saw fit to
stamp with eternal infallibility what was proper to the child development of the race, or perhaps mere local circumstance. . . .

The human family is like a child in a continued series of revelations; and what is proper to one age is not always adapted to another;
. . .

. . . Much of the revelations held most sacred, are the experiences
of departed spirits in various stages of progression; and if we go with
them they will give us better experiences; but if we entomb and
worship them, they become our hitching post on the highway of
progression.

. . . Worship the source of this testimony and prophecy, but not
the medium. Worship the primary cause—intelligence—perfected
mind. For according to the best authority, "in the beginning was *mind*,
and *mind* was in the beginning with God, and the *mind* was God." And
mind was revealed to man, and he became a living soul—a reasoning,
reflecting and accountable being. This first and greatest revelation is
the unqualified essayer of all others.
. . .

If all revelation were in the past, it shows poor design in placing
the eyes in the fore part of the head, or giving the feet the direction
they have. The physical, mental and spiritual vision, prophecy [*sic*]
forward, onward, upward.

True prophecy is a science, by which the higher intelligences
reveal to faith, what experience will record in the book of knowledge.

(*The Shaker* II, 5, pp. 34–35) [1872]

34

In Union There is Strength. (Anon., Enfield, NH)
. . .

It is not the too conservative, probably, who retard progress, and
postpone improvements, so much as the ultra radical. While the former
may be clinging too much to old forms, the latter, paying little regard
to these in their eagerness for variations step aside from the safe,
narrow track of obedience, and loss ensues, with poverty of spirit. The
former class, seeing their evil results, are thereby made more cautious,
and tenacious of time honored institutions.

Thus the day is deferred when the desired alterations may be adopted with full accord and harmony. . . .

I suppose there are as many grades of progress on the gospel journey as there are travelers. One will advance to a certain position, another to a stage further on, and still another takes a degree beyond this. Notwithstanding it is said that we cannot be stationary, I think that by yielding to indifference, we are exposed to the danger of becoming fixed, and fossilized; and a fossil Shaker is not a very attractive character.

(*The Shaker Manifesto* XII, 1, pp. 10–12) [1882]

35

We Are Able. *Jessie Evans*

. . .

He who walked the streets of the material Jerusalem is no more, the Christ that reigns today in the spiritual Jerusalem, the Christ that is ever cognizant of the needs, the sins of the world that "God so loved" is an omnipresence. His spirit inclines as two or three meet touching anything we would ask. In our human thoughtlessness we, too, like James and John, may ask for an *end*, but Christ will teach us that the *means* only are for us; we may desire an *effect*, but it springs from its corresponding *cause*.

The life which Jesus lived is a life of processes. Was ever intimation given by him of a goal, a resting-place for his workmen? The eternal knows no boundary lines, and recognizes neither time nor space. . . .

(*The Manifesto* XXIX, 11, p. 165) [1899]

36

Necessity of Expansion. *Oliver C. Hampton*

One of the laws of the universe of finite beings and things is progress—improvement—evolution [i.e.] rolling out or unfolding from lower to higher degrees of perfection. Between the finite spirit of man and the Infinite spirit of the All Good there is an eternal attraction. . . .

. . . through the above named attraction, resurrection is possible.

THE SHAKERS

For in spite of all drawbacks the blessed attraction of the love of the Infinite Father and Mother is in eternal and persistent energy and activity, and so, sooner or later we shall all be saved.

... Now *forms* are evanescent and changeable, but *principles* are eternal and unchangeable. Every discreet unfoldment of higher truth to finite man requires a new form to express itself in. This is because it is some little different from any thing which preceded it. Especially is this true of unimportant externalities.

. . .

Forms, fashions, customs, external rules all have to bow to the fiat of evolution and progress toward that which is more perfect. This need not alarm the most conservative Believer. For unless we keep pace with the progress of the universe our individual progress will be an impossibility. We shall be whirled off at some side station and relegated to the limbo of worn out—superannuated and used-up institutions. . . .

The Christ of the universe is met face to face in that sublime order and organization acknowledged and maintained among us even "God manifested in the flesh" by which the weaker and less experienced are ministered to by those further advanced and these again by higher and higher circles of intelligence, wisdom and love. Our foundation rests upon this eternal and impersonal principle and is impregnable to any and all assaults from below. And whatever new forms or changes may be necessary to meet the continually changing scenes of time or eternity inside or outside of Zion, will be made conducive to our well-being, protection and progress, so long as we adhere to this fundamental principle of organization and yield unfailing obedience and allegiance thereto.

. . .

(*The Manifesto* XVII, 3, pp. 57–58) [1887]

37

Past, Present and Future. *Antoinette Doolittle*

. . .

The progressive degrees of development have been under the control of teachers adapted to the condition of the people, and their powers of receptivity. Hence, the word of the Lord at one time, was not the same as at another; not that God, or truth changed, but lessons were given, as the people were able to receive.

(*The Shaker* II, 8, p. 61) [1872]

38

[Untitled Item.] *Anon.*

Was the God of the Jews, the Creator of heaven and earth? The Shakers say not.

The God that directed the Jews was a tutelar divinity; not the Father of the Christ. One believed in, and directed war; the other taught of an enduring peace. . . .

Very many complications of opinions may be unraveled by learning the distinction made by the assertion: "The God of the Christians is not the God of the Jews."

(*The Shaker* I, 6, p. 44) [1871]

39

The Christian's God and Christ. *G. B. Avery*
An address delivered at Alfred, Me., Aug. 29th, 1880.

. . .

Our God is a *living God,* a God of love; but the God character manifest to mankind has widely differed, in different ages; the race has been progressing in knowledge, and with this progress there has been a change of the idea of God.

. . .

(*The Shaker Manifesto* X, 11, p. 248) [1880]

40

Better and Better. *Wm. H. Bussell*

Eternal life, in the Christian sense, means not merely endless existence, but perpetual growth in knowledge, in wisdom, in grace both external and internal, and in love, which includes reverence to the infinite Creator and to all who are formed in His likeness. Education in its full sense means nothing less than this. Like the gospel of Christ, it is for all human beings without distinction of sex or color. . . .

. . . Intellectual conceptions are one thing, the inspirations of spiritual life are another. Ideas, if in accordance with truth, are good in their several places. A conception cannot take the place of a life, but it may lead to a life. The conception of God, however feeble at first, may lead, by prayer, to the very life of God. Cherish the beginnings of all good; no matter if they are feeble, they will ultimate in perfection after a sufficient time.

(The Shaker Manifesto XI, 5, pp. 97–98) [1881]

41

Circumcision and Beards. *F. W. Evans*

. . . We have Jerusalem churches[17] in all our societies of Shakers, composed of apostles and brethren who have, like the Jerusalem church, borne the burden and heat of the day. . . .

These habits [i.e., customs they brought from their day] became, to them, sanctified, by being incorporated with true gospel faith and practice. . . . [Re: newer members bringing new customs, e.g., beards] As in the other case, in the primitive church, God has settled it before and for them, the Holy Ghost having been just as free to give gifts to the unshaved as to the shaved. In all things they have been, and are, approved by the powers of the world to come. Will not the shaving believers call to mind the words of Peter: "What was I that I should withstand God?" . . .

Judgment begins at the house of God. If the people of God, unto whom Christ has appeared a second time, without sin, unto salvation, cannot increase with the increase of God from faith to faith, through the seven travels by which they, being Gentiles by descent, habit and thought, shall progress up out of the labyrinth of error—the corruptions that are in the world through the lusts of generation, of property and digestion [i.e., anti-vegetarianism][18]—to the law that in itself, when divested of traditions, comments and interpretations, is pure and

---

17. The context is the resistance of the Jerusalem Church to Peter's baptism of the uncircumcised Cornelius, Acts 11:1–18.

18. One of the Elder Frederick Evans' personal convictions was the need to reform diet to pure vegetarianism; this in itself is a good example of Shaker progressivist views

holy, so much so that heaven and earth would both pass away and be no more, as easy and as certain as the law upon which they rest could pass away....

The marriage of the lamb and bride means a union of the law and gospel—this, and nothing else. Certainly it was not the marriage of Jesus and Ann, according to our first childish thoughts, as first-cycle theologians....

All the conservatism of human nature [e.g., Egyptians, Jews, Dark Ages, &c.] ... is in the present people of God, the Shakers. They must be overcomers in all these respects, as none before them have been— must be baptized into the spirit of truth as to rise above educational prejudice and prepossessions....

(*The Shaker Manifesto* XI, 7, 149–151) [1881]

42

The Heavenly Brideship. *H. L. Eads*
[In answer to Evans: "Circumcision and Beards," *S.M.* XI, 7, pp. 149–151]

There are two very important things which every true follower of Christ in the Second Appearing must ever appear very sacredly to conserve, among many others. 1st. The pure unalloyed testimony of the Gospel of Christ's second appearing in the line of the female., 2nd. The pure union of the *spirit of Christ* among Gospel Kindred—true Brethren and Sisters of the family of Christ—....

Now, in the name of our suffering, bloodsweating, tortured, crucified and God-chosen Father of the New Creation, Jesus Christ, and in the name of our imprisoned, tortured, much abused, suffering, and God-chosen Mother Ann Christ, and in the name of the bleeding hearts of their faithful children we must protest against this denial, before the world, of the long prophesied of and Heaven-born truth, that the scriptural "Lamb and Bride" are persons as vice–regents of God, and not things. The Churches that embodied and still conserve

---

that all of life—material, practical, spiritual, religious—was sanctified by the Christ Spirit and thus open to progressive revelation. Elder Frederick's (and others') commitments to special practices did not in any way reflect religiously sanctioned customs or precepts—in the Shaker phrase, they did not have "any notions" (cf. Introduction, note 14, p. 17, "nothing odd comes from God").

their life baptism may be considered, figuratively, in the same sense. It is our ineradicable faith and understanding that Jesus and Ann were the chosen ones, as vice-regents of God, to inaugurate the Gospel plan of Christ's First and Second Appearing. . . .

. . . Their united voice is, "My sheep do hear *my* voice, not the voice of the typical law. And they follow us. To follow one is to follow the other, for all their work, testimony and life are one. Come unto us, all ye ends of the earth and be saved. . . ."

To quote further from the article under consideration it is stated, "Unless we do right about food, generation and property, there is no use multiplying words about salvation in this world, or any other." The way to do right about food is to govern the appetite, not to eat too much of anything, this was Christ's doctrine, which can't be improved; some people make themselves as sick in eating buckwheat cakes and molasses, as others do in eating oysters. The way for the followers of Christ to do right about generation is to let it entirely alone, not soil our bodies nor our spirits therewith, but leave its whole management with the lower floor generators. We anticipate this is what the writer from whose article we quote meant, but we fear it would not thus be generally understood.

(*The Shaker Manifesto* XI, 8, p. 170) [1881]

43

The Marriage of the Lamb and Bride. *G. B. Avery*
[In answer to Evans: "Circumcision and Beards," *S.M.* XI, 7, pp. 149–51]
. . .

To the understanding of every enlightened biblical reader and true follower of Christ Jesus, in His anointed capacity as Christ manifested in the male order, was the Lamb of the marriage twain denominated in these Scriptures, Lamb and Bride." And if the Lamb recognized in Scripture as the commissioned agency "to take away the sins of the world," is to be understood in any sense other than directly personal, it can possibly be in no other than the church of Christ's first appearing. . . .

The faithful flock of Christ's second appearing will not lose sight of the simple fact that *Christ*, manifest through Father Jesus (as He became by baptism), and the church of that dispensation, was the

Heavenly Bridegroom—the Vicegerent Father of the New Creation. A spiritual organization, to *introduce which* the *Law* was but a *school-master, not a Bridegroom!* Nor will they lose sight of the equally important fact that *Christ,* manifest through Mother Ann, after she received her spiritual baptism, was the Heavenly Bride, and the church of this latter day dispensation of Christ, in the second appearing, *still manifests* the same Heavenly Bride character—the Vicegerent Mother of the New Creation "Jerusalem which *is* above, is free, which is the mother of us all." . . .

The righteousness of generation [as in the *Law*], in its most perfect state, is, nevertheless, *not* an elementary righteousness of the work of the Heavenly Bridegroom and Bride, and cannot, therefore, be wedded to the Gospel of Christ in any sense. It must, therefore, be protested that the "marriage of the Lamb and Bride" does *not* mean a "union of the Law and Gospel."

With honest souls, begotten of the Christ the Bridegroom, and born of the Christ Bride (a spiritual creation), there cannot be in exercise any personal strife and ambition to be greatest; nor can there be contention and ill-feeling; while each one, in efforts to set forth the truths of the Gospel of Christ, will feel himself or herself a learner forever, as we are all only children in the school of Christ.

(*The Shaker Manifesto* XI, 9, pp. 201–202) [1881]

44

The Heavenly Brideship. *Thomas Smith*

Allow me to congratulate you on the article, in August number with above title; because it opens rather a new era, that is, one brother can express his thoughts as to the correctness of points taken by another, how otherwise can we grow?

History seems to be full of strange facts, of which none are more striking than the constant failure of the expectations of religious bodies; supported by prophecy, embedded in tradition, confirmed by reiteration, positive with bigotry, becoming chosen peoples of God; they finally decay and lose their hold upon the race, for good.

The cause seems to be that they restrict their ideas, beliefs and rewards to very narrow circles; a few are chosen, a few saved, one man controls the salvation of the world; or one set of men only possess authority to interpret all truth, especially any new truth, or idea.

Every era seems to demand change, new men, new thoughts, and the question of vital importance to us, as well as to all others is, how far are we from the best light of our times?

The article "Heavenly Brideship" in the August number seems to be a brotherly criticism of "Circumcision and Beards" in July number, but are the positions taken correct, is it not another skirmish in the continual struggle between those on the one side, who believe that the Gospel of Christ, first and second, takes hold of every act of our lives— Generation, Nutrition, Property and Government; and all their elaborations; and those who believe that when Jesus Christ came, then all these things ceased to call for attention on the part of his followers; in other words, Jesus Christ came to destroy, make null the Law, instead of fulfilling it. Which did He do?

The Law was a schoolmaster to bring souls to the Gospel. No man upon entering college throws away the rudiments of his early training. . . . he ceases his former lessons only because they have become an incorporate part of his being. No man, erecting an edifice, after completion, tears out his foundations, and throws them away; else when storms come his building falls. Now why does not this law hold good in the higher ethics of our latter-day life? If Israel walked by law and statute in all things pertaining to life here, for hundreds of years, and the net result was Jesus Christ, why not continue the process, for further results? Is it not just possible that we are suffering for the same processes?

. . .

If the restraints put upon the sexual relation by Moses, and in Christ's day [ended] in celibacy; that [sic; and (?)] the restraints put upon property ended in community of goods, by what process of reasoning can we escape the conclusion that the restraints put upon the use of animal food ended in its entire rejection? They must stand or fall together.

The work of preparation was too vast, too far reaching and elaborate, to find consummation in one man or set of men; it was universal ultimately. So with the Bride and Bridegroom; are they not terms, broad and comprehensive enough to cover systems of thought reaching from the past to the present? merging the stability of the Jew with the broader and deeper light and knowledge of the present Gentile? And how does this detract in anywise from the dignity or kinship of Jesus Christ or Mother Ann?

THE SHAKERS

He was the first born of many brethren; she the first born of many sisters; what either of them endured of physical suffering is of minor importance, as compared with the great systems of thought which each headed in their time. Thousands of men and women have borne equal physical pain and for righteousness sake. But Jesus and Ann led the van. He represented the Fatherhood of God, she the Motherhood of God, but more than this He represented the training and culture of ages, the stability and permanence of truth in the *Divine Man,* while she was the protest of the agony and suppression of the *Divine Woman* calling for recognition; pressed down by government, social custom and blind ignorance. She reached beyond her condition and claimed equality with her brother, Jesus. Why should her system reject His culture? Why should the basis of past progress be rejected by her followers? Is there no grandeur and beauty in the consummation of the Divine promise that "all sickness and pain, all suffering and everything that hurts or harms, in all God's holy mountain shall be removed?"

Go with me throughout the quiet homes of our dear brethren and sisters from Maine to Kentucky and what is there more needed than health? . . .

There exists a grave inconsistency in our saying, "The way for the followers of Christ to do right about generation is to let it entirely alone," and then say in relation to its fellow subjects, do as the Gentiles do.

Generation and its kindred subjects are all laid under the same discipline of the Law, vis., curtailment and restraint, and we say in relation to generation, this restraint points to extinction, for a higher life, but its fellow subjects are of no importance.

Because the Law was first, does not necessitate the assumption that the Gospel is subordinate, by any means; the lesser always precedes the greater, the greater conserves the lesser, not destroys it. "Because the law was weak through the flesh" the Gospel removed the flesh, and the law became strong, not a nullity. Then when the truths of both dispensations are embodied in human society, will we be able to sing the song of Moses, the servant of God, and the song of the Lamb; then differences of opinion will not constitute men heretics or lunatics, but the Law having given us Truth and Justice, the Gospel will give us Love which melts and merges differences of opinion into the Brotherhood and Sisterhood of Christ.

(*The Shaker Manifesto* XI, 10, pp. 217–219) [1881]

150

THE SHAKERS

45

Love. *F. W. Evans*

"By this shall all men know that ye are my disciples, if ye have love, one to another"—so said Jesus.

Unity, of ideas and opinions—oneness of sentiment is good. To see eye to eye in doctrine is desireable–beautiful; but to love and be loved is better than all else. . . .

It remains for the Shaker Church to not let the Gates of Hell prevail against her, but to produce unity of thought by freedom of thought—uniformity of doctrine, by spiritual unity—by such love of truth that gives her a fair field and a free fight with error, in which, who ever knew put to the worst?

Let brotherly love continue, notwithstanding differences of doctrinal ideas arising from constitutional or educational conditions of body or mind. . . .

My confidence in God remains unshaken, that peace is a result of righteousness—that the millennium is a possibility, when the within shall be as good as the without—. . . and brothers and sisters can exchange ideas and reason together . . . as Christians in whom brotherly and sisterly love still continues in full operation.

(The Shaker Manifesto XI, 11, pp. 241–242) [1881]

46

Responsive. *Thomas Smith*

[In answer to H. Eades, "Bridegroom and Bride," each item of criticism is taken up; then the contrast in principles . . .]

If I might summarize my conclusions on these matters, they would run as follows; on the one side, Jesus Christ and Mother Ann revealed all truth; gave us *all* that we need; all God has for us; no need of any further progress. If this be true *succeeding Elders* hold *all truth.* This truth consists in living a celibate life, obeying without question, authority, then you will save your soul.

Your body may suffer the torments of the damned; disease and weakness may cripple useful lives; egotism and bigotry may assume place and position; property may blind justice; trade corrode the heart;

selfishness dictate against a divine gift; human will shape government in its own interest; our crops may rot and fail; pestilence and pests wipe out of existence human beings and human toil; but with all these the Gospel has nothing to do.

On the other hand, the Gospel of Christ is for all nations, kindred, tongues and peoples in all words; it is broad, liberal and saving. Jesus is only our Elder Brother, Mother our Elder Sister; they did their duty grandly and faithfully; they spoke the truth committed to them; did their work, and occupy a position in the plan of salvation, from which nothing can dislodge them. They only showed what other men and women would do when baptized with the same Christ Spirit, and actuated by the same devotion to truth and progress. They never closed the door to new truth.

This Gospel is one of Peace, not only to the warrior, but to the whole earth, to all animated creation. It will conserve the welfare of the body as well as of the soul; it will deal mercy in preference to animal slaughter; will teach us to use all the blessings of life for human comfort; it will teach equality of the sexes in the administration of government; show us that every age and epoch must have new revelations of truth to act upon, that these new truths are as essential as fresh air, or new machinery, or the thousand and one improvements which Progress has given us since Jesus lived.

It teaches us that Christ is a Spirit that can reach the hearts of *all* men and women, baptizing them as it did Jesus and Ann. Does this deny Christ? So far from it, it exalts him into a far more potent power for good; gives him a reverence so much superior to authoritative reverence, that all the tenderness and devotion of sincerity, responds to its call. This Spirit says to men and women associated under its organization, Ye are all Brethren and Sisters together, no one per se greater than another. These Brethren and Sisters choose the best and most unselfish to lead them, and they acknowledge the divine unction upon whomsoever the choice may rest; these leaders are not infallible men and women, who can do no wrong; but are the uplifted ensign of a consecrated, devoted body of human souls, and responsible to that body, legally and morally.

In this Spirit there is room for growth, not less obedience, but more, because of clearer conceptions of duty. There is room for a home to be developed wherein heaven and earth may be realized; a home where brethren and sisters can dwell together in unity, and reach out after every good thing; where the greatest shall be least, or servant of all.

May God speed the day when we shall actualize more of this home, where there shall "nothing hurt or harm in all God's holy Mountain;" where even the "pots in the kitchen shall have Holiness unto the Lord written upon them;" where all men and women shall be taught of the Spirit, needing neither Priest or infallible Pope; building up no more Catholic Systems, but a brotherhood and sisterhood in God.

(The Shaker Manifesto XII, 2, pp. 25–28) [1882]

47

Consistency. (*Anon.*, Mt. Lebanon)

. . .

. . . Much has been said pro and con concerning the influence which music, pictures, and flowers have upon the mind. Some even suppose that their tendency is to draw our minds from spiritual duties. What are our spiritual duties? If our surroundings are uncongenial, we shall be more or less unhappy; and to alleviate this unhappiness, and render life pleasant is, indeed, a spiritual duty. The most conservative person would view a beautiful landscape with pleasure, and consider the effects every way beneficial; and a copy of that same landscape, whether on canvas or paper, affords a corresponding pleasure.

A beautiful rose may be admired while on the bush; and it is no less beautiful when taken into our dwellings, nor its fragrance less acceptable. Many quote from the Bible, "Thou shalt not make unto thee any graven image." But the Bible contains many commands highly inapplicable to our day and civilization; and any one who should be reckless enough to attempt to put them in practice, would soon discover his mistake: and among the first to rebuke him, would be those who always quote it so glibly, whenever they have a hobby that needs propping up. The questions of today must necessarily be settled upon their merits, and in accordance with the intelligence and reason of today; and not by the opinions and prejudices of past generations. Our right to use our reason is as clear as that of our ancestors: and we are not bound to believe what experience has proved to be in error because they did.

"A thing of beauty is a joy forever." Never was truth more fitly spoken. The Apostle says: "By the things which are seen, we know of the things which are not seen." If we were blind, we should know very little either of the "Things which are seen, or the things which are not seen;" and a thing of beauty could be no joy to us. But as we are not blind, and as we are promised all beautiful in another world, and as the same God is supposed to rule all worlds, why should we be denied the limited enjoyment of that here, of which we are to enjoy such a superabundance hereafter? As we reserve our best clothing for the Sabbath, why should we not have our best books, papers, pictures, or whatever may conduce to make us more like the sons and daughters of God, where we can enjoy them on the Sabbath? May not our fine clothing detract as much from our spirituality as our books and pictures? Let us be consistent. . . .

If the basic principles of our system are correct, we ought to be the happiest people in the world; and consistency would demand that we reject nothing not in conflict with those principles, that would tend to increase our happiness or better our condition.

We fully agree with Br. Thomas Smith when he says that "in logic as in Christ, we all are one." We would also call attention to this fact, that the final verdict of leading authorities upon all matters pertaining to our well being, as a people, can be our only criterion.

(*The Shaker Manifesto* XIII, 2, pp. 39–40) [1883]

48

[Letter: Ministry of Alfred to Ministry of Mt. Lebanon Re: organs and musical instruments]

. . .

The writer has always considered *singing* to be an essential part of our worship, not merely *listening* to singing or other music. Ofttimes the deepest emotions of the soul are voiced, while singing the beautiful songs of Zion; for that reason, all have been encouraged to unite in the song when not exercising.

Anything that would tend to deprive the body of worshipers of their right to praise God in the song, and to confine the singing to a select and educated few, should be discouraged. For this reason, singing in score, or harmony, should be considered in the narrowest limits.

These ideas may seem to be behind the times, and yet be correct. If they are extreme in one direction you will, doubtless, get enough that are extreme in an opposite direction to balance them.

THE SHAKERS

The soul of the writer is grieved over the drifting of Believers toward those things which the world delight in; and the christening of *progression* seems none the less conforming to the world, and, in most cases, the gratifying of that pride which the Gospel of Christ and Mother was intended to crucify.[19]

But I forbear. You know that our feelings are as yours, to have that only admitted into our families which will help to lift souls into a new life, above the world, with its lusts and vanities. Anything that would pander to these, delays that resurrection.

. . .

(*The Manifesto* XX, 2, p. 36) [1890]

49

[Editorial Note Re Organs—*Eld. Henry Blinn*]

It is a nice thing to be able to pass an opinion, and to be sure in our own mind that our opinion is carried to the convincing point. The opponents of the use of instrumental music seem to have it all their own way, even though their experience in its use has been very limited. It is a pity that those who enjoy the harmony of instrumental music should be judged as having no "real interest in our seasons of religious devotion."

This form of expression reminds us of the remark of a good brother:—"An organ," said he, "may assist those who sing, and we may be sure that it will not say any bad words, and this is more than can be said of some who are good singers." If the organist is so naughty as to be vain, it will be a wonder if some of those who have a fine bass or soprano voice will not be found in the same company. It has been said that to sing in harmony has "a decided tendency to a dead formality," and possibly that may be the case, and yet some of us would walk sorrowfully over the road, if obliged to return to the manner of singing of an earlier date.

(*The Manifesto* XX, 6, pp. 135–136) [1890]

---

19. The Societies of Maine, beginning with the controversy over the succession of Father Joseph to Father James in 1787, have tended to more conservative positions; and so, for example, Elder Otis Sawyer of the Maine Ministry made a complete collection of Shaker publications for the New Glouster (Sabbathday Lake) library but refused to include any of Elder Frederick Evans' writings; in the musical instruments controversy the Maine Societies were the last to introduce organs into worship, while Canterbury was the first.

three

___

SHARING THE CHRISTLIFE

Part One: Celibacy

Introduction

Certainly the outstanding commitment of the Shaker Way is the life of celibacy. It has been a point of general misunderstanding on the part of commentators, and in the early history the cause of bitter hatred and violent persecution. In drawing together the representative texts it becomes clear that right from the beginning Believers had very different understandings of their call to the virgin life and yet they were unanimous in recognizing this call as central to the *metanoia* of living the Christlife. In the ultimate transformation of Resurrection already begun through their celibate consecration, Believers were arising out of the human nature of generation into the Christ nature of regeneration.

Among early Shakers we find a range of experiences which color their particular projections of the meaning of celibacy. Some view it very negatively as an opposition to marriage and the entire dynamism of sexuality. Yet others see it primarily in positive terms, as a gift and value embraced in the process of human divinization in Christ. As the selections indicate, in the development of insight stretching over two centuries Shakers ultimately evaluate celibacy as a purely positive gift, not as a rejection but as having its full significance in a complementarity with marriage.

Whether we consider Shaker celibacy in terms of its origins or of its development through the principle of progression, it is always the experience of each person, never an abstraction, and therefore each insight must be related to the larger context in which the experiencers find themselves: their culture, religious presuppositions, and all that would constitute the whole way of life.

First of all we must remember that all of Western civilization has been infected by a Manichaean world view: the material/tangible side of existence is evil (or at least always suspect) while the immaterial/spiritual side alone is good. The eighteenth and nineteenth century context in which Shakerism arose and first took shape looked on sexuality and marriage from a Manichaean–influenced perspective. Christians spoke of the sacrament and ordinance of matrimony as "elevating" an animal instinct and relationship; they generally took for granted that the sinful act of the Fall in Genesis was sexual; they taught that the procreation of offspring was the sole morally acceptable purpose of marriage and that sexual pleasure as such was not to be sought but merely tolerated. Marriage represented the baser human instincts, acceptable only as a "cure for concupiscence," or, as Paul put it, *it is better to marry than to be in torment* (1 Cor. 7:9). It is small wonder that early Believers so often expressed their call to celibacy as a repudiation of the very root of human depravity!

There was another negative context for marriage of which we must be aware. Women in the eighteenth century (and well into the nineteenth) had few legal rights. Although they could own and inherit property, they had to have a male legal guardian to administer it. Marriage transferred significant rights to the husband so that he controlled and virtually owned all her property and inheritances. In addition to all the tangible legal disabilities, women suffered from the less tangible but even more demoralizing "double standard" which allowed virtual sexual freedom for the husband while demanding absolute fidelity of the wife. The simple fact is that for all too many women of the recent past, marriage was at best a dubious escape from the rule of a father to rule by a husband. The selections relating the Shaker experience of celibacy, especially as this progresses in understanding throughout the first hundred years, witness to the sense of freedom, dignity, and true equality achieved by sisters and brothers in the new open relationship of Christlife.

Celibacy is also seen as crucial for the other essential gifts of Christlife: sharing in community and witnessing to peace. Shakers are convinced that a free sharing in both temporal and spiritual gifts is not really possible except among the celibate simply because the married have a properly exclusive concern for each other and their children. Their first obligation is to support their life together, and only then to use what is left over for others. Celibate Believers, on the other hand, are free to commit themselves first to an open and inclusive relationship, receiving into their lives the many who come and whose needs they can be ready to fill because they have no prior commitments. Of course this openness is not to be imagined as an absolute, since both personal capabilities to serve and the resources available for service are necessarily limited; the issue is one of priorities. For the communal form of life celibacy proved indispensable. While other attempts at communitarianism quickly failed (Owenism, Harmonism, Oneida Perfectionism, Amana, and many more) largely because of conflicts in family/children values, the Shaker communes survived the better part of two centuries.[1]

Similarly, celibacy also makes possible a full witness to the nonviolence of peace. Without the obligation to defend children or spouse, the Believer is free to suffer violence rather than engage in it. As with the case of the freedom to enter relationships inclusively with others, this freedom to pursue Christian peace is not absolute, and Shakers from time to time have found themselves in situations of conflicting values. Thus, in the Civil War many young Believers felt called to fight for the Union Cause as the battle against slavery; they saw their concern for fellow men, women, and children caught in the violence of slavery as the call to put an end to a greater evil than the violence of a war of liberation. (Their acceptance back into the communities after the War evidences the respect for honest conscience on the part of fellow Believers who interpreted the call to peace differently.)

Many commentators have ignored these and related elements in the context of Shaker celibacy and have focused on the personality of Mother Ann, at least as they reconstruct it. She was raised in dire

---

1. The popular presumption that the present ending of the Shaker communal Societies is due to celibacy ignores the existence of the Shaker Way since 1747. Celibacy has always necessitated the active conversion of new members (since there are no "born Shakers"); this pressure has always been a Shaker *concern* but it has also been the source of special benefit in that Believers enter with an adult sense of commitment through positive choice.

poverty, married at an early age apparently against her preference, shared the common Manichaean world view against human materiality, and had four children who died in early childhood. This last, in commentators' views, turned her against marriage: her children died, so marriage must be sinful. The tragic social context of the era is ignored: about half of all children died in infancy, and the poorest classes suffered the highest loss of life. Ann Lee could never have been under any illusions about children's chances of survival. Her loss, no matter how hard to bear, did not represent the trauma experienced in contemporary society over the loss of a single infant. Much more important, a testimony from early Believers (4) clearly witnesses the fact that celibacy was practiced by James and Jane Wardley as elders of the first Shaking Quakers some years before Ann Lee joined them in 1758.

In the first selection (1) Elder John Dunlavy locates celibacy positively in the nature of the Resurrection Life Believers lead in Christ. The Church, as the Body of Christ, is celibate and thus distinct from the world; this separation is positive, not negative. In the next texts (2, 3) the relationship of celibacy to marriage as spiritual to natural reflects the teaching of Mother Ann's ministry, while the following (5) illustrates the negative expression so often characteristic of the founders' period. Father James Whittaker was usually extreme in his negation of marriage, reflecting the Manichaean side quite sharply. Although he was one of the three of the First Ministry and so revered in Shaker memory, later Believers unhesitatingly criticized his extremism. They certainly "progressed out of" his view and into one of positive complementarity and harmony between the two callings of adult life. The personal reflection of Elder Henry Clough (6) is especially noteworthy for its positive stance (Elder Henry was called in 1788 to be assisting elder to Father Joseph Meacham). Joseph Dyer, writing as a former Shaker, witnesses (7) to a positive celibacy as an "impartial and universal love," and the reflection on the life together of Benjamin and Mary Whitcher (8), the founders of the Canterbury Society, places celibacy in the inclusive relationship of an open community of faith.

The next group (9–13) represents somewhat conservative viewpoints appearing throughout the nineteenth century (conservative here meaning more negative-leaning than positive). Elder Calvin Green (9) defines virginity in spiritual rather than physical terms, achieved regardless of past natural relationships by coming into Christ-nature.

THE SHAKERS

Elder Giles Avery (10) speaks of a new male/female relationship transcending "lust," and the irreconcilable difference between the worldly order of marriage and the kingdom of Christ (11). Elder Daniel Frazer (12) excludes marriage from any movement into a higher order of life, evaluating it as the selfish opposed to the selfless. These are all mirrored in the final text of the group (13).

The next selections (14–18) are illustrations of positive analysis. The first is a criticism of negative asceticism as Manichaean (14), and then Elder William Redmon (15) addresses the integrity which should be proper to marriage. William Wetherbee (16) relates marriage to celibacy as a progression in which healthy offspring can become good Shakers. For Ruth Webster this is the relationship of seed time to harvest (17), an analogy which becomes a favorite among progressives. Finally (18), the value of the Shaker celibacy experience is projected toward the hoped-for-future unitive relationship among the Churches.

Eldress Antoinette Doolittle, the longtime colleague of Elder Frederick Evans at the North Family of Mt. Lebanon, relates marriage to celibacy in a continuum of the natural-into-the-resurrectional (19). Elder Watson Andrews (20) stresses the critical role of celibacy in communitarian life and this, in turn, as the developmental step into the ultimate of spiritual life. Elrress Antoinette identifies celibacy with the gifts of peace, community, and equality of men and women (21), and the next selection (22) identifies celibacy with the restoration of women's rights. Elder Frederick sees celibacy as necessary to communism (23) and also as part of the natural-to-spiritual development, which embraces forms of "secular" celibacy as well (24). The final item of this group (25) locates this developmental need in the context of the world at large with the Shaker experience contributing to a future evolution.

The concluding selections are illustrative of progressive views which seek the future, beginning with the very brief allusion to the married by Father Joseph (26) in spite of his separationist structuring of the first communities. The indication of a conflict in developing views (27) demonstrates the later Shakers' difficulties in envisioning how Father Joseph's notion might be implemented, Pelham's comment (28) specifying the problem area in terms of the realism of communitarian life. Once again Elder Frederick (29) proves to be the most willing to progress into the new, not hesitating to note the limitations in the work of the founders. The final comment (30), from Elder Alonzo

THE SHAKERS

Hollister, positively relates the meaning of marriage and celibacy to the Ideal of Love in two forms distinct but complementary, a view which becomes the established understanding bridging the conservative and progressive insights.

I

It is generally granted, in loose terms, that the people, or Church of Christ, are not of the world; but few consider in what respect, and by what distinguishing mark or characteristic, it may be known that they are not of the world. The distinction is generally viewed, or contemplated, as being internal in the Spirit, and therefore invisible, so that the people of God cannot be known or distinguished by physical or merely natural men; as if an internal work would not be clearly manifested by its visible effects. *"They are not of the world, even as I am not of the world."* As clear a line of distinction therefore as there is between Christ and the world, so clear is the same line of distinction between his Church and the world: for they do as he said; *Deny themselves, take up their cross daily, and follow him* in his footsteps where the world cannot go.

This discriminating line is so manifest that the world can see it, and discern the people of God from the world, and know that they are not of them nor of their order; that they have *put off the old man with his deeds,* and have forsaken the world for Christ's sake. No matter if the world call them devils, or impostors and deceivers, as they did their master, they know them, and can discover that they have gone away from them. They cannot always discover, in every case, who will follow Christ to the end; but they can observe the course which people must take, to come out of the world and follow Christ, or be his chosen. The world can see the Church of Christ distinctly enough to know that they are not of them, and to hate them for that only reason; because they are not of the world. Thus they hate his people as they hated him—*without a cause.* "If the world hate you, ye know that it hated me before it hated you. If ye were of the world, the world would love his own; but because ye are not of the world, but I have chosen you out of the world, therefore the world hateth you." (Jno. xv. 18, 19.)

. . .

But on what principle are the Church of Christ not of the world,

161

as really so as he is not of the world? In the first place; because they have rejected the first Adam, the father of the world, with all his works, and have put on Christ, being all baptized by one Spirit into one body, of which Christ is the head. "Seeing that ye have put off the old man with his deeds, and have put on the new man, who is renewed in knowledge after the image of him that created him." "For as many of you as have been baptized into Christ, have put on Christ. There is neither Jew nor Greek, there is neither bond nor free, there is neither male nor female; for ye are all one in Christ." (Col. iii. 9, 10; Gal. iii. 27, 28.) In the next place: They who are baptized into Christ, or by the one Spirit into the one body, of which he is the head and they the members, are baptized into his death, and thus die, or become dead with him, even as he is dead or hath died. "Know ye not, that so many of us as were baptized into Jesus Christ were baptized into his death? Therefore we are buried with him by baptism into death." (Rom. vi. 3, 4.)

Moreover, the Church of Christ are raised to life in him and live with him, even as he liveth. "For ye are dead, (or ἀπεθάνετε, ye have died,) and your life is hid with Christ in God." "Therefore we are buried with him by baptism into death; that, like as Christ was raised up from the dead by the glory of the Father, even so we also should walk in newness of life. For if we have been planted together in the likeness of his death, we shall be also in the likeness of his resurrection; (having the same death and resurrection with him;) knowing this, that our old man is crucified with him, that the body of sin might be destroyed, that henceforth we should not serve sin. For he that is dead, (dieth), is freed (is justified, δεδικαίωται from sin."

Thus the Church of Christ are dead with him, and alive with him, so as to be quite separated from the world; and the world see and feel that it is even so, and think it strange that they run not with them into the same excess of riot, or same pursuits, speaking evil of them and hating them, because they are not of the world, even as Christ Jesus is not of the world.

The sum of this discourse is, that the world, or the children of this world, marry and are given in marriage, but the children of God do not. For *the children of this world* are set in contrast with another class or character of people, who neither marry nor are given in marriage; and when their character is fully developed, they are found finally to be *the children of God*, being the children of the resurrection; which resurrection is set forth as the medium or principle by which they become children of God, and this can be none else than coming into Christ. For to as many as receive him, to them he giveth power to become the sons of God—He is the resurrection and the life. As Christ Jesus therefore did not marry, as the children of this world do, nor take any participation in their peculiar works, so neither do his Church. And this is the central and radical point in which both he and they are not of this world. This is the groundwork of the separating line between Christ, including his Church, and the world; in this centres that cross of Christ which the world hate, and without which no man can be saved from sin.

(John Dunlavy, *The Manifesto*, pp. 305–308) [1818/1847]

2

12. In conversation with some of the Believers at Watervliet, in the first opening of the gospel, Mother Ann said, "Those who choose to live after the flesh, can do so; but I know, by the revelation of God, that those who live in the gratification of their lusts will suffer in proportion as they have violated the law of God in nature." She also said to Daniel Mosely and others, "Do not go away and report that we forbid to marry; for, unless you are able to take up a full cross, and part with every gratification of the flesh for the kingdom of God, I would counsel you, and all such, to take wives in a lawful manner, and cleave to them only, and raise up a lawful posterity, and be perpetual servants to your families; for, of all lustful gratifications, that is the least sin."

Daniel Mosely.

(Giles Avery, ed., *Precepts*, p. 233) [1816/1888]

3

10. Again Mother Ann spoke to a number of married people as follows, "You must forsake the marriage of the flesh, and travel out of it, in order to be married to the Lamb; which is, to be married to Christ, or, joined to the Lord in one spirit."

Mother Lucy Wright.

(Giles Avery, ed., *Precepts*, p. 240) [1816/1888]

4

19. She then related some of her own experience, as follows: "Some time after I set out to live up to the light of God manifested to me, through James and Jane Wardley, I fell under heavy trials and tribulations on account of lodging with my husband; and as I looked to them for help and counsel, I opened my trials to Jane." She said, "James and I lodge together; but we do not touch each other any more than two babes. You may return home and do likewise."

(Giles Avery, ed., *Precepts*, p. 38) [1816/1888]

5

14. At Hancock, he [Father James] said, "Blessed are the sons of Zion who can look upon the daughters of men, and not lust after them; and blessed are the daughters of Zion who can look upon the sons of men, and not lust after them. We have an altar whereof no one shall partake, but those who rejoice in Christ Jesus, and have no confidence in the flesh; for our altar is God's altar, and the wicked shall not eat thereon or therefrom." And again he said, "The drunkard shall not eat on our altar."

Hannah Goodrich, Senr.
(Giles Avery, ed., *Precepts*, p. 280) [1816/1888]

6

I did not set out to obey the Gospel because I felt pressed with conviction for sin, not because I was afraid of going to hell, but because the requirements of the Gospel appeared to me as reasonable. I obeyed it from choice, to do that which was evidently right. I was drawn into it and kept in it by my love for that which was right and good.

(*Elder Henry Clough*)
(White and Taylor, *Shakerism*, p. 102) [1905]

THE SHAKERS

7

... everyone that had the true love of God in possession, felt an impartial and universal love, which was not contracted to an individual, ...

(Joseph Dyer, *A Compendious Narrative*, p. 19) [1819]

8

Mary Whitcher. *H. C. Blinn.*
. . .
Through a religious conviction of duty to God, they [Benjamin and Mary Whitcher] changed the order of their relation from that of the narrow and selfish interest of husband and wife, to the more universal and Christ-like order of brother and sister; and from this day watched over their children as parents in the Lord.
. . .

(*The Shaker Manifesto* XIII, 1, p. 9) [1883]

*   *   *

9

... If they have been married, how then can they be virgins, or are such to be excluded? ... suppose they have been "in the flesh"; this no more prevents them from becoming virgins in the spirit than it does the wicked from becoming righteous.... Therefore I say, as they come into Christ, and are one with him, so they are virgins, according to his nature. It matters not what they have been; for old things are done away, and all things become new in that element. ... when souls are gathered into Christ, they partake of his nature.

(Calvin Green, *Atheism, Deism*, &c., n.p.) [1830]

THE SHAKERS

10

Soul Travel. *G. B. Avery*

. . .

Next enters Christ, the evolution of soul to a recognition of God, not as an unknown Monster, to be *feared* only, but a Heavenly Father, with whom the Son might walk and talk familiarly and lovingly, and take lessons of *soul life*—spiritual wisdom. . . . But the march of the soul stops not here. Still on she climbs the ladder of destiny, and next perceives a revelation of God, not only as a *Heavenly Father*, but a *Heavenly Mother* also. Now man begins to learn his true selfhood, to recognize woman his counterpart, his finishing half, not his mere vassal, but his loving comforter, and spiritual compeer! In this revelation *love* is no longer *lust*, but is the fruit of purity and peace; this relation of the sexes, though born from the heavens upon the earth, is not of earthly destiny, it is to inaugurate a Kingdom of Heaven for man's residence, not only in the life to come, but while he is a sojourner on the shores of time.

(*The Shaker Manifesto* XI, 6, pp. 122–125) [1881]

11

[Letter of Giles B. Avery, Jan. 6, 1880]

. . .

In following Jesus, the Shakers do not object to marriage, *as a worldly institution*, but think it, when used in a normal manner, the most fitting social relation for a worldly kingdom, but only when freed from the abuses of the sexual relations which embrute man and degrade woman, and which now extensively, if not almost universally, envelop the marriage relations. . . .

. . .

But let it everlastingly be kept before the eyes of the people, and burned into their very soul's escutcheon, that marriage and its legitimate fruit, generation, *belongs entirely and exclusively to the worldly order, and has no part nor lot in the kingdom of Christ!*

(*The Shaker Manifesto* XI, 8, pp. 178–179) [1881]

THE SHAKERS

12

Marriage. *Daniel Frazer*

Marriage is not a Christian Institution. Why? Those who marry, fulfill the desires of the flesh and of the mind. . . . Because Community of goods cannot be maintained therein. . . . Those who for Christ's sake—for the higher life's sake, forsake the marriage order, with its private relationships and property, shall have in my kingdom of communal life an hundred fold.

. . . the Law of the marriage order is "Me and Mine". Touch me and mine and I will fight. The law of Communal life is,

> "Each shall care for others:
> And each to each shall bend;
> And all shall fare alike,
> Hence wars shall have an end."

[Marriage's] . . . function is to multiply and replenish the earth. The order of Christ's kingdom is to harvest the earth. . . .

From the foregoing, we find, that virgin purity is the order of Christ's kingdom. The order of Marriage is not purity, therefore, it is not a Christian Institution. Even should that order become perfected, it still would be of the earth, earthy. It will ever remain under the Law of carnal or animal commandment. "Multiply and replenish etc." Should the perfected man and woman come up to the standard of purity manifested by the animal creation, they will do well; but let them not presume to enter the Holy of Holies. Animal life—emotions, have no place therein. Angelic purity, communal life, and divine emotions, can alone enter and abide in the Holy of Holies.

The law of the order of Christ's kingdom is "The love of others, at the expense of self"; and its temporal procedure corresponds thereto. "Unto this last, even as unto thee, will I give a penny." All shall fare alike, as in the virgin order of the Shaker church. The Law of the marriage order, as generally manifested, is, "The love of self, at the expense of the neighbor." Therefore it is not a Christian Institution. Its temporal procedure, is to monopolize the productive forces of creation for selfish ends. And thus prevents the possibility, of all, to fare alike.

167

. . .

Private property is inseparably connected with the marriage order. . . .

(*The Manifesto* XIV, 1, pp. 1–2) [1884]

13

My Brother, My Sister and Mother. *Anon.*

. . . "Whosoever doeth the will of my Father which is in heaven the same is my brother and sister and mother."—*Matt.* xii–50.

. . . Some one had informed him that his mother and his brethren were anxiously waiting to speak to him. Perhaps they had not realized, as yet, that he was divinely commissioned to establish a new and spiritual relation where the fatherhood and motherhood was to be centered in God. . . .

. . . being fully baptized into the spirit of the resurrection order, he gave an impressive lesson, which was not misunderstood by the multitude, nor by his own natural relation. "Where is my mother" said he, "and where are my brethren?"

Risen as he had into the spirit of eternal life, all this relationship of the flesh, the inheritance of the old Adamic order, had been left to perish where it legitimately belonged. Stretching forth his hand towards his disciples, he said, "Behold my mother and my brethren are those who do the will of my Father in heaven."

Nothing could have been more clearly expressed or brought more directly to the point, in demonstrating the relations of the earthly order and that of the Kingdom of God. . . .

The universal love of God through the life of Jesus Christ must be lived to be known. There can be no compromise. One order belongs to the world and has its relations in the flesh, while the other belongs to Christ and has its relations in the spirit.

(*The Shaker Manifesto* XII, 2, pp. 37–38) [1882]

*   *   *

THE SHAKERS

14

[Editorial, re: "the bodily"]

. . .

It seems unfortunate that such excellent, God given regulations [i.e., "the Mosaic code, notwithstanding the mistakes of the author" *supra*] should not have been more abiding but on the introduction of asceticism among the early christians they very singularly held that the body was the great obstacle in the way of spiritual progress. It must be starved into subjection, flagellated as a mortification for its sins, and then subjected to all the uncleanness of their surroundings.

This slight estimation of the body still clings more or less tenaceously, in its varied degrees, to the christian as well as unchristian races.

. . .

(*The Shaker Manifesto* XII, 8, p. 184) [1882]

15

Life in God. *Wm. Redmon*

. . .

To the young man or woman in nature, whose life is to begin as the future father or mother, these inquiries should arise: Do I start with integrity in every purpose and design in this highest, earthly prerogative, to do the will of my heavenly parents, in perpetuating my likeness and representative in time? . . .

In the matrimonial union you have pledged yourselves to verity and integrity without reserve; and in keeping this solemn declaration in accordance with the laws of nature, depends your future fruitfulness and blessing. . . .

(*The Shaker* I, 12, p. 91) [1871]

16

Physical Improvement. *Wm. H. Wetherbee*

. . . physical culture and improvement should go hand in hand with spiritual progression.

169

THE SHAKERS

... Those living in the order of nature, in the marriage state, should so live as to produce healthy offspring; such as will make good Shakers. The world stands in need of more Shakers, to act as a balancing power; to keep in check the increasing tide of human depravity. It is for the world's interest to have more good Shakers on the earth.

(*The Shaker* I, 10, p. 77) [1871]

17

The Second Eve. *Ruth Webster*

According to the allegorical account, men and women were created having equal rights; but in consequence of the woman taking the lead in the transgressing [of] the law given them, she was told that her "desire should be to her husband and he should rule over her," thus making her condition little superior to that of a slave, ... the Messiah was promised, ...

. . .

In process of time Jesus came, and it was said of Him, that he should "save his people from their sins." He was called the "second Adam." Now, if there was a second Adam, should there not be a second Eve? Jesus was called the "son of man;"—after the spirit descended upon him he was called "Christ," the "son of God." He was said to be "God manifest in the flesh." As he said; "The words that I speak unto you, they are spirit and they are life; the flesh profiteth nothing."

God is also known by his works, "even his eternal power and Godhead." All things that are made are male and female, hence, the same principle exists in Deity. If the second Adam was the representative of the Eternal Father, there should be a second Eve to represent the Eternal Mother.

. . .

In Christ's first appearing there were some indulgences permitted, short of bearing a full cross; but it was said that his second coming should be "without sin unto salvation." Purity of life, purity of heart and an entire consecration to God is the aim of every true christian believer. Indeed, "holiness to the Lord" is our motto, and all that will not bear this inscription should be rejected.

THE SHAKERS

. . .

There are many earnest men and women who are zealously engaged in the different reforms, and as God works by human agency, as well as spirit influences, much good will be the result. When the cry is heard, —"Babylon is fallen;" and the call is heeded, "Come out of her my people that ye be not partakers of her plagues," many will gather to the spiritual order to live the Christ principle of regeneration. Those who are not ready to be harvested from the earth will observe times and seasons and beget their offspring according to law. These will constitute the natural order or new earth. When their children shall be called into the spiritual order, they will not be like those who are begotten in drunkenness and lust, so that it will take ages to redeem them. . . .

(The Shaker Manifesto XII, 4, pp. 82–83) [1882]

18

The Church of Christ—To-day and in the future [Editorial]

We have strongly advocated an Ecclesiastical Council, to determine what really is The Church of Christ; not as augured by the various theological academies, but one fashioned after the primitive arrangement of affairs, that tended to make brethren in deed and in truth of "all who believed." Certainly this would be a Paradise—a heaven on earth—if all would live as Jesus lived ... Yet there stands the grand examplar Christ—a CELIBATE. THE COMMUNITY SPIRIT is acknowledged as right by the various churches, but the practice is limited to accommodate individual selfishness to an extent that leaves the churches with their *rich and poor....* If heaven to come—if it comes upon earth—means PEACE, what shall the churches do with the elements of war, strife, contentions? . . .

Are the churches of to-day ready for the advent of the Christ? Are they ready to welcome the Jesus of old, renewed in all the glory and power of the heavens, to introduce anew his humble testimony, of CELIBACY for the kingdom's sake on earth? Are they ready to equalize all their members, after the pattern, when "all who believe are together, and none possess aught he or she calls her or his own? When none are MARRIED? When no one says this or that is *mine?* When peace and quietness reign?"

171

THE SHAKERS

Such is the Church of Christ, and such is to be the grand church of the future, in vaster numbers than ever were counted! And what will bring about this grand evolution? Simply, the overwhelming conviction that in the absence of the Christ, the self-denials of the same Christ have been wanting. Simply, that until those same denials are inaugurated, the Church of Christ cannot be again established.

The Church of God, of Christ, in the future, and in the present, will present some of these noble, unselfish, primitive Christian Church features. Are the churches ready for the change?

(*The Shaker Manifesto* XI, 1, pp. 17–18) [1881]

*   *   *

19

Correlations. *Antoinette Doolittle*

. . .

Let everything be called by its appropriate name, and applied to its proper uses in the sphere to which it belongs. There is a natural and a spiritual love; the natural is first, has its place on the generative plane, and was God–given to subserve useful purposes in that order. The love existing between parent and child was given for a noble purpose; it is a bond that holds them to the performance of duties while necessity lasts, and although that bond is oftentimes severed in an untimely season, yet it is good in its place. But when the spirit calls souls to a higher life—into the resurrection order in the Christ sphere—the natural which was designed to pass away, after having performed its uses, gives place to the higher spiritual love, which infills and permeates the whole being, and is the beginning of eternal life in human souls.

(*The Shaker Manifesto* XI, 9, pp. 193–195) [1881]

THE SHAKERS

20

Communism. *Watson Andrews*

. . .

Nature, first of all, must needs provide for the reproduction, care and culture of the race ... by endowing man and woman with the parental instincts; an unlimited partiality for their own offspring. Without this, the race could not have survived a day; and with it, there was necessitated private families, private property, and private residences. Hence all attempts to maintain community of interest and of residence, while retaining the family relation must ever fail. ...

The human race depends for its existence upon the family relation; and the family relation, as we have seen, depends upon isolation of interests and of resistance for its existence. Likewise, the human race depends for its completeness and permanent existence upon identity of interests and residence, and both phases of human life are alike called for by the nature of things.

The family relation, therefore, is a great primal necessity; perverted though it is, yet it is a fundamental necessity nevertheless; the seedfield of the human race. It antedates the birth of the race; it produced, and it sustains the race; and the last echoes of its knell will be heard only by the last of the race.

The communistic relation also is a great necessity; a kindred necessity, of even more importance. And although not primal, it is final, and completes what the other begins; being the harvest-field of the human race.

The necessary self-love of the one, with its consequent antagonisms, and the equally necessary social-love of the other, with its consequent harmony, are alike but parts of The Divine economy in the affairs of men, for growing and harvesting a crop of human souls divine. And "the husbandman that sowed the seed is the Son of man, the field is the world, *and the reapers are the angels.*" In the first, self-preservation is the standard of excellence; in the last, self-abnegation. In the first, except a man provide for his own household, he is said to be worse than an infidel; and in the last, if he do not "forsake and hate" his own household, *he is an infidel.* Beside these, there is no true way for men and women to live upon this planet; all others are but these in incipiency or decay, presaging or recalling normal, human society.

The family relation requires that a man be governed by the selfish sentiments; an almost exclusive care for himself and family. Directly or

173

indirectly, whatever he plans or executes, has for its object the support and comfort of his own household. He contributes, it may be, to the support of the state; to liberal institutions and various public enterprises; but it all means only this: that his nature prompts him (and very properly) to provide for his own in preference to another's. He gives in charity where he can, without depriving his own, not otherwise; self must have the preference, or the race would speedily become extinct. And this is by no means the result of calculation mainly; but it has its source in man's original nature—in the necessities of the case.

The true communistic relation, on the contrary, requires that a man be governed by the liberal sentiments—an almost exclusive care for his fellow man. Whatever he engages in has for its object the well-being and happiness of his fellows; for he has learned that the way to be happy is to make others happy. And the only way to do this permanently, is to make a full sacrifice of all selfish considerations; all natural, partial, private relations and possessions—"father, mother, brother, sister, wife, children, houses and lands; yea and his own (peculiarities of) life also."

No matter what the society ... there must needs be a common bond of union; a universally pervading element, in which all interests centre, and toward which all aspirations point. . . .

In natural, generative society, this harmonial bond is the reproductive instincts (erroneously called love), culminating in the family relation, with its "trouble in the flesh"—its care, its anxieties, its fears, and its sorrows. Antagonistic in its nature, and limited in duration, its pleasures are necessarily limited, and speedily pass away.

In spiritual, regenerative society, this harmonial bond is love—love to God supreme, and neighbor as self; culminating in the communistic relation, with its freedom from "trouble in the flesh"—the cares, the anxieties, the fears, and the sorrows of the family relation. Harmonial in its nature, and continuous in duration, its pleasures are necessarily unlimited and never pass away. For, having reference mainly to the spiritual of man's life, which is eternal in its nature, the true religious communistic relation is equally eternal; —a life—habits of thought and social intercourse which time cannot affect, and which death does but sever from whatever of annoyance things of time occasioned. Instead of stripping the soul of its treasures, death does but place it in the full enjoyment of all that constituted its happiness while on the earth. And this is eternal life, the voluntary relinquishment of all that death can take from the soul; and the formation of tastes and habits, while in time, which will eternally endure, and in the exercise of which souls are forever increasing in wisdom, in purity and in happiness.

And as fast as men progress to the condition of understanding these great truths—of comprehending the grand system of nature—of God, with regard to man; that it necessarily embraces a *harvest* as well as a *seed-time*, a *regenerative* as well as a *generative* dispensation; that these two states are necessarily of an exactly opposite character, inasmuch as the one is a purely *natural* state, indispensable in the development of *natural* beings, and the other a purely *spiritual* state, equally indispensable in the development of spiritual beings; that the ripening of the spiritual depends upon the decay of the natural, as really as the ripening of the grain depends upon the decay of the stalk; and therefore that what is pleasurable in the one is painful in the other; what is life to the one is death to the other, and *vice versa;*—so fast will they comprehend that all pertaining to the natural, generative order, either in this mode of existence or any other, must be stripped off from the immortal mind of man, as the chaff from the grain, before he can become capable of those complete soul-blendings with the Divine Source and his fellow man, which alone produce the harmony, and ensure the happiness of heaven.

(*The Shaker* II, 10, pp. 75–76) [1872]

2 I

Covenant by Sacrifice. *Antoinette Doolittle*

. . .

The true Christ-spirit always seeks to gather into one. False christs and prophets are seductive, and seek to divide and scatter. . . . We are not able to see how *one* principle upon which the primitive pentecostal church was founded could with safety have been omitted. . . .

Shakers, or believers in Christ's second coming, by a baptism of the same spirit, have been led and directed to found an institution upon the same principles that the first Christian church rested upon; that is, virgin life, nonresistance, community of property, with the addition of dual government, where the rights of woman are recognized, and the "counsel of peace" is between the male and female; and this institution seeks to gather all that is good and true to its embraces; but it requires a sacrifice of *all*. . . .

THE SHAKERS

If the Shakers ever lay down their testimony in regard to the principle of a celibate life, so soon will they leaven back into the spirit and element of the world, and disintegration will follow as a sequence! The system of ideas and principles that have held believers together for a century, if faithfully maintained, will bear them on and prosper them spiritually and temporally through the centuries yet to come. There is room within Zion's boundary lines for all the progress that increasing light may call for, upon the basis of more cross, and denial to the pleadings of carnal mind; but we need to be very careful not to heed every call for *change*, and name it *progress*, when in reality it is a spirit of innovation seeking to weaken instead of strengthening Zion's bulwarks. It is always safe to try the spirits who come to minister to us.

(*The Shaker Manifesto* XI, 8, pp. 173–175) [1881]

22

Woman's Rights. *Anon.*
. . .
. . . since the duties of maternity must necessarily restrict the action of the female, and those of paternity as necessarily leave the male unrestricted; it follows, that whatever should subject the female, in any department of the animal kingdom, to male rule, must be productive of disorder. . . . shall we admit this, and thus easily account for the disorders of society; thus easily solve the "mystery of iniquity"–?
. . . And since the principal difference in their [i.e., mankind's] habits relates to the procreative right, we can but conclude, that herein is seen the principal cause of the physical degeneracy and moral depravity of the human race today. . . . we easily see the necessity for the second appearance of Christ, or rather, the manifestation of the Second Christ, "the Comforter," in her own order, to restore to woman, not only her long-lost rule (of herself), but a power in addition, enabling her to preserve and employ her charms in a far more noble cause than that of generation (noble as that is when conducted in an orderly manner), to wit, in that of regeneration. And here she has no cause to complain of the usurpation of her rights by the man; for the life of purity which, following Christ in the regeneration necessitates, places them precisely in the relation of brother and sister, where they are alike mutually dependent and mutually independent. . . .

(*The Shaker* II, 7, pp. 53–54) [1872]

23

[Correspondence—D. Madden/F. W. Evans]

... The religious forms to my mind are not in keeping with the age of progress in which we now live, as religion is progressive as well as the moral and intellectual states are progressive; and any system of worship, adopted one hundred years ago, would necessarily be tainted more or less with the prejudices and teachings of that day. ... Now as you can only receive accessions from those without, and as the world of matter and all things are progressing, you will necessarily have to take in those of advanced thought or confine your additions to the illiterate or ignorant. ...

—D. Madden (Pawling, Pa., Oct. 30, 1880)

. . .

We shall feel much interest in the progress of any attempt you and your friends may make to establish a better system than this we are living under. I think there may be a successful cooperation movement among men, on the basis of marriage—of great benefit to all concerned.

But a successful community must be built upon the foundation of Christian celibacy.

—F. W. Evans (Mt. Lebanon, N.Y., Oct. 31, 1880)
(*The Shaker Manifesto* X, 12, pp. 272–274) [1880]

24

Letter: *F. W. Evans*

. . .

... If men and women are immortal in their existence, what will be the mode and functions of that existence, is a matter of some interest to rational thinking people. ... "That which is natural first, afterwards, that which is spiritual." Do these terms represent ideas? To me, they do ... The Resurrection means a Spiritual Order, with a Spiritual relation of the Sexes. New Heavens and New Earth. I was under the impression, after about 50 years experience, that I had found a relation of a pure, heavenly quality, not to *one* woman only, but to an hundred fold, as compared with what the World's order affords. . . . "Eye hath not seen, nor ear heard" the things God has prepared for his people, in this Resurrection relation in the union of the Sexes, "in the Lord."

Even in the Natural Order, there are those who live intellectual Celibates, Platonists, like Andrew Jackson and Mary, who claim to have lived, for many years, in Platonic Love, as brother and sister but that does not constitute them Shakers. They are intermediate between the two Orders, Generative and Resurrection. From that class, Male and Female, when we have a true Republic, I look to have all the Government Offices filled, leaving the married people at home to care for each other. . . .

(*The Manifesto* XII, 3, p. 66) [1882]

25

[Untitled item—from the *New Campaign*]

Shakerism is a desperate remedy for a desperate disease [i.e., celibacy, for materialism]. . . . it is manifest that there can scarcely be even a decent degree of saintliness till men and women are *able* to have a celibate life, so long as duty, inspiration or reason shall dictate. If there be a possibility of living out a partial affiliation of fraternal love and sexual passion, without the cast iron rules imposed by monogamous marriage and the Shaker brotherhood, the road to it lies *through* Shaker grounds, at least.

(*The Shaker* I, 11, p. 87) [1871]

*　　*　　*

26

But there will be a way open whereby you may find some relation to the work of God.

(Calvin Green, *Biography of Father Joseph*, p. 47) [1827]

THE SHAKERS

27

The Two Orders. *J. S. Prescott*

. . .

We would not object to an intermediate link being thrown between the rudimental and spiritual orders, to bridge over the chasm. . . . This may be necessary.* . . .

*[FOOTNOTE] Very many have proposed an "intermediate link;" but this link invariably contained the elements of the lusts of the flesh—not in their plain and proper dress, but in the disguise of improvements to the present system. Admitting that there is an advance called for, to be made by us, we yet want no suggestions or links, that intend the least amalgamation of flesh with the Spirit. The chasm between these is not sufficiently wide, and should be wider, and more distinctly and practically understood. We thus remark, to prevent any misconception of the above. —ED. [G. A. Lomas]

(*The Shaker* II, 11, p. 83) [1872]

28

Truth, Faith, and Reason—No. 2. *R. W. Pelham*

. . .

As the generative order necessarily requires a separate interest and the possession of personal property, it is forever repugnant to the Christ order which requires a relinquishment of personal wealth.

(*The Shaker* II, 4, p. 32) [1872]

29

[Re: celibacy & marriage]

. . . This idea [i.e., celibacy alone as man's proper calling] was held by Shakers themselves, until I came forward as a theologian. I soon saw that there were to be *two orders*—the natural and the spiritual; . . . Ann Lee *began* the process of unravelling "the mystery of godliness and of iniquity;" but she saw only in the light of one cycle. Now we see—begin to see in the light of the second cycle, and two orders are recognized, where, heretofore, only one was admissible, . . .

(F. W. Evans, *Elder Frederick W. Evans*, p. 122) [1893]

30

... Man's present body of flesh is not such an accident; for it is the inevitable product of great steady progressions under law, fixed, determined to the one end. And so it is with the Ideal now unfolding within man; what it will be, it must be; our business is to forecast the inevitable, and conform to it.

... And within it, part of the whole, is contained an Ideal as to Marriage.... This Ideal upon Marriage is traceable in its unfoldment....

... In a word, that Ideal is Love. It is the perfect harmony of good will, a spirit of passionate concern for and joy in each other's being; which shall rule in every member of the society of ideal beings. It is love ... fully present ... equal-shining along every line of the space it inhabits....

... the light of this love is always there for those who will receive it.

[Self-centeredness] is the root of evil. A root with two stems. One stem is selfishness in property, the other is selfishness in persons.

... sex–love is not wide, for all; not universal, but precisely narrow, forgetting all in one.

(Alonzo Hollister, Mission of Alethian Believers, pp. 17–20) [1899]

Part Two: Community

Introduction

The call to live the Christlife is a call to the experience of community. This is an ancient Christian realization: those called to believe are called into Christ—in the powerful image of Paul, becoming member–for–member the living Body of Christ. Somehow, mysteriously, the human community and the whole reality of Christ are one. The Church—the gathered community, *ekklesia*—is *the fullness of him who fills all with All* (Eph. 1:22).

As we have seen in previous sections, the Shaker vision is centered on a vivid recognition of the identification of the community of Believers with the total Christ, now come again in the clouds of witnesses. The tangible living of the Christlife must always clearly emphasize the experience of community, both as the inner spirit and its outer mani-

THE SHAKERS

festation. Historically Shakers have developed different concrete conceptualizations of this call to community. The first Believers, from 1747 through to 1786–1787, did not live in communal groups and apparently did not even envision such a form of life. Although some would look back to Mother Ann's ministry and see implied expectations for a future communalism, there is evidence which conflicts with this hindsight. For during her ministry several meeting houses were built (such as the one at Ashfield, Massachusetts), located so as to serve a relatively large area along established travel routes. These meeting houses included small second floor rooms for traveling ministry, an indication that they expected Shakers would continue to live scattered throughout the countryside and towns. At Harvard, Massachusetts, Mother Ann bought the "Square House" and used it as a center for the eastern Shakers, and it served her as a base from which to make numerous short trips throughout the area. There are matter-of-fact references to people being called to the "traveling ministry" as, later, there are references to the passing of that ministry. The most impressive evidence is the brief but strong resistance to Father James' decision to gather Believers into a communal Society at Mt. Lebanon in 1786–1787, building a new kind of meeting house there with apartments for the permanent residence of ministry.

Even after the final communal organization was completed under Father Joseph, becoming a covenanted member of a commune was never a requirement. Believers who lived privately (and there have always been many) were recognized as enjoying "full Gospel relation" in the Church. Living privately did not mean living without the sense of community. Not only did each individual Believer enjoy open relation with all others and with the gathered Societies, but, more important, each *believed* precisely because of the experience of the integral Union in Christ and each realized that such inner experience was to be made tangible in a practical reaching out to others. However unstructured and informal it might be, a real sense of Christ-community is of the very essence of Shakerism—and hence Mother Ann's practical admonition, "gather something to do good with" (1).

The first selections (1–4) reflect the roots of the experience which develops into the communitarian Societies, while the selections from McNemar (5), Dunlavy (6), and Youngs (7) present the initial formal reflections on the communal "Church Order" which arose through that experience. Dunlavy's presentation well illustrates the close interrelation among celibacy, community, peace, and equality.

THE SHAKERS

In Father Joseph's view the communal Church Order was a Faith–response, positively to the call to perfection and negatively to the need to separate from the world. Throughout the nineteenth century the issue of separation seems always at the forefront of any inquiry about progression; the openness of the expectations implicit in progression suggests regular reevaluation of the function of separation. Eldress Antoinette Doolittle (9) and Elder Daniel Frazer (10) represent relatively conservative positions on separation, which they see as positive. Because of the inner progression being achieved, separation highlights the new *freedom*, the freedom from enslavement to *things*, which allows personal and interpersonal growth into ultimate spiritual maturity. More conservative Shakers saw the separatist character of their communes as guaranteeing a positive environment for the flourishing of the Spirit; the line of separation, therefore, must be clearly drawn. But for Sister Aurelia Mace of Sabbathday Lake (11) the experience of separation leads to a new openness: because one has been kept free from enslavement to false worldly standards, a free progression into all the potential gifts coming through the arts and sciences is possible. The line of separation is thus not an absolute but a dynamic function allowing the assimilation of every good gift, wherever found. The communitarian experience, therefore, led to a paradoxical development: separation fostered an inner growth in freedom to seek a new progressive synthesis of gifts, some coming from within and others coming from outside. Believers were committed to an ultimate optimism for "the world" because of their sense of community: the community of Divine Union in Christ could not be confined to a separate few but inexorably extended to embrace all, one way or another, either now or in the unlimited unfoldment of Eternal Life.

Speaking of the original separational ideal of Father Joseph, Elder Calvin Green (12) notes the need, nonetheless, for a place of positive contact with the world, the "outer court" of the Temple. It was often those who were charged with the responsibilities of this outer court—the gathering Family in each Society in which inquirers were welcomed, and the trustee deacons and deaconesses who dealt regularly with the world's people and external affairs—who became the most noted progressives, such as Elder Frederick Evans of the North Family (gathering order) of Mt. Lebanon, or Deaconess Aurelia Mace of Sabbathday Lake. Sister Martha Anderson (13, 14), one of those at Mt. Lebanon most active in interaction with the progressive movements in the outside world, illustrates the growing awareness (often, as here, critical) of the larger contexts of community and its historical forms and character. This broadening of horizons throughout the later nineteenth century corresponds with the development of Shaker ecumenism and expectations of drastic social change. Commitment to community no longer means negative separation either from other Churches (previously thought of as anti-Christian) or from the larger secular society (previously thought of as dis-Believer). Early Christian traditions of monastic community, the Shaker experience, and the evolving world society can now be seen as in a continuum of progression.

This inevitably raises the open question of the future. Elder Watson Andrews (15), with the metaphor of the Church as a hospital for healing the sick and staffed by those who themselves had been sick but were now advanced in their recovery, brings the understanding of the perfection–seeking community into coordination with a world capable of movement toward perfection. Elder Oliver Hampton (16) relates the progressive expectations for community to the process of giving and receiving in community with others, to distinguish the organizational (however admirable) from the deeper value of the interpersonal, recognizing that any real progress into the further potential of the gift of community must come from the interrelating of the many gifted individual persons who together are community. The brief statement of Elder Andrew Barrett (17) illustrates the matured realization that the range of gifts proper to fulfilling life must be broadened. In Shaker terms, there must be the head–minded as well as the hand-minded who share their very different gifts (many early Believers had been very suspicious of the head–minded and tended toward a narrow view of what was *useful* for community). The anonymous excerpt (18) makes it clear that the communitarian form of the Societies was recognized as derived from more fundamental principles and not an ultimate value in itself, and hence was open to change and even eventual discontinuance. Community and commune were not necessarily synonymous.

Finally, the brief extract from Elder Calvin Green's *Biography of Father Joseph Meacham* (19) is crucial to understanding the Shaker freedom in foreseeing the eventual ending of the communitarian form of life. Just as the First Elders did not establish communitarian Societies, so Father Joseph, who gave the Church its predominantly communitarian Order, did not presume that this was or could be an absolute form. It was nothing more than a specific shape in a larger process.

THE SHAKERS

When it had served its purpose it would pass away so that a new form could arise. In speaking of this process of successive forms as "seven general & distinct travels" one should take the number "seven" in its Biblical sense of unlimited number. The reality that perdures is *community*, not one of its potentially countless shapes. It is community as an actual living of the Union Christ is: the Divine–human Union and the extended interpersonal participation in that Union.

I

10. Soon after the opening of the gospel at Enfield, N.H., some of the Believers in that place, having more zeal than wisdom and understanding, imbibed a notion that they were not to continue in this world but a few years, and concluded that they need not make any further provisions for a living, in consequence of which they made a very undue use of their property, by squandering it away in a profuse manner, which brought great trials upon some others of their Brethren, particularly upon Jacob Heath. Jacob, soon after, in company with Cornelius Goodale, went to see the Church, which was then at Ashfield, and opened his trials to some of the Elders respecting the matter. On Mother hearing of it, she called Jacob and Cornelius, and after instructing them concerning these things, she bade them go home and set out apple trees, and raise calves, and make provisions as though they were to live a thousand years, and gather something to do good with.

> *Jacob Heath.*
> (Giles Avery, ed., *Precepts*, p. 210) [1816/1888]

2

Benjamin Whitcher. *H. C. Blinn*

. . .

After accepting the testimony of renewed light [ca. 1782], and learning from Mother Ann and the Elders, the benefits of a spirit of universal interest for all, he from this time forward, opened his house to all who accepted the same form of faith, till he numbered, in his family, not less than forty-three persons. All sat at one common table, and were engaged in the business of the place, either in the house or on the farm.

. . .

The principles of a joint interest, however, were not fully taught till the gathering of the [Canterbury] Society in 1792.

. . .

(*The Shaker Manifesto* XII, 12, p. 268) [1882]

3

Job Bishop I. *Henry C. Blinn*
[From the Canterbury Records]

He was born in New Lebanon, N.Y., Sep. 29, 1760. His early years were spent with his parents, and so soon as his age permitted, he assisted his father in his work on the farm.

In 1779 he became quite interested in a religious revival of which he writes, ["] I entered fully into the spirit of the work, and received great light. I was often blessed with the presence of the spirit of God, and believed that the gospel of Christ required a daily cross against sin. Although zealous prayers and religious exercises often had the effect to produce spiritual sensations, yet they were not permanent and left me a subject of temptations.

I was encouraged by the revival to look forward with hope for a manifestation of the light of God, and fully believed that the second coming of Christ was near at hand. Elder Joseph Meacham who was one of the principle [*sic*] leaders in the revival warned us to take heed, that we might not oppose the work of God, as it was revealed to us. He believed that in this work, a virgin life would be required, but as he saw no way to protect the people in it, he thought it was not prudent to preach the doctrine.

The spirit of this revival continued through the summer, and then gradually declined, leaving its subjects in great tribulation. They had renounced the creeds and ceremonies of the churches, but their meetings though still continued had lost their power. The speakers recently so active now sat in silence with bowed heads. Those who rose to speak or to pray lost the power of utterance and were obliged to resume their seats in silence.

THE SHAKERS

We passed the winter exhorting each other to faithfulness, while we anxiously waited for the accomplishment of the prophetic spirit of the revival. The work came.

In the spring of 1780 we learned of a people near the city of Albany, N.Y. who were reported to have received a singular kind of religion, and that they possessed a large degree of divine light and spiritual power. Many went out to see them, and returned fully persuaded that they were the true witnesses of God. The interest increased and I felt a great desire to satisfy myself concerning these strangers and their religion.

Early in June, in company with several others, I made them a visit. We arrived on Saturday evening and remained till Monday. We found them all kind and social. Elder James Whittaker explained to me the doctrine which they taught; reasoned from the scriptures and manifested great knowledge of the spirit and light of the gospel of Christ. We attended their meetings. The singing was inspiring, the speaking powerful and heart searching. The wisdom of their instructions, the purity of their doctrine, and the Christ like simplicity of their deportment, all reminded me of the apostolic faith.

I returned home in a state of mind hardly to be described. A deep impression had been made upon my feelings, and a new scene had been opened to my view. I saw that the work was of God and my salvation depended upon it.

The cross that was before me was an evidence of the spirit of this testimony. . . .[2]

The three witnesses who came from England had all prophesied of a gathering of the Church into order.[3] A successor to Father James, however, had not been appointed at the time of his death, although Joseph Meacham had been named as an assistant in this great work. The prophecy concerning him had a corresponding bearing upon several others among whom we find Elders Calvin Harlow and David Meacham.

As no preponderating excellence appeared where so much native

---

2. In the preceeding paragraphs Mother Ann is mentioned just incidentally and without any emphasis.

3. The idea of "prophecy" here is quite common in the earlier literature as a way of assimilating "new progression," seeing it implied in a previous stage of development but which could not unfold until its proper time; another instance of this is found above in the third paragraph reference to Joseph Meacham's expectations concerning the virgin life in the imminent *parousia.*

talent and intellectual power were the endowment of each, combined apparently with equal religious zeal and spiritual attainment, it seemed impossible for aught save Divine Wisdom to decide the election. No eye but that which is single to the glory of God might look in upon that praying band, who were seeking to learn whom God had chosen to lead his people to the promised inheritance where all should share alike the blessings of a bounteous Providence, so great was the power manifested in the heavenly influence, so eloquent its utterances, so encouraging its promises that a beholder might well say as each declared the message given, 'Surely the Lord hath chosen this' yet no such power was vouchsafed to the burdened spirit of the chosen one as he meekly listened to the divinely inspired eloquence of his fellow laborers. When all the candidates had ceased, still waiting for a decisive manifestation, the voice of a youth, Elder Job Bishop, was heard, calm and decided, declaring with a power which left not a shadow of a doubt on the mind of any present, that the silent listener, Joseph Meacham, was the anointed of God to lead his people."

Father Job always regarded this as a revelation from God. An out growth from their united prayer while in that sacred conference in the church at New Lebanon. Immediately after this prophetic announcement, Elder John Hocknell kneeled in prayer before the assembly, giving utterance to this expression only, "Blessed be God."

Overshadowed with the divine presence these reverent and prayerful children of God fell upon their knees and the floor was wet with their tears. . . .

(*The Shaker Manifesto* XII, 3, pp. 53–55) [1882]

4

. . . First that which is natural and afterward that which is spiritual, was a remarkably true saying of the Apostle. Those who were gathered from the selfish, worldly order to that of universal inheritance, learned by experience the truth of what the Apostle had spoken. That it was a gradual growth into the life of Christ, and every step measured, we may readily admit from the progress that was made by the pioneers of the work. . . .

To sacrifice all this [i.e., possessions and self-direction of private interests] to the Lord and for the good of humanity, all they possessed, time, property, yea and their own lives also, that they might become disciples of Christ, and Brethren and Sisters of the household of faith, was such a work as had never before been known....

(Henry Blinn, *Church Record*, vol. ii, p. 32) [1879]

5

... The first point of faith in relation to the testimony, is to believe that he who bears it is a *true messenger* and *witness* of Christ, in whom the spirit of truth continually abides; and that whatever instruction, reproof or counsel is ministered by such, it comes from Christ, who speaketh *in him*. Therefore all who are taught in this manner are strictly and properly *taught of God*, and in obeying what they are taught they yield obedience *to Christ*.

... It then remains to follow that spirit which goes contrary to sin, and manifests its purity by its fruit, according to the scriptures, and the inward test of conscience. This is the spirit of Christ, and it sets them immediately at work to do the righteous will of God. And first of all to confess before God what they have done contrary to his will and the light of their own conscience ... by following the spirit of truth, he ... discovers, that according to the scriptures, God never accepted a confession of sin, which was not either made to those whom he had set in order in the church, or at least with the face toward the temple which was typical of his last habitation, viz. man. But the greatest evidence the true Believer receives, of this being the order and institution of heaven, is the divine light which he receives in consequence....

With an inward sense of the power, protection and presence of God, the Believer travels out of the use of shadows and signs, ceremonies and forms of worship, to which he might have been strongly bigotted while in bondage under the law. There is no more occasion for calling upon God afar off, when he has taken possession of his body and lives and walks in him, nor of calling to his memory a departed Saviour, by signs and shadows of his dying love, when the only Saviour that ever redeemed a lost soul, is formed and living in him, and executing every branch of his office.... Bodily exercises, dreams, visions and ecstacies, which had had but a momentary effect on the blind and obdurate heart, and furnished at best, but a fleeting joy, gradually give place to the sun of righteousness, that shines continually the same, without cloud or eclipse. Hence in the progressive work of the testimony, a blessed reality, an enduring antetype is wrought in the

Believer, which fully answers to all that he could possibly have conceived of, while longing, praying and hoping for the kingdom to come. As Believers become more and more leavened into the nature of Christ, they discover with increasing accuracy, the latent corruptions of a fleshly nature, and the secret wilss of Satan in injecting his poison into the heart. And as they discover, so by the cross they overcome and gain an increasing victory over that which is death to the soul, by dying to it—the spirit of the testimony runs through all the Believer's deportment, in public, in private and in secret, so that in no circumstance is he released from the work of self-denial, . . . by crucifying the flesh, its affections and lusts wither of course, and they grow into peaceable, gentle, kind and loving spirit, in which they can live together from one year's end to another, without feeling a hard thought, much less expressing a hard word one against another. And in such a spirit and deportment as cements them together in one fellow feeling, and promotes the peace, purity and happiness of the whole, the progress of the testimony mainly consists.

Moreover all who receive the testimony in the spirit of it, are taught thereby to be diligent and faithful in things temporal as well as spiritual, and to serve God with body and substance, as well as with their spirits. Hence the testimony has a proportionate progress in the frugality and honest industry of Believers, whereby they lay up in store a good foundation, not for their own pleasure and aggrandizement, but for the honor of God, and the relief and succour of him that needeth.

(Richard McNemar, *Kentucky Revival,* pp. 82–85) [1807]

6

Now the immediate production of love, in the members of Christ's body, and that also by which the world are to know and believe them to be the people of his love, is union—such a union as the world know not. "That they all may be one; as thou, Father, art in me, and I in thee, that they also may be one in us: that the world may believe that thou hast sent me. And the glory which thou gavest me, I have given them; that they may be one, even as we are one. I in them, and thou in me, that they may be perfect in one; and that the world *may know* that thou hast sent me, and *hast loved them, as thou hast loved me.*" (Jno. xvii. 21–23.) This then is the state of the body of Christ here on earth, in sight of the world, that they might know and believe the work of God—perfect in one. This evidence, in the estimation of Jesus Christ, is sufficient to convince the world, who are the people of God's love—and who is he that will scruple the propriety of his judgment? But where such a union is not manifested, as evidences the present agency and indwelling of the Spirit of God, as being his holy habitation, the true evidence of Christianity is wanting.

This union is of a different nature, separate and distinct from all the union which can possibly subsist among the children of the flesh, professed Christians or others: "The unity of the Spirit in the bond of peace." (Eph. iv. 3.) Therefore it is that true believers are able to maintain and increase in that union which the world cannot touch; gathering together, more and more, as they increase in the work of God in Christ Jesus, as it was prophesied of them; "Therefore they shall come and sing in the height of Zion, and shall flow together to the goodness of the Lord, for wheat and for wine, and for oil, and for the young of the flock and of the herd; and their soul shall be as a watered garden; and they shall not sorrow any more at all. Then shall the virgin rejoice in the dance, both young men and old together: For I will turn their mourning into joy, and will comfort them, and make them rejoice from their sorrow. And I will satiate the soul of the priest with fatness, and my people shall be satisfied with my goodness, saith the Lord." (Jer. xxxi. 12–14.) "Now, therefore, ye are no more strangers and foreigners, but fellow-citizens with the saints, and of the household of God; and are built upon the foundation of the apostles and prophets, Jesus Christ himself being the chief corner-stone; in whom all the building, fitly framed together, groweth unto an holy temple in the Lord; in whom ye also are builded together for an habitation of God through the Spirit." (Eph. ii. 19–22.)

Numerous other passages might be quoted to prove that Christians are united by one Spirit into one body, as the habitation or temple of God. And as like causes produce like effects, the unity of Spirit within produces unity of operation without, for as is the fountain so are the streams. Therefore it is that believers are united in a manner and degree which the world cannot imitate, and the rule of Christ is proved true by experiment. . . .

. . .

Thus the Church and people of God are united in one body, and in one Spirit, and enjoy the mutual benefits of one consecrated and united interest and inheritance in all good things, whether temporal or spiritual. And all those who yield to the truth of God, impelled by the same Spirit, know nothing better to do with all they have and are, than to give all up to God, to be enjoyed by his people; for this is according to the genuine operation of the one Spirit of Christ, as it is written; "Inasmuch as ye have done it to one of the least of these my brethren, ye have done it to me." (Matt. xxv. 40.) This fulfills the word of the Lord, by the prophet, to his Church, in the day when her deliverance should come. "Arise and thresh, O daughter of Zion; for I will make thine horn iron, and I will make thy hoofs brass; and thou shall beat in pieces many people: and I will consecrate their gain unto the Lord, and their substance unto the Lord of the whole earth." (Mic. iv. 13.)

The world have no such union, neither can have, because they are governed by a different principle, incapable of producing it; not a principle of purity in the Spirit, but a fleshly principle of lust,[4] as it is written: "All that is in the world, the lust of the flesh, the lust of the eyes, and the pride of life, is not of the Father, but is of the world." (1 Jno. ii. 16.) God is Spirit; and when man fell from God, he fell from the Spirit into the flesh; hence the flesh is considered as being in opposition to the Spirit. God is love; and therefore when man fell from God, he fell out of love into lust. The love of God unites, but the lust of the flesh separates and divides. "From whence come wars and fightings among you? come they not hence, even of your lusts the war in your members?" (Jas. iv. 1.) The world therefore cannot live in Gospel union; jealousies and divisions arise too easily, because they are in the flesh, and walk as men, that is, in the fleshly fallen nature of man. "For whereas there is among you envying, and strife, and divisions, are ye not carnal and walk as men?" (1 Cor. iii. 3.)

. . .

It is a question with some whether the Spirit of Christ leads to so great a union as to possess a united interest in all things, as well outward as spiritual; or whether it is necessary to practise such a union to be Christians indeed? This question can exist in that heart only where selfishness prevails above every other principle; for out of the abundance of the heart the mouth speaketh; and where the Spirit of Christ prevails it says, Look not every one to his own things, but every one also to the things of another.

---

4. Note here the clearly extended meaning of *lust*, including all forms of possessive desire and grasping; the intended contrast in experience is clear: God loves–gives, fallen man lusts–grasps—God as *spirit*, fallen nature as *carnal*, in the King James Biblical vocabulary use.

But the very existence of such a union proves it to be of God, and in the Spirit of Christ. For fact proves principle; or, the existence of any effect proves the existence of the cause producing it. And the existence of any effect which cannot be produced by any cause save one, proves invariably the existence of that cause. But it is proved, in fact, that such a connection in a united interest cannot be supported by any cause separate and distinct from the Spirit of Christ dwelling and acting in the people who are thus united. Yet such a connection does exist in a united interest; it therefore proves the agency and indwelling of the Spirit of Christ, and that this union is according to the mind of Christ, and proceeds from him as his own work.

(John Dunlavy, *The Manifesto*, pp. 266–267; 268; 271) [1818/1847]

7

23. All the Believers, who came together in the full order and covenant of a Church relation, possessed all things jointly; neither said any of them that aught of the things which he possessed was his own; but every thing was possessed in a perfect law of justice and equity, by all the members.

24. However, there were some, who gathered together into large families, and stood in a family relation, whose circumstances did not immediately admit of a joint union and interest in all things; and who devoted their services, and the use and improvement only, of their temporal substance, for the joint support and up-building of each other; while their real and personal estates remained in substance, as they were at the time of their coming together.

25. Such were not considered as standing in perfect Gospel order, but held a certain relation to the Church according to the order in which they stood.[5] It may, therefore, be proper to make a few remarks on the nature of the Church Covenant, in which alone the perfect order and equality of the Gospel can be enjoyed.

26. *First.* As one of the most essential principles of the Church,

---

5. The distinction is between the Church Family and the Novitiate Family in each gathered Society, the latter not yet free to enter the final covenanting of all their possessions as a United Inheritance; the remaining Order, the Gathering Family, is not mentioned here since its participants would be only in the stage of exploring the possibility of entering the Novitiate Order.

was to maintain a perfect law of justice and equity, both in relation to themselves and others; therefore parents, who had estates, and children under age, could not bring their substance into the united interest of the Church, after it was established, unless the inheritance of heirship was secured to them until they became of age.

27. And provided the parents or children were gathered, with their substance, into any family, in the like capacity, the inheritance of the children was secured until they became of age. And it was an established principle in the Church, that children who were faithful and obedient to their parents until they became of age, were then entitled to their natural and just portion.

28. *Second.* As the Church was established upon the principles of Gospel liberty and freedom, and as no one could be bound contrary to their own faith and desire, having a perfect understanding of the nature of their undertaking; therefore, children in minority, could not be fully considered as members of the Church, until they became of mature age to judge and act for themselves.[6]

29. Nevertheless, children who had faith, and who were wrought upon by the Spirit of light from God, (of whom there were many that received faith with their parents,) enjoyed equal rights and privileges of all things in the Church, according to their needs, and the measure of their faith and understanding.

30. *Third.* As the gathering together of the Believers, into the order and liberty of the Gospel, immediately respected their separation from the perplexing cares and entanglements of the world; therefore such as were under obligations to creditors or heirs, were not considered in full membership in the Church, until they were perfectly free from all just demands of those who were without. Yet, all such as were diligent in paying their just debts, and faithful in all matters according to their light and understanding, were as really owned in their order, and accepted in their relation to the Church as any others.

---

6. Societies received orphaned or unwanted children on this basis; to secure the right of these children to remain (in an era in which children had no legal rights), the Societies received them under the legal form of apprentice indenture, which vested guardianship in the Trustees who then protected their moral right of freedom of choice, property, etc.; this arrangement, needed for the sake of the children, is often misrepresented or misunderstood as if Shakers were somehow "buying" children to make them into Shakers. We should recall that there were laws enacted to protect animals from abuse before such laws were extended to children!

31. *Fourth.* As the gathering of the Church, was not from any worldly motives, to lay up in store of this world's goods, but solely as a religious duty and privilege, for mutual benefit; therefore, all had an equal right as members, jointly, in the use of all the things in the Church, and according to their several needs, whether they brought in any temporal substance or not. And in those who brought in substance, more or less, was that Scripture fulfilled, *He that gathered much had nothing over, and he that gathered little had no lack* (Exo. xvi. 18; 2 Cor. viii. 15).

32. *Fifth.* As all the members of the Church are equally holden, according to their abilities, to maintain and support one united interest, in union and conformity to the order and government of the Church; therefore, all labor with their hands, to maintain the mutual comfort and benefit of one another by honest industry and acts of kindness—not by compulsion, but of choice, from a principle of faith, justice, and equity.

33. Ministers, Elders, and Deacons, all, without exception, labor with their hands; excepting at such times as are taken up by each in their particular gifts and callings, which all tend to the mutual increase and benefit of the whole. And no member or members are required by any law or custom in the Church, to go beyond their abilities, or to act contrary to their own faith. But all are equally holden by the unity of the Spirit and their covenant, to conform to the established principles and rules of the Church, or they cannot keep their union.

34. *Sixth.* As the Gospel is perfectly free, and the free exercise of conscience can in no wise be retarded; therefore, all who believe in the Gospel of Christ's present appearing, ever remain in perfect liberty, without any breach of order, to use and improve their own temporal interest as a separate possession, or to unite with others of the same faith, in one joint union; either of which must be according to their own faith and discretion, provided they maintain the true faith of the Gospel.

35. *Seventh.* The order and regulation of the Church, in all spiritual matters, is entrusted, by the unity in the gift of God, to the Ministry and Elders, or elder brethren and sisters, of each community and family. To them is also committed the charge of sending out ministers to preach the Gospel to the world of mankind.

36. None of the Ministry hold any title to lands or property, as individuals, more than any other members; nor have they any pensions

or salaries; but whatever they need for their support at home, or expenditure abroad, they receive at such times as they need it.

37. The concern and regulation of the temporal matters of the Church is entrusted to the Deacons, appointed to that office by the joint union of the body. To them, their assigns and successors in the Gospel, appointed to the like office, is entrusted the whole of the joint interest in the Church, to support and maintain the same in behalf of the Church, and their heirs in the Gospel forever.

38. And their office and care it is, to have the principal concern in dealing with those who are without; and to provide all things necessary for the comfortable support of the Church, jointly and equally, according to the number and need of each family in the Church.

39. Besides the first order of Deacons and Deaconesses,[7] there are also Deacons and Deaconesses in each family, whose care it is to see that every member in the family, from the eldest to the youngest, enjoy their just and equal rights, according to their several needs, of all temporal things possessed in the family.

40. In the order and government or regulation of the Church, no compulsion or violence is either used, approved, or found necessary. So that, according to our faith, in the full and perfect establishment of *Christ's government* among his people, no kind of corporal punishment is or can be exercised on any person, among those who stand in the first order of Gospel liberty.

41. Neither Ministers, Elders, nor Deacons, nor any others, either in spiritual or temporal trust in the Church, are appointed to their several callings by their own individual choice, nor by a majority of votes among the people; but by a spontaneous spirit of union, which flows through the body, by which every useful talent is brought into exercise for the time being, for the benefit of all considered.[8]

42. *Unto every member of the body is given a measure of the Spirit of Christ to profit withal* (1 Cor. xii. 7.), in which, by a faithful improvement of their created talents, every member becomes prepared, and thus grows up into a fitness to fill that place and order, in the spiritual house of God, for which they were created; and their real qualifica-

---

7. From their primary area of responsibility these are commonly referred to as Trustees or office deacons/deaconesses.

8. Since no community was allowed to exceed about one hundred members, each brother and sister was well known to all; when a vacancy in an office occurred, all would know who was most gifted to fill that responsibility.

tions appear and become mutually useful to the body, so that every improved talent and gift of God, given to individuals, thereby becomes a real gift of God to the whole.

43. As there can be no arbitrary appointment of members in the human body, to which the body of Christ is compared, and no one member can be appointed to fill the place or office of another, but each member fills its proper place and office, by a spontaneous influence and a mutual concurrence of every other member; so is the appointment of members in the Church of Christ.

44. But as the human body has a leading part, which is the head, by which all the other members of the body are directed, and as the head directs and governs by the general consent of the members, so it is with the Church or body of Christ.

45. The revelation and gift of God is given to the Ministry, as the head of the body, in relation to lots of office and trust, and other matters of importance; and through these, communicated to the other members. Yet nothing is considered as established in the Church until it receives the general consent and united approbation of the body; and thus, by the body, in union with the head, every thing important is established.

46. And each member of the body throughout, is also dependent on another. *The eye cannot say unto the hand, I have no need of thee; nor again, the head to the feet, I have no need of you. Nay, much more those members of the body, which seem to be more feeble, are necessary* (1 Cor. xii. 21, 22.).

47. Such as are entrusted with the greatest care, are the greatest servants; and such as feel care, concern, and labor for the welfare of the whole, are verily the servants of all, and are the more highly beloved and esteemed for their works' sake, and counted worthy of double honor (1 Tim. v. 17.).

48. Those little, simple, and very comprehensive words of Christ Jesus. *Whosoever will come after me, let him deny himself, and take up his cross and follow me* (Mark viii. 34. Luke xiv. 26, 27.), were received and established among the people of God, as a foundation and lovely principle, from the time they first heard and received the Gospel of Christ's second appearing, unto the present day.

49. Hence no true member of the body sought to obtain the pre–eminence, or to usurp authority over another; but each to build up, and support the welfare and comfort of the other, and consequently all were busy, peaceable, and happy; and every blessing, spiritual and

temporal, ensued, as naturally as rays of light flow from the sun, or the fruits of the harvest from the heat and moisture of summer.

(Benjamin Youngs, *Testimony*, pp. 444–448) [1808/1810/1823/1856]

* * *

8

The Difficult Lesson. *Anon.*

. . .

Let others cleave to the earth; to earthly institutions and practices as seems to them proper; such cannot reasonably expect that we, who have had our lives *cut off* from the earthly plane, can remain satisfied with the nourishment of earthly pleasures; but having become ripe for the Christian harvest . . .

We are being schooled into eternal life. We have forsaken the loves of the word [*sic*][9] as well as its lusts, because neither are [*sic*] eternal. We realize war to be the product of earthly loves and relations, we will not fight, nor vote for those who do fight; nor for those who believe in marriage, private property, or who engage in fleshly lusts of whatever description. . . .

(*The Shaker* I, 11, p. 82) [1871]

9

Thoughts by a Shaker Sister. *A. Doolittle*

. . .

The people known as "*Shakers*," have not sought to be numbered with popular Christians—the sects called orthodox. They have dwelt alone. . . . There they patiently wait . . . and watch for the bright morning star to arise.

(*The Shaker* I, 10, p. 76) [1871]

---

9. I.e., world.

THE SHAKERS

10

Baptism. *Daniel Frazer*

. . .

Better far to look around and see, that the close of the nineteenth century has for me, for you, for all, special baptisms, and higher resurrections than have yet been reached; increasing in us a separation from the world.

It is a mistake to suppose that by lessening the separation, we will draw people to our principles. The City set on the hill must keep its place, or lose its attractive power.

Come, let us gather to our Anointing, and greatly rejoice in the glorious surroundings of our "isolation" from the world—the heavenly fruit of virgin purity.

(*The Manifesto* XV, 4, pp. 75–76) [1885]

11

The Christ of the Ages. *Aurelia G. Mace.*
[Commendation of Paul Tyner's "The Christ Ideal in Shakerism" as published in *The Humanitarian*]

. . .

The Revelation which she [i.e., Ann Lee] received was a harvest from the generative life. Also that the mission of Jesus upon the earth was to teach a higher life to those who were able to receive the doctrine.

. . .

. . . Christ had appeared in thousands before our Mother lived, and also before the days of Jesus.

New truths have been revealed to the disciples of Mother Ann from time to time, ever since the Shaker Order has been established. Our brother, Paul Tyner is right in this, fast upon the downfall of this generative life has come the enlightenment.

. . .

The arts and sciences, in a future day, will flourish under the patronage of those living the highest life,—The Shaker Life. Heretofore the work of drawing the lines between flesh and spirit have been so great that there has been no time to give to any other thought but that of watching all the avenues to keep out the evils that might enter and destroy the good that had been gained. In the New Heavens and the New Earth, all that is pure and elevating in Art and the Sciences will be understood and appreciated.

(*The Manifesto* XXVI, 4, pp. 45–46) [1896]

*   *   *

12

... the Perfect work has begun and the outer Court must be left out, nor can any that are therein be held in communion by the Church, for its influence would be the same as in the First Appearing, and the Church would not stand, therefore it must be cut off. But there is an outward Order in the world, which is preparative to the gathering of souls to the inner Court. For while it is left in the world, the influence and light thereof, draws towards the true Church of Christ and not from it. Therefore the followers of Christ can own and bless those who compose this Order, in their proper sphere; as raised up by ministering Spirits and doing a providential work that is drawing towards, and preparing the way for the extension of the Kingdom of Christ, now rising on Earth, while at the same time it is an external medium of protection.

(Calvin Green, *Biographic Memoir,* p. 130) [1850]

13

Asceticism. No. 1. *Martha J. Anderson*

In all eyes, and in every clime, the golden chain of heavenly principles has been outwrought, in individual life and character. They, who in their mental development, expressed the highest unfoldment of the spirituality of their time, have ascended above the basic plane of animal desire and indulgence, to the cerebral region of inner consciousness the God-life of the soul, where they could enjoy the blessedness of spiritual communion untrammelled by worldliness and external temptation to sin. . . .

THE SHAKERS

The oriental doctrine that matter was the origin of evil, hence the body was an enemy to the soul, influenced many in earlier ages, to withdraw from all human society, and abide in seclusion. Such uniformly adopted austere rules of action and rigorous abstinence from all the pleasures of the senses . . . [they counted] earthly things of little importance compared with the joys of that higher spiritual state, attainable by contemplation of God, and communion with the invisible world . . . many unbalanced minds, conjoining the purely religious element, with the notion that all materiality was in its nature evil, and detrimental to spiritual growth, carried the idea of celibacy to extreme results, which tended to create abnormal physical conditions, and rendered the spirit while under mortal bonds, incapable of acting out its highest convictions of right.

. . . Religious institutions established at later periods [i.e., the later desert fathers], for the protection, accomodation and regulation of the religiously inclined; were blessed with the salutary influence of labor, which proved beneficial in checking the visionary tendencies of the enthusiastic devotee.

There were various phases of cenobite life among those who embraced Christianity, and measurably comprehended the grand principles of the virgin life and community of property. Saint Martin acted under the idea that all mercinary employment detracted from the sanctity of the monk's life; hence, his disciples lived in holes cut from the rocks, or built narrow wooden cells, which they inhabited and worked just enough to barely raise a meagre subsistence. . . .

(*The Shaker Manifesto* XIII, 2, pp. 31–32) [1883]

14

Asceticism. No. 2. *Martha J. Anderson*

Saint Basil speaks glowingly of the supreme satisfaction derived from the pious exercises of a religious life, where labor occupies the hands, the proceeds of which are used for charitable purposes; where holy and divine thoughts inspire the mind, and pure christian love absorbs the interests and affections of the heart. He pronounced him a slave to carnal nature, who loved a brother in blood, more than a brother in the religious community. He says: "Can you imagine felicity more desireable, than that of imitating on earth the life the angels lead in heaven?"

THE SHAKERS

Saint Anthony, the Father of Christian Monasticism, not only established houses for men, whose inclinations and convictions led them to embrace the Christ-life; but, under his direction at a later period, institutions were founded for females who took upon themselves the sacred vow of virginity. Chrysostom speaks thus of them, "Transport yourselves in imagination into Egypt, there you will see a new paradise, more beautiful than the richest gardens; innumerable troops of angels in human forms; an entire nation of martyrs and virgins. There the weaker sex rival the most fervent solitaries in their virtues. It is a life worthy of heaven and not inferior to that of angels."

Communism, truly christian, is socialistic; the fullness of that love which Jesus exhibited in his life and character; revealed his perfect manhood. . . . But the order of male and female, could not have been consummated under the then existing forms of government, civil and spiritual in the eastern world; they were exclusively masculine in spirit and sentiment, expressing the attributes and qualities of man, to the entire exclusion of the feminine elements of love, mercy and refinement. The doctrine of Trinity, was the out-growth of man's one-sided conception of Deity, revealed to his understanding as purely masculine in form and spirit. It was only when a Heavenly Mother was revealed, in the full beauty and perfection of love, tenderness and benign goodness, through the instrumentality of one of Her inspired daughters, that an angelic state of human society was organized, molded by divine laws, and based on the exalted principles so clearly enunciated by the lowly Nazarene. The spiritual communistic order, remained to be established in a land where woman was ennobled; where rights of conscience were acknowledged and the inspiration of continual revelation could have free course. This, the highest and most perfect type of human association, requires a greater degree of self-denial, than is needed to sustain celibacy where the sexes are arbitrarily separated. Not that self-abnegation that injures or destroys the body, in order to stifle and subdue inordinate passion; but, voluntary sacrifice of all that belongs to the lower loves and desires. . . .

As we progress in truth, we may glance toward the historic past, and mark the characters that have made their impress for good on humanity; no less the philosopher, the sage and scientist, than the religious devotee. Wisdom has revealed her choicest treasures through the intellective genius of many minds, who have labored with zeal and devotion in their various spheres for the elevation and improvement of the race. But, "the one thing needful," the power of redemptive principles, has come to human hearts through the world's great Saviors; those spiritual lights, that have arisen like stars from the darkness of ignorance and error, and shed a glowing radiance over a sin benighted earth. . . .

Thus out of the depths of mental philosophy, and innumerable forms of religious belief, we gather wisdom, knowledge and truth; safely garnering the precious sheaves of wheat, harvests from the world's history; adding good to good; rejoicing in the ever recurring cycles that bring to humanity, broader and clearer views of eternal righteousness and truth.

(*The Shaker Manifesto* XIII, 3, pp. 53–54) [1883]

* * *

15

The Church of Christ. *Watson Andrews*

Nothing is plainer than if there is a Church of Christ on earth it is the embodiment of his Spirit, and of course under the control of that Spirit; and it is equally plain that a Church or body of people organized as a religious Society, and which is governed by the Spirit of Christ, will, nay *must* bring forth the fruits of that Spirit. . . . Jesus promised his disciples he would send them another Comforter, that would "lead them into all truth." Observe now what this Holy Ghost—Spirit—did lead them into.

. . .

The result of this was a number of churches, or more properly, a number of branches of the one Church of Christ, and the "All Truth" Jesus declared the "Comforter"—could be come nearer suggesting Mother, but his time had not come to say that. . . .

. . .

Upon the four cardinal principles enumerated above [i.e., virgin purity of life, community of goods, parental control, filial respect], the Pentecostal Church was established by the direct inspiration of the Holy Spirit, and all the branches of that Church, so long as they retained their integrity, taught and practiced the same. . . .

THE SHAKERS

... Sinners, the morally sick, then, are those whom he came to call, and of which, it is evident, he is to build his Church.

But surely, you will think, the Church of Christ cannot be composed of sinners; certainly not, on any other principle than that sick people form the occupants of our hospital.

This proves the Church of Christ to be a hospital. A moral hospital for the morally infirm; and those who, having been admitted as patients, and who have submitted to the treatment sufficiently long to become healed, or even comfortably convalescent, are to be, we may reasonably suppose, retained as assistant physicians, nurses and caretakers of those still suffering under moral infirmities. Hence, wherever the Church is established, it will be known by the characteristics of a well regulated hospital, viz., that of healing the sick. ...

Metaphor aside, The Church of Christ can be no other than his body, animated and hence controlled by his spirit. ...

(*The Manifesto* XXIV, 1, pp. 10–11) [1894]

16

Communal Relations. *O. C. Hampton*

In a Community of Believers, the interests of one are the interests of all. There are no privileged parties possessing a right to absorb into themselves a greater number of communal interests than any others. ... While all are eligible to the privileges, gifts, comforts and blessings of the Community, still all cannot belong promiscuously to any and all the Executive committees [which variously direct the differing activities of the Community].

The reason of this is found 1st, in the great inequality of physical and mental ability; 2nd in the immense versatility in talent, genius and experience. Consequently absolute equality of mere standing as it regards the occupancy of offices of care and burden among Believers is an impossibility. ...

...

Finally, this inequality obtains throughout the material and spiritual Universe in the shape of inevitable gradations of intelligences from infinitely high and holy, to infinitely low, ignorant and imperfect. But all these series are ever ascending to higher and higher planes of perfection and goodness, and consequent happiness and glory,

THE SHAKERS

through the all-potent instrumentality of the great Law of Evolution and progress. So that each individual of the series will eventually enjoy not only all he is capable of enjoying, but also find himself elevated as far above those below him as he may find others above him.

And in this sense as the series is infinite, without center or circumference, each individual is as much the center as every other, and consequently all will consider themselves equally blessed as soon as they are sufficiently developed to understand or comprehend the full scope of this subject.

But again, here come in sight another of the beautiful laws of the Universe, namely, that throughout the whole realm of existence, "The lower or less progressed are blessed and elevated by the higher and more progressed," and from the very nature of progression, cannot be otherwise elevated. The Units of relation between intelligences are such, that no individual is independently capable of progress. If he rises at all, it must be through attraction toward a greater body of intelligence than he himself possesses, ... But this greater mass is found in an individual or individuals, immediately above him either visible or invisible, but most likely both. . . .

These . . . serve as a strong argument in favor of correctness of our theory and practice, relative to our governmental machinery of Ministry, Elders, Trustees, Deacons and Instructors. Indeed it seems to me the best proof of inspiration from on high having been given to the founders of our Organization in the original establishment of the same.

Now, I do not pretend to deny that the powers delegated to burden bearers in our community may not be and have not been, and will not be hereafter, more or less abused at times, and the rights of individuals ignored, through the weakness and imperfections of our common undeveloped rudimental status. But this in no wise militates against the theory here advocated, any more than the pains and sickness of gluttony militate against the propriety of eating good and wholesome food.

Besides, by the gradual diminution of our rudimental ignorances, arrogances, conceits, cruelties, jealousies and lusts, all such unholy use of power will be done away and the attractive and divine energy of Love, Mercy, Patience, and Humility, take its place. . . .

Our organization is a self–mending machine and friction and antagonism must finally be eliminated from it and forced to "flee to the uttermost parts of Egypt." We shall progress in personal purity and practical righteousness toward each other and both our Administration and ourselves shall and will be all for peace, reconciliation and at-onement with God and each other; not a system of force and coercion, but of wisdom, love and attraction.

I may not see it in this life, but I feel it and know it and rejoice with joy unspeakable and full of glory in the halcyon prospect.

(The Shaker Manifesto XII, 5, pp. 99–101) [1882]

17

Work. *Andrew Barrett.*

. . .

We are building up a community of interest, and it will readily be granted that to do this, every individual talent should be employed to the best advantage; . . .

We do not wish to be understood that we refer wholly to manual toil; this would be as disastrous to society as though all were engaged in purely intellectual pursuits. In whatever sphere of action we may be placed, let us not allow any excuse to seduce us from our duty. . . .

(The Shaker Manifesto XII, 6, pp. 128–129) [1882]

18

Among the Shakers. *Anon.*

. . .

Although the Shakers may be looked upon as one of the best examples of successful Communism, it always seemed to me that Communism was with them an incidental rather than a fundamental doctrine. They did not begin by teaching Communism. There seems to be no evidence of any Communistic theories in the days of Ann Lee, their founder. They had a new religion, and Communism was found to be the best means of presenting it. Their religion struck at the roots of family life, and left them dependent upon one another. They acknowledged no husband or wife, no father or mother but God; consequently, they were all brothers and sisters to one another—united, as the followers of a persecuted religion always are, with their union made still stronger by the dissolution of family ties. People who had houses and lands gave them up for the good of the whole, and they all looked forward to the speedy coming of the Kingdom of Heaven on earth.

THE SHAKERS

The establishment of Communism amongst them seems to have been only the following out of the acts and wishes of the members themselves, rather than any doctrine which was forced upon them; and although they advocate Communism now, and speak of it as a better way of living, they do not appear to insist upon that feature so much as they do upon certain others; and it is a fact that will be noticed by all readers on this subject, that those communities never have succeeded which have started with Communistic theories for their basis. The successful communities have always had something more potent than this to keep them together. It has been a bond of common faith and feeling, rather than the distribution of material benefits; and this speaks well for human nature, showing that people are not really so much actuated by a love of common property as by a love of common sympathies. . . .

(*The Shaker Manifesto* X, 1, pp. 5–6) [1880]
[Reprinted from the *American Socialist*]

19

Also his revelation of the future state of the church was far seeing. He said that he saw by revelation a perfect church completed on earth and he labored with all his powers to gain and establish its system & order as far as possible. But after having done all he was able, he then found that but one general order, that is the united system [i.e., communitarian], as a foundation had been gained, & further predicted that it would take seven general & distinct travels of believers to bring to maturity that perfect church order, which he then saw by revelation would ultimately be accomplished.

By general travels was understood the periods, from one general opening of the gospel to another, including all the degrees and changes in each one.

(Calvin Green, *Biography of Father Joseph*, p. 39) [1827]

four
_____

GOD: FATHER AND MOTHER

Introduction

The origin of the Shaker affirmation of God as Father and Mother is rooted, of course, in their experience of the ministry of Mother Ann. It is not simply a question of their primary founder's having been a woman. Rather it is the experience of a ministry in Christ undertaken by a woman in a way proper to a woman. Mother Ann never proposed for herself or any others in ministry that being a woman or a man was an indifferent matter. Male and female were not merely interchangeable—one doing whatever the other did—but were complementary in their distinctness. Humankind comes in two matching forms, male and female, and is incomplete when one or the other is missing or when the two are not enjoying each other's equality.

That Mother Ann saw her own ministry in a distinctively feminine mode is clear from the regular use she made of the scripturally based *bride, wife* and *mother* symbolism of traditional mysticism. We should be aware that all these are indeed symbolic statements, not intended to be taken at their surface meanings. They express intensely unitive personal experience in terms of fundamentals of womanhood in such a way that theoretical definitions are not initially needed. Thus, since being *child to a mother* is an experience common to all people, a *mystical motherhood* expresses an experiential relationship which can first be directly *felt* as personal reality, and then subsequently explored in its implications, as personal response is understood in terms of a wider "objective" reality. And so the earliest Believers recognized Ann Lee as their *spiritual mother* because of their own experience: they had been brought into a new kind of existence through the ministration of this woman. But this was their experience *as persons,* and so it was more than an abstract new kind of existence, *they were alive in a new way,* most vividly expressed by *reborn.* This new way of living was a transforming Union in Christ—they had been *reborn into Christlife.* And this had not taken place through intellectual analysis or speculation, nor from a "bolt out of the blue," but through this woman who was able to touch the depths of their personhood as a love-creating person. They had been *reborn into Christlife through her as their Mother in the spirit.*

Almost as important to the affirmation of Motherhood in God is the early Shaker experience of equality of men and women together as the living Christ now come again in-through-with them. Their Quaker ancestors had both men and women as religious leaders, and all participated freely in meeting, yet they had not seen this as a total equality demanding fundamental changes in the structures of both religious and secular society. From the outset of Mother Ann's ministry it was clear to Believers that the Gift they found through her as a woman did not suggest she was to be regarded as simply an exception to otherwise male-oriented structures. Even in the very fluid patterns of the First Ministry we can see truly equal participation of sisters with brothers in the evolving life. But we must be alert to another factor. The Shaker sense of equality and equal participation did not suggest to them an indifference; the distinctions between men and women were significant. The human race in these two different forms needed the interaction of them both to be complete. And this was true of the human community of the Church and therefore true *somehow* of the reality of Christ which the Church, men-and-women, manifests.

The gathering of Believers into the Church Order of the communal Societies between 1787 and 1797 translates the general experience of equality and complementarity into tangible structures. In effect there are two parallel orders throughout the Societies, living as integrated communities but with two vertical lines of leadership: deacons and deaconesses, family elders and eldresses (pastors), and ministry elders and eldresses (bishops). In each, one of the sisters and one of the brothers is senior, so that at every level there are two co-seniors, with whichever of the two as "senior senior" bearing the ultimate responsibility to the community. While the horizontal structure inevitably exhibited patterns of work divided according to sex (often enough, however, cutting across what the "world" regarded as "man's work" and "woman's work"), this typically reflected a useful division according to physical strength Many occupations were shared in by both sexes equally, such as weaving, the herb industry, and printing, among others.[1] The very pattern of the living quarters and work areas contributed to and reflected the palpable sense of functioning equality. Brothers and sisters lived in the same communal dwelling house, each group occupying retiring rooms at the opposite ends of the building, but with common corridors, meeting rooms, and dining rooms. Most often the houses were provided with two outside doors and two sets of staircases—stressing both the equality of each order, and as a support to celibate living.[2]

The lived experience of equality together with the personal impact of Mother Ann as "spiritual mother in Christ" laid the foundation for the emergence of the doctrine of God as Father and Mother. Discovering the reality of Christ in a constantly extending incarnation embracing themselves as men and women, it was inevitable that they began to see, first, maleness and femaleness as somehow integral to the historic Christlife now unfolding; second, as somehow bound up in the mystery of the Eternal Christ; and, finally, as somehow within the ultimate mystery of the Godhead. The qualification *somehow* is stressed here to indicate (as the selections amply witness) the awareness of Shakers over a period of a century or more that they were in a *process of developing* an important insight and doctrine. Although at any one

---

1. Although many culturally traditional work divisions (women housekeeping, sewing, etc.) were maintained, participation of women generally in a wide range of income–producing work (weaving, chair seating, etc.), either with the brothers or as a sisters' industry, gave these traditional tasks positive socio–economic value. The fact that *all* occupations contributed to the total pattern of the commune and without involvement in any form of internal remuneration reinforced egalitarian recognition.

2. The double doorways, staircases, etc., were useful in the early very large communities to support the separation of the sexes as celibate families. This is sometimes thought excessive by commentators, but we should recall how the often violent anti-Shakers viewed as scandalous unmarried men and women living in the same undivided building. The double doors were regarded by Believers as a testimony to the outsider of the genuineness and seriousness of their attempt to live celibately together. They also testified to the equality of brothers and sisters: each group had its own entry and so did not have to defer in false courtesy to the other.

point some might be satisfied that a final revelatory doctrine had been established, even elaborate theological statements proved to be anything but final.

The doctrine of Divine Fatherhood-Motherhood evolved, developed, and underwent great changes in expectations, from the early triumphal proclamations of the absolute truth possessed in this doctrine uniquely by the "one true Church" (as with Benjamin Youngs), to the later wonder of the God of infinitely expanding universes mirrored *for us* in our human duality man-woman. What remained constant in Shaker experience was the sense of aptness in seeking in *our* response to the mystery of God a recognition of *ourselves* as truly belonging unitively with God. To speak of God as Father-Mother is to look up through our human experience to the One we *begin* to recognize as in Union with us the way we actually are. God Father-Mother is not actually an image of God, but the image of ourselves in God. Earlier Shakers might have thought they had a "true image" of God in Divine Fatherhood-Motherhood. Later Shakers realized this was a self-image that pointed them in the right direction so they could move more and more deeply into God as *they* actually were.

The first brief selection (1) is a fundamental statement of the fine distinction in Shaker experience between a simplistic identification of Mother Ann and Christ-the-Savior and her ministering presence in Christ as the actual human being through whom they come to experience *Christ Saving*. Her admonition "be wise and careful how you speak" is one of the countless indications from the oral tradition of their awareness of the always present hazard of misrepresentation.

The series of texts from the works of Elder Calvin Green (2–7) illustrates the range of thought in Shaker Christology as he addresses aspects of the image of male and female in the human manifestation of the Eternal Christ/Logos. Elder Calvin, a conservative-to-moderate, writes after Youngs' *Testimony of Christ's Second Appearing* (1808, and following), in which the doctrine of God as Father and Mother and manifested in a twofold Christ Spirit through male and female human agents is presented for the first time. In the biography of Father Joseph, Green notes (2) an earlier presence (ca. 1795?) of an undeveloped doctrine. The remaining selections explore various aspects of the developed doctrine: an argument drawn from the Genesis creation story (3), which becomes a favorite Shaker apologetic argument during the rest of the century; the Church as the Body of Christ (4) necessarily a community of men and women; a corrective (5) for extremism in statements about Mother Ann.

The condensed Christological statements concluding this section (6, 7) bring together the major themes which are explored by all the authors: the recognition of Christ is in the context of a complex ordering of creation oriented toward an ascending series of evolving forms of personal life; the Divine Eternal Christ, the Logos, at the apex manifests the Godhead Father and Mother; Jesus is a *real man* in a human nature developed to its highest degree; Jesus and the Anointing (Christ) Spirit are related *from the beginning* yet he must historically *rise into* the nature of the Christ Spirit and so initiate the rise of all. The Christ Spirit and Jesus are in a true unity, but it is dynamic, always allowing the distinctiveness of the human and the Divine to be evident. Here as elsewhere we see the struggle to come to grips with the integrally One Jesus-Christ and also affirm real humanity. This reflects a rough parallel in the quest to understand the reality of Ann Lee in the Christ experience. A number of understandings are proposed, including a form of Christological adoptionism, but we must keep in mind the evolving character of theological *travel in the Gospel* and not settle on one as the "established" doctrine.

The selection from Dunlavy's *Manifesto* (8) is important for two reasons: it ignores the Father-Mother doctrine, and this twenty years after the first publication of Youngs' influential *Testimony*. Dunlavy stresses God as known by the experience of *traveling into* the *whole* God manifested in Christ; as God is Spirit and all receive this Spirit then all receive the Fullness God is. Dunlavy's extending incarnation does not actually mention Mother Ann (as was also the case in Father Joseph's *Concise Statement* in 1790)! The three selections from Youngs (9, 10, 11) present the Church as Christ, the Anointing/Christing initiated by a man, and the completion through a woman.

The next section illustrates the later move to moderate the Father-Mother doctrine of Youngs and his more enthusiastic followers (especially the enthusiasts of the 1837–1857 mystical revival). The first two texts (12, 13) from late in the century are future oriented. Elder Frederick, as usual the most daring of Shaker explorers, looks to the secular scientific-humanistic sphere for a new era in Christ-consciousness, and is sweeping in his abandonment of earlier enthusiasm centered on Mother Ann. Elder Hamilton DeGraw sees the issue in terms of an open-ended development of humanity: Ann Lee witnessing to a spiritual motherhood in an advancing "evolution of soul" among the *many* saviors of the human race.

The concluding three items of this section (14, 15, 16) reflect the previous generation during the period of *Mother's Work* (1837–1847) but from the perspective of new seekers trying to relate the mission of Mother Ann to the larger context of a wider Christian context. They "tone down" the then current enthusiasm as well as the elaborated vision of Youngs. The impact of the feminine in the "woman-half" of the Church as the Body of Christ is affirmed, and implications from this for the imaging of Christ and Godhead are appreciated, but any tendency toward deification of Mother Ann is avoided. The editorial comment (15) is interesting, indicating again the commitment to openness in evolving doctrine from unfolding experience.

Complementing these progressive views are the more conservative expositions of Elders Abraham Perkins and Giles Avery (17–21). The very brief excerpt (17) embodies the basic experiential reason Believers tended to emphasize the difference between the human Jesus and the Eternal Christ: a mythologized Jesus, so often part of popular Christianity, is irrelevant to real human life. This allows for a better understanding of Elder Giles' concern with Jesus, an absolutely natural human being, "becoming" Christ with the descent of the Holy Spirit at his baptism. It is not *adoptionism* in the meaning of the Christological disputes of the Patristic Period, but an attempt to affirm the truly human in the human-Divine Union. We should also note (18) that he does not identify the outpouring of the Motherhood of God with Ann Lee, but beginning with the spiritual baptism of all Believers, including the very first who gathered under the Wardleys in 1747; Ann Lee subsequently (1758) enters this Union of Believers and its baptism in the Mothering Spirit. The Christ-Bride manifestation ministered through Mother Ann constitutes *all* the people of the Bride Church of Christ as the Second Coming (20). Finally he makes clear (21) that Believers' Christology is derived from their sensitivity to the integrity of the human as male–and–female, as against the popular image of the exclusively male Father–Son–Spirit.

The final section looks to the rise of a full universalism in Shaker insight: first, the recognition of fellowship in faith with earlier eras, especially the Patristic and Medieval (previously thought of as caught up in the reign of anti–Christ); next the outreach to other Churches in a beginning ecumenism and extended to all religious traditions as manifesting the Christ Spirit of Truth; finally, the vision of an infinite cosmos with countless planets peopled with other races also finding the manifestation of the One Spirit in their midst. Elder Frederick attempts to project the experience of Christ into this greatest possible universalism (22), even though some of his notions may be eccentric. Elder Oliver Hampton (23) affirms simply that a new cosmology of an infinite universe demands a correspondingly new Christology. This is rooted in the infinite evolutionary progression of personhood (24), God evolving/creating ever higher progressions, manifesting the Infinite Love–Wisdom which is the Divine Father–Mother. Eades, Sears, and Pelham (25, 26, 27) stress the purely analogous character of the image of God as Father and Mother as derived from the experience of Jesus and Ann. The anonymous anti–Trinitarian "maleness" stance (28) provides the context for Hampton's "Tria Juncto in Uno" (29), an extraordinary testimony to the impact of experience as the foundation of the development of religious insight. A century and a half of rejection of Trinity by Shakers is here resolved! The false "three male image" of popular thought is rightly rejected; the analogy of Fathering and Mothering is extended from a Duality into a Trinity of Father–Mother–Union. God Father and Mother in Union manifested through human reality is the Anointing/Christing of men and women into one: the One Church, the Fullness of the One Christ *in whom there is neither male nor female.*

I

I once said to Mother Ann, "Mother is my Savior." "Abijah," said Mother, "You must be wise and careful how you speak: It is Mother in a Savior, and a Savior in Mother."
(Abijah Worcester)
(Roxalana Grosvernor, ed., *Sayings* [SDLms.], p. 98) [1845]

2

I learned that he had an inspired view of the order of Father and Mother in the nature of God, & also of the Divine Christ in the heavens who had been the mediator between him & all his works from

the beginning; but thro' motives of wisdom did not manifest it publicly, for the time had not yet come.

(Calvin Green, *Biography of Father Joseph,* p. 42) [1827]

3

To have just conceptions of the real character of that Divine
PRINCIPLE or BEING whom we call GOD, it is necessary to understand the nature of his attributes, which stand in perfect correspondence with each other, and which are fully displayed in his Word and
Works, and clearly manifest his Divine perfections. "For the invisible
things of him from the creation of the world are clearly seen, being
understood by the things that are made." (Rom. i. 20.)

It is certainly most reasonable and consistent with infinite Wisdom, that the image and likeness of God should be most plainly
manifested in man, who was made the most noble part of the natural
creation. Accordingly we read, "And God said, Let us make man in
our image, after our likeness. — So God created man in his own image;
in the image of God created he him; male and female created he them."
Hence it must appear evident that there exists in the DEITY, the
likeness of male and female, forming the unity of that creative and
good principle from which proceeds the work of *Father and Mother,*
manifested in *Power* to create, and *Wisdom* to bring forth into proper
order, all the works of God. If it were not so, then man, who was
created male and female, as father and mother, could not, with any
propriety, be said to show forth the image and likeness of God. But the
manifestation of Father and Mother in the Deity, being spiritual, does
not imply two *Persons,* but two *Incomprehensibles,* of one substance,
from which proceed all Divine power and life.*

*[FOOTNOTE.] This shows something essentially differ-
ent from "three distinct persons in one God," all in the
masculine gender, as established by a council of catholic bishops in the fourth century, and which has been the prevailing
creed among their blind and bigoted followers to this day.

The Almighty is manifested as proceeding from everlasting, as the
first Source of all power, and the *fountain* of all good, the *Creator* of all
good beings, and is the ETERNAL FATHER; and the Holy Spirit of

THE SHAKERS

Wisdom, who was the *Co-worker* with him, from everlasting, is the ETERNAL MOTHER, the *bearing Spirit* of all the works of God. This is according to the testimony of her own inspiration. (See Prov. viii; and iii. 17, 18, 19.)

(Calvin Green, *Summary View*, pp. 91–92) [1823/1848]

4

As the Divine Spirit and Will of God, in these last days, has been manifested in Christ, through the first two messengers of salvation; so the same Spirit continues to manifest his will, through the same line and order, in the church of Christ, and will ever continue to do so, as long as Christ shall continue to have a true church on earth. Therefore, as the ancients worshipped the God of their fathers; so worship we that God who has been revealed to us by our spiritual parents in the gospel, whom God hath raised up, and sent to open the way of salvation to us. We worship neither man nor woman; but we honor and obey the Spirit of Christ, whether revealed in man, woman or child.

The natural creation, and the things therein contained, are figurative representations of the spiritual creation which is to supersede it, as we have already shown. . . . The first parents of the natural world were created male and female.

As the true church of Christ, which is his body, is composed of male and female, as its members; and as there must be a correspondent spiritual union between the male and female, to render the church complete, as a spiritual body; so it is essentially necessary that such a spiritual union should exist in the head of that body, which is Christ; otherwise there could be no source from which such a correspondent, spiritual union could flow to that body. It must be admitted by every reasonable person, that the order of man cannot be complete without the woman. If so, then the church cannot exist, in its proper order, without male and female members; for, "neither is the man without the woman, nor the woman without the man, in the Lord." (1 Cor. xi. 11.) And it would be very unreasonable to suppose that the body of Christ should be more complete and perfect, in its order, than the head. This would give the body a superiority over the head.

This spiritual union between the male and female, in the body and in the head of the church, is that which the apostle calls *a great mystery*. (Eph. v. 32.) And indeed it is a great mystery to the lost children of

215

man, who seem to have no conception of any other union between the male and female, than that which is natural, according to the order of the flesh. Nor do they seem to know any other design in the creation of the female, nor any other essential use for her than that of carnal enjoyment in a sexual union, and the production of offspring through that medium. But the work of Christ, being a spiritual work, the union must therefore be spiritual; and it is impossible for souls to come into this work, and enjoy this union, unless the Spirit of Christ become their life.

Since then, Christ must appear in every female, as well as in every male, before they can be saved; and since that Divine Spirit has appeared in one man, whom God has chosen as the Captain of our salvation, and an example of righteousness to all men; is it not reasonable and consistent that the same anointing power (which is Christ) should also appear in a woman, and distinguish her as a leader, and an example of righteousness to all women?

It may be asked, How can Christ appear in a woman? With the same propriety we might ask, how can Christ appear in a man? Christ is a Spirit: "The Lord is that Spirit." (2 Cor. iii. 17.) In that Spirit is contained the only power of salvation. If Christ could not appear in a man, then no man could be saved; so also, if Christ could not appear in a woman, then no woman could be saved. Christ first appeared in Jesus of Nazareth, by which he was constituted the head of the new and spiritual creation of God. The Spirit of Christ was in the primitive church; and the Spirit of Christ is also in every one of his true and faithful followers. The Spirit of Christ is the same, whether revealed in man, woman or child.

(Calvin Green, *Summary View*, pp. 215–217) [1823/1848]

5

... And in no other sense has Ann Lee ever been termed a Mother among us; a Mother in the spiritual Israel; because by receiving and yielding obedience to the testimony of Christ revived and brought forth by her, we have been delivered from the bondage of sin, and found a relation in Christ, and a part in the glorious liberty of the children of God.... She did not pretend to teach a new doctrine; (however new it may appear to many,) but to renew the doctrine of

Jesus Christ in its purity. In so doing she fulfilled his will; and she always pointed us to his blessed precepts and examples for our guide, and always acknowledged and declared him to be her head and Lord.

(Calvin Green, *A Discourse &c.*, pp. 46–47) [1830]

6

Christ is a Divine Spirit or Being, the immediate offspring of the Eternal Parentage; "to us," the first emanation and Son of the Creator—God. 2nd.—In the unity of this Divine Offspring, there were the Spirits of male and female, which in their progressive developments to completed Order, as Head of all Creation, were the perfect likeness and representation of the Eternal Father and Mother—the Creator—God—"Blessed forevermore." This Divine Christ has ever been the first, and primary Mediator between God and all *His* works. The first natural man was formed in a figure and likeness of this Divine arrangement, and in his progressive developments to the full Order of God's likeness in the natural or earthly state,—he figuratively passed through all the degrees of progress to maturity—that did the Divine Christ ("to us," the first Offspring of the Dual God,) in his progress to perfect Order.

All the virtues and goodness ever manifested on Earth were emanations from this Divine Christ through proper Angel Agents. But in all ages previous to the manifestation of this Holy Spirit for the redemption of the human race, and to lay the foundation for the New and Spiritual Creation, in mankind, Christ followed them, and through his Agents, ministered all the power and goodness that was adapted to their State as as Children of the World. Hence St. Paul says, "Israel did all drink of that spiritual Rock that followed them, and that Rock was Christ." (1 Cor. x. 4.)—Yet it is said the "Law ordained by the ministry of Angels." (Acts, vii. 23—Gal. iii. 19—Heb. ii. 2.) But when Christ was revealed in human nature, He then called them to follow him, or they could have no part in His New Creation, which was not of the world, but out of the world, in a far higher Order and Spiritual Sphere. . . .

Jesus was the first Agent of the Kingdom of Heaven in the human race. He was the first man that was able to bear the struggle necessary to overcome "him that had the Power of death." The first Adam by transgression had allowed the "Enemy" to supplant him in his natural "Dominion," who thus became "the Prince of this world" and "brought death into the world which passed upon all men." . . .

. . . Man at creation became alive to the knowledge of spiritual existences, whereby he rose into correspondence with the Angels next above him. His guardian Angel was his Lord, and evidently all the God he knew. This Angel acted in correspondent union with the Order before him, and so on through every higher Order to the Almighty Creator. Man's fall was the loss of this union and *sinking* into the Animal Life. . . .

It was necessary that the Agent by whom Christ should be revealed for the Redemption of the human race, in order that he might be their Head, and leader in the New Creation, should be formed of the full and strongest properties of human nature, and grow up in their midst.—He must be a real man working in the midst of man's nature, where Death and the Serpent reigned. Born of the female, the medium through which all are born, Jesus was brought forth in the midst of the human race, and was formed of that nature in its highest degree. For that female was the production of the strongest and most developed Branch of the human race, which had been supernaturally preserved and nurtured for the purpose of producing a Son, capable of being the Head of the New Creation of God.

Jesus was ministered to and inspired by the Spirit of Christ from his beginning, and by his faithful obedience, he subdued that nature in which he was formed, and rose out of it into the nature of Christ, and became the "first fruit of the Resurrection"—the "First born of many brethren." He opened the way of Redemption, by overcoming him that was stronger than man, by dispensing his overcoming power, and setting the example of subduing and traveling out of that nature by "which man is held in bondage," and became the Redeemer of all who receive him. i.e., his Spirit. . . .

(Calvin Green, *Biographic Memoir*, pp. 94–98) [ca. 1850]

7

. . . *Christ*, the real offspring of God was a Divine intelligence, (according to the original,) which proceeded and came forth from the Eternal Parents, therefore was the seed of God. Jesus was a real man . . . in which all the properties of the world, soul and body, were concentrated in their highest natural order. . . . Jesus was formed of all the properties of human nature, in their highest living order; therefore he was the highest being that could be brot[sic] forth of the properties of nature; hence reached the order above, and formed a proper medium for the Divine Spirit of Christ, to enter into human nature. . . .

Therefore, it is plain, that no one begotten of the seed of man, could be the proper medium to introduce Christ into the world. But Jesus Christ did not proceed of, or from, the seed of man, therefore, he was the proper medium to receive the seed of the heavenly order, that is, *Christ* the quickening spirit. Hence, he was the prepared body, spiritual and temporal to usher that divine spirit into the world.
. . .

Christ was the power of God, and the *Wisdom* of God, Was this Jesus? . . . the name [Christ] may be applied to the medium [Jesus] properly enough to such as understand; in the same manner as we say *Mother* Ann Lee, when we all know that Ann Lee, personally, is not the Mother of any of us; but we allude to the Mother spirit revealed in her, and we are so understood.

. . . when Jesus was begotten from the dead . . . this was effected by the operations and inspiring power and wisdom of the Divine spirit of Christ, and was animated and filled with the fulness of the elements and life of the *Divine Son*. Therefore, Jesus became truly the Christ of the race of man, that is the first anointed, and Father of the regeneration, thro whom, Christ was, and is, revealed in the world, and thus he ascended on high, far above the Angels, even into the Christ elementary order, for he ascended with Christ, as his first fruit, which he descended and came into the world to redeem.

(Calvin Green, *Incontestible Position &c.*, n.p.) [ca. 1830]

*   *   *

8

[Following an exposition of the Attributes of God. . . .]
I have been the more careful to make some practical remarks on the character and attributes of God, that readers may be impressed

with some influential sense of what a man must be, when he becomes a son of God in Christ; that he must be like God in all the graces of the Spirit; for as Jesus Christ, who was the first true tabernacle of God among men, which the LORD pitched, and who is the head of the body, the Church, had the fullness of the Deity dwelling in him bodily; so each and all of the members who, in union with the head, constitute the true body or church, which is Christ, are partakers of the same Spirit and same divine nature, that God may be all and in all. "And of his fullness have we all received, and grace according to grace." "And the glory," said Jesus to the Father, "which thou gavest me, I have given them; that they may be one, even as we are one."—"Now if any man have not the Spirit of Christ he is none of his." (Jno. i. 16. and xvii. 22. Rom. viii. 9.)

. . .

Nevertheless, let it be remembered, with respect to the attributes of God, that no one of them, neither all of them together, comprehend God so as to enable us to know definitively what God is. He is incomprehensible. We cannot know God except as he reveals himself in his character, his attributes and his works. We cannot have any just conceptions of God as lacking any one attribute belonging to the perfection of his character, and yet when we view all these to the extent of our sphere, there is yet that behind his Essence and Being, of which we are ignorant. All these attributes, or perfections, are qualities none of which can exist abstractly or alone. Thus if we speak of his holiness—holiness is a quality which implies a being, as it were, previously extant, to be holy, or a being capable of containing holiness. If we speak of love, love is a quality or attribute of some being presupposed by the very naming of this attribute. If we speak of goodness, goodness is also an attribute or perfection of some being or existence presupposed or at least included in the thought; and so of the rest. Yet so intimately and essentially do these perfections belong to the very essence of his nature and being, that we may say in truth and with safety, that *God is truth, God is light, God is love, God is holiness;* for there is nothing in God but what is *truth,* there is nothing in God but what is *light,* there is nothing in God but what is *love,* there is nothing in God but what is *holiness;* and so of the rest. On the whole, no one can have any just conception of God otherwise than as his character is revealed by his word and works; neither can any have a just and correct knowledge of God, even by revelation, any farther than as they grow into an acquaintance with him by travelling into the same nature in the work of redemption and holiness, by the Gospel.

Nevertheless, according to the privilege given to us in the revelations which he makes of himself, to teach us our duty and our relation to him, we may talk freely of his character and his works, in the things which pertain to our salvation and redemption. For God hath revealed himself in Christ, that in our sphere we may know him with certainty in all his character, and speak of him with safety. So that while on the one hand, we are unable fully to comprehend all or any one of the perfections of Deity, God being incomparably superior to man; on the other hand, there is nothing in God which, in our sphere, and to the extent thereof, we may not know with certainty and safety, as fast as we overcome evil. For although no man hath seen God abstractedly, at any time, yet the only begotten Son who is in the bosom of the Father hath revealed him—*hath revealed God, whole God,* in himself who is the *brightness* of his glory and the *character* of his person or *subsistence.* And nothing short of the correct and perfect knowledge of God in his whole character can ever complete the happiness of man, who was created in the image of God. And for this cause he hath sent his Son into the world, in whom dwelt all the fullness of the Godhead bodily, to be our example and to reveal God to us, that we might find salvation in being conformed to the image of his Son, and so to God himself, and in no other way. Thus God's people live as knowing the unknowable, and seeing him who is invisible.

"GOD is a SPIRIT," or more properly and emphatically, "GOD is SPIRIT." This is perfectly consistent with the Greek text, and conveys a much more noble sentiment of God, and fixes on the mind a more noble impression, than to say, he is *a Spirit,* as though he were a circumscribed or limited being. There are many spirits, all limited and dependent beings; but there is one God, independent, and in all his character and perfections unlimited. But God is SPIRIT; and is therefore the proper fountain from whom all created spirits proceed. Moreover God is Spirit; it is therefore no marvel that he is not satisfied with fleshly or material worship; "God is Spirit; and they that worship him, must worship him in spirit and in truth." (Jno. iv. 24.) And no marvel that God will increase the work of the Spirit in his people until they are finally redeemed in the Spirit and the flesh made void. And what if we should say the *God is Spirit,* comes nearer to pointing out what God is, in his real Being or Essence, than any other name, character or attribute, ascribed to him by the Spirit of revelation, not even excepting the name by which he was made known to Moses, I AM THAT I AM, or I WILL BE WHAT I WILL BE, expressing his unchangeableness and independence? We can have some understanding, according to our sphere, of the existence of a Being who is Spirit in the abstract, as a primary Being or foundation existence, independent of any distinct being, attribute or quality, and yet as it were the proper basis for all good qualities, and without all and everyone of which we cannot conceive of that Spirit, that Existence, whom we call God. Spirit is a real existence; a proper agent; a subject of power, of righteousness, holiness, love, and the like. A Being who is Spirit is also the proper subject of volition and free agency. But if we speak of love it is not an independent idea; it presupposes some subject or agent to inherit and exercise that love. If we speak of justice; it presupposes a Being who is just, distinct from the idea of justice, as its possessor's seat, or the place of its habitation. If we speak of light; though by some supposed to be a real body, it seems nearest the truth to say, that it presupposes some being capable of illumination and reflection, and that where there is no body to contain light there can be no light. If we speak of power or wisdom, it is a dependent idea, presupposing a Being powerful or wise; and so of the rest.

But when we say that *God is Spirit*, we express the idea of an existence, not material yet real, capable of volition and agency; I say we conceive and express the idea of the Being of God, according to our sphere, for beyond that he is incomprehensible to us, we know nothing; and the circle of our knowledge is small in the infinite I AM. Yet when we say God is spirit, we can conceive that that Spirit is capable of volition and agency; and is also capable of possessing in himself as his essential qualities, attributes or perfections, *power, wisdom, righteousness and justice, holiness, truth, goodness, love, mercy, light, independence, self-existence*, and the like. Accordingly, when we speak or read of the Spirit of God, it is God the Spirit; if of the Spirit of truth, we have respect to God the Spirit, who is Truth; that Spirit who could not exist or ever have existed without truth; if of the Spirit of holiness, it is God the Spirit, who is holy, essentially holy in his very nature; if of the love of God, or Spirit of love, it is no other than God the Spirit who is love, "For God is love, and whosoever dwelleth in love dwelleth in God and God in him;" if of the Spirit of unity in the bond of peace, it is none else but that Spirit who is God, and is one, in himself and all who know him, being in them and to them, the uniting bond in abiding peace towards God and one another. Thus when a man receives the Spirit of Christ, he receives God who is Spirit; and when the spirit of Christ abideth in any man, he hath abiding in him that God who is Spirit; and he hath both the Father and the Son. "At that day ye shall know that I am in my Father, and ye in me, and I in you." "If a man love me, he will keep my words: and my Father will love him, and we will come unto him, and make our abode with him." (Jno. xiv. 20, 23.)

(John Dunlavy, *The Manifesto*, pp. 28–31) [1818/1847]

9

1. The Church of Christ has its foundation in the revelation of God, and that foundation is *Christ.* But who, or what is *Christ?* The name *Christ Jesus* signifies *anointed Saviour. Thou shalt call his name JESUS; for he shall save his people from their sins.* (Mat. i. 21.) And as the man Jesus was, for that very purpose endowed with the spiritual unction or anointing power of the Holy Spirit of Christ, which proceeded forth and came from God; therefore being baptized into the divine nature he was called Jesus Christ, i.e., the *anointed.* (1 Cor. xii. 13.)

2. Hence the Church is called the body of *Christ,* which signifies the body of the *anointed,* or the body of those who have received the Holy Spirit, and have been baptized into the one spiritual body; therefore the Church of Christ is the Church of the anointed. Christ Jesus was not the *body* of the anointed, but the *Head;* and as the body hath many members, so also is *Christ,* or the *anointed.* These members are those human beings in which the *anointing* spirit hath its abode. And hence it is written: *The anointing which ye have received of him abideth in you—which is Christ in you, the hope of glory.* (1 John, ii. 27; Col. i. 27.).

3. Therefore, *Christ* or the divine *anointing* in the body, or Church, is not a man or woman, but the unction or anointing of his Holy Spirit, of which the anointing oil with which the Jewish kings and prophets were formerly anointed, was a figure. Neither is the *anointed* one member, but many: not a particular person only, but a body of people. And as every thing must have a foundation or first cause, so the body of the *anointed* originated from one, and this *one* must be considered as the foundation pillar or first father of all who constitute that body.

4. The world is not one person, but many; yet all the world sprang from one man, who is therefore considered as the foundation pillar or first father of the human race. But as the first man was not alone in the foundation of the *old creation;* so neither did Christ Jesus, in his single person, complete the order in the foundation of the *new creation.*

5. Had there never been any written account of the foundation of human society, or the constituent order of the world, the world itself would be a standing momument of the essential parts of which it is composed, namely of man and woman; the father and mother of all living. And as every individual in the world sprang from a father and mother, the conclusion is self-evident, that the whole sprang from one joint parentage, or first father and mother, as the foundation pillars of human society.

6. And upon the same principle might the foundation pillars of the *anointed* be discovered, were there no written or verbal account of the beginning of such an order; for no effect can exist without a cause, and by the effect, the cause which produced it is made manifest: and this truth is still more evident since the pointed predictions of the ancient prophets are recorded, and fulfilled in the Church of Christ in the present day.

7. Then *first,* as the Church is constituted of mankind, who are anointed with the Holy Spirit, and separated from the world, it follows that *man,* anointed with the Holy Spirit, was the first foundation pillar of the Church. And *second,* as the Church is not composed of the man without the woman, but both are united in the Lord by an inseparable bond of spiritual union, it follows of course that such a union and relation sprang from a first *man* and *woman* who were thus united.

8. And this man and woman, united in the bond of an everlasting covenant, and anointed with the same spirit, must be the foundation pillars of all who are thus united by the same anointing. And whether they are immediately and personally known or not, yet, by the spirit of harmony and union flowing through the anointed, there is a relative knowledge of their nature and union; as much as the world relatively know, by experience, the nature and union of their first foundation pillars, or parentage, whose image they bear.

9. And as the order in the foundation of the old creation could not be complete by the first man without the first woman; so the order in the foundation of the new creation could not be complete in the man

alone; for the man is not without the woman in the Lord, nor the woman without the man.

10. In the natural creation, the man was first formed, and afterwards the woman, who was *the mother of all living;* and the man was not of the woman, but the woman of the man, and by the woman, was the order in the creation of man completed; and the first covenant was between them both, for the increasing glory of the natural creation.

11. Christ Jesus, that is the anointed Jesus, was the *second man,* the *beginning of a new creation of God:* but, as has been observed, no order in the creation could be completed by one alone; therefore, according to the invariable order and relation of things, the ultimate display of the new creation required a corresponding female, that the new covenant might stand between them both, for the increase and glory of the new creation.

12. The first man was created male and female jointly, but neither was male nor female separately, until the woman was taken out of the man; so in the first appearing of Christ, that spirit of anointing which constituted Christ, was male and female jointly, but not separately in visible order: Nor could any abiding and perfect spiritual union and relation exist in order, between the sexes, until the woman was raised up, in her appointed season, and anointed to complete the order in the foundation of the new creation, for the redemption of both man and woman.

13. The woman was the *first* in the transgression, and therefore must be the *last* out of it, and by her the way of deliverance must be completed. Nevertheless, by her faith, and in her subjection to the man, she was justified and accepted in the primitive Church; but her true order could not be gained; but only in the line of prophecy, as relating to the second appearing of Christ, was she allowed to teach, until the time of her redemption came.

. . .

26. As sin first took its seat in the woman, and thence entered the human race, and as Christ in taking upon him the nature of fallen man, in Jesus, to purify and redeem him, made his first appearing in the line of the male only; therefore the mystery of iniquity or MAN OF SIN was not fully revealed, nor the mystery of God finished, in Christ's first appearing.

27. And therefore, it was also necessary, that Christ should make his second appearing in the line of the female, and that in one who was

conceived in sin, and lost in the fulness of man's fall; because in the woman the root of sin was first planted, and its final destruction must begin where its foundation was first laid, and from whence it first entered the human race.

28. Therefore, in the fulness of time, according to the unchangeable purpose of God, that same Spirit and word of power, which created man at the beginning—which spake by all the Prophets—which dwelt in the man Jesus—which was given to the Apostles and true witnesses as the Holy Spirit and word of promise, which groaned in them, waiting for the day of redemption—and which was spoken of in the language of prophecy, as "a woman travailing with child, and pained to be delivered," was revealed in a WOMAN.

29. And that *woman*, in whom was manifested that Spirit and word of power, who was anointed and chosen of God, to reveal the mystery of iniquity, to stand as the first in her order, to accomplish the purpose of God, in the restoration of that which was lost by the transgression of the first woman, and to finish the work of man's final redemption, was ANN LEE.

30. As a chosen vessel, appointed by Divine wisdom, she, by her faithful obedience to that same anointing, became the temple of the Holy Spirit, and the second heir with Jesus, in the covenant and promise of eternal life. And by her sufferings and travail for a lost world, and her union and subjection to Christ Jesus, her Lord and Head, she became the *first born of many sisters*, and the true MOTHER *of all living* in the new creation.

31. Thus the perfection of the revelation of God, in this latter day, excels, particularly, in that which respects the glorious part in the creation of man, namely, the woman. And herein is the most condescending goodness and mercy of God displayed, not only in redeeming *that amiable part of the creation from the curse, and all the sorrows of the fall,* but also in condescending to the lowest estate of the loss of mankind.

32. So that by the first and second appearing of Christ, the foundation of God is laid and completed, for the full restoration and redemption of both the man and the woman in Christ, according to the order of the new covenant, which God has established in them for his own glory, and the mutual good and happiness of each other, and their spiritual posterity.

33. And in this covenant, both male and female, as brethren and sisters in the family of Christ, jointly united by the bond of love, find

each their correspondent relation to the first cause of their existence, through the joint parentage of their redemption.

34. Then the man who was called JESUS, and the woman who was called ANN, are verily the two first visible foundation pillars of the Church of Christ—the two anointed ones—the two first *heirs* of promise, between whom the covenant of eternal life is established—the first *Father* and *Mother* of all the children of regeneration—the two first visible Parents in the work of redemption—and in whom was revealed the invisible joint Parentage in the new creation, for the increase of that seed through which "all the families of the earth shall be blessed."

(Benjamin Youngs, *Testimony*, pp. 379–381; 383–384) [1808/1810/1823/1856]

10

18. The man Jesus, through the medium of a woman, inherited the seed of Abraham, *the nature of human depravity* (Heb. ii. 16, 17.), with which he entered the world, and in all things he was made like unto his brethren; yet, by perfectly following the divine light, he was, in every sense, taken out of, separated from, and placed above (John viii, 29.) every correspondent attachment to all that was carnal in woman, which came by the fall.

19. And by the energy of that eternal word, which he received from his Father, he overcame the spirit and power of human depravity, and was sanctified and set apart in the work of redemption, as the first born in the new creation. And by that word which liveth and abideth forever, he was constituted an high priest forever over the household of God, after the order of *Melchisedec* (Heb. vi. 20.).

20. And all who came into him, that is, not into the natural body of Jesus Christ, but into his divine nature, were in him, and by him, through the energy of that same eternal word, taken out of their correspondent relation to the depravity of the fall, and constituted the spiritual body of the *second Adam,* comprehending male and female, as the body of Christ. And this was the work of Christ in his first appearing, *to make in himself, of twain* (i.e., of man and woman) *one new man; so making peace* (Eph. ii. 15.).

21. Then the Church, which was the body of Christ in his first appearing, did constitute one new man, consisting of man and woman; but that body alone could not increase and multiply, after the order of

the new covenant (any more than the body of the first male and female, while in the state in which God first created them, when he called *their name Adam*) until the spiritual woman was taken out of the spiritual man, and placed in her own proper order and correspondent relation to her spiritual head.

22. This was the reason why the Apostle, speaking of Christ's second appearing, and of the Church's increase in that day, says: *That day shall not come, except there come a falling away first, and that man of sin be revealed,* even *the mystery of iniquity* (2 Thes. ii.). Hence, it follows, beyond all contradiction, that the work of redemption was not yet complete.

23. Therefore, the work of God, in the first mother of the new creation, was to reveal the mystery of iniquity where it first entered, and to separate the woman from her correspondent relation in the flesh, after the order of the old covenant, and to place her in her proper order as a *spiritual woman,* according to the new covenant, in a correspondent relation to the first *spiritual man.*

24. As it was by the revelation of Christ, and the energy of the same eternal word which liveth and abideth forver, that the woman was taken out of, and separated from her correspondent relation to the fallen state of man, and made a spiritual woman; so in her, and by her, the glory and perfection of the spiritual man, Christ Jesus was revealed.

25. It was only by the spiritual man, Christ Jesus, and her corresponding relation to him, that she could receive the attribute of spiritual woman. And it is only from the certain existence of sons and daughters, or spiritual children, that those who begat and brought them forth, can receive the attributes of father and mother, or spiritual parents. So that if the son has a corresponding relation in the new creation, so likewise has the daughter.

26. It is not to be understood in the spiritual work of God, that one natural body, either of man or woman, is either taken out of, or joined to another; but as man and woman are terms used to express the joint body and relation in the natural creation of man; so they are used in regard to the spiritual work of God.

27. To this spiritual relation the Apostle refers, and brings the natural as a figure of the spiritual, when he says, *For this cause shall a man leave his father and mother, and shall be joined unto his wife, and they two shall be one flesh* (Eph. v. 31, 32.). And therefore, as the very essence of male implies also the female, the same applies to the woman, to leave

mother and father, and be joined to her corresponding relation in the same spiritual work.

28. *This*, says the Apostle, *is a great mystery; but I speak concerning Christ and concerning the Church.* To the same thing he refers, when he says, *He that is joined to the Lord is one Spirit* (1 Cor. vi. 17). And from such a union and correspondence, arises the substance of all those spiritual attributes in the new creation, or work of redemption, such as the *bridegroom*—the *bride, the Lamb's wife*—*brethren* and *sisters*, and the *sons* and *daughters* of God.

29. Hence the Apostle, speaking of the final separation between Christ and Belial, light and darkness, the believer and infidel, saith, *Wherefore, come out from among them, and be ye separate, saith the Lord, and touch not the unclean thing; and I will receive you, and will be a Father unto you, and ye shall be my sons and daughters, saith the Lord Almighty* (2 Cor. vi. 17, 18.).

30. Then, if the Church, which is called out, and separated from the unclean, is composed of sons and daughters, they must needs have both a father and mother, and these must be the first foundation pillars, and joint parentage of the Church.

31. Therefore, as there was a *natural Adam* and *Eve*, who were the first foundation pillars of the world, and the first joint parentage of the human race; so there is also a *spiritual Adam* and *Eve*, (manifested in Jesus and Ann, the first joint visible Parentage) who are the first foundation pillars of the Church, and the invisible parentage of all the children of redemption. And as the world, truly and properly, proceeds from father and mother, in the line of *generation;* so the Church as truly and properly proceeds from father and mother in the line of *regeneration.*

(Benjamin Youngs, *Testimony*, pp. 387–389) [1808/1810/1823/1856]

II

1. ... concerning the order in the existence of Deity, the order in which man was created, and the correspondent manner of man's redemption, may be comprised in the following words; as from time to time, has been made known by the revelation of Christ, in this day of the second manifestation of that Divine Spirit, with infallible proofs of their truth and reality, namely:

2. That in the ALMIGHTY BEING, whom we call God, there

existed, before man was created, and before the worlds were formed, an ETERNAL TWO IN ONE SPIRIT; who, in plain Scripture language are termed ALMIGHTY POWER and INFINITE WISDOM. That the first holds the seat or throne of the ETERNAL FATHER; and the second, that of the ETERNAL MOTHER; and that by the union of these ETERNAL TWO, the heavens and earth were created and set in order; and by their united power and wisdom they are sustained.

3. Secondly. That before the world or order of creation was formed, and before man was created on the earth, there existed, in the Christ element, an order of spiritual beings, male and female, designated *Sons of God* and *Morning Stars* (Job, xxxviii. 7.), in union with the Eternal Father and Mother from whose living essence they were a proceeding; and who were the prototypes of the human race. And, after the earth, and every living creature thereon was formed, God, through means adapted to the end, created man, *two in one nature,* *"male and female,* created them, after his own image, and in his own likeness," and called their name Adam.

4. Third, That, notwithstanding Adam, the first man and woman that God created on the earth, by disobedience to the laws of their Creator, fell from the rectitude in which they had been placed; and their posterity following the example of their parents in transgression, having likewise fallen, the design of God to raise man to an elevated spiritual order, was not thereby thwarted; but, that his purposes in that respect, might be accomplished, He mercifully, at sundry times, and in divers manners, promised a restoration and redemption through the agency of his Divine Son and Daughter, the mediators of his own choosing.

5. That this promise, which continued to be renewed for many successive ages, was couched and involved in prophetic language, in types and shadows; in allegories; in obscure sayings, and dark similitudes, which were not, could not be understood by mortals, until the *"times and seasons"* in which God would fulfill his promise, and accomplish his work of restoration. (See Hosea, xi. 10.) And these times and seasons, as well as the order and manner, in the accomplishment of his work, the *"Father reserved in his own power."* He suffered not man to have the knowledge of this: *"no, not the angels in heaven, neither the Son, but the Father only."* (See Acts i; Mat. xxvi. 36; Mark, xiii. 32.).

6. Fourth. That in the fulness of time, the Father sent into the world his beloved Son; the true representative of his character, the

"express image" and likeness of the Eternal Father, to redeem the fallen race; He was revealed in Jesus of Nazareth, who existed in *the form of a servant,* and was the *"body prepared for him,"* which was "made of woman," as the Apostle expresses it, and as has been clearly set forth. (Isa. lix. 20; Gal. iv. 4; Heb. ii. 16, 17.)

7. It was hence, in this line of life, that the Spirit like a dove descended upon him, (Jesus) with a voice and testimony *"This is my beloved Son, in whom I am well pleased."* This was the *Christ,* the *Anointing Spirit of the Holy One; the Son of the living God,* of whom the voice spake. Thus Jesus became the author of eternal salvation, the *"first begotten from the dead."* The *"beginning and first Father of the new heavens, and the new earth, wherein dwelleth righteousness."*

8. Fifth. That the Son revealed the character and will of his heavenly Father; and that, for the day and time being, *"he finished the work his Father gave him to do."* But there was still a far greater work for him to do in a future day. The time for the *"setting up of his kingdom"* on earth had not yet come; and he *must needs go away;* but at the time appointed of the Father, he would come; he would come in *"his own glory, and in the glory of his Father, and of the holy angels."* (Luke, ix. 26.)

9. That the time for his *"marriage"* should come, when the *"Bride* should have *made herself ready;"* and that, at his coming again, he would appear in union with his Bride. Until that time, his kingdom could not be "set up" and established on earth; nor could that happy period advance, when, *"Of the increase of his government and peace there shall be no end;"* (Isa. ix. 7); when *"nation shall not lift up sword against nation, neither shall they learn war any more"* (Micah, iv. 3.). Then, and not till then, should his kingdom appear.

10. Sixth. That it was not possible for the kingdom of Christ to be established on earth, and for him to appear in "power and great glory," as he promised, until the two Anointed ones; the Son and Daughter; the two first foundation pillars of that kingdom, should both be made manifest on earth, and the testimony of their witnesses established among men.

11. That the Son having been made manifest, and the testimony of his witnesses established, (but not so of the Daughter,) it was necessary, therefore, that the *"heavens must receive him, until the times of restitution of all things, which God hath spoken by the mouth of all his holy Prophets since the world began."* (Acts, iii. 20.)

12. The "times of restitution of all things" had not come. The

woman, that congenial and essential part of man's existence in the new creation, (as well as in the old,) had not yet been restored to her proper place and order. Therefore, the order of God in the work of man's redemption, and the *restitution of all things*, was not, and could not be completed in the day of Christ's first appearing.

13. It was for this very reason, that he had to come, and promised to come, the "second time." And it was from this very cause, and the long distance of time between the two advents, or Christ's first and second coming, that the adversary (Satan) took the advantage and *"scattered the power of the holy people;"* and the sanctuary of the saints became "trodden under foot" for the space of "forty and two months," or at least 1260 years. (See Daniel.)

14. The true Church of Christ, and its saving power, was supplanted; a false Church, (and finally innumerable false Churches,) false doctrines, and corrupt power and dominion, under the *Christian name*, were established on its ruins, and prevailed, even until the time when the promise drew near, for "Christ's second coming," and the "cleansing of the sanctuary."

15. Seventh. To accomplish the order of the new creation, and the order of man's redemption in both the male and female line, when the fulness of time had come, according to promise, God, the Eternal Father and Mother, sent forth into the world their beloved Daughter in the chosen *one prepared*, who descended, not from the princes and nobles of the earth; but she appeared in the *"form of a handmaid."*

16. Who, being the *"chosen vessel"* of God's will, became subject to the death of a carnal nature by the cross, through obedience and sufferings, and was invested with the power of God, and "excellent majesty from on High;" and was *"clothed in the glory and brightness of her Lord and Redeemer, and with the garments of salvation. Hence she was the second Heir, in the covenant of promise of eternal life;"* and having received the "Anointing of the Holy One," she was the true representative of the Daughter, the Mother Spirit in Christ, the *"express image and likeness of her Eternal Mother;"* and by the same anointing, the Christ, abiding in her, she became the *first Mother of the children of the regeneration.* Of this Parentage, the *"whole family and household of God, in heaven and on earth, is named."* (See Eph. iii. 15.)

17. As the testimony of Christ's first appearing, in and with the Son of man, was confirmed by many witnesses, in all of whom we believe, with unwavering faith and confidence, even so it is now. The testimony of Christ's second appearing *in and with the Daughter*, is also

confirmed by many living witnesses; by thousands who, through her ministration and Spirit, (derived from the Son) have received the power of salvation from all sin, and daily partake of the bread and waters of eternal life. These are they, *who follow Jesus Christ in the regeneration;* and that have "forsaken all for Christ, and the kingdom of heaven's sake." *"By their fruits ye shall know them."*

18. And finally, after the Son and Daughter, the Two Anointing Ones, the first and Divine Parents of our redemption, had both, in their appointed times, been revealed on earth, in the form of those whom they came to redeem, and after they had finished the work on earth which the Eternal Parents had given them to do, they then left, with their first born Son and Daughter and their cross-bearing children, their united spirit and counsel for building Zion.

19. And when, by the power of their united testimony and example, they had laid the foundation for the "second (spiritual) temple," conjointly with the first, and the *"Desire of all nations"* had come; then, and never till then, could the Church, the beloved city, New Jerusalem, begin to appear as *"coming down from God out of heaven, prepared as a bride adorned for her husband."* (Rev. xxi. 2.)

20. All these things have come to pass in their proper times and seasons as predicted by the Prophets. The *evidences* of this fact, of its truth and reality, are before the world. *"And the Light shineth in darkness, and the darkness comprehendeth it not."* The Divine Son and Daughter, through these two Anointed Ones of the Most High, have appeared, and have been made manifest on earth. Not in earthly pomp and splendor, according to the lofty and vain imagination of "blind guides," did, or was Christ to appear, either at his first or second coming; but in low humility and sorrow of soul did he come, both the first and second time; in the male, and in the female. (See Isa. liii. 1, 3, & liv. 6.)

21. These, the two Anointed ones of God's own choosing and appointment, have borne their testimony, and left the example of forsaking all for the kingdom of heaven's sake; of confessing and forsaking every sin, and every sinful thing; of living a pure and holy life of self-denial, and bearing a daily cross against all the allurements, temptations, and propensities of an evil and corrupt nature; of renouncing the world, and *crucifying the flesh with all its affections and lusts,* which is crucifixion and death to all the elements and rudiments of the fleshy, sensual and sinful nature of fallen man.

22. And thus, by the united spirit and testimony of the two

Anointed ones, they have broken asunder the bands of death, and brought *"life and immortality to light."* To the *"willing and obedient,"* both man and woman, they have brought salvation and deliverance from the bondage of sin and corruption.

23. They have, moreover, visited their children, their true and faithful crossbearing followers, with their spiritual presence, and bestowed upon them of the rich treasures of the invisible world, and endowed them with the power and gifts of God from on high. They have established the *Zion of God's likeness* upon earth, the *beloved city,* the *Heavenly Jerusalem,* wherein no unclean thing can enter and abide. And they have adorned Zion with the elements of order and beauty, harmony and love. Hence her walls are *salvation;* and virtue and truth, righteousness and peace, *reign* within her borders. And this *beloved city* can never be overcome. (See Rev. xx. 7–10.)

24. These are the *"marvellous works"* of the Lord our God, which he promised to perform in the latter days. And thus, beyond all doubt, will God, in his own due time, fulfill his word, and accomplish all his purposes, and his work, with all the nations and inhabitants of the earth.

25. Although the day has actually come, that shall *"burn as an oven,"* and the judgments of God are rolling on the earth with increasing calamity, while *devouring fires,* and *destroying floods,* while *earthquakes,* and *hail,* and *wars,* and *famine,* and *pestilence,* are stalking through the earth, to punish the world for its iniquities. (See Luke, xix. 41–44.) And also while the proclaiming angels of God, through marvellous signs, and wonderful providential and spiritual operations, which are more and more increasing in the age and day in which we live, are loudly calling, and solemnly warning the inhabitants of the earth that God is drawing near to visit the world by "pouring out his Spirit," in mercy as well as judgment. (See Rev. xviii. 1–4; xix. 17–21. [Note. The conjunctive voices, powers, and influences of these two angels, are evidently the supernatural agencies which cause the extraordinary phenomena of this age and time, and which, in their strange manifestations, have confounded all the natural wisdom of man.]) Still the children of man do not know the day of their visitation.

26. Yet, to them that *"fear his name, shall the Sun of righteousness arise with healing in his wings."* (Mal. iv. 2; See Mat. v. 6.) They that *"Hunger and thirst after righteousness shall be filled."* (Heb. ix. 28; Hab. ii. 14; Isa. ix. 9.) They that, in true humility and sincerity of heart, desire

and look for Christ's second coming, to them will he appear the "second time," to their *joy and salvation;* and the *"knowledge of the Lord and his glory shall yet fill the earth as the waters cover the sea."* Amen.

(Benjamin Youngs, *Testimony*, pp. 533–537) [1808/1810/1823/1856]

* * *

12

Messiahs. *Hamilton DeGraw*

. . .

The question will be propounded, who was Ann Lee? She was the founder of the order of Shaker Communities that have flourished for the last century in the United States. But the founding of a sect is a small matter when compared with the far reaching results of her complete mission.

At the time of the great tidal wave of spiritual baptism that visited our Societies prior to the advent of modern Spiritualism, she said through one of the inspired media that her mission would directly be closed and cease with her people and that she would go where she was not known or wanted.

In all ages the higher revelations have first come to illuminated souls that far in advance of the body stand as an advance guard, and many times a forlorn hope, "who take into their breasts the sheaf of hostile spears and break a path for the oppressed." Such constitute the Messiah of their time and race, and such was Ann Lee.

Her testimony so little understood one hundred years ago by only a chosen few of her direct followers, now through the evolution of soul is being accepted in its fullness or in part (according to development) by more than the organized body of her immediate followers.

As the on-rolling ages unfold to human perception higher and more exalted thought, enrolled among the illustrious and illuminated saviors of the race, Ann Lee will hold the position of Mother in the new dispensation already dawning for the redemption of the race.

(*The Manifesto* XXII, 4, pp. 77–78) [1892]

13

Conservatism Vs. Progress. *F. W. Evans*

. . .

Our Spiritual Order parallels that [i.e., the new idea of republican-ism]. A true Christ Church was the idea thrown out to all Christen-dom—all things new—new theology—new temporal arrangement—new sexual relations—new order of human society.

To build up this *new* creation, material had to be taken from the *old*. That old material was divided into two parts—*Orthodox* and *Skep-tic*. The founders of the *first* cycle of our Order were from the ortho-dox class. They have had their day and their say—have done well. The founders of the *second* cycle will be from the ranks of the skeptics—Rationalists—the founders of the American Government. They will have their day and their say. Hope they will do as well.

In our first cycle, we have had celibate life, community of goods, and a few fragmentary new theologies, not yet fitted into much of a system—about as much of a Christ Church as the United States gov-ernment has been a Republic. . . .

. . .

In the first cycle, the question came up—"Can an infidel to old theologies—to anti-Christianity—become a good Shaker?" [i.e., con-verts *not* from the colonial churches]. . . . Or have they, by desecrating sacred words and things—professing the name of Christ, and living out the character of Antichrist—committed the unpardonable sin against the Holy Spirit of Truth? Having been *Idolators*—worshiping *Jesus* as *God,* are they not tempted to worship *Ann* as *Goddess?* Having, while yet Christians, lived in generative lusts, they now bring down the God of the universe, to this little unfinished planet, to engage in the work of generating a human being—Jesus (see Dunlavy)—thereby building up generation as a pure, holy spiritual work and institution, right in the Holy Temple of God in Christ's second appearing—Church. This too, in standard works which aims to hold forth celibacy—a resurrection as the pivotal idea of the new order of true Shakerism—an order which holds that in the Adamic condition, free from sin, Generation was only natural, earthly, animal.

As the Heavens are above the earth, so is Resurrection above Generation.

Can such Orthodox material ever be redeemed—saved? If so, there is hope in their latter end—and great hope for the infidels. . . .

THE SHAKERS

Let us have the new cycle, as fast as the present generation can bear the new truths that will be its foundation stones.

(*The Shaker Manifesto* XI, 6, pp. 125–126) [1881]

14

Condition of Society, and its only hope, in obeying the everlasting Gospel Part III.

. . .

Character of Christ's Second Appearing.

"God has ever manifested himself in the character He sustains at the time, and among those who witness (and are affected by) the manifestation. His resources are infinite, and hence he always appears in character. To Abraham, the venerable, quickminded, patriarchial shepherd, He appeared as a guest to enjoy his hospitality; but to the martial leader of Israel's invading host, He stood forth with sword in hand ready to bathe it in the blood of his foe. . . . God adopts means to the object He intends to effect. . . . So I conceive the assumption of "The body" the seed of Abraham, "that through death he might destroy death" and its author, the Devil. The great sacrifice, *"The offering of the body of Christ once for all,"* was a manifestation of God to man, totally different from that revealed concerning him when *"He shall come to be glorified in his saints,"* and to qualify them *"to judge the world."* Then He veiled his glory by the flesh of humanity. Now He will invest the humanity with the glory of His Divinity. His saints will be sons of God "declared with power" by the resurrection, or the change equivalent to it. *He,* He, He will appear, and do all that he has promised, only however, in the way that *is* promised, not as erring man has usually conceived. *"We shall see Him as He is"*—not as he was. He *was* a man of sorrows; appeared a child of the first Adam; but He is coming again to receive His people; we shall be like Him, for we shall see *Him as He is*—as He is, not as He was. The Lord himself shall descend not the man himself; or if you please, the Lord (Christ Jesus) himself, not the man (Christ Jesus) himself. He will appear as he is, and we shall see Him. Hallelujah! Now the *living soul* has Christ formed in him the hope of glory. He has been engrafted with Christ's word and Spirit; this is the germ, the earnest, the bud. Well, under the genial influence of God's grace it will come out in the second Advent a full blown rose. The process will be complete. The word of Christ, now in

237

Him, will expand, (by that working by which He is able to subdue all things to himself) into a full likeness to Christ! Jesus is "the Head of the body" of his church; yet we should remember that this head is not human, but Divine. I am reminded of Acts 1:9–11. It is a precious passage to be fulfilled in the second Advent, but we should not put "the veil, that is, his flesh" over it. The first man was of the earth, earthy. This earthy, this natural, which is first, is not to appear again; but the spiritual, the second Adam, who is *"the Lord from heaven,"* He will invest the redeemed with the glories of His Divinity, rather than allow them or their nature to vest it in humanity. Oh, how much more desirable that we should be elevated to the divine, rather than have the Son himself descend to the human again. Jude ver. 14: "The Lord cometh in ten thousand of His saints" &c. The veriest tyro in Biblical learning knows that the Greek preposition *en* means *in*. True, He will be *with them,* He must of course attend them in the judgment. . . .

. . . instead of bringing down the divine to human, I see God's plan is to raise that which is still human to the Divine. This makes my soul magnify the Son: then these things of glory magnify my enjoyments. Our Divine Savior was no more seen by Paul, in his manhood, I believe, than Moses or Joshua. . . .

With this view of the *character* of Christ in his Second Appearing, we feel ourselves safe with Paul, in knowing Christ after the flesh no more. "What think ye of Christ, whose son is He?" Was a question propounded by our Lord to the Pharisees: and *they* say David.'s. Let the reasoning of Christ upon the Pharisees' reply, be applied to those who give a similar reply by saying he is the son of Mary. If she in spirit called him Lord, (which they will not deny), how is he then *her* son? Still, we *admit* that there was a natural reason for calling the son of Mary, Christ; just as natural a reason as there is for calling a man's clothing, the man himself. . . . We admit that Christ was known by "the world", by the body which he took on Him, or with which he clothed himself: But that clothing was worn out—*"offered once for all,"* "profiteth nothing"—was not a body prepared for a second advent, but for *sacrifice;* and the pure in heart, who alone can see God—such as could see the Father who dwelt in the *man* Christ-Jesus, will be prepared to glorify Him *in his saints.*

Manner of Christ's Second Appearing.

. . . "He shall come to be glorified in his saints"—when "He shall gather together his elect from the four winds"—in "the dispensation of

238

the fulness of times," during which all things in Christ will be gathered together in one; both which are in heaven, and which are on earth, even *in him* (Eph. 1:10). In this collected body, Christ is to be seen with the same kind of an eye that can see God. Here his people are to be tried, and the chaff separated from the wheat. Here "every branch *in* me [Christ] that beareth not fruit he taketh away."

The order in which this perfecting work is carried forward, to make the saints like Christ's glorious body, is presented by Christ, under the various symbols of "the vine"—the "sheepfold"—the "mustard seed"—the "garner"—&c. It is described by Paul under the figure of a body, in I Cor. 12: where "all the members have the same care one of another". As our space is limited, we will dwell upon this figure, briefly to show the manner in which the body of Christ's Second Appearing developes itself.

Adam was a "figure of him that was to come," Rom. 5:14. He was placed at the head of the old creation, as Christ was head of the New. "The invisible things of him [God] from *the creation of the world* are clearly seen, being understood by the things that are made, even his eternal power and God-head." Rom. 1:20. This head of the original creation is the "God-head" because it was by Him placed at the head of that creation "from the foundation of the world," (not before). Keeping in your mind's eye the figure of the human body—look further at the development of the God-head of the old creation—that which is first— the natural body. Its head comes forth on this wise. "In the day that God created man, in the *likeness of God* made he him; *male* and *female* created he them; and blessed them and called THEIR NAME *Adam.* This was true when none but the man was seen or known at the head of that creation. The female had not yet appeared, though she was in the man, and constituted a part of him—so that he could not have been Adam without her. "He called *their* name Adam." But when the work of creation was in a proper state for the God-head to be further developed, or the Government of God established; the *woman* appeared in her proper place—an "help meet" for man—taken out of him, and thus the Generations of the first Adam began. Now we have a right boldly to reject a "Second Adam" unless he be a proper antitype of the first.

. . .

. . . God made the "last Adam" *male* and *female*, and called their name Christ. The elements of the New Creation were in disorder until the woman appeared—bearing the same cross, and living the same life

239

that the man did: —Opposed by the same spirit, persecuted and imprisoned for preaching and practising the same doctrines: She participated
in the same mental anguish and travail of soul, and shared the same
spiritual gifts. Such is the spirit developed in our Mother; and as proof
of its goodness, we have only to refer to the fruits of this parentage. . . .

The God-Head being thus developed, the work of the new creation commences. The first Adam's work was a work of generation:—
That of the Second Adam, a work of regeneration. The first Adam's
work was in the natural creation—that of the Second Adam, to create
them anew, —to bring them out of Adam into Christ—out of the world
into an order "not of the world."

. . . While the principle of the parentage [i.e., male–female] exists
in every part of both the animal and vegetable creation, why exclude it
from the Gospel work? Especially since it is by these "things that are
made," that the "Eternal power and God-head," were clearly to be
seen. While the body of Christ is constituted of males and females, (as
the "woman is not without the man, nor the man without the woman"
in the Lord,) so also the same necessity exists for male and female in
the Head, as in the Body.

(*The Day-Star* XII, 12, pp. 47–48) [1847]

15

Letter from Geo. A. Sterling (Sharon, Ct.)

. . .

Historical testimony establishes as a fact that the Lord, many
years ago, commenced a witness among the Shakers, that Jesus Christ
would manifest his second appearing in his body, the Church, and, that
this witness commenced in a female, for glorious reasons, best known
to God, which we shall all soon know, and adore, as the wisdom of the
great Omniscent. . . . By this witness a truth regarding *one feature* of
the manner of Christ's second appearing, was established beyond the
powers of hell. The other feature is, that after the translation of the
saints, He himself, personally will descend and appear. . . . To this
witness, as commenced by a female, was in due time, as we all know,
added some truths regarding a feature of the worship, and social
conditions of the wanderers come home to Zion: such as David's

dancing before the ark on its return—having all things in common—neither marrying nor giving in marriage.

. . .

Does the reader ask: why say, made His second appearing in her? Why not simply say: witnessed through her of his second appearing, to be manifested in His body? Why make her a *reality* as well as a witness? The answer depends upon what is meant by the second appearing of Christ in his children, and the full nature of the work the Lord wrought in her.

. . . Now whenever it shall please the Lord Jesus, or the Lord Jesus the anointed, to anoint his body, as the Father by the Holy Ghost anointed his manhood, then the Church will become anointed flesh, or Christ; for although the Father anointed Jesus by the Holy Ghost at His ascension the Holy Ghost was given unto Him to empower Him to anoint His body or church, Act. 23:33. Jesus being perfect God, and perfect man, two natures united forever in one person, of course it was not his divine nature that received this anointing, but His human nature *to qualify it for the Divine nature to act through*. The same anointing which his human nature received whilst on earth, our human nature may receive, and therefore qualify it to act the Christ—ever remembering that the everlasting distinction between Jesus Christ the head, and the body is in that in Jesus is combined both God and man; whereas the body is only anointed with the Holy Ghost. . . .

. . . The question is, did the Lord commence a manifesting work of this nature in her through whom the Believers testimony began? I am not acquainted with all the particulars of the work, but looking at it as a student of God's word, I affirm that there is nothing unscriptural, or incredible in it—nothing that conflicts with orthodox doctrine, but is in strict concordance with the truth that the Lord will establish his kingdom by His second appearing in his body.

I am sure I hazard nothing in affirming that the Lord began a great work in her years ago preparatory to the great day of judgment for the Believers, give a testimony to this so peculiar, so self-denying, and true that it could come alone from Him. . . . [Ann Lee and the Believers] were not only anointed with the Holy Ghost and power, and performed a work of *subjection*, corresponding with the manner in part in which Jesus began his work, and was also an expression of the work now to be done by the full body of Christ. If it *was* done; it was not a mere show but a *reality*, and Christ accordingly made His second appearing manifested in them. . . . this anointing of Jesus fell on her, making her simply a woman anointed whereas Jesus Christ is the Godman anointed.

It therefore conflicts not with the doctrine of the Eternal incarnation of the Word ever acting as the Son of man; but witnessess only unto that degree of anointing of flesh, by which alone, according to the word of God, the kingdom of God can be established. True, errors of interpretation have been connected with this mystery, but this does not overthrow the witness itself—its foundation standeth sure. It is claimed that if this witness is of the Lord, its interpretation, and all else taught in connexion with it, would be pure truth. Which objection amounts to this: that if God makes one a witness to a few truths, He is at the same time bound to keep them from all error; whereas, his word teaches, that to his compacted body, with a full perfecting ministry, does this alone belong. . . . Errors, then, so connected, [i.e., inferential &c.], furnish no evidence against the *main fact* witnessed unto. The mistakes of the Believer, so far as I have seen, are inferential ones, and just such as we all would have fallen into under like circumstances. The truth of Christ's second appearing in his people, given out by the Holy Ghost, unconnected with a full interpretation, its accordance with the analogy of faith not explained, was calculated to make a tremendous overthrow of what is called orthodox doctrine. Instead therefore of astonishment and censure upon their condition, I would adore that grace of God which has enabled them to hold firmly, but in great weakness unto the end, that which they had received. In them is fulfilled, Rev. 3:8. . . .

. . . I repeat, the witness of Christ coming in the clouds of heaven, and the witness that now He will manifest this second appearing in his body the Church, are concurring and inseparable testimonies; and that there remains no *Scriptural reasons* why all who went forth to meet the Bridegroom should not be united instantly in the unity of the spirit and the bonds of peace.

In conclusion, permit me to say one word to the Believers. You will ere this have perceived the order of God's blessing to his householders—that it is from without. . . .

[Editor's note: ". . . We do not endorse the doctrine of Bro. Sterling, nor shall we make one attempt to contravert them; for he is passing very rapidly in a "straight way," where any errors he may have, will be wrested from him sooner, and far more effectually that we could do it. . . . It will rejoice our hearts when we see Bro. George in the midst of those Glories which he anticipates for the "organized body of Christ."]

(The Day-Star XII, 13, pp. 54 col. 3, 55, 56 col. 2) [1847]

16

[Open Letter of] Robert Thomson to Thomas Kimpton.

. . .

... But we must be born again, and born of the same spirit of which he was born—anointed with the same holy anointing with which he was anointed—born not of the will of the flesh, nor of the will of man, but of God. That holy *birth, baptism* or *anointing* comes by holy obedience and in no other way. It consists not in new impules of feeling, neither does it consist in a change of perceptions, notions or theories; for if it consisted in either of these we would be conscious of having experienced the new birth many a time. But we are convinced it is a gradual and progressive work, and, as Jesus was "the way, the truth, and the life," his way, during his life on earth, was the way of the cross against the fleshly, animal, or natural mind. It is a way that requires a sacrifice of all that the natural man holds dear to him. It is a narrow way, and the straight gate of forsaking all leads into it. . . .

. . .

Your great objection to participating in that united interest of the "Shakers," you say, is that "They believe that Ann Lee in person was Christ in the Second Advent, and they worship her as such." With regard to their worshipping Ann Lee, or a "dead woman," as you say, you greatly err, for it is not a fact; and with regard to their believing that Ann Lee *in person* was Christ, is also a mistake. As far as I understand, they do not consider that the *person* or flesh of anyone profits anything at all. They with the Apostle "Know Christ no more after the flesh." (2 Cor. 5:17). But as the Apostle again says, that the life of Jesus should be made manifest in our mortal flesh, (2 Cor. 4:10, 11), they believe, that it was thus manifested in her person, and that she was *anointed*, or *Christed*, with the same spirit that he was, for there is but one spirit. (Eph. 4:4, 5). And is it such a shocking thing in your imagination that to hold that the anointing spirit made its appearance in such a humble person, and a female, is enough for you to keep separate from a people whom you can know by their fruits to have "An unction from the Holy One," who are his little ones, that "keep the unity of the spirit in the bond of peace?" If they do not the works of God believe them not; but if they do, though ye believe not as they do, believe the works, that ye may know and believe that the Father is in them, and they in him. But will you reject them, because they call Ann Lee *mother?* You do not see any propriety in this, and neither do I, satisfactorily; but as I know that some of them who do call her Mother, in a spiritual sense, give evidence of further advancement in the work of God, than I feel to have done, I am willing to bear with them in that which I either in weakeness or strength, can not approve of. They do not reject me on this ground, and why should I, a mere child in the work, feel competent to lead them who have more completely subdued the carnal mind? For remember that it is goodness that brings heavenly wisdom, and not mental acumen. I believe that Ann Lee had, in an eminent degree, the spirit of Christ, but I can not call her Mother until I find out that she, or her spirit, and that something different from the Lord's spirit, had any thing to do in begetting me into a spiritual life. But as I presume to be only travailing into that life, it will not be strange, if I make some mistake concerning my parentage. Again, as she began this life of continence, purity, and order for the second time, after its first introduction in Jerusalem, it may be plausible to call her mother on that account, but to my mind it is no more than plausible. I would be willing to admit that she is an elder sister, in respect to that particular work; and, as I have never been taught in the Scriptures to call even Jesus more than elder brother, (Rom. 8:29; Heb. 2:11,) and God, or the Holy Spirit, Father, I can not accede to the appelation of Mother. But these or any other doctrinal views differing from mine, as long as they do not clash with the order of Christ, and steadfastness of the faith, I am bound to make a matter of forbearance. Without forbearance in such things, no people can ever exist in the "Unity of the Spirit, in the bond of peace." We design to make nothing a stumbling stone, or rock of offence, that does not conflict with the evident teachings of the Spirit; and so long as these people give evidence of its predominating influence, we feel satisfied that they are the body of Christ.

(*The Day-Star* XII, 13, p. 54. May 5, 1847)

* * *

THE SHAKERS

17

[Untitled]. *Abraham Perkins.*

... the adversary has cunningly established the Son of God in the God-head, as a part of Deity, too exalted in life and character to be imitated or followed; ...

(*The Shaker Manifesto* XIII, 5, p. 100) [1883]

18

The Living Christ. *G. B. Avery*

The English word *"Christ"* appears to have been derived from the Greek word *"Christos"-anointed;* and this is a derivation from the word *"Chrio,"-*anoint. Whether Christians have properly or improperly applied this form to Jesus, it is thus used in their Scriptures. "Jesus" means *Saviour*, hence—Christ Jesus is made to mean *"Anointed Saviour."* Thus the Spirit of Christ would truly mean, the spirit of him who was anointed–Christ–Jesus. This anointing, received of the Father, by Jesus, made him "One with the Father;" and the same received by Christ's followers make them one with Jesus Christ, as he was one with the Father; thus constituting them Christs, with Jesus, who was the Living Christ.

In reply to the oft repeated question, "What is the Shaker Theology concerning Christ, and what do Shakers teach their children on this subject?" We answer: (1) Shaker Theology teaches that Jesus, abstractly considered, aside from his baptism, and when born of Mary, was not the Christ, nor Christ Jesus.

(2) He became Christ by a spiritual baptism of the Father, God, constituting him the heavenly *"Bridegroom."* This baptism caused Jesus to be born again, of the spirit of God; by this baptism he became "A creature" of the resurrection order; and *in this order*, "The first born of every creature;" "The first born among many brethren;" "The Elder Brother." In this capacity he was *The* Christ of his day, or Master. "One is your Master, even Christ, and all ye are brethren."

(3) We teach our children that Jesus, when born of Mary, was not possessed of the nature of angels; that "he took not on him the nature of angels, but the seed of Abraham, wherefore it became him—Jesus—

to be tempted in all points like unto his brethren" of the seed of Abraham, meaning children of this world.

(4) That Jesus, in order to become Christ, had to be born again of the spirit of his Heavenly Father—into a spiritual Resurrection Order—a "New Creation"—thus making Jesus "a New Creature," "a quickening Spirit," "The Lord from Heaven", "The Second Adam." He was now constituted Christ Jesus (i.e.) the anointed Jesus. This anointing, Jesus being true to his mission, he has never lost; hence he is still the "Christ Jesus"—the "Anointed Saviour."

(5) That Jesus, and all his faithful followers who crucify and overcome the world—the generative worldly life in themselves, as Jesus set the example, and thus become harvested from the world, as Jesus was—become eunuchs, spiritually, for the "Kingdom of Heaven's sake," constitute the Christ Order now manifested on the earth, and to all the souls of men, both in this and in the spirit world, and yet, that this Order was not completed in the dispensation of Christ's *first* appearing.

(6) Christ Jesus, and his faithful followers, constituting the true Christ Order, were for ages lost from the earth; but Jesus and his true disciples maintained it in the spirit world, and constituted still the one true body of the Christ.

(7) The John Baptist unction, or forerunning spirit began to be manifested on earth the second time, in the latter part of the seventeenth century, in Vivarais, France, extended into England in the early part of the eighteenth century, and, about the middle of this century the revival of the manifestation of the Christ Spirit, an unction from the Motherhood of God, began to be poured out upon a little band of united souls in England, headed, for a time, by James and Jane Wardley. Of this unction, Ann Lee at length became baptized, and eventually received the acknowledged, leading gift, as the "Elder Sister of many Sisters in the Christ Order,"—as Jesus became the "Elder Brother" of many brethren. Thus she became the anointed Bride, for which Jesus, the anointed Bridegroom, waited. And spoken in its collective or united capacity,—Jesus Christ and his *true* Church, and Ann Lee, and her *true* church—constitute the manifest Christ Body, being "one" in spirit as Bridegroom and Bride. Thus it is that the Apostle John saw the church *as* the Bride of Christ, which should be manifested in the dispensation of Christ's Second Appearing; his first Christian Church revealing the Fatherhood of God, the second the Motherhood of God. This church is Christ now made manifest on earth; the true followers

246

of Christ Jesus are "one" with him as he is "one" with his Father. In like oneness is the Bridal Christ Church, united with the Mother in God.

(The Shaker Manifesto X, 1, pp. 2–3) [1880]

19

Jesus, the Son of Man—Jesus Christ, the Son of God, Christ the Lord from Heaven. *Giles B. Avery*

. . .

The reason why the Jews failed to believe of Jesus as *becoming* the Messias, the Christ the Son of God, was because they knew the parents of Jesus; but they looked for their Redeemer to be born of God; and they understood not the second birth. . . .

. . .

. . . Jesus . . . went to John to be baptized of him in order to prepare him for the higher baptism of The Holy Ghost and fire of Divine life and inspiration. It thus became Jesus to "fulfill all righteousness," which required that God's work should be performed in order, each step of the soul's progress in grace in its proper place; first, John's baptism into confession, repentance and remission of sins; this Jesus received of John.

After this baptism, the Holy Ghost, the Christ, in visible form, like a dove, descended upon Jesus, his soul having been prepared by John's baptism, and he now became born of the Spirit of God; a Son of God—he was now JESUS CHRIST.

But . . . by this baptism he was not *sufficiently* a "Son of God" without being born again; spiritually regenerated, in order to become a "Son of God" after the Spirit; . . .

. . .

But, the baptized Jesus is now become *Jesus Christ,* or "The Christ of God"—the viceregent of God on earth, or Emanuel "God with us;" God manifest in the flesh. But his younger brethren have also become viceregents of God on earth, and God through these also was, and still is, manifest in the flesh. . . .

. . .

Thus, to portray, in one view, all these special characters, we have synonymously:

First. Jesus—Son of Man; of the seed of Abraham—flesh and

247

blood; who *could* sin, if he would; having a sinful nature; who said: "Why callest thou me good?" Offspring of David, who had to be born again—became

Second. Jesus *Christ*—the baptized Jesus—the Son of God—became a quickening spirit; of the seed of God—who could not sin— (being *redeemed* from sinful nature); *one with* the "Root of David; Born of God—the first begotten from the dead—the "first born of many brethren;" sent of God—anointed—Saviour of the world!

Third. Christ: The Pre–eminent and original Son of God; The Quickening Spirit; *The* Root of David; Baptizer of Jesus; who made the worlds (of the New Creation); and the (New) Heavens are the works of his hands.

(The Shaker II, 2, pp. 9–10) [1872]

20

What is the Matter? *G. B. Avery*
[Points of Shaker Doctrine]

5. That the first appearing of Christ was through the male sex of humanity—this constituted the Heavenly Bridegroom—"He that hath the Bride." The souls, however few or many, who were obedient to Christ, manifested through the male line, constituted the Bridegroom, Church of Christ, "He that hath the Bride, is the Bridegroom." John iii, 29. This is not man, not the man Jesus, abstractly, but Christ. 6. A bridegroom, must, necessarily, have a bride. The heavenly Christ Bride is the manifestation of Christ, the "Second Time, in his Glory"—that is, the female sex of humanity. And, those souls, however few or many, who are obedient to the same Christ Spirit, manifested in, and through the female line, constitute the Bride Church of Christ—Jerusalem which is above, —which is the Mother of us all,". . .

(The Shaker Manifesto XII, 6, pp. 125–126) [1882]

21

What is Infidelity and Who Are Infidels. *G. B. Avery*

. . . All truth is, in its nature, adapted to progress. All genuine revelations from God to man are comformable to this law.

THE SHAKERS

. . .

. . . As used in theology, *fidelity* means faithfulness to the testimonies of a Creed of religious faith. Hence *in*fidelity is *un*faithfulness to such testimonies.

Thus, since we have opposition of religious Creeds in what is *called* Christendom, *in this sense*, we might have *Christian Infidels*, as well as heathen infidels. . . .

. . .

. . . so is God unknown *to*, and incomprehensible *by* man, except by revelation; and the God, or the character of God, revealed to the human family of one era of the world's history is widely different from that revealed in a subsequent age. And, further, the God revealed to one nation, or class of human benngs, differs widely from the God revealed to another class of human beings in the *same* era of the world's history.

Thus, one class of believers in God are *infidel* to another class of believers in God! But, this infidelity is easily seen to be simply *relative* infidelity; that is, the creed of one class of believers in God is *Infidel* to the creed of another class. . . .

The lowest, most primitive idea of God . . . symbolical representations of gods, their idols, are in human form, because this form exists intuitively in the human mind as the highest manifestation of God's creative power.

. . .

[Thence, an apologetic for the "Duality" Doctrine]

The Church of Christ, then, being constituted of a heavenly family of Brethren and Sisters, living in the innocent and dependent capacity of the *Children of God* (not of husbands and wives), in a *pure*, celibate, angelic state, as live the Angels of Heaven, and governed, in an immediate capacity, by the *Heavenly Father* and *Mother, God*, but in a *Mediate Capacity*, by the Older (Elder) Brethren and Sisters of the family, and *practicing* the life–teachings and examples of Jesus Christ, *is* the *Christian Church!* And, thus to live, is *fidelity* to the Church, *"par excellence!"*

Then, may not Infidelity to the Church consist: First, in ignoring the *Father and Mother, God*, as the leading authority of the Christian Church, and substituting a Triune God, of three males, Father, Son, and Holy Ghost, all equal in age—that is the *Son* as old as his *Father*, and older than his Mother (Mary), yet, having two Mothers, the Holy Ghost Mother being the same age as her Son? And secondly, as

249

Mediatorial authority to lead this Church, substituting Popes and Cardinals, all of the male sex, as infallible viceregents of this Trinitarian, Masculine God. And thirdly, for the Church laity, instead of simple Brethren and Sisters, of *grace,* and of the *regeneration* . . . substituting *husbands* and *wives*—*men* and *women* living in *natural* generation—. . . .

(*The Shaker*, I, 4, pp. 27–28) [1871]

*　　*　　*

22

Pre-Existence of Christ. *F. W. Evans*

[The following reasonings, by our revered Elder Evans, are ideas peculiar to him, and with all the truths they may contain, are not yet the accepted ideas of the leading authorities of Shakerdom. It may be that we have not yet sufficiently progressed to make their adoption orthodox, but at present, but little is known among us of a Christ sphere or heavens; nor of the pre–existence of Christ; nor whether there are three, seven or eleven heavens; nor of tutelary divinities for this or other worlds. We therefore present the Elder's opinions that any who choose to adopt them may do so, while we are still content to find a sufficiency of theological food in the simplicity of Jesus' life and testimony.] Ed.

Some object that this is a gnostic idea. Taking Webster's definition of Gnostic, I do not see why it may not be a true idea. "All natures, intellectual, intelligible, and material, are derived, by successive emanations, from the infinite fountain of Deity; these successive emanations are termed eons." Is it not so? All agree that God is the Creator. This merely aims to explain the mode of creation. If Jesus was born a natural man—a Jew, and when between thirty and forty years of age, became a Christian, is it not quite as proper to say Jesus *was* the Christ, as to say Jesus *is* the Christ[?].

Was not Jesus the first Christian man, and Ann Lee the first Christian woman? Were they not both baptized with pre–existing Christ Spirit? Does not that idea leave other nations beside the Jews as Christian, and other races as recipient of the Christ Spirit? And further, could not a pre–existing Christ Spirit be a Saviour—a resurrection power—to the intelligent inhabitants of other globes? If Christ be not pre-existent, whence came the spirit in the form of a dove that lit upon Jesus, and who, and what was that dove, if not "a foreign spirit?"... God is Spirit, a Supreme Being, existing in the God element,.... And yet we say God is omnipresent, omniscient and all good; that all things are in God; and God rules and governs, by His agents and officials, in all creation. The affairs of a race—a nation—a society—an individual—a sparrow—of this and all inhabited globes, are directed by the spirit of Deity, through rulers of his selection and appointment. One is Ruler—a tutelary Deity—of a race. Another of a globe, with their subordinates, powers and principalities—Gods many and Lords many. Jackson says: "God is the great Father (and Mother) spirit of all spirits—the great type of whom all other spirits are but indications and corresponding organizations—the Creator, Sustainer— Father and Mother of all." Kiddle says: "Man must, from his spirit and from his heart, or the depths of his spiritual being, go to God in prayer, or the holy angels, who do the will of God, cannot visit him and assist him. He prays to God because it is only by God's will he can be aided, and then the aid comes from God, through His ministering spirits who bring it—Thus His attributes are described as personal—Love, Mercy, Wisdom, heedfulness to prayer." All these imply personality, either of primary or secondary beings.

If God be dual—Father and Mother—the first emanation, we will suppose to be a materialization of the spirit world, or sphere, by some termed the Christ sphere, or Heaven. Its inhabitants may be as Gods and Goddesses, who are sent as ministering spirits. By them worlds are made—visible and invisible.

We will then assume this sphere to be the fountain of inspiration to the Prophetic or Resurrection order of men and women, in all worlds, who speak as they are moved upon by holy, Christ Spirits.

When we admit that there is a third heaven, reached unto by Paul and Swedenborg, we admit gradations from earth to Deity; and if there be higher and lower orders of being, there must be one nearest to Deity, and that one would be but a Mediatorial Order to all others.

Is there any sphere beneath the earth sphere, or above the Christ Heavens? Are we necessarily limited to the precise degree of knowledge that those from before us have attained unto in spiritual things? "The spirit searcheth all things, yea even the deep things of God." If Paul had knowledge of *these*, why may not we have knowledge of seven heavens? If Jesus not only *was*, but *is* the Christ, except Jesus be in us, then are we reprobates, which is an awkward saying that we would avoid using.

(*The Shaker Manifesto* X, 1, pp. 3–4) [1880]

23

Hampton Logic. *O.C. Hampton*

. . .

Where there is no circumference there can be no center; consequently this Divine influence is distributed wherever the visible or invisible machinery is found for its transmission in the whole concatenation of individualized intelligences throughout the universe. The direction of this power of the All Father and All Mother is forever toward higher and higher degrees of perfection in goodness and intelligence, from lower and more imperfect conditions. It may be asked: Do you not, by this argument, destroy the theory of a personal God outside of and independent of the universe of forms and forces? Answering the question indirectly, we think we furnish a "local habitation and a name" for the Father and Mother God, more consistent than any other theory can develop; and indeed any other theory or ascription of personality to God, will not bear the rigid scrutiny of logic or common sense for a moment; so at least it seems to the writer. The universe then is the house of our Father and Mother, and all progressive manifestations are the results of their influence and presence. This must be so, for if the universe of mind and matter is boundless and infinite, no God can be predicated as having a separate, personal existence outside of it, because there is *no outside*, and, consequently, *no room* for such existence.

. . .

Jesus being the most holy, as well as the most intelligent organizer of which we have any history, and Mother Ann Lee having organized her Church precisely after Jesus' model, and both being based upon the two eternal laws of the universe (above stated) [i.e., *common good:* greatest good to greatest number; *subsidiarity:* the less is blest of the better]. Therefore, it would seem to be proved that the foundation of the Church of Christ's second appearing is sure, steadfast, eternal, one upon which we may forever build in safety, passing on from grace to grace and from glory to glory forever, evolving from age to age higher degrees of intelligence, goodness and felicity during all the endless ages of the interminable future.

(*The Shaker* I, 11, p. 84–85) [1871]

24

God. *Oliver C. Hampton.*

. . .

. . . the twin principles of Love and Wisdom. These principles are the moving forces of the Universe, the primary essence of our Father and Mother God. These are intelligent, spiritual, sympathetic, emotional.

These are male and female. In a word these are God. But we do not know whether there is or is not a personal identity of these primary forces, distinct from the Universe of visible manifestations which they seem to control. Indeed in which they seem to live and move and have their being, —we do not care. However, our most satisfactory view is, that there seems to be an unending category of individualized intelligences extending endlessly and infinitely higher and lower, and all located along a line of everlasting evolution and progress to higher and higher conditions of perfection toward which they will forever and ever approach, but never reach.

We do not know and cannot conceive of any end of this that would be satisfactory to the reaching party and therefore do not believe there is any end. "God is all of this visible and invisible phenomena of Infinite love and wisdom, permeating all the realms of the Infinite Universe and moving it on in all directions, toward eternally higher and higher, holier and holier, happier and happier conditions. We mean the totality of this whole phenomena [*sic*] visible and invisible, finite and Infinite, past, present and to come is directly or indirectly, God. God is omnipresent, all present; Omnipotent, all potent or powerful, and Omniscient, all Intelligent."

Now we can conceive of the personality of such an Infinite, limitless being, in no other way only that all this vast Universe is His embodiment.

Is not this Universe the divine manifestation of Infinite Love and Infinite Wisdom and so the image of the Godhead bodily? This is a subject too deep and goes too far into the absolutely unknowable and incomprehensible for you kind reader or us to fathom. Still in the infinite concatenation of intelligences from the lowest scullion in creation to the highest Archangel, and yet there is no highest, we shall both be able to find friends and helpers innumerable, for as there is no end to the Heavens, we shall never be in want of myriads of friends and spiritual guides always ready and happy to lead, direct, help and comfort as under all trials, sorrows and temptations and to gradually locate us in realms of peace and rest.

(The Shaker Manifesto XIV, 9, pp. 193–194) [1884]

25

Duality in Godhead. *H. L. Eades*

... *God* is spoken of in two senses, the *infinite* and the *finite*, or subordinate sense....

.... It is admitted by us all that the attributes ascribed to Deity, some are considered masculine, some feminine; and hence comes the idea of father and mother of the universe. We admit the revelation of these attributes of The *Eternal Unity* by son and daughter; that is to say, *God as Father*, or the *fatherly character of God* was *revealed by the Son, Christ Jesus*, and *God* as *mother*, or the *motherly character of God* was *revealed by the daughter (Ann Lee).* Thus "God manifest in the flesh;" not of *man only*, but also of *woman, male* and *female*, constitute the *duality of God*, and dual only in this subordinate sense. Being equally manifest in and through finite human beings, who are dual, male and female. Thus the apparently conflicting ideas of unity and duality are reconciled.

(The Shaker I, 2, p. 15) [1871]

26

Duality of the Deity. "C. E. S." [C. E. Sears]

... Thus it is equally true whether we say that God is male and female, or that an infinite perfection of the male and female principles is God.

. . .

Here we find a consistent way to look through nature to nature's

THE SHAKERS

God. Can there be a more natural or consoling idea than to view God as our Heavenly Parentage, father and mother?

(*The Shaker* I, 1, p. 6) [1871]

27

The Omnipresence of Deity. *R. W. Pelham.*

. . . We may say we feel the power of God within us, but would be shocked to hear one say, "I feel God within me." It will do very well to say that no soul can be saved without the operation and indwelling of the spirit of God; we should be startled to hear one say he could not be saved without the indwelling of God in his soul. . . . wherever the power of God is felt or perceived, there is the God of Power, since it is as absurd to suppose the power of God without God, as to suppose God without power. Where the spirit of God is, there is God, for God is spirit; . . . Happy are they who heartily and habitually believe in this Omnipresence and infinite goodness of God, the Heavenly Father and Mother, and who are reconciled to everything which He permits; who see his footsteps in every thing without them, and feel Him "working within them to will and to do of his own good pleasure," being conscious that they are daily and faithful co-workers with him. By Father and Mother, I do not mean two distinct persons or beings in Deity, but that in the one Infinite Spirit or Divine Essence, there exists the attributes of Father and Mother, just as much the one as the other. But Father and Mother are the names of *relations*, not of *essences*, and belong to that class of things which logicians call accidents.

(*The Shaker*, I, 11, p. 86–87) [1871]

28

God, —Dual. *Anon.*

. . .

If we interpret the biblical account [Genesis creation of man—male and female—in the image of God] literally, as christian sects usually do, we must believe that man was an exact copy of God in miniature, in form and in structure; and if man is male and female,

God must be male and female. If, again, we give a spiritual construction thereto, making due allowance for the figurative language of the ancients, we must believe that great principles were involved instead of mere physical formation, and that man's anatomy represents the male and female principle in Deity.

We do not attempt the presumptuous folly of proving two *persons* in the God–head. This would be as absurd as to assert that there are three.[3] ... Our God does not compel us to believe inconsistencies of himself; nor does our religion consist of mystery. Common sense and the yearning of our souls for parents, teach us of a Heavenly Father and *Mother* too. ...

Do we believe in Jesus, the Son of God? Most certainly, and we also believe in Ann the Daughter of God. Why not have a daughter as well as a son? We believe He has many sons and daughters. ...

Throughout creation we find manifest the dual principle—in the mineral, vegetable and animal kingdoms. This triple Deity [i.e., Trinitarian] has no illustration in the world of ours. The idea originated in the abnormal brain of some visionary monk. The arguments adduced to sustain such a theory are fallacious and have no shadow of scriptural foundation even, save the occurrence a few times in the New Testament, of the words Holy Ghost, and which only means Holy Spirit. ...

(*The Shaker Manifesto* XII, 1, pp. 6–8) [1882]

29

Tria Juncto in Uno. *Oliver C. Hampton*

My intuitions lead me to recognize in the over-soul of the Universe, the two qualities of wisdom and love. I find that in finite man, these two qualities can, may and do act as it were separately. ... The absent quality in each case is merely lying dormant in the human soul and is not yet developed into normal activity.

.... Jesus Christ supposed man to be capable of absolute perfection, that is, infinite perfection, else why did he say, "Be ye therefore

---

3. Here as elsewhere Shakers are presuming the popular notion of Trinitarian "person" as "individual entity," not the meaning of *hypostasis* intended in the actual doctrine; Shakers reject what is also rejected in orthodoxy, i.e., that three male entities compose the Trinity. For a positive Shaker expression compatible with orthodox Trinitarianism, see the following "Tria Juncto in Uno" of Elder Oliver Hampton.

perfect, even as your Father in heaven is perfect." Our Father in heaven—the Over-soul of the visible universe—The Divine Intelligence or whatever one may call it, differs from our humanity on the lower plane in this way, viz., That the Infinite Father possesses in exact equality, the energies of wisdom and love and from these, a third active attribute, a perfect union thereof ensues. Here is a trinity of aspects or conditions not possible to be experienced on the lower plane of humanity with its abnormal, unequal and imperfect conditions. This Trinity in Unity is what constitutes the difference between the rudimental plane of existence and the grand and glorious Christ plane....

(*The Manifesto* XXIV, 3, pp. 56–57) [1894]

five

GIFTS AND ORDERS

Introduction

In the Shaker vision everything is gift—not just those realities of our lives which arrest our attention, but all the literally countless realities from the smallest to the greatest. Ultimately we realize all is the Gift of the all–giving God Who is Love.

To receive a gift is to acknowledge *need*, the need the gift fills. It is here that the paradox of pride and humility is centered. For Shakers, to be humble is not to be humiliated or lessened. On the contrary, by realizing what we lack we can then reach out for the gift we need and thereby be enriched. One of the common symbols for this true humility and its fulfillment is the image of *coming down into the valley from the heights*. The mountain top of prideful self-exaltation is barren and windswept; the valley to which we descend when we see ourselves rightly is blessed with well-watered soil to bring forth fruit in abundance. It is the farmer's image of bottom land, rich and fertile.[1]

For Believers the ultimate Gift is God–in–Christ giving Himself to us all so that we can become anointed with the Divine Nature and so live the Christlife. It is a gift to fill our need, felt in our urge to transcend the limits of natural existence and death. To accept the gift

---

1. See Elder Joseph Brackett's *Simple Gifts* (25): "the gift to come down where we ought to be . . . in the valley of love and delight."

258

is to acknowledge we are not absolute in ourselves—in a Shaker phrase, to dethrone ourselves as our own lead, and accept the Divine Lead. Taking the Christ Gift means an active embrace of a new kind of life: to rise out of mortal life and into the Resurrection. This involves the essential Christian commitment to *metanoia* expressed in the mystery of the Cross: dying to (the false sense of) self and rising into unity with the Eternal Christ, thus becoming a single new kind of human being.[2] Shakers speak of this as *crossing one's nature*, taking up the cross against that life which leads only to death, and following Christ into the regeneration of Eternal Life. (And it is here that they see the essential link between the ultimate Christ Gift and the gift of celibacy as the actual process of *metanoia* in regeneration.)

The experience of this transforming gift of Christlife and of all the many related gifts which day by day made the living of it possible led Believers to examine closely the meaning and functioning of gifts generally. Their experience brought them to realize the full impact of Paul's reflections on gifts as stated in the principle: *All these are the working of one and the same Spirit, who distributes different gifts to different people just as she chooses* (1 Cor. 12:11). Gifts are given to and received by *individual persons*, not groups or communities. The difference in gifts is fitted to the difference appropriate to each person as a distinct individual. Hence the gifts which one receives cannot be received by another, and so one cannot give them away to another. The *gifted person* can *share the effects* of the individualized gifts with others. And in this community-of-persons all are enriched by each gifted person sharing life with all the others. There is no gift or charism of a community; rather, many gather together to share in their very different gifts, each having received in a distinct manner the ultimate Self-gift of God in Christlife. Consequently, Shaker senses of community, whether as the gathered communitarian Societies or as the less tangible communion in the Christ Spirit, always accentuate the uniqueness of each person; persons are not reduced to a collectivity.

We can see this illustrated in the stated communitarian principle: From each according to ability to each according to capacity. Each is to be fulfilled distinctively in terms of what range of gifts *can be received*. (This is in radical contrast to the Marxist "to each according to *need*," which is a fulfillment on the basis of *utility* since the individual is

---

2. "... until we have become the perfect human being, fully mature with the Fullness of Christ Himself" (Eph. 4:13).

thought of as having identity only as a part of the collectivity and not as a person.) Again in Pauline terms, Believers realize that in bringing together all their different gifts they are building up the One Body of Christ—themselves—growing in all ways into Christ, growing as persons loving/giving to one another (Eph. 4:12, 15, 16).

Recognizing one's needs and realizing there are gifts through the Spirit to fill them creates the expectation of religious wealth, instead of religious poverty. Living in response to gift means enrichment, especially in the sharing whereby the lack one has experienced is supplied from the abundance of another. But since all gifts are meaningful only in the light of the Gift of Christlife, this wealth in gifts is not to lead to a selfish building up of treasure, but to the power to give to fulfill others. This is simply the logic of *metanoia*: becoming as God is, Fullness Itself, needing nothing, and thus able to fill the needs of others. It is the meaning of Divine Power: *the power to give*. And so we find Mother Ann and all after her exhorting Believers to build up a treasure so that they would have something to share with others, something ready when someone in need came, an inheritance for generations still to come. The ultimate wealth, of course, is the Christlife which can be given by sharing. But this cannot be done except in the context of sharing all the gifts of life. Hence all the life of gift and sharing is unified in its limitless diversity rooted in the uniqueness of persons.

Earlier Believers sought ways to conceive of this unity and diversity which would avoid the two dangers either of falsely hierarchizing the gifts or of atomizing the community into merely ideosyncratic individuals. Mother Ann established the dynamics for a unified perception in drawing attention to the difference between a *leading gift* and the many *witnessing gifts* of life. (This was especially important in worship: one central theme or insight or reality would *lead* all the worshipers into a sense of communion together at that particular moment, and from among the many gifts they possessed they could bring a gift to share which *witnessed* appropriately to this one communal moment.)

Ultimately it was Mother Lucy Wright who resolved the issue with the principle: *the Union is the Gift*. Union identified the personal reality of the giving-receiving-sharing: God giving Himself in Christ to everyone, each responding and growing into all God is, and so all becoming One in the One Who fills all with the All. The Union is both God One–with–us and all of us One-in-Christ. Thus, *the Union is the*

THE SHAKERS

Gift speaks simultaneously to the Divine Self-gift of Christlife and to the countless moment-to-moment gifts which make the actual living of the Christlife possible. Ultimately there is only One Gift, which has countless personal manifestations.

As with all of life, the insoluble dilemma of good–and–evil is to be found in the universality of gifts: if everything is a gift in the Spirit, how is it that things come into life which should not be, things which are destructive, which actually oppose life in the Spirit? While not being able to solve the dilemma, Shakers identified it in their life–by–gift: there are both *forwards gifts* and *backwards gifts*. All gifts should come into our lives the right way, but some are twisted, perverted from their proper purpose. Having identified a gift as *backwards*, we then seek to turn it around or, if that is not possible, to find a way to make good the damage. Once again, this discernment points back to the commitment to *metanoia*, the dedication to change *whatever should not be* in life so that people can become all they can be.

While not wishing to fall into the triumphalistic superiority feelings of the Pauline Corinthians in their pride over having "better" gifts, experience quickly taught Believers that not all gifts were of equal value. But this was not because some *thing* was more valuable than some other. Since the differences in things as gifts reflected proper differences among persons, such a distinction would effectually proclaim that some persons were more valuable than others. Rather, the differing values among gifts relates to the character of life as a process, a *travel* in growth toward greater and greater maturity and finally toward the realization of the full maturity of Christlife. Therefore Shakers speak of the superiority in gifts as *come–up–higher gifts*. Any gift which calls the recipient to a higher development of life, to more maturity, is superior for that reason at that moment. Living and its gifts are to be seen in a continuum from immaturity to maturity, from promise to fulfillment. A gift is "greater" insofar as it manifests *progression*, and not abstractly but as practically realizable at that point in life.

Experience also taught Believers that come-up-higher gifts were typically *simple gifts* as well. Perhaps the most impressive characteristic of Shaker life-values has been *simplicity*. Believers use the word often as the epitome of spirituality. It embraces authenticity, unadorned practicality, honesty, service—the insistence that every one and every thing should be no more nor less than it is, and it should appear as such. Mother Ann had put it: Be what you seem to be, and seem to be what you really are. We associate simplicity most readily with styles of Shaker architecture, furniture, and other tangible gifts. Simplicity in design means the object must be functional, properly serving the human need which calls for it. Simplicity also means avoidance of useless ornamentation; let the design, the materials, and the function all "show" and become the cause of aesthetic pleasure.

Simplicity is even more important in persons than in things. Believers see their development away from early enthusiastic gifts (such as the physical whirling, shaking, and dancing, the noise of strange tongues and ecstatic inspirational messages) as a progression into simpler gifts of inner peace, the in-depth perception of the total Christ shared together, the "filled silence" of Divine Presence. To have become more simple could almost be measured: to be less needing of things, including "spiritual things," while growing into depth. The gift to be simple is a gift to come up higher.

Growth in insight of living by the gifts of God includes the recognition of what Believers refer to as the *orders of God*. As implied in the notion of come-up-higher gifts, gifts are not received as isolated items but integrated into the whole personal life and shared in a whole community of personal lives. Therefore gifts come into orders (arrangements, structures, patterns) or have to be made into orders. Some orders are thought of as given by God since they seem to be inherent in the very constitution of things. For example, the Gospel Order of living the Christlife, with its base in the commitment to *change* from the narrow limit of creaturely existence and enter into the Divine Existence, presupposes a step-by-step progression, each gift or set of gifts successively filling a need in that Order. Other orders are the orderings of gifts we make as the exercise of our creativity.

Everything is indeed a gift but we are not passive in our receiving. We must find ways to put the gifts together both to grow in them and to share them. We must develop the potential the gift represents, since only rarely does anything come full blown into our lives. Mother Ann spoke of this as *laboring* for our gifts, *laboring* to make them fully ours, and *traveling* in them. Once again, *travel* and *travail* are virtually interchangeable words in her time. So our *labor, travel,* and *travail* in growing in our gifts indicate both the dynamic experience of movement—the travel from grace (gift) to Grace (Gift) and from glory to Glory—and the bringing forth of new life. It is the labor and travail of the inward groaning of the "one great act of giving birth" supported by the Spirit (Rm. 8:22, ff.). What we are given are truly *our* gifts, and as we use and develop them they more and more belong to us. They empower us to live *this way*, but *we* do the living. It is as the baptismal prayer of Paul in Ephesians puts it, *may He give you Power through His Spirit for your inner self to grow strong....* (Eph. 3:16). The inner self grows in Power, the Power does not "grow" the inner self.

This creative dynamic is even more evident, perhaps, in the devising of orders for our gifts. Even in the case of an order thought of as given in the very constitution of things, the specifics of relating the gifts must be worked out, and usually with possible alternatives. And as gifts are always open-ended, calling for our growth and travel in them, even more so are the orders we create since they must be ready to receive new gifts in progression.

Here we encounter one of the most realistic of Shaker insights into gifts. There are *gifts forever* and *gifts for-a-season,* and our experience testifies that very few gifts are forever. In receiving a gift and beginning to travel in it the first question should be, is this a gift for-a-season and if so can its period of usefulness be discerned? Several times in Shaker history we see a radical change take place on the basis of discerning the closing of a season. Believers in the first century could not have initially imagined that the gifts of worship in the dance would ever be put aside, yet by the 1880s they came to realize that what they had thought to be a gift forever had proved to be a gift for–a–season.[3] Even more impressive is the gift of communal life in the Societies and the great Church Order inaugurated by Father Joseph and consolidated by Mother Lucy. Though most Believers took for granted that the communitarian form of life in one shape or another would always be the very life's breath of the Society, it too proved to be a gift limited to a season. As that became evident, they remembered the admonitions and prophecies of that fact, beginning with Father Joseph's own vision of seven cycles of change.[4]

The closing of a season is reached when a developed gift has served its growth purpose and is consequently displaced by the next gift(s) in progression, or when a larger context for the ordering of gifts is replaced or fundamentally altered. Thus, the earlier ecstatic gifts were displaced by more inward gifts of reflection/meditation/contemplation, in which the emotional enthusiasm of being young in the Spirit was succeeded by the subtler emotions of deepening maturity. And

---

3. See below (36).
4. See Section Three, text 19, p. 206.

thus also, as the socioeconomic base of life became generally reoriented from rural, dominantly agricultural and hand-manufacturing communities to urban industrial-technological mass society, the communitarian ideals achieved in the earlier period became less and less functional and participatory. Of course, it would be possible to *preserve* the previous gifts as elements in a static heritage or as an alternative subculture, but this does not respond to the essential Shaker commitment: the progressive *metanoia* in living the Christlife.[5]

The initial text (1), most probably by Eldress Anna White of Mt. Lebanon, represents the progression of a century and a half. Worship as gift embraces humanity, the natural world, all life and activity, and the eucharistic character of meals. Most important is the recognition that any form is authentic only insofar as it is a useful expression of "the gift and leading of the Spirit." This reflects the admonition in the Preface to the *Millennial Praises* published eighty years before in 1813 (2). Mother Lucy, though reluctant to put a book of worship into print lest it thereby become an established and unchangeable Order, finally authorized the *Millennial Praises* to meet the practical needs of communities scattered from Maine to Kentucky. The Preface is designed as a corrective for any tendency to absolutize this as a form. It is a remarkable testimony to the unconditional commitment of the leadership to *travel* and *progression*—in other church traditions we regularly find authoritative hierarchial statements attempting to establish the irreformability of the forms of worship! The Preface accentuates not only the fact that all forms are but outward signs of the inner reality and

---

5. This is the ultimate root of the current division in attitude between some of the members of the Society at Sabbathday Lake and the Society at Canterbury together with the Ministry. The Sabbathday Lake members are convinced every effort should be made to continue and to revive the old form of life in the communitarian Societies. The Ministry and Canterbury members are convinced that the communitarian gift has had its proper season, now ended; for them the question of the future is open, but it must be in a very different form from the communitarian. Some cannot imagine a Shaker Way except in village–communities; others cannot imagine as authentic the attempt to preserve a form as an absolute instead of embracing the progressive travel from gift to gift. At the very least we must observe: the earliest period (1747–1787) did not envision a communitarian form of life; the beginnings of that development in 1786–1787 were a practical response to persecution; Father Joseph at his death in 1797 foresaw a succession of forms for the Church stretching into the future; not all Believers lived in gathered Societies and yet they always enjoyed full membership in the Church; by the period 1875–1895 serious questions were being raised about the continuance of the communitarian Societies; growing throughout the twentieth century was the presumption that the old form was passing away, which finally became the set policy of the Ministry in 1958.

hence governed by their relative usefulness as expressions, but also the expectation that forms as gifts are inevitably gifts for-a-season.

The next section begins with the earliest known description of Shaker worship (3) at Niskeyuna shortly after Mother Ann's death. The anonymous non–Shaker author provides the oldest version of the consecration prayer used toward the closing of the meeting together with the hand gesture of gift-receiving and gift-giving.[6] The recollection by Jemima Blanchard of the teaching of Father James and Mother Ann (4) illustrates the dynamism of gifts, sharing and laboring. The brief testimony of Abijah Worster (5) points to the pastoral need to be patient with youthful enthusiasm so that those newly gifted will find support in their subsequent travel in progression. The next texts (beginning with 6) accentuate the fact that gifts have their value to the person and community in building up the Christlife. The simple gifts of song (usually wordless) and quiet gesture of Mother Ann should be noted; here and elsewhere the community memory that she did not exhibit any of the enthusiastic gifts is unanimous. The portion from the *Precepts* (7) demonstrates the roots in experience of how incidents can grow into "memories" of the miraculous; here we see episodes of feeding people in the process of being transformed in the minds of some into a "feeding of the multitudes" wonder story. Mother Hannah Kendal's testimony (8) accentuates the relation of personal gifts to the sharing in community; the motif of "feeding" is another common instance of the wide-ranging Shaker sense of Eucharist as the total nurture in the growth in Christlife. The anonymous item (9) and Elder Hervey Eades' exposition (10) relate the Shaker practice of confession to gift. For Believers confession is not actually a *penitential* act, felt

---

6. The gesture of hands held palms up and before the worshiper is purposefully ambiguous, indicating both receiving and giving simultaneously. There are several versions of the consecration prayer, both from the period of the First Ministry and throughout the nineteenth century. A later version was widely used:

This is our altar,
our altar is love.
And none can build this altar
or sacrifice upon it
but the pure of heart—
those who see: God is Love!
We offer living sacrifice
upon our living altar—
Communion, Union, Love—
We will love one another!

psychologically as a negative, but is the positive movement into the life of regeneration. It is an act of liberation.

The next section relates personal gifts to larger contexts: first, gifts of inspiration and how these can be accepted by others (11); next, a very important ordering of gifts to Union (12), in which the personal character of creativity and progress is stressed in coordination with a unity of life with others; and, finally, an interesting instance of insight into the difference between an inspired orginator and the equally but differently inspired editor (13). All of these are pointed illustrations of a growth in recognizing the uniqueness of individuals as the receivers of gifts, and the positive tension between the gifted individual and the community to be enriched. Especially noteworthy are the insights that a truly inspired gift might not be shareable with others (which in no way suggests it is not a true gift), and the realization that creativity and progress take place out at the tips of the branches (the individuals) of the Tree of Life and not in the trunk which supports them and derives its further increase from them.

The following section surveys a variety of aspects of worship, prayer, work, and natural faculties as these manifest gifts and call for orderings. Youngs (14) presents what became a standard statement on worship in the gift of the dance; the final two paragraphs are especially noteworthy. Chauncy Dibble's comment (15) on dancing as worship was made on the eve of the closing of the season for that gift (about 1888–1890). The editorial note (16) draws attention to the limitation inherent in forms: they can support worshipers, but of themselves cannot be the vitalizing power for those worshiping in spirit and truth. The editorial excerpt (17) focuses on the sense of prayerfulness which must characterize worship otherwise it ceases to be fruitful; the citation of Mother Ann's "Every breath is a continual prayer to God" highlights the Shaker awareness of the universality of gifts. Elder Andrew Barrett's reflection on prayer (18) carries this forward, "Our prayers must be in our lives." Next, work as worship (19) sees that working at one's gifts improves them, encourages others to grow, and is worship "respecting the gift, respects the Giver"—God the master workman. Elder Abraham Perkins (20) points to supposedly secular elements (intellect, wealth, fame) as potentially sacred gifts. Elder Oliver Hampton notes (21) that the visible Order of the Church—ministry, bishops, elders, trustees, deacons—demonstrates a law governing gifts, "the less is blessed by the greater," with the expectation that eventually the progress they encourage into wisdom and love will bring about their replacement in a new Order. Elder Oliver (22) considers the interaction of the gifts of emotion and intellect as integral to each other and to full progression. And finally (23) Charlotte Byrdsall assimilates the early enthusiasm for at times extravagant spiritualism to a maturing insight into the Divine indwelling more and more clearly recognized as universal—and so reverencing science and religion as brother and sister, seeking all come–up–higher gifts which can be ours through human knowledge and Divine wisdom.

The series of extracts from Elder Henry Blinn's *Church Record 1784–1879, Canterbury, N.H.* (24) provides insight into the century-long development of patterns of worship, especially the various "spiritual exercises" (worship dances) and the ecstatic gifts of the 1837–1847 period; the chronological record makes evident the constant process of change. A group of gifts of prayer and inspirational reflection is brought together (25) as illustrative of the mystical charism of the Shaker Way. They are typically gifts embodying simplicity and union. The first, Mother Ann's prayer, expresses the universality of union with all creation. The two prayers of Father Eleazar of Harvard, Massachusetts, center on love's uniting people and triumphing in Eternal Life. The next four are brief inspirational gifts from the Mother's Work period, perfect illustrations of the intensity of which simplicity of insight and form are capable. The morning and evening prayer responses (said following a period of silent inner prayer) are the oldest recorded forms from the Sabbathday Lake Society. The two longer worship songs are out of outstanding importance. "Build Me a House" is an inspirational song, given to commemorate the building of the meeting houses of the first communities. "The Gift to be Simple," given by inspiration to Elder Joseph Brackett of the Maine Societies' Ministry, is certainly the most famous of all Shaker songs. It embodies all the spirituality of traveling the Gospel Way in two principles: simple freedom is to come down where we ought to be (in the valley of love and delight) and to turn ourselves around (*metanoia*) to be headed in the right direction for our travel forward into Christlife. The music of the song is also Elder Joseph's gift. The "gift of a flock of doves" is an appeal in simplicity to examine one's own experience: can you, yourselves, see? The concluding four texts (26–29) reflect on the nature of inspirational gifts, insisting on the difference between the subjective mode of experience and its inner essential meaning. As gifts are always ordered to progression, they involve stages of *metanoia*, learning and maturation.

THE SHAKERS

The last section deals with reflections on the significance of Eucharist in the gift of worship (30–36). The general Shaker rejection of a ritual Eucharist was rooted in their previous experience of popularized Protestant Eucharistic thinking: bread and wine as the sign of his absence until he comes again. As their experience was of Christ wholly present, they saw the meaning of Eucharist integrated into their living of the Christlife. When Mother Ann was charged with heathenism for not having a ritual Holy Communion, she answered: On the contrary, you have Communion four times a year, we have Communion three times a day! The Eucharistic signs of eating and drinking are the sharing of Christlife and at each meal Believers, member–for–member the living Body of Christ, sit together in Union within Christ sharing that One Life as they eat and drink. This sense of feasting in Christ is further extended to all life, since "all life and activity animated by the Christ Spirit of Love is worship." Gathering for prayer, reflection through the witnessing gifts, and sharing inner life are all further moments of this Eucharistic Feast. The concluding citation from White and Taylor (36) testifies to the progression in gifts: now "deeper, with less noise and outward demonstration." It is a mind-centered mysticism of consciousness opened outward, seeking to know all that exists through all modes of knowledge, and opened inward into the unique depths of personal existence—in Eldress Anna's simple phrase, "Shakers are thinkers."

I

The worship is prayer and praise to God, as the Almighty Creator of heaven and earth, Fountain of eternal light, love and goodness, One in essence, Dual in manifestation, Father and Mother, manifested and expressed in humanity and in all the beauties and sublimities of the natural world.

Shakers regard all life and activity animated by Christian love as worship. They invoke the Divine Father-Mother in silent prayer together before each meal, partake of their food in a worshipful spirit and go about their duties in a cheerful, happy, helpful temper, feeling that "Labor is worship and prayer."

. . .

No form of worship, however sacred, is regarded as established, only so far as it expresses the gift and leading of the Spirit; no form but

268

may be changed or dispensed with. The life of the spirit, not the form of expression, is regarded as essential.

(Anna White [?], *Present Day Shakerism*, pp. 5, 7) [ca. 1895]

2

. . .

It is not expected that the people of God will ever be confined, in their mode of worship, to any particular set of hymns, or any other regular system of words—for words are but the signs of our ideas, and of course, must vary as the ideas increase with the increasing work of God. Therefore, these compositions, though they may evince to future Believers, the work and worship of God at this day; yet they can be no rule to direct them in that work of God which may be hereafter required of his people. As the work of regeneration is an increasing work, and as there can be no end of the increase of Christ's government and Kingdom; so all that his people have to do is, to keep in the increasing work of God, and unite with whatever changes that increase may lead to, which, to the truly faithful, will be a continual travel from grace to grace, and from glory to glory: so that the spiritual songs of Believers, as well as every other part of their worship, must be according to that degree of grace and glory in which they are given. Therefore, these hymns, wherever they may be sung by Believers, must be limited to their period of usefulness: for no gift or order of God can be binding on Believers for a longer term of time than it can be profitable to their travel in the gospel.

(*Millennial Praises*, Preface, pp. iii–iv) [1813]

*   *   *

3

Their form of worship is, I am informed, as we saw it and therefore a description of what passed while we were there will give you some idea of it—They were singing in this unknown language a very solemn tune, at the end of which they always begin again with Oh! and in such a loud and hollow note accompanied with a catching of the breath as if they were strangling and the most violent contortions of their whole body as cannot fail to shock every one who first sees them—

After singing in that way for sometime, one of the men who appeared the most decent and sensible and who I am informed was formerly a preacher in New England, began a lecture evidently for us—He said we had no doubt heard of Christ's second coming which was foretold to happen, that the time was now come and that he was manifested in the flesh by them; that he had come in righteousness without any sin and that what we had seen was the power of God manifested in them; that what he felt and saw he could not but speak of, that all who wished might be converted, and that he could from the bottom of his heart declare that all those things which we saw were from God, and that theirs was the only religion by which man could be saved—he also said that he knew their religion was despised, but such was the fate of the predictions of Noah, of the prophecies of the Prophets and such was the fate of his blessed Master; that they were supported under all their trials and persecutions by visitations from heaven in the same manner as Paul was converted and as Peter saw a vision when a sheet was let down by the four corners from Heaven—He railed against the pride and luxury of the world and said they had been taught to despise the things thereof except so far as belonged to the necessaries of life—He then quoted a number of texts of Scripture upon which I suppose they found their principles and the form of their worship—such as that the time shall come when men shall "beat their swords into plowshares," which time they say is come to them; and where St. Paul says he was with the brethren "in fear and much trembling" authorizes their shaking—"Turn ye and ye shall be turned" which is their apology for turning round on their heels— "Clap your hands and be joyful O ye people, shout aloud for joy," "Praise God in the dance and with songs" which are also parts of their worship—

After he had run thro his Lecture, they began their singing and two persons more afterwards lectured much to the same affact [sic] and between each Lecture they held their solemn singing in that stile for about an hour accompanying it with groaning sighing and shaking, the Person who lectured to us first, mentioned David's dancing before the Ark in honor of his God and quoted the text of Scripture above mentioned about praying God in the dance; he then began to hum The Soldiers Joy, a country dance tune, and the whole assembly men and women began a violent dancing without any kind of order, the men keeping on one side of the room and the women on the other; during the dance one of the men who had lectured went over to the women's side and touched four of them, when they instantly began to turn round with a velocity that is really inconceivable to any one who has not been a witness to it—they had been turning in this manner for some time, when astonished with the length of their vortical motion, I thought I would observe my watch and see how long they would continue, and for the space of eighteen minutes afterwards they went round with the same surprising velocity, until they were called off by a clapping of hands in which they all joined for the space of five minutes; they then began their solemn singing, then their jig and then clapped hands and continued at that kind of worship for some time—during one of their jigs the old man who had set them a dancing went dancing up to a likely young girl and held out his hand to her, as if to give something, when immediately she fell into such a fit of shaking as exceeded any convulsive fit I had ever seen and continued it for such a length of time that the exercise made the sweat come from her face as if water had been thrown on her—The old man then came up to us as he frequently did during the dance and told us to observe and admire the powerful working of God in his people.

After having proceeded for some time in the manner as above related, the men got together in a cluster holding out both hands, as if supporting something, then one of them spoke to this effect, the rest all repeating as by way of response, "This is our altar and our altar is love and none can build this altar or sacrifice upon it but the pure of heart and such are we—therefore we will sacrifice on our altar and we will love one another"—They then began to shout and clap their hands, the women joining them and renewed their jig—presently after, they got together again in the same manner and repeated something like this, "The dead should be buried, yes we will bury the dead, but we are alive and we will sacrifice on our altar, communion, union, love, we will love one another"—they then continued their shouting, &c.

(Untitled Ms. [Letter or Journal excerpt],
Connecticut Historical Society Collection.)[7] [1785]

---

7. Copy of the text made available through the courtesy of the Connecticut State Historical Society.

4

Father James said "Kneel to God." Then he added, "All that is in the sound of my voice, remember what I say. It is my feeling and desire whenever you are in a room or go to a door where people are kneeling that you kneel with them and not wait for them to arise." Mother used to teach us to unite with the leading gift of the meeting; that if any one was taken with great gift of power or repentance that seemed at variance with the leading influence that they should labor to get out of it as soon as they well could and unite with the rest. And tho she bore much with young Believers in this respect, yet as soon as they were able to bear it, she always strove gently to bend their feelings to unite with the leading gift.

But sometimes when any one had a very powerful gift of repentance, or any other gift, it would last a while after the rest got thru; but if they tried to give it up as soon as they could Mother would be satisfied, yet she would remark that those who found it very hard to have their gifts in union would have a hard travel.

Mother taught us to be strictly devoted in the worship of God. She would speak in substance as follows. "Labor all the time when you have a privilege to worship God, to gather of the substance of the gospel to lay up for your own souls or to give to others; not to be pining your clothes, to take out a pin or put one in unnecessarily; but have your souls devoted to gain the gifts and power of God." When she set out to seek the Lord, she durst not have her mind on any earthly thing, but gave her whole soul and body to labor for the saving power of God.

> (Jemima Blanchard)
> (Roxalana Grosvernor, ed., *Sayings* [SDLms.], p. 28–30) [1845]

5

Mother said [re immature Believers]: "They have received the power of God and are full of zeal, but lack wisdom to know how to improve their gifts; and if you strike at their zeal, they will be likely to lose their gifts and go back to the world and be lost."

> (Abijah Worster)
> (Roxalana Grosvernor, ed., *Sayings* [Pms.], p. 48) [1845]

THE SHAKERS

6

Sister Jemima said, Mother used to encourage them to labor for the gift of tongues, visions, turning and the like, and taught them that all they did to beautify the worship of God, whether in singing or speaking or improving in any gift, would be a peculiar treasure to them.

That no one should be idle in time of worship, if they could do no more than to lift one hand.[8]

(Jemima Blanchard)

(Roxalana Grosvernor, ed., *Sayings* [SDLms.], p. 58) [1845]

She said she never saw Mother under any violent operation of the power of God. She seemed to possess within herself an inexhaustible fountain of that power which she would often communicate to a whole assembly by singing, not in a loud voice, and gently motioning her hands or by speaking a few words.

Father William and Father James used to labor in the worship with great power and zeal, and administer gifts to all around. But Mother's presence merely, the sound of her voice or the movement of her hand, when under the immediate influence of the Spirit of God, was far more powerful than the united gifts of all the others on the earth.

She was the supporter of all their gifts and the centre of their influence, and thus they ever seemed to consider her.

(Jemima Blanchard)

(Roxalana Grosvernor, ed., *Sayings* [SDLms.], pp. 64–65) [1845]

Mother once said to me "Treasure up the gifts of God; the time will come when you will need them; and if you are faithful to treasure up the gifts of God, then they will wake up in your soul."

(Abijah Worcester)

(Roxalana Grosvernor, ed., *Sayings* [SDLms.], p. 96) [1845]

---

8. There are many versions of this "lift one hand" exhortation (cf. *Precepts*, p. 230). One, particularly, stresses *union* as the basic gift in worship. During a worship meeting Mother Ann noted that while some were overwhelmed with emotion and were dancing, whirling and otherwise under "physical operations," others were seated along the walls of the room with arms folded, impatiently waiting for the enthusiasts to calm down. Mother Ann stopped the worshipers, drawing attention to the disunity they were manifesting. Those not gifted to join in the operations of the others should not pretend to a gift not theirs. But to show all their union she asked them to at least wave their hands every so often. (Such a phrase as "we had better wave our hands" came to be used as a signal that union was being lost and something should be done to regain it.)

7

19. The people in Harvard were mostly poor, and, at the Square House, where Mother and the Elders had their residence, there had been no stores of provisions laid up, and, though vast numbers of people came from various parts to visit them, and great crowds were almost daily fed there, yet, through the abounding goodness of God, they were never known to lack a meal of victuals, but always found enough to satisfy the multitude, which, at times, seemed almost miraculous. But Mother Ann felt that it was the duty of Believers to provide for their temporal support, and not always be seemingly idle dependents on the bountiful, and, apparently miraculous hand of Providence. She therefore called Jonathan Slosson to her room one day, and spoke to him concerning these things; and reminded him of the small quantity of provisions they had possessed to entertain so many people. "We are fed here," said Mother Ann, "apparently by the miracles of God; a great many people come, bringing little or nothing with them but their sins; yet they are fed, and have a plenty. I know it is by the miracles of God, as when Jesus fed the multitude with a few loaves and little fishes; so it is now, but, it cannot always be so." She then asked him if he could not assist them in devising some means to procure bread for the multitude.

(Giles Avery, ed., *Precepts*, pp. 71–72) [1816/1888]

7. As no previous preparation had been made for the entertainment of the Believers in Ashfield, consequently there were no stores of provisions laid up for the multitude; and, though the quantity on hand was sometimes very small, and great numbers of people were continually coming and going; yet, being constantly attended with the blessing of God, they found no lack; but always had enough.

8. Sometimes Mother ordered the people to sit down upon the floor, or on the ground, and a small quantity of bread and cheese, or some other kind of provision, was served round to the multitude, much in the same manner as Christ fed the multitude, with a few loaves and fishes; and the power and blessing of God evidently attended them, so that a small portion sufficed for a large number, and all were satisfied.

9. One particular instance of this kind which took place in the winter, is well recollected, by many. There being a very large collection of people from various parts, and scarcely any thing to eat, Mother

called on the family to give the people something to eat. They answered, "There is no victuals to give so many people." Mother again said, "Give them to eat." The people were then ordered to sit down, and a very small quantity of bread and cheese, cut into small pieces, was served around to the multitude, of which they all partook, and had a plenty. After they had eaten, Mother said, "It is by the miracles of God that you have been fed, as when Christ fed the multitude, O! ye of little faith."

(Giles Avery, ed., *Precepts*, pp. 108–109) [1816/1888]

8

[Mother Hannah Kendal:] "Brethren and sisters, you must labor for strength; you have been fed with milk long enough, and now I want you to have a little meat to strengthen you. I want you to labor for the power of God and the life of the gospel, which is love, union and simplicity. You must labor to unite your feelings together as the heart of one man, and treasure up the gifts and orders of God and keep them, that your souls may have something to feed upon. The gifts of God are given to feed and strengthen your souls while you are on your journey."

. . .

"Attend strictly to your meetings, for when you are out of meeting, and there is a gift of God administered you lose it, and you do not realize how much you lose in this way. It is the order of God, to attend to your retirements,[9] meetings and meals, and not let trifles hinder you; and when the signal is given, either for retireing time or for meals, drop your work, go into the house and sit down and retire, and have no loud or unnecessary conversation."

(Mother Hannah Kendal)
(Roxalana Grosvernor, ed., *Sayings* [Pms.], pp. 105, 106–107) [1845]

---

9. "Retirements," "retiring time" refer to times set aside for meditative prayer and reflection, and especially before coming together for common worship.

9

Notes from the Life Experiences of Mother Ann Lee. *Anon.*
. . .

The gifts and calling of God are given to souls in nature's darkness; not because they have repented, but the gifts are intended to lead souls to repentance.

Some one asked, What is repentance? and were answered, To cease from committing sin, is the only repentance that God accepts, and this no one can do except by an honest and faithful confession of all sin to the chosen witnesses of Christ. . . .

(*The Manifesto* XII, 3, p. 59) [1882]

I O

Shakerism. *H. L. Eades.*
[In answer to an Exshaker's article in the *Boston Investigator*]
[Re: confession-] . . . But, I need not quote scripture further; besides the spiritual and scriptural injunction, there is a reasonable necessity that the Elders should know the weak points of each applicant in order to be able to throw around them the proper safe–guards and succor them. Besides, it is incumbent on the Elders, and a duty they owe to the Church, to know what kind of material is admitted into the body. The writer of this has been a confessor for near half a century, and quite willing to anticipate Ex–Shaker's exposure of the Confessional.

There are but two motives which should induce any persons to seek entrance into the Shaker Church. viz: First, to get rid of all the sins of a past life, by letting them go before into judgmett, and 2nd, To place themselves in a condition where they can live a better, higher, purer, more useful and a more sinless life than is possible to any one, while remaining in the world. . . .

. . . But many come from selfish consideration, to obtain a living without rendering an equivalent. Such ones usually fight shy of the Confessional, and come forward, not to confess, but to conceal their sins and weaknesses from the light of God's order, and sometimes need enlightening to help them, hoping they may receive a conviction which has not yet reached them. . . .

My uniform course with applicants has been to inform them, that the first step to be taken, is the confession of every transaction of life, within one's immediate remembrance, which the confessor [i.e., one confessing] knew, or now thinks, was wrong and sinful.

The earnest, honest applicant, then begins and goes straight forward and gives a satisfactory account of himself, puts his name to the Novitiate Covenant, and comes into full fellowship with the body of Christ.—So, God, in His Order, and God in the penitent, remits the sins and lifts their burden from the soul. . . .

Some, foolishly choose to put off the mortifying ordeal until they shuffle off the mortal, expecting then to appear before some big imaginary Deity, seated on a large white Throne, perhaps inside the rings of Saturn, or somewhere else among the stars! But, the scriptures, properly understood, justify no such belief. In this, such souls will find themselves mistaken, for God has His Order, composed of finite agents, in both worlds, to which all must bow, whether angels or men.

1. As to confessing all the acts of a married life I will say:—It is only necessary to confess what the enlightened mind now sees to be wrong.

2. We know nothing about "the recording angel blotting out sins by our intercessions." I have shown how sins are forgiven, by God, in the saint, and God within the sinner. The latter with repentance and honesty, the former with love and charity. But it is all labor lost with one sin willfully covered, God, in the sinner, will not bless and lift the burden from the soul, and God in the saints cannot. . . .

4. It is sometimes charged that the Shakers require confessing every week! Just so, if one sins every week, not otherwise! . . .

7. Shakers are not required to subdue every natural instinct, as ex-shaker testifies. Our desire is to change the carnal for the pure and spiritual! Is this objectionable? . . .

(*The Manifesto* XII, 4, pp. 77–79) [1882]

* * *

I I

Ideas of Inspiration. *Jason Pool*

The Church was established by Divine revelation, and the leaders, afterwards, were, no doubt gifted with inspiration to lead the people. It is quite possible for a person to be inspired and not be fully aware of it, the quantity being very small. . . .

Reason, in man, is of a progressive nature, and on this account he was destined to come to a point where he could see and understand for himself.

. . .

Neither am I obliged to receive a thing because another says it has been revealed to him. It may be a revelation to him, but it is not therefore a revelation to me: neither am I bound to believe it on his testimony. If the thing be revealed to me by the Spirit, I know it to be true by the testimony of the spirit, but if it be revealed to another, I cannot receive it without the proof.

(*The Shaker Manifesto* XII, 8, p. 203) [1882]

12

Progress and Order. *O. P.* [*Oliver Prentiss*]

. . .

An organized body is not obliged to accept any increase of testimony: but if any member, or a family manifests an increase . . . they ought not to be crushed down, nor retarded by the inertia of the body.

. . . Shall an increase begin at the center, or at the extremities? . . . [an allegory of a tree:] I am an assemblage of individuals; every bud I bear, is a tree in embryo. . . . I am a community; composed of many members working harmoniously together. My progress, growth and strength, have been at, and from my extremities. . . . I have indeed manifested a degree of diversity in Unity, but there is a tree by the river, which yields twelve kinds of fruits, and its leaves—divine ideas— are for the healing of human ills. It manifests a greater diversity than I do, it being a higher organism.

Human Society is like me, an assemblage of individuals, and is truly an organism, and if of the highest type, twelve manner of fruits may be forth coming. Low organisms do not admit of much diversity.

It is the province of my roots and trunk to support the buds, and it is their three–fold office, to strengthen the trunk, bloom and bear fruit. Unity of action is Order; growth and fruit is Progress. Order will become stonefied, if not fully compatible with Progress. Progress cannot be established, unless compatible with Order. Where Order is stonefied, an increase will be out of unity.

My conditions of growth, are light, warmth, moisture, air. The conditions of the tree by the river of life, are divine light, love, and an atmosphere which invigorates and gladdens all divine forms. Its every bud, is a divine human spirit, accessible to Progress, and ever tending to Order.

(The Shaker Manifesto XIV, 2, pp. 30–31) [1884]

13

... [Paulina Bates' <i>The Divine Book of Holy Wisdom</i>] was written in the line of the female. But Holy Wisdom said by Inspiration that She could not create new faculties in the Instruments chosen, but all that any Spirit could do was to inspire the faculties that were created in them. Hence, tho one might be the most suitable to bring forth an original inspired message, the language and arrangement may be deficient, and often may be improved so as to be better understood. This department is more adapted to the male sex. It does not depreciate the value of an inspired Gift in any one, for another to have a gift to improve what the first has brot forth; but to the contrary, it shows "The Unity of the Spirit"—that there are diversities of Gifts but the same Spirit, and that Spirit is from the same God that worketh all good.

(Calvin Green, Biographic Memoir, p. 115) [ca. 1850]

*   *   *

14

1. Whatever may be called the worship of God, it is certain that no external exercise therein can be any thing more than an outward expression of an inward spiritual sensation of love and obedience to God, arising from a knowledge and understanding of his will. And, as nothing is more expressive of love and respect to God than obedience, therefore the most perfect and acceptable worship is performed by those who keep the commandments of God.

2. Hence the words of Jesus Christ, "*If you love me, keep my commandments.* (John, xiv. 15.) Why call ye me *Lord, Lord,* and do not

the things which I say? (Luke, vi. 46.) In vain do they worship me, teaching for doctrines the commandments of men. (Mat. xv. 2.) But the hour cometh, and now is, when *the true worshippers shall worship the Father in Spirit and in truth:* for the Father seeketh such to worship him. (John, iv. 22, 23.) *Thou shalt worship the Lord thy God, and him only shalt thou serve."* (Mat. iv. 10.)

3. As man is an active, intelligent being, formed for social communion; so in every age, there have always been certain external forms of Divine worship, which, in different dispensations, have been various, according to the manifestations of the will of God in each, and the various operations of his Spirit, for the time then present.

4. The manner of worship in the first appearing of Christ, was not reduced to any form, but according as true believers were moved by the Spirit, in various circumstances. They worshipped God in prayer, vocal or silent, in praise, in thanksgiving, in exhortations, and in feasts of charity, by which they expressed their love and union to each other. And, as *there were diversities of operations,* we have good reason to believe that dancing was one of them. (i Cor. xii. 4.)

5. This various manner of worship continued mostly, with all the true witnesses, until near the time of Christ's second appearing, when many, like the guards of the night, sat in solemn silence, waiting for the break of day, denying their own wisdom and judgment, and performing no act of worship but such as they were moved to by the inward light and evidence of the quickening Spirit.

6. Being thus wholly cut off from the fruitless inventions and precepts of man, and wholly dependent on the Author and Fountain of life, they devoted themselves to do his will in all things wherein it might be made manifest. Hence the light, and truth, and revelation of God increased among them, until by the special operation of his power, they were moved to go forth and worship God in the dance; which had been expressly signified by the Law and the Prophets, as the peculiar manner of worship to be established in the latter day.

7. And, as the work of full redemption, and the worship of God attending it, were to be introduced in the line of the female; therefore it is particularly worthy of notice, that through the order of the female, both the example and promise were given, through all the Law and the Prophets, which may evidently appear from what follows:

[Paragraphs 8 through 23 review scriptural passages relating to the dance in worship: Ex. xv. 1–20; 1 Sam. xviii. 6; 1

Chron. xiii. 8; 2 Sam. vi. 14–23; Lam. v. 15; Dan. v. 23; Ezra, i. 7; Jer. xxx. 18–24.]

24. Thus it is evident, that the promise of God for the restoration of this solemn exercise, was given in the line of the female, to virgins, or such as were pure and undefiled before God; and it was to such only that this worship was to be restored in the latter day.

25. But as these things could not be but in part fulfilled in Christ's first appearing, therefore he renewed the promises, which were made through the Prophets, saying, "*All things must be fulfilled which were written in the law of Moses, and in the Prophets, and in the Psalms, concerning me;*" (Luke, xxiv. 44.) which, in this particular, was most expressly alluded to in his parable of the younger son, who returned to his father's house, and being stript of his old garments, and clothed with the best robe, and there was *music and dancing*. (Luke, xv. 25.)

26. But the elder son was offended, and would not go in; which was particularly expressive of the effect of this manner of worship, in making a separation between the old leaven of malice in a hypocritical profession, and the unleavened bread of sincerity and truth.

27. Therefore, those who found their belief on the Bible, may know that there are nineteen passages recorded in Scripture, which speak *of dancing as the worship of God*, and not one passage in the whole which speaks against it *as sacred devotion*. Hence, all opposition to it, as devotion to God, is entirely unfounded in Scripture. It is evident that the faculty of dancing was created of God, to be used in his honor; hence, although the wicked have abused it in the *service of the devil*, they have abused *singing to a far greater extent*, and for much baser purposes.

28. For there is not a single corrupt propensity, which has not been excited and fostered *by singing;* yet it has been adopted by nearly all professors of religion, as sacred worship. But singing, either vocal or instrumental, is the very life of dancing. Without it dancing would be like a body without a soul. Therefore, to *condemn dancing*, and justify *singing*, is, at least, like condemning the *body* for actions and justifying the *soul*, when the soul is the real actor. Who cannot see the inconsistency?

29. It is not merely the external performance of the present worship of God, by which any are justified; but the same being given by the special gift and revelation of God, according to promise, it is therefore an outward manifestation of the Holy Spirit, which is effec-

tual, in the hearts of the faithful, to the destruction of the nature of sin. And, as unity and harmony of exercise is [*sic*] emblematical of the *one spirit* by which the people of God are led, this unity and harmony of worship is beautiful and glorious.

30. And thus, by uniting together in one faith, to worship God in diversities of *gifts and operations*, according to his own appointment and effusions of the Spirit, believers are baptized into one Spirit, and grow up together in Christ as the members of one body. This manner of worship to the people of God, is not empty, nor carnal; but mighty through God, joyful as heaven, and solemn as eternity.

(Benjamin Youngs, *Testimony*, pp. 584–588) [1808/1810/1823/1856]

15

Dancing in Worship. *Chauncy Dibble*

Singing and dancing are inherent in the dispositions of human beings. It is to those in the vigor of life an outward expression of a thrill of pleasure.

. . .

Form in itself is only an outward expression of worship.

Revivals of spirituality which stir men's souls with deep convictions often produce outward operations.

. . .

'Twas thus our leaders learned the beautiful order of marching in circles, and other exercises, sacred on account of the sincerity of their souls; and because kindred spirits drew near, and the door of inspiration was opened.

. . .

There can be no circle of mediums more congenial or attractive to spirits than a company of pure and innocent brethren and sisters united in the spirit of Christian love.

In such society and under such conditions the higher class of inspirations predominates; and false spirits are easily detected and excluded.

(*The Shaker Manifesto* X, 2, p. 32) [1880]

16

Notes [Editorial]

... It is the life of the Christian order, and a church devoted to the worship of God, in the beauty of holiness, must be a live church. The dull routine of forms and ceremonies may be more or less necessary for an organized body of worshippers to hold in check the earthly relations, but they have no vitalizing power which shall make of an assembly, worshippers in spirit and in truth. ...

(*The Manifesto* XV, 7, p. 162) [1885]

17

[Editorial Re: worship]
. . .
Shall we not, as Believers, find in this a lesson [i.e., the fact of fall off in church attendance] which will admonish us to more carefulness? We certainly need not fear to learn a good lesson, as taught by the experience of those not of our faith. We also have prayer meetings. Are they so organized that all wish to be present? Shall we not make them fruitful seasons of spiritual love and life, in which every member of the household shall hold a privileged place?

The spirit of prayer must of necessity grow with a body of christians as they grow in the spirit of righteousness. The explanation which Mother Ann gave to prayer is the embodiment of all that helps to lead the soul home to God.

"Every breath," said she, "is continual prayer to God."

It may take the form of a petition for protection, for guidance or for determined resolutions. Whatever it may be, let us give it as a free will offering to the cause of right and truth.

(*The Manifesto* XII, 3, pp. 62–63) [1882]

18

Prayer. *Andrew Barrett.*
. . .
I pray for divine aid and divine things—for the help of the Divine Spirit to develop within me that understanding and wisdom which

will direct me aright. . . . While in the attitude of prayer I breathe in God's eternal love. The old idea of prayer was, that God could be dissuaded from doing evil unto his creatures, if they curried his favor. The new idea of prayer is that God helps those who help themselves, and that we must co–operate with the Divine Spirit, otherwise we may not receive the Divine blessing.

Prayer should embody the will to act as occasions offer; our prayers must be in our lives. . . .

Is there not a beautiful thought connected with prayer for the dead? Were it not sad to feel that when our loved ones pass away, they are wholly separated from us? Through prayer we may still hold communion with them; by the spirit of prayer we may gather the inspiration and clothe ourselves with the mantle they were clothed with. In blessing them we receive their blessing. . . .

(The Shaker Manifesto XIII, 1, p. 16) [1883]

19

Work as a Mode of Worship. *C. B. Bostwick.*

. . .

How can we best show our respect, or in other words, worship, to the Giver of all good? reasoning by analogy I would say, by increasing our endeavors to make the best use of the gifts God has bestowed on us whether bodily or mental. We all have a gift either small or great; it matters not how small, be earnest in trying to make the best of it. . . . Get all the available knowledge in the direction your gift leads and go ahead . . . learn your business thoroughly from every source, it does not matter where, men, books or nature, but don't be content to do a thing because "it has been done so for the last generation or two and will do for you," it won't do for you, be sure of that. "The Lord requires his own with usury," and the usury can be best attained by improving your gift and making your land produce more than your predecessor by the skill you bring to bear on it.

By doing this you have three causes of satisfaction: you are doing the will of God by improving your talents, you have increased the yield of your land, and you have also the satisfaction of being a direct encourager, (by example, which is better than precept), of others in the same path, and lastly, all the time you have been working, you have been worshipping God by doing his will. This will be found to be the case throughout all the gifts of God; if the gift be small make it of use by constant practice of it; if it be large, then, my friend, a greater responsibility rests upon you, "the greater the gift, the greater the burden." An earnest worker is one of God's true nobility; he is trying to do all he knows, and by respecting the gift, he respects the giver. . . .

There is as much worship in good workmanship done in the right spirit, as in any other act; the spirit of the thing done and not the act itself is the key to tell whether anything done be worship or not, but God, the master workman, who has made the minutest insect with as much care as the mammoth elephant, sets us the example of good works. Imitation is the sincerest praise.

(*The Shaker Manifesto* XI, 2, pp. 29–30) [1881]

20

Fragmentary Thoughts. *Abraham Perkins.*

. . .

It is said three powers rule the world: to wit,—intellect, wealth and fame. Even in the church of Christ, to become successful in missionary labors, each power is a necessity. Ignorance blinds and lays waste; and says Goethe, "Nothing is more terrible than *active* ignorance." Wealth, though the love of it may be the root of all evil, is mighty to revolutionize men and nations and accomplish the greatest reforms in civilization and morality. Lastly without some of the excellence of fame, suspicion and jealousy are upon the heels of progress to destroy confidence, and thus retard and counteract good, effective operations. With the best use of these powers, they are unavailing in the kingdom of Christ, to bring the baptism and fire of the heavens, unless associated with the spirit of the Messiah and governed by the principles of the angel world.

(*The Shaker Manifesto* XII, 7, p. 150) [1882]

21

God's Church Government—Present and Future. *O. C. Hampton.*

From what we have been taught, and what appears in the administration of government in our Pentecostal community, we infer that this ministry at the mother church, the subordinate ministry of the several bishoprics, the elders, trustees, deacons, etc., constitute the official administrative machinery of the community, or what is more generally called the *visible order* of the church.... we may logically infer that this same order will be continued in the next state of existence as in this; the same necessities attending us there which we find ourselves under here. And doubtless this order of things rests upon the great law of the universe, viz., *that the less is blessed of the better*.... To be sure, the sweet attractions of wisdom and love may in the course of one or two hundred thousand years be substituted gradually for present sagacity, executive and administrative energy and ability; ...

(*The Shaker Manifesto* X, 9, pp. 193–194) [1880]

22

Relation of Intellect and Emotion. *O. C. Hampton*

... The origin of these [dualities] may be traced to the no less palpable principles of wisdom and love, a duality observable in all the dispensations of Divine Providence, and for aught we know to the contrary, a duality constituting the Infinite mind itself. This matter of duality receives amongst mankind the several names of positive and negative, active and passive, male and female, love and wisdom, discreting all things into a constant duality without any exception. Intellect and emotion in man are merely finite manifestations of the dual principles of wisdom and love, transmuted to the sublime offices of reason and religion in man. The first is necessary to develop, define, explain, to illustrate the character as well as necessity of discipline, self-government, church government, organization, order and regulations, necessary to the existence of a self–perpetuating community. The second is necessary to the development of the religious sentiment, together with all the Pentecostal gifts, inspirations, ministrations from the spirit world, prophecies, tongues, healings of disease, together with all sympathy for human suffering, going out of one's self to do good to others. Unless these principles of wisdom and love are equally and normally developed in the individual, his or her efforts to attain to spiritual perfection must necessarily be abortive.... Intellect relates to all matters within the domain of reason. Emotion relates to all those indescribably grand and important matters within the domain of religion and inspiration, often transcending the bounds of reason, but never necessarily contradicting her suggestions. Intellect enables us to search into all truth which can be discovered by logical research, experiment and analysis.

Emotion presents to us the beauty of holiness, the peace of righteousness, love to each other, sympathy and tenderness toward the suffering, the glory and perfect splendor of purity, and often opens up a vista of sublimity and glory far-reaching even unto the serenest recesses of heaven itself. And yet intellect and emotion are so perfectly correlated that one is in every way and under all circumstances necessary to the other, in the highest and most harmonious development of which humanity is capable. If one is so far overborne by the other that spontaneity in the direction of either is forestalled or annihilated, the abnormal results of mental and spiritual disaster and sorrow are sure to follow, and persistently continue until the normal equilibrium is restored. . . . We must be thoughtful upon this matter of healthy development of mind, or we may have to regret having spent a useless life among the Arctic icebergs of an intellectual North Pole, or in traversing an equatorial Sahara of emotional enthusiasm, neither of which will confer much happiness upon the individual, and still less blessing and benefit to the community.

(*The Shaker Manifesto* X, 10, pp. 217–218) [1880]

23

Who Are True Spiritualists? *Charlotte Byrdsall*

Through faith in the immortal laws that govern our existence we are spiritualists. Salvation consists, or is dependent upon, the relation that human beings bear to the spirit and matter that constitute life. . . . Let nothing obstruct or hinder the powers that would unfold industry, true cultivation, religion, revelation, and science, for upon the unfoldment of these depend our destiny.

By a willingness to accept scientific truth, the physical and moral laws and principles upon which life is built, and by which it is sustained, we form the basic foundation of a true understanding how to advance in wisdom until in the ever unfoldment of spiritual and eternal truth we intuitively comprehend the divine, and inbreathe and outbreathe the faith, the love and genuine religion, which bind humanity in the golden cords of justice, mercy and peace, and unites the

THE SHAKERS

lower to the higher by successive degrees; and in return the knowledge of the goodness of God is transmitted through spirit unto spirit, from spirit unto mortal, and from mortal unto mortal.

Science and religion are brother and sister, and point upward to infinitude, the father and the mother, God. The object of science is to attain the bounds of all righteous presents, and of religion not merely to symbolize but to actualize that attainment by bringing into existence a true brotherhood and sisterhood. . . . By a proper use of spiritualism we may acquire a relation to the forces and changes of the universe, which afford the material that enshrouds our spirits.

If we avail ourselves of a knowledge of a future life, which blind creeds, bigotry, and dogmatism cannot change, the balance of existence is ours. Only as we harmonize with the elements of growth can we be adapted to the modes and means which simply and truly embody spiritualism.

. . . spiritualism does not consist of some phenomenal wonder, but of the development of the indwelling, God–implanted germ in the hearts of manhood which will be a key to the chambers of human souls, and reveal true character. It will be a health restorer, by imparting the knowledge how we should live to avoid disease, and the proper medicine to be used, and show the real utility of life in mortal form, and its continuance in a future state of existence.

In seeking this valuable knowledge we must not lose sight of individual responsibility, nor embrace the idea that we may be safe in remaining in a mediumistic state of mere passivity to unseen forces. There is work for all to perform. We cannot justly claim to be true spiritualists while subject to halting, doubting, wavering spirit in regard to the influx of spirit life and power by agencies which Divine wisdom employs to minister to our needs.

Spiritualists, who are worthy to bear the name, should be guileless, ready to grasp the Christ-principles, irrespective of person; to call home the erring, uplift the fallen, and unite with spirit voices that call, "Come up higher." Woman must act well her part and use her God–given power to expand, beautify and immortalize existence, and to blend and unite human hearts and teach them to walk in the illumined pathway that leads to realms of peace.

(*The Shaker Manifesto* XI, 8, pp. 172–173) [1881]

*   *   *

24

Elder Henry C. Blinn, *Church Record 1784–1879*, Canterbury, New Hampshire

[One half hour reserved for meditation before all meetings for worship.] "the Lord's time." (Vol. i, p. 16)

[Open air marching–processions (akin to those within the house, especially prior to meetings as their initial exercise) an early practice although first recorded at Canterbury in 1825.] (Vol. i, p. 16)

[In 1825, the first instance of "unusual gifts" at worship:]
... the gift of bowings and whirlings, and even by some persons being obliged to roll on the floor. (Vol. i, p. 16)

[In 1843, procession into the fields to bless the coming crops:]
The Brethren and Sisters marched in order ... and scattered the seed of blessing.... (Vol. i, p. 29)

[Six brothers and six sisters as "Sweepers" in the *Sweeping Gift* in 1844:]
A deviation from all former manifestations was the peculiarity of the dress of these mediums. The Brethren wore a scarlet band, two and one half inches wide, on the right wrist. Attached to this was a card with this inscription: "War hath been declared by the God of Heaven, against the Beast, and with the help of the saints of God, upon earth, he shall be slain." (Vol. i, p. 35)

[Summary of the development of worship forms]

1782: Spontaneous, unpatterned charismatic acts—"shouting; singing; preaching; dancing." (Vol. i, p. 7)
1792: "Slow and solemn exercise"—a type of square with bowing; worded hymns and anthems were laid aside for wordless songs "which had been known by Mother Ann and the Elders, as solemn songs"—this continued for the next sixteen years. (Vol. i, p. 8)
1798: "Marching exercise" introduced; from the beginning at Canterbury until 1870 the "Square Order exercise" was in use, giving way finally to the "Stepping March." (Vol. i, pp. 8–9)
1792–98: A period during which the outside public was not admitted to the services of worship; a time of consolidation for the *Gospel Order* of the Church introduced by Father Joseph. (Vol. i, pp. 9–10)

1801: "Stepping March" introduced from Mt. Lebanon. (Vol. i, p. 10) "Union Meetings" organized the previous year. (Vol. i, p. 11)

1808: Worded hymns introduced, originating from Ohio (eventually gathered and published in the *Millennial Praises*, 1813) (Vol. i, p. 11)

1815: Anthems introduced; (the first: "The Cherubim" from Mt. Lebanon, in the *Sacred Repository*, p. 12); since 1792 most preaching and public speaking done by the Ministry and Elders; during this period the "Slow March" introduced. (Vol. i, p. 12)

1822: "March in the circle." (Vol. i, p. 13)

1824: Circular exercise, with the singers in the center. (Vol. i, p. 14)

1825: A brief period of ecstatic gifts comparable to the later period of *Mother's Work*, 1837 through c.1850. (Vol. i, p. 16) "Skipping" introduced. (Vol. i, p. 17)

1826: "Square March" introduced to replace "Stepping March," until 1831; speaking by all family members at meeting was gradually encouraged at this time. (Vol. i, p. 17)

1828: "Changeable March" and a form of circle exercise from Mt. Lebanon introduced; subsequently laid aside. (Vol. i, p. 17)

1829: Second and North Families conduct public services, while the Church Family worshipped in private. (Vol. i, p. 17)

1837: On the 27th of June the Mt. Lebanon Ministry came and instructed the Canterbury community on the "remarkable outpouring of the spirit. . . . To them it was an increase of light, life and spirit power. . . . The order of the meetings was now changed and adapted to the times." Whirling, shaking and singing, as individual movements in the spirit were characteristic. In December the first visions occurred to several instruments, aged between 10 and 20; they would "personate," [i.e., speak in the *persona* of the spirit]: (Vol. i, p. 18)

This ministration of spirit gifts began in a very curious manner. The seeing and hearing were among the first gifts to be received. To these were added the gift of tasting, smelling and feelnng. . . . Inspirational messages, instructive and salutary, were now received. . . . These visionary gifts gradually passed away and by the close of 1838 they had given place to several other phases of inspiration. An inward impression warranted the mediums in giving exhortations, admonitions and messages of love in the name of the persons whom they had heretofore seen in visions. A great variety of presents were received from the spirit land. . . .

[A gift of whirling and of rolling on the floor "mostly confined to the young men."] As would naturally be expected, some individuals were more susceptible of these influences than others, and were able to see and hear and taste in a spiritual sense, the varied treasures which they received from the hands of the spirits. [—A variety of symbolic gifts of food, flowers, garments, musical instruments, and the like.]

In 1840 the mediums who had heretofore spoken all their messages, now commenced to write them in full, as directed by their spirit guides. Here, again, diverse forms of inspiration were manifested; some of the mediums heard the spirits speak, and wrote their messages as a reporter would take a speech; others saw the spirit paper and read from it as one would read from a book. This class were copyists or transcribers for the spirits, while others were impressed so thoroughly with the word of the person for whom they were to write, that they wrote almost unconsciously. In the advancement of the work the messages became more extended and more substantial. Even books were received and copied under the influence of inspiration, while hymns and anthems were sung as directed by these spirit guides. . . . In the autumn of this year, 1840, the mediums were impressed to deliver some of their messages in languages that we could not understand. . . . Most of these manifestations were proceeded by the gift of bowing or jerking or by the gift of whirling. (Vol. i, pp. 20–21)

1841: The "Narrow Path" exercise was given, a slow march introduced from Mt. Lebanon; a square order, one foot placed directly before the other—heel–to–toe—with the hands either at the sides or held as if reading from spiritual books entitled "Spiritual Reflection." (Vol. i, pp. 21–22)

Holy Wisdom's Work, begun on November 27th, 1841. Meetings held to receive messages through instruments (initially three individuals); the messages were exhortations to the leaders, and a call for the inspection of all things:
. . . the plain, simple and good were blessed, while the

costly, fanciful or superfluous were disapproved. (Vol. i, p. 23)

The Prophet's Work (Elisha). Evening meetings with singing, dancing, speaking in tongues, spiritual messages; lamentations for imperfections and penitence. In a special exercise, small circles were formed (brothers and sisters separate), with joined hands, moving from right to left [i.e., counterclockwise], accompanied by bowing, jerking and tongues—"the whole house seemed to be given up to the confusion of tongues." (Vol. i, p. 24)

Indian spirits—came through instruments for spiritual instruction; the instruments would "deport themselves very much as we might suppose the indians would in their native state." They departed after eight weeks. (Vol. i, p. 25)

The Spiritual Sweep, introduced from Mt. Lebanon, October 1, 1842.

... Four brethren and four sisters were chosen for the work and a season afforded them for meditation and preparation that they might be the active and true mediums of Father William, Father James, Father Job and Elder Benjamin, also of Mother Ann, Mother Lucy, Mother Hannah and Eldress Molly Chase. [*The Spiritual Sweep* consisted in a ritual procession through all the buildings to purge them of all disorder, while one or more "sweeping songs" were sung; this order was closed in 1850.] (Vol. i, pp. 25, 26–27)

... The establishing of order seemed to be the great object, that the Society might be one in harmony. Those flights of zeal, belonging more particularly to the revivalists, consisting of shouting and powerful bodily operations, were now carefully laid aside [beginning in 1792]. New forms of exercise for worship were introduced, and the songs were made to correspond. (Vol. ii, p. 35)

[The ceremony of the Washing of Feet; a gift introduced from Mt. Lebanon in 1828 and continued in use until 1840.]

On the 4th of November the Ministry of New Lebanon, wrote to the Believers, in the several Societies, informing them that it was a general gift for all to unite in the example of Jesus, in the ceremony of washing the feet. ...

[All in the community went to their retiring rooms; there each group two–by–two beginning with the eldest one would wash and dry the other's feet. The ceremony was performed four times yearly on the first Saturday of December, March, June, and September. The previous evening the Elders would instruct the community in the gift, solemnly reading the opening section of the Last Supper scene from John's Gospel.]   (Vol. ii, pp. 217–218)

25

(9) "O that the fishes of the sea and fowls of the air, and all things that have life and breath, yea, all the trees of the forest, and grass of the fields, would pray to God for me!" (—M. A.)

(Giles Avery, ed., *Precepts*, p. 10) [1816/1888]

[Father Eleazer:]
"There is but one table, one bread, and but one God,
and one union, and you ought to be one people."
                    (Father Eleazer)
                    (Roxalana Grosvernor, ed., *Sayings* [Pms.], p. 98) [1845]

[Father Eleazer:]
"Love fills my heart and hope my breast,
With joy I yield my breath.
'Tis love that drives my chariot wheels,
And death must yield to love."
                    (Jemima Blanchard)
                    (Roxalana Grosvernor, ed., *Sayings* [Pms.], p. 38) [1845]

In a basket of flowers ye can see the wonderful work
      of the Creator.
Look on him and admire His work, a perfect work.
O Earth and Heaven, praise ye the Lord!

Open the windows and the doors and receive whomsoever
[*sic*] is sent.

THE SHAKERS

A Staff of Love from Jesus Christ the Savior
whereon to lean in tribulation.

> (Untitled sheet of inspirational texts and vignettes, dated 1848;
> Sabbathday Lake Library)

Prayer at Morning, after silence:
One: Now 'tis the call to arise.
All: And be wise!
Prayer during the Day, after silence:
One: Now 'tis the Christlife to live.
All: And to give.
Prayer at Evening, after silence:
One: Now 'tis the gift to be still.
All: And we will!

> (Untitled Ms. of prayers and hymns, dated 1790;
> Sabbathday Lake Library)[10]

Build Me a House, saith the Lord,
and let every heart contribute
as you raise it to My Spirit.
With My Glory I will fill it
and My Power shall be round about.
Let the wise who have long known My Way
bring these gifts:
Holiness of heart, holiness of life.
Let the young bring their best
to be inwrought for me.
And ye shall all together write:
Holiness, Holiness, Holiness to the Lord God,
Holiness upon all things in His House forever!

> (Worship Song, ca. 1870; Canterbury, New Hampshire)

'Tis the Gift to be Simple, 'Tis the Gift to be Free,
'Tis the Gift to come down where we ought to be,
And when we find ourselves in the place just right,
'Twill be in the valley of Love and Delight!

---

10. The *Prayer during the Day*, omitted in the SDLms., has been supplied.

THE SHAKERS

When true Simplicity is gained
To bow and to bend we shan't be ashamed.
To turn, turn will be our delight,
'Till by turning, turning we come 'round right!
                    (Inspirational gift–song, Elder Joseph Brackett of the
                    Ministry of the Maine Societies, ca. 1850)

[Symbolic gift of a flock of doves:]
  ... they will soar, and soar, and soar, until they find a resting
place. On those who will receive them, they have brought a meek and
quiet spirit, mild and gentle; so it will be very easy to see who receives
them. Are there not some in this assembly that can see These Doves?
                    (MS.—SDL—*Enfield Church/Thursday evening
                    September 2nd 1841.* &c. Ms. p. 7)

26

[Re: Spiritual gifts]
  ... These gifts ye may give wherever and unto whom ye think
proper; they are only to simplify and bring low the imaginations of the
high minded.
                    (MS.—SDL—*Enfield Church. From Elder Benjamin, Oct. 2nd 1841*)

27

[The gifts of the 1837–57 period] seem to have had an educative
force and to be, on a spiritual plane, of the nature of kindergarten work
in modern educational methods—preparing minds and hearts for the
reception of higher spiritual truths; training the powers of the soul
through pictorial and simple object lessons for dealing with spiritual
facts ... seems to have been the plan of development of these unseen
teachers.

                    (White and Taylor, *Shakerism,* p. 235) [1905]

28

Christian Experience. *Patience Vining*

Friend Editor; —I am one of the few left of the eighteenth century. . . .

My experience of seventy six years includes many more blessings than I am able to recount. From the early date of six years I have been made the recipient of God's love, and the life of the Believer has been beautiful to me. . . .

When I was young I often saw brethren and sisters under the control of spirit influence, and was in a quandary for a long time wondering how a spirit could move a body without the will of the one moved. I made it a subject of prayer. One day while alone and in deep thought on this subject, I felt the manifestation of the spirit of God on my body and knew what it was.

This proved satisfactory. I had received a spiritual baptism, and was never troubled any more about it. . . .

(*The Shaker Manifesto* XII, 3, p. 51) [1882]

29

[Untitled letter *Anon*. Re: Spiritualism]

. . .

We have always with very great pleasure placed our name among the spiritualists, and that name to us has a significance that far transcends all the dreams and visions that fall to common humanity. The best spiritualism that can manifest itself in an assemblage of Shakers must be that testimony which is the outgrowth of a pure heart. Visions which allow us to see ourselves are preeminently visions of God, and the exhortations of righteousness coming from a consecrated life are far better than any angel messages from a foreign sphere, so far as the prosperity of our Church is dependent upon them. . . . when we know that it [i.e., mediumistic spiritualism] is only the development of a natural faculty, the same as singing or speaking, we assign it to its legitimate place. . . .

We do think that while there is much that is sweet and choice in what we have shared as spiritual gifts [esp., re: 1837–1847], there has also immense harm reached us from the same mediums. The pioneers of our gospel work were gifted in visions but they were at the same time indefatigable workers on the earth.

. . .

Now, in all this confusion of thoughts and feelings; in all this anxiety of dreaming and ghost seeing which is among the Believers in every Society and family, we are not surprised that they are seeking beyond our own order for a shadowy satisfaction, and they will be fortunate if they get even a shadow. Another generation will not know the spiritualism that was with us from 1837 to 1847. The good they cannot know, to appreciate, and much of it would require an able, religious interpreter or it could not be understood. . . .

Now, Dear Elder, why do we need to wait for the coming years for an inspiration from on high? Is not the revelation of the work of God a growing revelation that shall make us what we profess to be, sons and daughters of a living God? Truly, and this spiritual health, prosperity and happiness is in our own hands.

(The Manifesto XIV, 7, pp. 159–160) [1884]

*　　　*　　　*

30

The church, or assembly of the faithful, established by the apostles at Jerusalem, "were of one heart and one soul;" and we have no account that they ever kept any external sacrament, as the Lord's supper, in any other manner than by eating and drinking together, daily, as Jesus Christ set them the example while he was with them. "And all that believed were together, and had all things common: — and breaking bread from house to house, did eat their meat with gladness and singleness of heart." (Acts, ii. 44 & 46.) It is true that when the gospel was preached to the Gentiles, those who believed did not generally come into a united interest; and therefore could not eat and drink together daily; hence they came together at appointed times, and held their love feasts, and ate and drank together, in remembrance of the last supper of the Lord Jesus with his disciples. But as soon as they fell into disorder in these things, the apostle Paul interfered, and set proper regulations among them, and said, "As often as ye eat this bread, and drink this cup, ye do shew the Lord's death till he come." (1 Cor. xi. 26.)

Hence it appears that, tho it might be done to commemorate the Lord's death; yet after the second coming of Christ, it could no longer be necessary; because the reality must then be made manifest. But where can we find any evidence to show, that the apostles and primitive christians ever pretended to a ceremonious consecration of a little bread and wine, and to make a formal distribution of it among the members of the church, and call it *the sacrament of the Lord's supper?* This practice was first introduced into the church by Gentile philosophers, who professed the christian faith, and whose object was, (as Dr. Mosheim[11] says,) "to give their religion a mystic air, in order to put it upon an equal footing, in point of dignity, with that of the pagans." (See Eccl. Hist. vol. i. p. 199.) This was undoubtedly the origin of all those ideas of the mysterious virtues which have ever been attached to that ceremony.

It is however certain, that if the bread and wine in this ceremony, are to be considered as symbols of the body and blood of a dying Savior, they must be symbols of an absent Savior: for there can be no kind of use in representing the Savior by signs and symbols, when he is really present. Wherever Christ has a true church, there he abides, and there is his body and blood. The church of Christ is fed with the bread of life, and refreshed with the water of life; and this is the body and blood of Christ, and these united, become the life of his true followers, and of which they all partake by their union to the body. "If we walk in the light, as he is in the light, we have fellowship one with another; and the blood of Jesus Christ (that is, his Spirit and life) cleanseth us from all sin." (1 John, i. 7.)

Thus the true sacrament of the Lord's supper is found in the spiritual union of the saints, who have fellowship one with another, by walking in the true light which is in Christ; and thus they partake of his Spirit and life, according to his own testimony: "I am the bread of life—I am the living bread which came down from Heaven: if any man eat of this bread, he shall live forever. —Except ye eat the flesh of the Son of man, and drink his blood, ye have no life in you. For my flesh is

---

11. Johann Lorenz von Mosheim (1694–1755), ecclesiastical historian, one of the founders of the University of Gottingen (where he became chancellor and professor of church history in 1747); the founder of modern pragmatic ecclesiastical historical criticism.

meat indeed, and my blood is drink indeed. He that eateth my flesh, and drinketh my blood, dwelleth in me, and I in him." (John, vi. 48–56.) This is partaking of the Lord's supper in very deed; and they who truly do this, have the promise of eternal life; and none can ever possess eternal life, unless they enjoy this holy communion, and really partake of this food, in its true spiritual sense.

No person can reasonably suppose that Jesus meant that we must literally eat his flesh and drink his blood, in order to obtain eternal life. His language on this occasion, as on many others, was used figuratively, to imply his life and his Spirit. His meaning was, that those who partake of his life and Spirit, will live as he lived, and walk as he walked; that is, in perfect obedience to the will of God. "My meat is to do the will of him that sent me," said he; and that which was his meat, became also the meat of his true followers, who thereby became the members of his body, and were made partakers with him, of the bread of life which was manifested in him. This is the food of heavenly minded souls, and this is the true sacrament, and there is no other. "To him that overcometh will I give to eat of the hidden manna." And again; "I will not drink henceforth of the fruit of the vine, until the day when I drink it new with you in my Father's Kingdom." (Matt. xxvi. 29. & Rev. ii. 17.) This remained to be accomplished at the period of his second coming.

Hence we may see what the true supper of the Lord is; and what his supper with his disciples was designed to typify: and when souls really come to partake of this bread, and drink this wine, they will no longer contend about shadows and signs. Jesus Christ did not say, "Except ye eat *that bread* and drink *that wine,*" which is called the Lord's supper, "ye have no life in you." Yet the professors of christianity, who have been so solicitious about the performance of the outward ceremony, instead of commemorating the dying love of the Divine Redeemer, by partaking of his Divine Spirit, and exercising it in love one to another, have manifested the most bitter animosities towards each other.

(Calvin Green, *Summary View*, pp. 240–241) [1823/1848]

3 I

"A new commandment I give unto you," said Jesus, "That ye love one another, as I have loved you. —By this shall all men know that ye

are my disciples, if ye have love one to another." (John, xiii. 34, 35.)
Here is a plain and positive command given; and those who faithfully
obey this command, cannot live in contention and strife; but will love
one another, not in profession and word; but in practical deeds of
kindness and charity. This is a plain and visible criterion by which all
men may see and know who are the true disciples of Christ. But a great
profession of religious love, with all the ceremonies of consecrated
bread and wine added to it, without a corresponding practice, is no
evidence of discipleship: for such are often as full of contention and
strife, as those who make no profession at all.

But the greatest practical evidence of genuine love and disinter-
ested benevolence that can be manifested on earth, is found where all
are of one heart and one soul; where the rich and the poor can meet
together, and eat and drink at one table, and cheerfully partake of one
common blessing and interest, and mutually share in each others
comforts and afflictions, both in things spiritual and temporal. Here
souls, by eating and drinking together, in christian love and harmony,
may daily partake of the Lord's supper, according to the manner in
which the primitive church partook of it. Here they may show forth
the Lord's death, in very deed, by their own example, in showing that
he died to a selfish, partial nature; and that they have become partakers
of that death, and have consequently risen with him, into that life
which the world, with all its professions of religion, have never obtained.

Herein they plainly show to all men, that they are partakers of
that real body and blood which is the true life of Christ; and are fed
and nourished by the true bread and wine of his spiritual Kingdom.
And in them is truly fulfilled the prayer of the Lord Jesus to his
heavenly Father; *"that they may be one, even as we are one."*

(Calvin Green, *Summary View*, pp. 243–244) [1823/1848]

32

The Sacrament. *Elijah Myrick.*

"And as they did eat, Jesus took bread, and blessed, and brake it,
and gave to them, and said take, eat; This is my body."

Which was his body? Those whom he was addressing? Who had
continued with him in his temptations? To whom he appointed a

kingdom as his father had appointed unto him? Who were to be the body through which Christ would continue to be manifest? Or was it the bread which he passed round as a symbol of union?

And while he was committing to them this great trust—this life—this new testament for many, for the remission of sins, did he not pass the cup as a seal of unity—a confirmation that they were one living body?...

(*The Shaker* VI, 10, p. 73) [1876]

33

[Letter:] *Mary A. Gillespie* [S.D.L.]
. . .

Now another scene presents itself to view—a table spread with food to sustain the physical part. We read of a Prophet in ancient days, who was fed morning and evening by the fowls of the air, also of the children of Israel, who were fed with manna in the wilderness, and perhaps, at some future time, others may read of *us* who are assembled here today; who knows but it may be so? We frequently hear of family gatherings in the natural order, where children are called home, where fathers and mothers, and brothers and sisters, re–unite around the family altar. And now we are all home again in the land of our Fathers, and as we sit at the table, let us raise a shout of thanksgiving that we have been spared to enjoy this rich feast with *Gospel* parents, and brethren and sisters. . . .

(*Shaker and Shakeress*, Social Gathering , August 19, 1873, p. 7) [1873]

34

[Letter:] *Richard Vanderbeck.*

I rejoice to meet with you, in this beautiful Grove of farm Canaan, today, where the sun pours its golden rays upon us, as if to make us feel cheerful while we share in this feast of heavenly things, which are pure in the sight of God and his Angels.

I always feel thankful to drink in, with you, this pure Gospel love which flows so free from soul to soul. It is good to be here, to sit beneath the shade of these beautiful trees, where the soft winds of heaven are blowing over us all. These gifts and offerings are food to my soul. . . .

(*Shaker and Shakeress,* Social Gathering, August 19, 1873, p. 8) [1873]

35

Home Notes: Mt. Lebanon—Ch. F. [Church Family]

I have just been filled with the life–giving spirit of the gospel, having freely partaken of the bread and waters of life fresh from the spiritual conservation of heaven. To–day the North family met with the Church in worship and the heavenly avenues were opened and the indwellers of the celestial temple were with us in spirit and in truth. Elder Giles [Avery, (deceased 1890)] was with us as a minister of the power of the world to come. He repeated some things that he had spoken before, viz: Hear ye my people! The Lord's work is in its infancy. You will be surprised at the manifestations of his power. There is light emanating from the Spirit world that will prove the fulfillment of the prophecies delivered to the Shakers during the period of time between 1837 and 1846. . . .

(*The Manifesto* XXVII, 2, p. 27) [1897]

36

In later years there has been a gradual change in the character of the worship in the hour of public or family devotion. While inflowings of spiritual power are frequent, and the gifts and leadings of the Spirit are heeded and followed, the tendency is toward expression of thought rather than bodily exercise. Shakers are thinkers; the spiritual current runs, perhaps, deeper, with less of noise and outward demonstration.

(White and Taylor, *Shakerism,* p. 333) [1905]

six

IN SPIRIT AND TRUTH

Introduction

As Travel in the Gospel, the Shaker Way is always in movement
from one moment to the next. It is always rooted in a dynamic sense of
history, looking back to a *genetic past* in which can be discerned the
potentials for a *creative present*, which in turn looks to an *open future*.
The expectations of the future are always to be positive: what will the
next gifts be? Believers in each era were concerned to understand this
process of progression as best they could and so regularly re–evaluated
their grasp of the past in terms of what was at hand in the present.[1] As
always, they found it much easier to read the past than to prophesy the
future. However much their present creativity might suggest the next
developments, the future always held the unexpected new factors—
gifts—and so true faithfulness required constant openness.

By the mid-nineteenth century, just about a hundred years after
the first gathering under the Wardleys, many Shakers saw signs of
decline in the communal form of life. Fewer new members were

---

1. There was a standing practice throughout the communities to hold "Year End
Meetings" between Christmas and New Year's, to review the previous year and all the
patterns of community life. At this time especially they would try to reach consensus on
any change which should be undertaken. It was a series of such meetings throughout the
Societies in the 1880's which reached a common recognition that the season for the gift
of dancing in worship had closed.

entering and their internal spirit at times seemed less zealous. Leaders more and more commented on the implications for the future, most often with positive expectations for change, even radical change, rather than a mere hope of recovery of the momentum to sustain the existing form. Walt Whitman, on a personal retreat at Mt. Lebanon in the mid–1850s, records in his journal an elder's sermon in which the Shaker Church is compared to a normal school for training teachers, and the elder suggests that perhaps enough teachers (witnesses of the Gospel) have been prepared. If so, Believers should look for a new and different gift to come.

Shakers have often noted the distinction between the truth they sought to live and their organized, tangible forms. They have been committed to the authenticity of the truth, but never to the form, which is only *useful,* and useful only in limited circumstances and for limited periods. Shaker "orthodoxy" explicitly insists that all forms ultimately pass away, and so no one can cling to them uncritically and be truly faithful. Believers, thus, enjoyed a very unusual sense of freedom for the future, but therefore were also forced to pay close attention to the present so as to be able to contribute creatively to the shaping of that future. Freedom for the future also meant freedom from the past, that is, from the past as a burden of demands for conformity and preservation. The past was yesterday's creative present open to its future, which today has come with its new gifts. The present, thus, fulfills the past by subsuming it into a new reality, not by perpetuating it. And this present, in turn, is integral to the future–oriented process of further growth into transformation.

We have already seen this commitment expressed in many ways, but perhaps most notably in Father Joseph's vision of the seven cycles of openings and change reaching into the future, and in the Preface to the *Millennial Praises* with its warning of the limits for present gifts. There are many reflections, especially in later writings, of the positive expectations for the future and freedom from the overburden of the past. For more than a century Believers have looked forward with anticipation: what would the new gifts be and how different would they be? Inevitably much of that question would have to remain unanswered, yet they gradually were able to envision at least the broad outlines of the shape of things to come.

The first selections highlight the basic freedom experienced in looking to the future. The teaching of Mother Ann (1) is of the greatest importance as the principle of community: the entirety of community and its implications can be found, if need be, in even one individual Believer. Community in the ultimate meaning of the One Christ is not a matter of groups or numbers. One anointed—*Christed*—in the One Christ can be the bearer of the incarnate reality of God-in-Christ-in-us. As all humanity was at–one in Jesus Christ in his dying and rising, so the Union of Believers in whom Christ comes again can be embodied in one who believes. Because of this principle Shakers have never been trapped into evaluating the validity of their lived experience in terms of numbers. Nor are they even committed to maintain any one form of life into the future as if this would insure authenticity. The reflection of Elder Richard McNemar (2) on the conversion experience of the early Kentucky-Ohio Believers states another basic principle of openness to the future: the rightful inheritance of all that proves to be true. The movement into ever greater light does not presume rejection but growing enrichment. The expectation for the future is, simply, *more!* Hence the future involves a twofold sense of freedom: a freedom from any preoccupation with numbers or forms, and a freedom to receive all true gifts however unexpected or revolutionary. The remaining three selections illustrate this freedom, first, in Father James' prophecy (3) of decline until but five were left, next, in Mother Ann's admonition (4) to be unconcerned about outguessing the future but rather labor in present gifts, and, finally, the 1827 prophecy (5) of decline to the point of extinction and then a new opening of the Gospel in totally new dimensions. Historically this last has played an important role in shaping Believers' expectations, coming as it did a full thirty years before the communitarian Societies had reached their peak in numbers and effectiveness. (It is an important factor in explaining why Shakers never sought to develop efficient long-term missionary activities to ensure survival of the existing communities.)

The next selections (6–21) involve positive visions of the future as characterized by unity and univeralism. The range of insight represented is remarkable, leading to an ecumenical commitment of the future, re–shaped Shaker Church—Elder George Lomas' editorial "Union of Churches" (8), Eldress Antoinette Doolittle's unity through progression in learning from *all* and not being reliant on mere tradition (11), the positive interchange with Catholics through the *Ave Maria* magazine editors (17, 18), and the extension of inter–Christian ecumenical commitment to one reaching out to all religious traditions (19, 20, 21). The authors represent the full spectrum of conservative-moderate-liberal Shaker thinking, but unite significantly to extend the ultimate horizon to include all that can prove true, whatever its source. This unitive hope is as authentic as one of the earliest Christian theological principles, as first stated in the second century by Justin Martyr: *The truth, whoever speaks it, is from the Holy Spirit.*

In the later nineteenth century Shakers came to identify their committed position as *Alethianism* (from the Greek *aletheia*, truth), even for a time formally adopting the designation *United Society of Alethians*. Alethian Shakerism represents the positive commitment to the future: authenticity is fulfilled only in the quest for unity and it is violated by separatism. The Alethian commitment is to unity with all that is progressive in secular life, to unity with other Christian Churches and traditions so as to inherit all truth, and to unity with all Religious Traditions whereby God is manifested through His inner Gift of increasing Light. Traveling in this commitment would be much more than a mere mixing together of a variety of elements, as Elder Giles Avery insists (21). It requires discernment and transformation, in which what prove to be gifts–for–a–season are put aside and the gifts–forever are renewed through further progression into come–up–higher–gifts. What is significant for the Shaker Way, however, is the fact that Believers have been committed to Alethianism for over a century. Whatever the re-shaping of Shakerism might be in a new opening of the Gospel, it must be truly unitive, not separatistic, and so participate in a growing revelation embracing progressive human life, unitive Christianity, and the whole manifestation of Light. The divisiveness heretofore characteristic of separate human societies, classes, and peoples must be healed. The Churches must find each other One in Christ since their separation cannot be realistic in a Christ who cannot be divided. Their diversity in gifts must also become an enriching unity. The discovery of all that is true in God is the progressive opening into enlightenment leading us from the narrow limits we imagine as proper to life in the Spirit to the recognition of a limitlessly expanding Spirit "blowing where She wills." Shakers could commit themselves to this future but could not unilaterally re–shape their way of life to embody it. A unitive Shakerism must be created with partners or it is just another form of separatism. The first Shaker visionaries were too early: no other Church was yet ready for a unitive vision. Not until the mid-twentieth century have significant responses come to the call for unity among human communities, the Christian Churches, and universal Religious Traditions.

One aspect of the call to unity-in-diversity is the need to locate what divides or, more positively, what unifies. The selections (22–26) provide us with an insight into the view taken by the more conservative Shakers. They are generally suspicious (to say the least) of creedal or theological traditions, opposing this tendency to represent the authenticity of Christianity by systems of thought with the insistence that the lived experience is more fundamental—to the point where these "conservatives" would discard doctrinal structures altogether! Elder Giles Avery, for over thirty years the colleague of Elder Daniel Boler who presided over the Mt. Lebanon Central Ministry, was a noted conservative. It is interesting here (25, 26) and elsewhere to see his conservatism rigorously linked with the commitment to progression.

If unity includes the secular world, Shakers had to come to grips with their sense of separation from the world. They attempted to do so through the application of the principle of progression (27–38), and here we see the elements of a debate which occupied the final third of the nineteenth century. There were optimists (29) who interpreted external events as the sure signs of an evolving humanity, which would soon begin to transcend the "worldly" limitations of nature and rise into regeneration. For them Shakers were the heralds of a new kind of secular world to emerge shortly. In contrast, the pessimists (28) presumed there must always be an ongoing struggle against "worldly" principles and practices, a struggle which would make even sharper the line separating Believers from "world's people." Generally, the optimists were more persuasive, as evidenced by the many practical innovations introduced from the "world" and the developing sense of coherence with the ideology of secular progress. Indeed, some of the selections seemed to reflect a naive acceptance of the "cult of progress," a common danger among Shaker progressives. The two selections from Elder Alonzo Hollister (31, 32) illustrate his position as the foremost spokesman for the developing Alethianist position. The last reflection (38), by Eldress Catherine Allen, who was to preside over the Mt. Lebanon Ministry in the period of World War I, expresses the unquestioning optimism for the coming unity of the religious with the secular, which then faded with the tragedy of the World War and the further moral-economic disasters of postwar affluence and the final disillusionment of the Depression.

While Shakers (as others) failed to forsee the coming failures in secular society, they dealt realistically with the principle of progression at home. The six selections (39–44) testifying to this stress the fact of change at the heart of progression. Progression does not signify mere increase or refinement of what is already present but a process of continued *metanoia*, change of consciousness. Thus commitment to progression calls for a continuing discernment as to what really constitute essentials (39, 42) and how the externals help support the recognition of these essentials by making a way of life which can be lived practically (40, 41). The old Shaker principle *Christianity properly practiced is practical and progressive* allows for and in fact insists on a constant testing. The test reveals whether or not effective change is taking place, rather than assurance that what has been is being maintained.

The next selections (45–60) are perhaps the most important of all, reflecting the range of expectations of fundamental changes called for by the future. The attempt at a new kind of Shaker life in a non–communitarian and urban form is witnessed to by Arthur Dowe[2] and the group of Believers in San Francisco (46). Apart from the earlier interracial community in Philadelphia under Eldress Rebecca Jackson, this is the only recorded instance of the concrete exploration of a truly new form. Unfortunately, little is known beyond a handful of letters (some published in *The Manifesto*) and pamphlets; the effort seems to have been swept away with the Earthquake and Fire of 1906. The two items from Simon Emery (47, 48) supporting Dowe's frustrated criticism of the established Societies and their inability to transform illustrate both the activity of non–communitarian Shakers and the openness of the established Lead to accept clear and demanding criticism—and publish it! The remaining texts testify to the awareness of communitarian Believers that their rural–agricultural experience cannot guide them into creating a form appropriate to the coming urban-industrial context. As Elder Oliver Hampton observes (51), renewal must be left to a future generation. DeGraw (49), Frazer (56), and Blinn (57) present a variety of insights of ecumenical and pluralistic factors which must characterize the future; especially noteworthy is Frazer's identification of Shakers as a priesthood and not a separatistic sect, and therefore called outward in service to a larger sense of community beyond the communitarian Societies' boundaries.

---

2. Dowe and the San Francisco Shakers published several short pieces—pamplets, broadsides—as part of their missionary activity; they represent late-nineteenth century Shakerism without notable innovation. Cf. bibliography entry.

THE SHAKERS

Finally, a variety of reflections (61–66) illustrate attitudes of openness to a future which cannot be predefined. They stress the difference between principles and organization, with commitment resting solely in the former (61, 62). There is hope for the future (63), but tempered with the need for emotional resignation in letting go of what is passing away, together with patience and the call to reach out to others (64). And once again, the overriding sense of the non–static process of Faith as Travel with all its unfolding changes is affirmed in the recollection of Father Joseph's vision of the seven cycles (65).

As the closing word (66), one which paradoxically looks beyond the closing of one era to the yet-to-come people of the next, Eldress Antoinette Doolittle's image of the empty candlesticks waiting to be filled with the new candles is certainly the most fitting witness to Believers' commitment to the future: not the mere continuity of themselves by attempting to preserve the *things* they have, but the continuity of themselves through others in a community of experience transcending times and forms.

I

3. Not long after the opening of the gospel at Watervliet, Mother Ann was speaking to a large number of the Believers, concerning those who were called by the gospel, and of their bearing and travailing for other souls, and she said, "If there be but one called out of a generation, and that soul is faithful, it will have to travail and bear for all its generation; for the world will be redeemed by generations." Elder William Lee, and Elder James Whittaker often spoke in the same manner, concerning the redemption of souls. *Hannah Cogswell.*

(Giles Avery, ed., *Precepts*, p. 186) [1816/1888]

2

This little company were so far from brooking the character of apostates from any true religion, that they considered themselves, if faithful, rightful heirs to all true religion that had ever existed in the Church of God.

(Richard McNemar, *Important Events*, p. 16) [1831]

3

... soon there will be not one left who ever saw the face of any of our *first Parents*. But the gospel will be kept in its purity, whether fiew [*sic*] or many are willing to endure its purifying fire.
. . .

Father James testified, that if there should be such a falling away that but five souls were left in the gospel, that five would rise up and spread the *gospel thro' the earth*. . . .

(Calvin Green, *Letter to Joshua Bussell* [SDLms.], pp. 21, 32) [1856]

4

2. A certain young man came to Mother with some peach and plum stones in his hand, and asked her if he might plant them? "Yea," answered Mother, "do all your work as though you had a thousand years to live, and as you would if you knew you must die to-morrow."
Lucy Wright.
(Giles Avery, ed., *Precepts*, p. 242) [1816/1888]

5

[Daniel Merton, visiting Union Village, Ohio, in 1827 prophesied:]
After great and peaceful growth, then change and decline—when annihilation seems inevitable, the church will rise again to a higher culmination of glory. . . .
Smaller and smaller shall you grow, fewer and fewer, till a child in its mother's arms can count the remnant, [then. . . .]
A new opening of the Gospel—a far grander and more universal revelation of these and other sacred truths will come. The faithful remnant shall become the germ of a new, far reaching life and the glory of the latter days shall outshine the brightest that went before.
(White and Taylor, *Shakerism*, pp. 369, 370) [1905]

*　　*　　*

6

Calvin Green: Pluralism.

... There never were so many *ravenous beasts* of *prey* ranging in the world, as there are at the present *time;* for as other [i.e., for as at other times?] are various stages and degrees in this immediate age, so there have been and will be various manners and degrees of operation each having its peculiar time of day; and like to the natural days and nights many different days and nights are going on divers lattitudes at once. So it is in the providential and spiritual work, hence arises the various scenes which are going on in various places in the world at the same litteral time, according to the nature of the spirits that have the ascendency in such time and place. Therefore as there are more enlightening principles in various degrees operating in the world to bring forth the natural and religious rights of man and ultimately preparing Lambs for the *fold of Christ.* . . . The revolutionary so powerfully operating in the world is the *lion* [i.e., to protect the lambs] in the order of providence in the outward work operating in many *Lions.* . . .

(Calvin Green: *Letter to Eld. Lorenzo Grosvenor;*
New Lebanon, April 11, 1852. SDLms.)

7

Right and Light. *Anon. "Septimus"*

The First Cause of all causes we call God; by descending terms, Father and Mother; Being and Will; Truth and Love; I am and I do; Spirit and Matter; Religion and Science. . . . The desire to be and do good, is religion. The desire to know how, why and when to be good, is theology. Spiritualism is the soul of all systems of philosophy.

. . .

The priests of Nature—Pythagoras, Diogenes, Plato, Seneca and the Stoics, enjoined self–control, and, to a great extent, self–denial of the senses, as did the Avaters [*sic*], like Confucius, Buddha, Zoroaster, Jesus; they touched each other.

The material worlds! the spiritual worlds! Why, is it not *all* spirit, in different stages of unfoldment, from the stand-point of Deity? *All spirit,* more or less externalized, down to the earths, which are first, gas and ether, then granite, rock and diamond. *All matter,* more or less attenuated, sublimated, etheralized, up to the lowest spirit sphere, and thence up to the heaven of heavens.

. . .

It should be distinctly remarked, that it was in goodness, rather than in intellectuality—in religion rather than in theology, that he (Jesus) excelled. . . .

When Paul came up, who was also of a good philosophical and intellectual stock, and had been educated in all the learning and culture of the Jews, he taught theology—the science of the religion of Jesus. It was an effort of the human mind to comprehend the height and depth, and length and breadth of the work of human redemption, and to systematize and explain it logically.

(*The Shaker* I, 5, p. 33) [1871]

8

Union of Churches—Editorial   [*Geo. A. Lomas*]

We have often urged upon the various denominations or churches, professing Christ as their Lord and Head, to try and come to some united opinion as to what constitutes genuine Christianity; and so to take action upon the subject as to have but one grand church, one united brotherhood of faith and life. Although some wise heads of the "Revs." have informed us that this "never can be done," we yet have an unbounded confidence, that sooner than many are aware this scheme will be consummated.

A very ably edited paper in New York city has for years labored to this end, and has the encouraging influences of very many of the most prominent clergy of our own and other countries. This periodical is "THE CHURCH UNION." Amidst the most discouraging circumstances it never has flagged, nor drooped its standard. And why should it? Churches having by profession one Lord, Christ Jesus, and the life of this head of the faith so explicitly and unerringly delineated and illustrated, why should there be any fears of a final union and a united Christ family made up of all the churches professing love for the Christian life? None whatever. *The Golden Rule*, of Boston says:

"The Bishop of Manchester, Eng., in the course of a sermon recently delivered at Rochdale, referred to the differences existing between various religious bodies, and said he should like to see a conference of representatives of all denominations for the purpose of seeing whether it was not possible even yet to adjust their differences and place Christianity on a common basis, in order that they might have a common Christianity running through the Sunday–schools of the land."

Now, this feeler, put forth by the anxious bishop, will work as a leaven among both clergy and laity; and but a few years can intervene, ere the popular demand of humanity, with greatly increased intelligence and human sympathies, will institute a conference for a union of the now divided churches; and the spirit, tenor, ruling characteristic of such conference will be to settle the question: How did Jesus Christ live? and the key that will unlock the bar to a complete union, and dispel such bar, will be the conscientious agreement of the representatives of such conference, that *as Jesus, the Lord and Leader lived, so should his disciples,—those joining his church, live.* And brethren of the various Churches, Ecclesiastic Denominations professing the Christian religion, we, your friends, the Shakers, are ready and anxious to have the conference called and to meet you there. Further, *we issue the call,* the same to be considered living and active, until both conference and Universal Church are consummated.

(*The Shaker Manifesto* X, 9, pp. 203–204) [1880]

9

The Happy Omen. [Editorial Note.]

"The present age perceives that there are bonds of union far more important than doctrinal divisions.". . .

We hope all our dear friends will read, and ponder upon the noble, wise unsectarian sentiments of the above paragraph. . . ."The world does move;" and with it its theological, biased prejudices grow less. Thirty years from now, who knows how much more men will love each other and how fewer creeds there will be, and what they are, how much nearer like Christ, who was positively non–sectarian!

(*The Shaker Manifesto* XI, 2, p. 41) [1881]

THE SHAKERS

10

[Editorial:] Signs of the Times

To every individual, given to fervent thought, the present status of the so-called religious world is wearing a very different complexion than ever before, and withal, a very improved complexion. Every denomination of the Christian profession has lost much of that which formerly made it a competitor for the laurels of infallibility, while a liberal tone, and better—a humane, brotherly feeling—now pervades, where hatred for anything that differed from "our church" once prevailed.

There are principles of godliness that are infallible, invincible, all–conquering principles, which in the progress of man, from the mere animal up to the angel, are irrevocably sealed as everlasting truths.

. . .

Admissions of the superior are invariably accompanied by confessions of error in preconceived opinions. Admissions and confessions are really good for the soul. Adjustments of differences in religious matters are being rapidly made upon the principles of righteousness and charitable love, and these principles will eventuate in a church universal—the millennium come.

(*The Shaker Manifesto* XI, 10, pp. 233–234) [1881]

11

Who Holds the Keys? *Antoinette Doolittle*

Jesus, when he was about to leave his little flock that he had gathered around him during his ministry, gave the keys of the kingdom to Peter. We do not suppose that Jesus meant to be understood that Peter was a *Rock*, or that as a *man* he designed to build his church upon him. But he perceived that Peter was blest with the gift of Revelation when he said, "Thou art the Christ." And Jesus, knowing that the time of his departure was at hand, was anxious to find one upon whose brow he could place the signet of Leadership, and baptize, as he himself had been baptized, one who would be able to lead, direct and protect the lambs of his fold after he had passed from their sight.

He felt that Peter was the fittest representative of christian principles, and the ablest expounder of the doctrines which he himself had taught that he would find for the time being. Peter also passed away in due time, and also a long line of his successors down through the ages. Did they retain or lose the keys, or who holds the keys of the kingdom now?

. . .

It is apparent to every close observer of the signs of the times . . . that Luther and Calvin doctrines are destined to pass away; that orthodoxy [i.e., Protestant] and heterodoxy must meet face to face, each to plead their cause and bring forth their *reasons* for believing, or disbelieving thus, and so, and if this would be done in a right spirit, truth would be advanced thereby.

Those who have been honestly linked to the creedal faiths of their forefathers and have conscientiously guarded them, would certainly lose nothing by liberal investigation. . . .

When the national civil rulers enact more just laws, bearing equally upon all citizens, irrespective of sex or color, deepening and broadening the basic foundation of American government, which professes and should be non–partisan, and will give a strong guarantee that all its subjects shall be fully protected in civil and religious liberty, leaving each and all free (while law-abiding) to worship God in accordance with their own convictions of right and duty, irresponsible of any earthly tribunal, then the *new earth* will be formed, abounding in fruitful fields. Wars will cease, and fraternal relations between nations be established to the ends of the earth.

Thus purified, the national banner will be uplifted, and never more be left to trail in the dust of low selfish aims and political intrigues. Then the *new heavens* will have a permanent foundation to rest upon, and divine revelation will illumine the spiritual pathway and open the doors to the inner spheres of the resurrection heavens, and harmony will prevail. Leading minds will fraternize, and the "Watchman in Zion will see eye to eye." This unity will only be accomplished by a heavenly baptism that will purify the heart and quicken the germ of immortality planted by God in all human souls.

When that good time comes we shall no longer ask, "Who holds the keys?" that will unlock the doors of Christ's kingdom. We shall find the "seal broken, and the mystery finished." There will be "an open door that no man can shut; and that all may know the Lord for himself or herself, from the least to the greatest."

We shall always have need of spiritual, heavenly guides and teachers, more advanced than ourselves, to go before us; but all may hold the

THE SHAKERS

keys of revelation within their own grasp. If *truth* be our motto, and we resolve to make *it* our nearest friend and companion, we shall find neither bondage, mystery, darkness nor death in it. All hail the coming day!

(The Shaker Manifesto X, 8, pp. 176–178) [1880]

I 2

Welcome Progress. [Editorial]

It is more than one hundred years since the founders of the Shaker Church, arriving in America, preached the good news of a present salvation from sin, and consequently from the punishments of sin through a life of self-denial, similar to that lived by Jesus, and which saved Jesus. *Purity, Peace, Equality* and *Unworldly ambitions* ranked first, a most worthy attainment. For the possession of these any, and every necessary self-denial was endured. Closely allied to these, but secondary in importance were theological beliefs, which, however unorthodox and heretical at the time, have since become the popular beliefs of the millions....["Hell" the torment of conscience; a non–physical resurrection; equality of sexes; God Father and Mother; anti–slavery; communism; anti–war.]...There have been no forward movements yet made by Church nor State but were anticipated and longed for by the little, obscure people, called Shakers. We would welcome more progress, particularly in the churches; we would welcome the relinquishment of the unstable hope, dreamed of in the *atonement* doctrine, and the substitution of the real life of Christ, which will save, and make us *at–one–ment* with Christ. We look for this consummation with positive certainty, and welcome its dawning from any circumstance and from every quarter. The Shakers have very much to gain before they assert their proficiency as a Christian people; but they have thus far been in the van of all the righteous demonstrations that have reformed Church and State for the better; and yet stand ready to welcome more, and an eternal increase of morality, justice and true religion. These forward movements have been made at the expense of proneness to selfish considerations; and extreme self-denial in the foundation of the Shaker life and Church.

(The Shaker Manifesto XI, 12, pp. 274–275) [1881]

THE SHAKERS

13

The Simple Gospel of Christ. *G. A. Lomas.*

....Why should Christianity be the prey of so many and much contentions? Why, when there is only "one Lord, one faith and one baptism," should there be almost numberless divisions of opinions as to what genuine Christianity really is? Why ... should there be such demands for Colleges, Universities, etc., for the training of the young, by the most skilled theologians and ingenious scholars, simply that they may know and teach what some ignorant, unpretentious fishermen learned from the lips and observed in the life-walks of the Master? These Universities and Colleges are not for the learning of the simple religion of Jesus. . . .

Is there any doubt in the minds of any professors of Christianity, or of those who do not profess it, as to what kind of a life Jesus lived?

There is oneness of knowledge, oneness of feeling in this respect. Let us have one Christian Church that will absorb all the previous Babylonyish professions—a Church that will be the universally acknowledged Christian Church, embracing all sensible men and women, who are not led by the ingenious evasions of the priests; but one that will be accepted, because it teaches that Christ's life was His religion and His Christianity; and as Christians that life must be ours.

(*The Shaker Manifesto* XII, 1, pp. 3–4) [1882]

14

Ancestral Tradition. *Antoinette Doolittle*

... thorough investigation on our part, often convinces us that many of those ideas are only traditionally ours, inherited, and have not come to us by close reasoning, nor earned by labor. Hence the necessity of great charity for the views and opinions of others, who think and reason differently from us; and in all cases "to be kindly affectioned one towards another." If the advancement of truth be our aim, then all can work harmoniously together.

....It is our privilege to take lessons from the wise and unwise, the progressed and unprogressed. Let all have a place to work according to their several gifts and attainments, "one after this manner,

317

another after that," according to the measure of grace through the gift of God to them and the ministration and effectual working of His power by the spirit of Christ.

. . .

The progressive spirit of the ages will roll onward the great car freighted with the ripest and best fruits of the centuries gone by; and let us say, as did Jesus, that it is not our purpose to destroy or annul any truth of the Law or Gospel; but pray and work to the end, that every jot and tittle may be fulfilled, and glorified. . . .

Shall we learn, and be warned by the past to look well to the present, and to hold fast our veracity, while we press on to know and understand the future, and prepare to meet whatever may betide, whether weal or woe, prosperity or adversity? If forewarned, we may be forearmed; and thus be able to stand where others have fallen; and then we shall be debtors to the wise and unwise.

(*The Shaker Manifesto* XII, 3, pp. 55–57) [1882]

15

Home Notes—Enfield, New Hampshire. *George H. Baxter.*

In this age of spiritual enlightenment, when the evangelical churches are blending in fellowship, and giving as did Jesus the Christ, free gifts of mind and soul for the elevation of the needy, it bespeaks volumes of praise to the doers of the work as well as the hearers of the word of salvation. It is pleasant to realize that the old fence of exclusiveness that once hedged in the various churches is crumbling away, and the living vines of truth are drawing mankind out of the furrows of dogmatic narrowness into the broad fields of Christian duty.

(*The Manifesto* XXVI, 11, p. 180) [1896]

16

One of The Signs of The Times. *Martha J. Anderson*

. . .

There had been a series of Tuesday evening services [at Unity Church, (Unitarian), Pittsfield Mass.], at which several prominent clergymen of various denominations had occupied the pulpit . . . for better acquaintance, to strengthen the bonds of fraternal love, and awaken an interest and desire to know more of the various phases of thought and belief, that build up sectarian barriers, and separate churches from associative work along the lines of organized effort for good.

... in one hundred and eighteen years, this was the first time that our neighboring townspeople had invited "Believers" to speak in one of their churches.

(*The Manifesto* XXIV, 5, p. 104) [1894]

17

[Editorial Item] *Henry C. Blinn* [re: *Ave Maria*]

It is with a peculiar sense of regard and appreciation we publish for the benefit of all the readers of *The Manifesto,* the following notice taken from a recent issue of the *Ave Maria* one of the most popular, and most extensively circulated magazines in the Catholic Church. . . .

As Shakers, interested in every movement that conduces to advance the kingdom of God among men by fighting the cursed vice of sensuality which is the chief cause of so much misery in the world, we never depreciate the movement because it comes from this or that peculiar creed or sect, we are only glad that it comes, only glad to help it on by our prayers and support.

We are thoroughly acquainted with the high standard of moral training which prevails in Catholic schools and colleges. The pupils are taught to regard the holy virtue of purity as a thing divine, before which angels prostrate in adoring love. They are taught to believe that its observance constitutes the noblest manhood or womanhood that this world has to offer.

It is not surprising that such a magazine as the *Ave Maria* should issue from such a source. While we may differ from the *Ave Maria* in our views of the eternal truths of Christianity, yet we are one in our belief that sin is detestable, that it is man's worst enemy, and that the only power that can conquer it is the pure gospel of Jesus Christ. . . .

[*Ave Maria* item:] The editor of our Shaker contemporary, *The Manifesto,* explains how the United Society of Believers came to be called Shakers, a nickname they have since adopted. The founders of this sect were God-fearing men, who dwelt much on the severity of the divine judgments. . . . the Shakers were the only sect, we believe, who meekly accepted a nickname invented in ridicule.

We wish we could share with our readers the pleasure derived from a letter lately received from the editor of *The Manifesto,* asking an exchange with the *Ave Maria*—a letter breathing a beautiful spirit of Christian charity. It affords another proof that God's flowers bloom upon every soil, and that many who are geographically outside the Church are not culpably outside it. If all Shakers are like the pious, prayerful, peaceful, God-loving, sin-hating Community from which *The Manifesto* emanates, they can not be far from the Kingdom of God.

(*The Manifesto* XXVII, 9, p. 142) [1897]

18

Home Notes—Shakers, New York (Watervliet). *Hamilton DeGraw*

When we read the editorial comments of the "Ave Maria" on the principles of our Communities, and coming from an organ under the jurisdiction of that powerful ecclesiastical organization, the Catholic Church, we realized the fact that the boundary line of sects and parties could not prevent the communion of kindred souls and all who love the truth were as brethren and sisters, regardless of the organization, religious or political with which they are associated.

Let those who think that the testimony of truth which Believers have held forth has fallen on barren ground, because of our disparity of numbers, remove their doubts; there never was a time when the testimony was working with that fullness as at present. The more advanced minds are going deep to the foundation of the causes which are producing the discordant effects portrayed in our political and religious life. The opening years of the twentieth century will witness a quickening of the spiritual forces that have been dormant . . .

(*The Manifesto* XXVII, 10, p. 155) [1897]

19

Writing on the Sky. *Alonzo G. Hollister*

. . .

The doctrine of the supernal life, if we are rightly informed, was made known to Buddha the sage of India, in answer to his searching desire to know and remove the cause of pain. Both Buddha and Jesus taught that though it is an object of hope to all, and the path thereto is open to all who choose to travel therein, it cannot be attained without a total sacrifice of interests in the lower life, and a vigorous and persistent prosecution of the object by whoever would win it. . . .

. . .Only that select portion could be disciples of Jesus, according to the terms laid down by him, which were in essence and practical effect nearly the same as those taught by Buddha for attaining Nirvana. . . .

ʿAnn Lee owning Jesus Christ as her head, Lord, and teacher, while laboring to know and remove the cause of man's loss from God, (a loss which man's conduct makes too evident to be rationally disputed,) revived anew the law and doctrine of the supernal life, with such advances in its application to earthly conditions as the growth of centuries, the different customs and habits of thought among the people to whom her message was directed, and its adaptation to the common mind and the equality of the sexes, demanded.

Ann was one of a group of souls, like minded, prepared as tinder to kindle with fire thus again brought down from heaven, and through their agency, and the co–operation of the Holy Spirit, the age of the seventh trumpet, and the woman clothed with the sun, which typifies divine light, has been ushered upon the earthly stage. . . .

Buddhism as a philosophy and rule of life would seem to have been a good preparation for the doctrines of self-denial Jesus taught. The renunciations and crucifixions in either system, were much like those of the other, in essence and in the results proposed, though differing somewhat in external routine, the christian routine being easier because more helpful, useful, and less solitary than the Buddhist discipline.

Shakerism is not distinct from pure christianity in the end sought, and the sacrifices demanded by it, being a new edition, revised and adapted to the present age of progressed thought.

Buddhism is at present attracting great attention from scholars and liberal thinkers because of its literature, language, and antiquity, and the influence these are supposed to have exercised upon the growth of human ideas and conduct. . . . whenever . . . the divine germ [in man] is allowed to freely expand in its own native element, it always asserts the same general principles of purity, gentleness, humility, self-sacrifice, patient willingness to serve, serenity, rectitude, harmony, and enlightened intelligence, whether in Jesus, Ann, Buddha, Plato, or any who look to them as teachers.

THE SHAKERS

...

Shakerism is a return to deeds, and possesses the same efficacy through the co–operation of the Holy Spirit, to transform the inward life, regenerate and purify the soul, and raise it to aeionian or eternal life, as had primitive christianity, and the eight fold path of Buddhism, and this too while discharging the ordinary duties of earth life, and performing the reciprocal offices of society in communion with kindred spirits in the body and out of the body.

(*The Shaker Manifesto* XIII, 5, pp. 97–100) [1883]

20

Religious Sentiment. *Martha J. Anderson*
...

The increasing liberality of the present time is a happy promise of the near future when sectarian bigotry—the bane of religion—shall have been swept away by the tide of intellectual expansion and true Christian faith, resulting in brotherly love.

...Dying, beyond resusitation, is that power that has molded mind in the narrow limits of soulless systems of dogmatic belief.

Great men and true women are clasping hands, and standing side by side, in work that pertains to the common interests of society and civil government, without questioning each other's differences on religious points. ...

No great truth, whether enunciated by Confucius, Buddha, Zoroaster, or Jesus, will ever be lost. The grandeur and stability of moral principles outlive all forms, ceremonies and traditions, ...

(*The Shaker Manifesto* XI, 5, pp. 102–103) [1881]

21

The Shaker Problem. *Giles B. Avery.*

[Response to the future of Shakerism—including the numbers issue, etc.]

... If such souls [i.e., whom God has called to live a life of perfection now] can be found among Shakers, Quakers, Methodists, Baptists, Episcopalians, Presbyterians, Catholics, or any other of the multitudinous cognomens of those professing religion, or those making no religious profession, such really are Shakers of worldly elements, principles and institutions; they are the laboring agents whom God hath declared, by the mouth of his prophet Haggai, should shake the world and its old heavens of pleasure in unrighteousness. Thus, "yet once it is a little while, and I will shake the heavens and the earth, the sea and the dry land; and I will shake all nations, and the desire of all nations shall come; and I will fill this (Shaker) house with glory, saith the Lord of Hosts." See Haggai ii, 6th and 7th.

. . .

Shakerism, while it recognizes and accepts all the revelations of God's will and purposes for man's elevation, salvation and redemption, . . . yet, it does not, in one Babylonish mixture, mingle the ordinances which were the laws of progress for man while under the ministration of each of these distinct and different dispensations, as do many man made theologies and creeds.

And though at present the numbers progressing in this prophetic shaking dispensation are small, and for a time and times, may decrease, yet the genuine Shaker's faith is consonant with the prophet's declaration: [above].

. . .

The present phase of "Shaker" experience with regard to numbers professing the Shaker faith, as well as the experience of the other denominations of religious profession, is merely a halt in the march of religious progress.

When names, and sects, and parties shall have passed away, true Shakers will be found to possess a kingdom eternal, while the world, and its elements, will be burned up by the fire of truth.

(*The Manifesto* XV, 3, pp. 51–53) [1885]

*   *   *

22

"What is Truth?" *Anon.*

. . . These [i.e., non–Shaker] theologies form the most monstrous Babylon ever existing. The majority are professedly Christian; but instead of converging toward each other into the Christ life ... a diverging from the principles of truth are [sic] continually consummating. We propose the burning of all the so-called Christian theologies, and substituting the simple, faultless life of Christ as a guide—this is all the theology needed; relieving us from the necessity of clerical legerdermain, pulpit wrangling, and the vast expense of that branch of colleges and academies used for theological purposes.

(The Shaker II, 7, p. 49) [1872]

23

One Faith. *A. G. Hollister.*

. . .

Concerning what may be termed theological interpretations of certain sentimentalities of religious opinion, or what some would call speculative theology, the ideas of Christians may vary; but in relation to the genuine Christian's duty of dying to worldly life, consecration of life to God, ceasing from sin, as interpreted in the life of Christ, by confession and repentance, and living a life of virgin purity and self-denial, there can be only one faith.

(The Shaker Manifesto X, 6, pp. 121–122) [1880]

24

Letter: G. B. Avery to Stephen P. Andrews.
[In answer to an invitation to a Colloquium "to forecast and inaugurate that grand reconciliation, mutual acceptance, and harmony, which, is believed may be the basis of the religion of the future."]

. . .

. . . "What is truth?" Jesus never answered it, except in reference to its religious character. In this capacity, he said, "I am the truth," that is, my life's mission; my testimony of theory and practice! Our answer to the question, in its universal bearing, is this, Truth, is the manifesto of those principles, that, in their application to the pursuits of life, eventuate in the development, elevation and perfection of humanity, and culminate in the glory of God.

. . . But to refer to religious truth, we would suggest that it is not an article made of the metal of human sophisms, or philosophy and tempered in a theological bath! It would be falsehood to assert that there are no expressions of a measure of truth in the sentimental frame work of the multiform theologies which are the products of the labored speculations of the human mind; because each one, and all of them have a few golden nuggets of truth mid the vast amount of speculative debris, that makes up the bulk of their denominational characteristics and differences.

But, Creeds which shroud faith and religion in mystery and inconsistency; which make God a revengful Tyrant—etc.—cannot be models of Truth.

. . .

. . . The great mistakes of the present churchal influence, are. I. An attempt to harmonize the Church and the world! II. An effort to combine, in one churchal organization, before there is a spiritual harmony in the understandings and heart's emotions of the different religious professors. III. A harmony of denominations, before there is a harmony and unity of faith. IV. To convert religion into a mere theology. V. To embody, in a communistic relation, souls who have not been baptized into, nor grown up unto, a union of spirit.

All communions formed on a mere external or material basis, for external purposes only, without reference to unity of spirit, must fail, for it lacks the foundational principle of success!

Thus, friend Andrews, you will observe, that the Shaker idea is, I. That religion is not theology. II. That no human institution of theology that can be devised, will ever, be a reliable basis for a unification of the human family in religion.

III. That the Truth, in religion, is already revealed, and needs no colloquial tinkering to render it perfect. IV. Shakers do not believe that the mere profession of faith in any special theory or dogma of theological opinion, constitutes true religion. This is accomplished only by living in harmony with the same principles of Truth that Jesus Christ lived.

. . . . True religion consists, I. Of faith in God, as a Supreme Being, unto whom all intelligent beings are accountable for the conduct of . their lives.

II. Of faith in Man as the Creature of God, unto whom the same regard for the good feelings of brother and sister, should be exercised as unto ones–self.

THE SHAKERS

III. In a practical obedience to the dictates of this faith, so that life's deeds will be a blessing to the doer, and work no ill to any creature of God.

While Shakers understand that Truth is an eternal reality, and that all phases of its manifestations are necessary, and living stones in its glorious temple, they do not believe that any formulated opinions of mere human conception, anchored at the dock of Creed has chained the heavenly Argosy of Divine Truth, with all her cargo of revelations, within the finite harbor of human attainments. She is out upon the boundless ocean of God's wisdom and love; and, though she may often come to human port, with her cargo, will never be chained to the dock of any finished Venice on a human strand.

(*The Shaker Manifesto* XII, 8, pp. 193–195) [1882]

25

Soul Travel, No. 2. *G. B. Avery*
[A general evolutional/dispensational presentation—ancient Greece &c.]

. . .

Now arose one Apollonius of Tyana, who aided in the introduction of Orientalism. By Philostratus, Philo's biographer, a parallel was introduced between this man and our Savior. Herein is to be seen what has been manifest in all ages of the world's progress, namely, the existence of parallel workers in the Lord's cause, as witnesses of the true leading evolutionists of the ages. All this class of persons have ever been ascetics, and lived lives of abstemiousness from pleasures and creative comforts. This man attempted a reformation of religious rites and morals, denied the efficacy of sacrifices, substituting for the same simple worship and pure prayer, scarce even needing words. But this man taught the transmigration of souls, as a means of evolution, purification and development for future bliss.

. . . He now [in the age of reason and science] recognizes a spirit God, but still incomprehensible by man. And still the soul is pleading for a nearer relation to its Creator and for *light*, more *light*, and with light, *life*, love and liberty.

The soul's travel cannot be halting here. Succeeding ages record her onward march toward her millennial goal. She is not even yet privileged, after her ages of wanderings in the wilderness of sin, to see as did Moses from Pisgah's top the promised land of liberty and redemption. True, her prophets and visionists visited it in their trance flights, and foretold its beauties and enchantments, but the masses were plodding still in darkness drear, yet seeking to satisfy themselves with material treasures—delusive hopes. Soul will not, cannot tarry here.

(*The Shaker Manifesto* XI, 9, pp. 197–199) [1881]

26

Soul Travel No. 4. *Giles B. Avery*

. . .

It must be admitted that conflicting interests, and collisions of multitudinous creeds and forms of religion (so called), contribute to destroy individual faith *in* such religion, and introduce and diffuse the deadly bane of atheism—a soulless, godless state of society. These creedal walls that bar the union, peace and fellowship of one religious devotee and worshiper from another of a different creed are just as fast vanishing as the light of Divine truth and the power of Christian love moves upon the human soul, and overcomes its prejudices, and links it into the one united chain of wisdom's revelations. And so fast is this work in operation, that, at present, ministers of magnanimous spirits and advanced minds frequently worship at one and the same shrine though trained in the theology of diverse creeds, or often exchange pulpits with each other.

Easy and quick transit by railroads, and instantaneous communication by telegraph and telephone, is [*sic*] beginning in a marvelous degree to conscociate [*sic*] the nations, harmonize their ideas of science, art, political and social economy; and, as is now beginning to be manifest, must, eventually, uproot also polytheism and polycreedism, and introduce the millennium of religious truth and its fruits of united graces.

Possessed of powers and faculties which, if kept tuned in harmony with the Divine mind, would make him almost a demi–god, man's normal state is to be a co-worker with God, as His servant, in producing such conditions for humanity and for all inferior creation. . . .

From the organization of the soul of man it is demonstrably certain, that, in his normal condition, he is so affinitively united to his Creator as to be, at all times, conscious of His Divine will, and as a dutiful child ever ready to yield explicit obedience to His behests, thus to dwell in the sunshine of His paternal affection and love continually, and drink at the well-springs of His superior wisdom and power. . . .

The experience of the human race illustrates the fact, that, to be able to attain unto the Divine wisdom and grasp the treasures of the heavenly home, a considerable degree of rational asceticism must be practiced in order to disengage the soul from earth bond [*sic*] shackles of time and sense; for, inasmuch as it is unharnessed from these, it is free to soar to heavenly realms in the paradisian fields of wisdom, glory and godliness; but, while bound by those shackles, it never can rise to heavenly mansions.

The soul, freed from the enthrallments of animal, earthly sensualism, is at liberty to walk and talk with God, and often privileged to see, with the prophetic telescope, future prospects and liabilities; at liberty to roam with angels 'mid groves of the trees of life, bearing the fruits of the spirit of such luscious flavor as to spoil all relish, in those who partake thereof, for mortal fruits that only minister to the earthly senses of the worldly man and perish in the using. . . .

Let thirsty, hungering, starving Zion so live and so labor, and they will have the key to unlock the heavens, and draw from her sacred fountains blessings to the satisfaction of every heaven-born soul.

(*The Shaker Manifesto* XI, 12, 268–270) [1881]

*　　*　　*

27

Fragmentary Thoughts. *Abraham Perkins.*

. . .

I have favorable auguries, by which my confidence is strengthened of a "good time coming;" and from the effects of the operation of an apparent inner work of the spirit, we have the best of evidence that a brighter day is dawning.

"As fast as people learn to think, they demand liberty," and greater light is sought and resources resorted to to obtain it; which, in the providence of God, in His own time, is dispensed, giving liberty in a corresponding degree with the acceptation of light. It comes not without sacrifice; and the greater the sacrifice required and conscientiously made, the greater the progress, purification and freedom of the soul. . . .

(*The Manifesto* XII, 4, p. 82) [1882]

28

Shakerism. *Floyd C. Field.*

What are the future prospects for Shakerism? This is a question which agitates the mind of many true Believers. This subject has a tendency to cause uneasiness or partial unhappiness to many of the old and well tried heroes and heroines. . . .

They feel sad when they see their beloved brothers and sisters passing away. . . .

But soon the spell [of remembrance of earlier times of fervor] is broken and they realize that they are living in a different age, an age of lukewarmness and worldliness, associated with some who care not for real spiritual growth; but they are waiting: patiently waiting; hoping, that, ere long the power of God will manifest itself as it has in days that are past. . . .

I believe a better day is dawning, the world is beginning to realize the terrible influence and prevalence of sensuality. . . .

Principles founded upon Infinite truth can never die! God will triumph.

. . .

(*The Shaker Manifesto* XIII, 7, pp. 153–154) [1883]

29

Natural and Spiritual Relations. *Martha J. Anderson.*

. . .

All true union and harmony of spirit springs from moral conditions and not from those human instincts that we hold in common with the animal creation. Sexual love and physical attraction, spring from the sensual nature, and is [*sic*] not man's highest estate of happiness. The true affection of the natural, should open to our thought the

universal love and affection, which, in the progressive state of unfoldment, shall exist between all truly good and pure natures. "In Christ
there is neither male nor female," which represents a condition of
human advancement, when fleshly lusts and desires shall be consumed
by the indwelling of God's Spirit. . . .

There is a growing tendency in this age of alliances, to concentrate
for mutual good. There seems to be two spirits at work in opposite
directions, one in the form of trusts and monopolies for individual
aggrandizement; another in the form of co–operation and guilds for
the fraternization and benefit of the masses, who are the wage-slaves of
the moneyed classes.

Progress, like the spiral motion of all things, tends to ever increasing life and activity, which draws humanity in its vortex, for the
process of unification of thought and feeling. What seems to be evil in
our present state of civilization will eventuate in good.

. . .

Mankind are evolving toward the spiritual, through the perfect
natural state, where self-restraint and continence, subdues the animal
and the savage in their natures, where love engendered in the coronal
region of the brain, holds in control the selfish propensities, that
develop their force in the cerebellum or lower portion of the brain.

The essence of true religion is chastity and love which bind the
soul to God. Human affections are never carried to their exaltation of
sweetness and beauty until they are made manifest in the sphere of
unselfish devotion. We should be nearer to each other as human beings
in those things we have in common with God, than in that we have in
common with the animals.

. . .

Why are the churches divided into sects? and why do men look
coldly on each other? Is it not because they place too much stress on
difference of opinion in minor matters, and chill the love of God in
their hearts? They expect to share their heaven in common in the
future, and yet drive themselves asunder while here. "In Christ there is
no schism." His love metes out no bounds nor limits.

The only true union and fellowship lies in the interest and upbuilding of a faith in man, "if we love not our brother whom we have
seen, how can we love God whom we have not seen."

Jesus taught the law of love as expressed in this text, and in
contiguous passage(s), which it would be well for all to read and
consider. The outcome would, if practically carried out in every day

life, result in the establishment of the Kingdom of heaven, for which he prayed, and which we all have desired might come on the earth. May we all be united in one common cause and kinship; to do good, to carry out the vital spirit of religion which is "Love to God and the neighbor." Then they who do the will of God the same will be our Father and Mother, our brother and sister.

(*The Manifesto* XXVI, 2, pp. 25–28) [1896]

30

"Blow ye the Trumpet in Zion." *Anon.*

In accord and concord the outside world, under divine influences, are this day an example for our beloved Zion. Let accord, concord, love and good–will permeate all branches of Zion; and truth-loving souls, under divine influence, will fill the waste places of Zion and extend her borders. Amen.

(*The Shaker Manifesto* XI, 12, p. 271) [1881]

31

Progress, Order and Individualism. *Alonzo G. Hollister*

. . .

That as God is a God of order, and order is Heaven's first law, "the nearer we approach the Kingdom of God, the more order we must come to," and, according to the most reliable evidence that can be had, Shakers are in the commencement of that Kingdom which is destined in its progress to "Break in pieces and consume all other Kingdoms," while to the increase of its own government, order and stability there shall be no end, consequently, Shakerism is aggregation, centralization, organization,—a building up, a progress into increasing degrees of order and government, while the progress of the world, and its systems, effected by the great increase of light, is towards disorganization, individualism, and final dissolution.

That this demolishing work, which produces so much clash, confusion, and distrust, in the mental, religious, and political world, is necessary that the Kingdom begun to be set up, may have room to expand.

(*The Shaker Manifesto* XIII, 11, p. 256) [1883]

32

The Pole Star of Faith. *Alonzo G. Hollister*

. . .

Jesus said he would build his church upon a rock; but if one coming after may contradict Jesus, both cannot be right. . . . If our standard varies so as to conform to individual ideas, is not this the same as to be without a standard, or without a reliable guide to the formation of opinions, and for testing our revelations, and then, what do we know; and what becomes of the ground of unity for faith and practice in the body?. . .

Is not the character and testimony of the first witnesses of the new creation, the Pole Star of our faith, and the visible lead like a compass to which we turn for counsel when clouds obscure our spiritual sky and for directions how to work the present work of God in union with the visible body of Christ?. . . Jesus testified, "I and my Father are one." If he was not perfect, how could he be one with the perfect, and how can his followers be perfect?. . .

The perfect ones, who properly improve the talents confided to them, become one with the anointing spirit, and that which is one cannot be divided, "The disciple is not above his master, but every one that is perfect shall be as his master.". . .

If we build our faith upon persons, and they fail, we fail also; but if, as our first Mother taught, we build our faith upon the gift and power of God in the gospel, we must have a light which transcends individual opinions by which to know the real from the seeming, the substance from the shadow. And that light, or test, must be the revelation of the beginning, supported by concurring testimony of all true witnesses, who are one in spirit, though testifying ages apart. We may call this light principle, but it was manifested to us through witnesses; for principles are not self-actors, but modes of action that require organization to be made apparent.

. . . upon the foundation which was laid in revelation by the first witnesses of the new creation, is room for endless growth, and increase without limit, and if it be said that we are laboring to support a theory, we answer it is not a theory of man's devising, and man cannot alter it. . . .

The Apostles saw the spiritual things of a future dispensation obscurely, but this did not prevent their seeing clearly to perform the work of their day, perfect in its order and time. . . .

THE SHAKERS

Should we not rather preserve a distinction between the revolutionary element which is disorganizing the false systems of the world, removing debris, and which is therefore transient in its character, and the new creating word which is building up a permanent Order that will increase forever?

(The Shaker Manifesto XIII, 7, pp. 145–148) [1883]

33

Tribute to Gospel Friends. *Catherine Allen.*

When contemplating the joy and ever unfolding glory, with which our Zion Home is rife, my heart fills with praise to the Dispenser of all good, and turns with thankful emotion to those whose sacrifice for truth in past and present time, has ultimated in this beautiful heritage; . . .

When the curtain of retirement is lifted, and we look for a moment on earth's restless throng, how repulsive and painful many of the scenes which unbidden rise before the vision, of political and social organizations, discordant with the laws of God and of nature. . . .

The prophet's fire still burns in the hearts of many in our own midst; and still bright visions thrill the souls of those who look with Faith's clairvoyant eye to the increase of the future, and around are angel messengers, prompting to deeper devotion, and more self-denial, which alone can open the portals to new degrees of revelation.

(The Shaker Manifesto XIII, 6, pp. 125–127) [1883]

34

Fervency of Spirit. *Elizabeth Martin*

When we view the ranks of our church, and number the souls whom the Father has drawn to his people, whom it has been our privilege in the past to assist, we think: Where are they who to–day should be the most active workers in the Lord's vineyard?. . .

Our love, as disciples of Christ, is too limited, too narrow, vague, indifferent, not intensified by an active concern,—. . .

We are students in the school of Christ;—for what purpose are students learning? Is it that they alone may know of the doctrine of

Christ's kingdom, be passively good themselves, keeping free from the grosser sins to which humanity are heirs, while they carelessly gaze upon a world of iniquity?... That our church suffers drouth to–day from the sloth and indifference of its members, its want of "fervency of spirit" is plainly to be seen.

It is not enough that we understand christian principles, and dwell in the church built thereon, thinking it will stand without our aid; God will ever work through agencies; the luke-warm and indifferent He "will spew from his mouth."...

... It is fully time for our church to arise, shake off her drowsy condition, and putting her trust in God, go forth into the harvest fields, and with "fervency of spirit," call down upon the ripened earth the pentecostal baptism just at hand.

(*The Shaker Manifesto* XIII, 6, pp. 124–125) [1883]

35

[Editorial—*H. C. Blinn*]

Prophetic minds, in the spirit of that divine gift, have informed us that, "The stroke or testimony that wakes up the children of this world will also wake up the Believers." Are we asleep! Have we fallen into a lethargic state, dreamily passing away our days, waiting for some form of electric shock to arouse us to more active duty?

Does the same manifestation of divine presence that acts upon all the sects in christendom, act correspondingly upon us?...

It is admitted that there is a worldliness in the christian churches. ... We should not become indifferent to the state of mind that exists in the religious world, as its influences are powerful and may become permanent even within our own order. We are informed that, "Out of every thousand church members only one in five attends prayer meeting, and only one in five of those attending can be depended upon to take any part in the meeting. There is a woeful lack of Christly earnestness in doing God's work."

These signals of distress should prove a warning to the observing or reflecting mind, and prevent in our own home, one of the most insidious means of disintegration. ...

When men will devote themselves to the cultivation of religious principles with the untiring intensity, and study the advantages of the situation with the same acumen, that they do for the accumulation of worldly treasures; religious communities will evidently flourish with corresponding marks of success. We need a revival, a revival of truthfulness and honesty, and a living kindness for poor humanity. We need a school of prophets from which men and women can graduate as saviors and redeemers. Preachers of the testimony of Jesus Christ, which is the sure word of prophecy, and the only effectual door of hope.

(*The Shaker Manifesto* XIII, 3, pp. 66–67) [1883]

36

The Good Time Coming. *Anna White*

. . .

All that is inherent in the human heart, that tends to uplift and elevate it from inferior conditions, and points to a higher and better life—something still beyond that has not yet been attained—is God–given. Even though the goal of anticipation is not reached, still the effort remains for succeeding generations.

As the "iniquities of the fathers are visited upon the children," in the natural order, so does the baptism and inspiration of the prophets and sages of one dispensation rest upon another. Each dispensation derives benefit from the preceding one. One is as essential to the other as are the rudiments of education to the scholar. . . .

Had the inspired prophets of past centuries lived to witness the fulfillment of their predictions—even to the degree that has been already attained—they would probably have felt that their hopes, desires and prayers had been met and answered in a large measure; . . .

We sing of our fathers and mothers who have preceded us, "*We* reap where *they* have sown, and the harvest fields have grown, and the fruits of faith and righteousness appear;" still the law and order that regulated them in their intercourse with each other would be thraldom to the liberty–loving people of our day, who incline to rush forward with a wild enthusiasm that soon comes to a terminus, and retrogression is sure to follow. . . .

To indorse all of the fundamental principles of Christianity and abide by them does not infer that we of the nineteenth century have not a work to do as well as our predecessors; far from it. "Of the increase of his government and peace, to order and to establish it with judgment and with justice, there shall be no end."

... —we too must increase and advance, as the light is revealed, and the way made manifest; *our* righteousness should exceed *their* righteousness. . . . we look forward to the better time coming, when all the nations of the earth shall learn the *cause* of war and bloodshed, when the land shall be free to the homeless millions, and where neither rich or poor, black or white, bond or free exist, and the knowledge of the Lord shall cover the earth. . . .

(*The Shaker Manifesto* XI, 8, pp. 171–172) [1881]

37

[Editorial Item]

Universality is the watchword of the age. If "God hath made of one blood all the nations of the earth," then shall mankind eventually become one brotherhood. The easy communication between the countries of the globe makes it possible. The exchange not only in the commodities necessary to physical life, but in thoughts, ideas, and religious experiences, seem to be the moulding or leavening process. Intelligence grows apace, and the barriers of narrow sectarianism, and the monopoly of God and heaven, must give way to the broader ideas of enlightened reason and soul expansion. God is love, and when man grows to divinity of character he too will be loved, and will enlarge the sphere of his activities.

(*The Manifesto* XXIV, 12, p. 279) [1894]

38

The Millennium. *Catherine Allen.*

. . .

Thus through Deific impulse the better life in man will be quickened till all realize the essential unity of the race, and gradually merge into one great family of nations, speaking one tongue, having one Bible and one religion, all written in the simple words: "Love one another."

(*The Manifesto* XXIV, 12, p. 275) [1894]

*   *   *

39

Home Notes—Mt. L.—N. F. [Mt. Lebanon—North Family] *Catherine Allen.*

. . .

The date of our writing is the 123 anniversary of the arrival in America of Mother Ann Lee and her eight brave companions, and marks an epoch in history which we believe will be much more widely and clearly appreciated in future years than at present. It seems a fitting time for all Believers who realize the value to mankind of the Gospel testimony, to recount the accomplishment of the past, consider the means of success and the causes of failure, distinguish between customs and principles, understand whether certain habits and rules had their origin in considerations of principles or of the necessities of the times, and while comparing present conditions of society with those which existed more than a century since let us adjust ourselves for present duty and future advancement.

(*The Manifesto* XXVII, 9, p. 140) [1897]

40

Essentials and Non–Essentials *Anon.*

. . .

To cling to a custom, for custom's sake, would deny to us the benefits of all modern blessings. . . .

. . . "The union is the gift," is a truism of our Mother Lucy Wright; and we must learn to be united on all points of doctrine, of custom, even if new, when proved to be essential to our well being, and when in conformity with our visible lead. The stubborn conservative, hurts the union—the gift—and ties the hands and hearts of our good Ministry, from yielding their consent to have Society improve in all that would make her beautiful, without departing a hair's breadth from the essential, heavenly, fundamental principles of our beautiful Gospel. If Society really needs an organ to improve it, then let us be united, regardless of past custom.

. . . We want to make home so delightful, so beautiful, that it will gather and retain individuals, and would not omit a single feature that did not conflict with the purity of life, . . . Therefore, begone, all opposition to music and flowers; to any and every improvement that will and can stand on our everlasting foundational principles. . . .

(*The Shaker* II, 9, p. 71) [1872]

41

Our Home. *Odillon B. Elkins.*

. . .

While the external conditions of our home may be shaped by us, and improved upon, the divine plan upon which this home is built, is perfect and unchangeable, and adapted to every soil and clime. The waiting may seem long to us, impatient, short sighted mortals, and none of us may live to see any great increase or spread of those truths which we have espoused, but in the unerring course of Providence this is sure to transpire in God's own time. . . .

. . . And this home was founded for the sole purpose, that all who will may seek and find the gifts of the spirit. These in their fullness are not to be had at less cost, than to give our whole life, and our own dear selves a free will offering to God. . . .

To some it is very distasteful to mingle religious topics with temporal, every day pursuits, or with our letter writing; but in a purely religious home this view seems inconsistent. As for me I would have every part of life,—every employment so tinctured, and so mixed with pious impulses, that to draw a line of division between them would be impossible. And to me the sentiments and motives of a true piety cannot seem misplaced under any circumstances in a community like ours; the words of eternal life are ever too scarce. . . .

(*The Shaker Manifesto* XIII, 4, pp. 85–86) [1883]

THE SHAKERS

42

What is Right. [Editorial Note.]

... it is below the dignity of matured religious enlightenment, to consider such inferiorities [i.e., "the feet–washings, the communism, the nearly hundred, or more, of arranged performances] Christianity; let us have CHRIST HIMSELF represented, and all these inferiorities will be unostentatiously, *imperceptibly*, but inevitably involved and represented.

Essentials are good; but the essentials are in doing good things in the right spirit; and the right spirit is the good essential thing, regardless of what *any* may consider *essential*.

(*The Shaker Manifesto* XI, 3, p. 61) [1881]

43

Mental Photography. *Catherine Allen.*

. . .

The more we comprehend of the science and laws of the visible creation, the better we can understand the originating forces and soul life of which the exterior is but a reflex, and the more we learn of our own curious dual life; because man is a complete microcosm of the universe, body, soul and spirit. There is not one substance of earth element, of the animal or spiritual creation, principle of science, or attribute of Deity, but has a germinal existence in the human brain.

(*The Shaker Manifesto* XI, 4, p. 79) [1881]

44

Progress. *Emily Offord*

. . .

The world moves forward truly, and no less in religion than in science, although many are bewailing the low spiritual state of the sectarian churches; all of which probably began with a measure of the spirit of grace and truth, but becoming fixed and creed bound, they had no opportunity for spiritual growth, and when an organization ceases to grow dissolution begins. The churches endeavor to derive sustenance from old and time worn theology, and therefore literally starve the people for the lack of a living inspiration and present revelation of light and truth. Why should they not pass away and give place to something better?

And what is true of others is also true of this, the Shaker Church. Like causes produce like effects. But one great blessing vouchsafed to Zion, is that her people are not creed bound; our gospel teaches endless progression. Light is ever beaming brighter, truth and wisdom gradually unfolding to every sincere, earnest seeker within her borders. Every opportunity is given for soul growth; it only remains for each individual to labor and struggle, and if necessary, to wrestle as did Jacob of old with the angels, to gain increasing righteousness and maintain a living church. The gospel requires from time to time, greater sacrifices, more cross, and greater self-denial, with increasing testimony against error, as proof of advancement in the spiritual life.

True religion is practical and logical; it takes cognizance of every act, spiritual, intellectual and physical; it teaches us to observe physiological laws as the law of God; that if these are disregarded, suffering and disease will ensue as the just penalty; that they are not imposed upon us by an offended Deity, but are the consequences of violated law. Effect follows cause as sure as night succeeds the day. It teaches us how, when and what to eat and drink ... etc. Good ventilation will also be included; thus our religion will save us from sickness which is much better than doing wrong and getting sick, and then wanting to be cured in some miraculous, incomprehensible way, and allowing us to go on sinning (or violating law). It is antichristian to try to be saved *in* our sins; the gospel saves *from* sin, and this is the only salvation worth seeking.

The increasing testimony will require the sacrifice of all superfluities in dress, and no less the pernicious habit of tight lacing. All things will be done to the honor and glory of God and the upbuilding of true and noble manhood and womanhood. The selfish principle of me and mine will then be brought into much more subjection so that no one will think of owning even a plant any more than they now do of carrying a purse. Flowers, those beautiful emblems of virtue, so fitly called the "stars of earth," will be ours to enjoy in abundance through consecration, by cultivating them for the sole purpose of beautifying our gospel homes, ornamenting and brightening the whole household of faith, and not to foster personal selfishness.

THE SHAKERS

The church of Christ's second appearing has always been and must ever be a progressive institution; but if the testimony does not continue to sound forth with an increase, and its members become inert, what will save it more than others from ruin? Nothing short of a renewal of the inspiration of the Holy Spirit, and an ever present revelation of God's truth, and strict obedience thereunto, will keep it alive, and promote its growth and glory. . . .

(The Manifesto XXI, 5, pp. 101–102) [1891]

*   *   *

45

Home Notes—Mt. L. [Re: Canaan closing] *Calvin G. Reed.*

. . .

The religious element is all in a foam. Even the Shakers are affected with the mania. One family after another is seeking other quarters or regions. The South family of Canaan formed the introduction; next the Center family became non est; and now the North family of Canaan are vacating and casting their lot with the people at Enfield, Conn. What next stands on the program of revolution? This is the moving current at Mt. Lebanon. A like tidal wave has swept over communities, and some of these have become extinct and others stand on the verge of an avalanche.

Our founders predicted seven essential changes would take place among us in spiritual degrees of evolution. The spirit world appears to be aroused with various aims for the improvement of mankind.

(The Manifesto XXVII, 4, p. 58) [1897]

46

[Letter of Arthur W. Dowe—San Francisco, Cal., April 29, 1894.]

. . .

I fully realize that you have become so fixed and settled in your present mode of life and worship that it would take more effort and labor to overcome the inertia and quietude you now enjoy, and get you started into a spiritual avalanche, than would be needed in fully converting a society which has no faith nor doctrine and setting it on its feet in the gospel road of salvation.

. . .

Since the present generation of Believers have never been through a great revival and reformation of spiritual power, their own experience does not fit them for the tremendous issues now before the world. In all the great questions of the coming age, the majority of Believers have no practical knowledge and consequently little practical sympathy. So to disturb their quiet sleep and rest and their dreams of security would be of very little use, and would only provoke needless discussion and friction. . . .

. . . when a people become fixed and immovable . . . God is accustomed to raise up a new people and the former is left to wax old and decay away.

. . .

One thing is as certain as that God is true, and that is that of the present form of Christian religion, no matter under what name, "Not one stone shall be left standing upon another." God has spoken.

In the meantime we must do our duty, day by day just as though we were to continue a thousand years. . . . As to what the outcome will be of the movement on this coast [i.e., California], God only knows. . . .

[Arthur W. Dowe—948 Mission St.—San Francisco
—a Shaker missionary of some years in S.F.]
(*The Manifesto* XXIV, 7, pp. 157–158) [1894]

47

[Letter of Simon Emery—Bangor, Me., Aug. 7, 1894.]

. . .

The Shakers have been praying for nearly fifty years for an increase, and all this time have been growing less. Now let them go to work in real earnest regardless of dollars and cents, to bring it about. . . .

All that is worth having is worth laboring for, and the article of our good brother, A. W. Dowe, in the July Manifesto is right to the point. . . .

(*The Manifesto* XXIV, 11, p. 251) [1894]

48

[Letter of Simon Emery—Bangor, Me., Oct. 4, 1896]

... You have been praying for nearly fifty years for an increase, for a tidal wave to flow to you from the outside world to fill up your scattered and broken ranks, and why has not your prayer been answered? The reason is very apparent as God never helps only those that help themselves.

... If each Society had done no more than I have done for the last twenty years by putting their literature before the world. ...

If all the Societies had been less absorbed in the root of all evil, and more interested in the spread of the light of gospel truth, there would not be that dearth there is among them now. ...

(*The Manifesto* XXVII, 1, pp. 13–14) [1897]

49

Home Notes: Shakers, N.Y. [i.e., Watervliet] *Hamilton DeGraw*
. . .

We have been both entertained and instructed, in the perusal of some of the works of Thomas A. [*sic*] Kempis. Living in what is termed the dark ages of the Christian era, his was a mind largely free from theological bigotry and had an understanding of spiritual gifts, which places him in the ranks, as one of the inspired teachers of the race. He was translated in the year 1471 at 91 years of age.

Our friend, Simon Emery hits the nail on the head in his letter in the Jan. *Manifesto*. We fully endorse the sentiments there exprest. Whoever receives the gift to minister the gospel, must let their light shine, and proclaim from the house–top, that testimony which has been unfolded to their spiritual understanding.

(*The Manifesto* XXVII, 2, p. 29) [1897]

50

Home Notes—Mt. L.—N. F. *Walter S. Shepherd*
. . .

During the meeting the question was asked by one of the Sisters, "What of the future of Shakerism?" and replied to by another Sister.

Which at the close of the meeting called forth a few remarks.

Whatever the future may have in store for the Shaker Institution, Shaker principles are imperishable and are finding wider and firmer acceptance continually.

The question for us is "Has the Shaker Society leaders to put it upon a basis for the better and more complete practice of its principles." Time will prove. . . .

(*The Manifesto* XXIV, 11, p. 260) [1894]

51

Home Notes—Union, O. *O.C. Hampton.*
. . .

We might travel quite around the world and preach the Gospel to every nation, baptizing them in the name of the Father, Son and Holy Spirit. But I fear we shall leave these blessings to another, and God grant, a more worthy generation. . . .

(*The Manifesto* XXIV, 2, p. 47) [1894]

52

Our Mission—Its Authority. *Jessie Evans*
. . .

The sacred Covenant which we have subscribed, is something more than a legal compact. The Virgin Church is not a Shaker village, however perfectly the material environments may be adjusted. . . .

The walls of our material homes will crumble as dust to dust, but what of the mission entrusted to us?. . .

. . . With the unobtrusive yet unflinching authority of The Christ, may we hold our rightful place among the churches of this land! . . .

(*The Manifesto* XXVIII, 4, p. 51) [1898]

53

Home Notes—Mt. Lebanon—N.F. *Martha J. Anderson.*
. . .

It is according to Elder Frederic's prophecy, that the next movement and awakening of the spirit would not result so much in the accession of members to the older Societies, as it would lead to the forming of new associations, with the same basic principles as a sure foundation on which to build, but with the increase and progress belonging to our own day and time.

(*The Manifesto* XXIV, 6, p. 141) [1894]

54

... Therefore, as the new States [republics] are progressing beyond the old, so will new Shaker societies progress far beyond the old, and it will only be a question whether the old will come into the new increase or become extinct.

(F. W. Evans on "The Future of Shakerism," in *Elder Frederic W. Evans*, p. 114) [1893]

55

Christian Success. *Anon.*

... We *believe* Christ to have appeared, just as we firmly believe in the existence of gold; but until we experience the value of gold, by real possession and the benefits of its exchange, of how much worth is our belief? Until we experience the salvation from the commission of sin, which Christ's mission promised, of what avail is Christianity to us?...

... Our success has not been in the congregation of vast numbers; never will be; at least we do not look for this.... Our numbers are not so large, as in periods that are past; we fearlessly admit this fact; but our principles are firmer than ever.... while living in happy anticipation of the approach of a blessed season, when mankind will become convicted of the need of Christian success, and gather to the principles that alone can satisfy the demand. "... in a community life, where so much self-denial is in exercise, that but *few* individuals will be willing to submit to its demands."

(*The Shaker* I, 8, p. 57) [1871]

THE SHAKERS

56

The Order of Shakers, A Priesthood, not a Sect. *Daniel Frazer*

Every act of this priesthood should represent a divine motive, and be outwardly illustrative of hygienic and moral law.

How much the spirits in person (those who have done wrong to themselves and to their neighbors) need help as such a priesthood can render, I am not prepared to say. . . .

The thoughts of many indwellers of clay do not, practically, extend much beyond their own mole–hill. Those who see the ages as they roll, *their* thoughts are more dignified. They see that the time allotted, and all the troubles assigned to man, are but brief, educational opportunities, preparatory to a life of higher aims, and nobler purposes. And that there will be those who will rise into the higher life, and being clothed with a divine humanity, form a priesthood, whose presence will say: "Peace, be still, ye elements of human trouble." At first, it will be traduced; but the never-dying afflatus flowing through them, from the "Throne of Eternal Brightness", will, in succeeding generations, call forth forms of love, beauty, peace and good will. Even the hems of their garments will be curative; and the sweetness of their spirits will *catalyze* into harmony, even devils.

. . .

That divinely vitalized beings possess a corresponding power [i.e., to be catalysts] I have not the smallest doubt; indeed, I have the most undoubted assurance that all such, whether in or out of the body, possess that power. . . .

. . .

At present society is wisely let alone, to discover and solve her own problems. Evils will certainly increase, for it is their nature to reproduce, incarnate, and make themselves felt.

Should a few of the spirits of what are called the dark ages, visit us, and compare notes, they would declare that our civilization is all alive with troubles. Hence, I have been for some years inclining to the opinion, that the time is already on the way, when Shaker institutions will become a necessity in the earth. Our ORDER is not exclusively for those who are its members; but also others—to be a priesthood to them—to change humanity into peace, to assist in introducing the crowning civilization of the ages; and finally help to wind up the terrestrial destiny of man. . . .

(*The Shaker Manifesto* X, 7, pp. 145–146) [1880]

THE SHAKERS

57

The Value of a Name. *Henry C. Blinn.*

. . .

Every religious denomination has a special work, which points more or less directly toward the life of our divine Teacher, and in this righteousness, will have the reward of "well done." Whatever this may be for humanity, we need not occupy their ground.

Our lines are well drawn. Our work is distinct from all others, and our name [Shakers] is significant of the work which we have espoused and will be our witness before the world. If like the wise virgins we keep our lamps trimmed and burning, we may hope to find a place in the ranks of the redeemed and be able to enter into the Holy City, the habitation of our God.

(*The Manifesto* XXVII, 7, p. 99) [1897]

58

Discourse delivered at Canterbury, N. H.—Shakers—June 19, 1887 [Initial signature "A"]

[Lengthy quotation from Horace Greeley]

. . . Now our numbers may be, nay, they are few, as compared with other churches and as a sect we have not spread as have others. But there is a difference between the spread of a sect, and the spread of ideas. In this sphere we claim that we have done some work, and that we have not labored in vain.

The Shakers are a small body, and if there is no success but what depends on worldly combination, organization or policy, never had any men and women less chance of it than we. Bound only by mutual love and good–will, with no creed but the gospel, thinking each one what he will, questioning ourselves and our actions sharply, finding all the fault we can with ourselves, looking out our defects and criticising them keenly as those only can who believe in immortal truth; certainly we are the least politic of all people.

Those who know of us say, "the Shakers are dying out," and "they believe in nothing." Yea, we *do* believe in *truth*. And here we stand, "as chastened and not killed, as dying and behold we live; as unknown and yet well known;" here we stand, this forlorn hope, if we are named such, we say rather this vanguard in the army of Christian progress, a vanguard which cannot be conquered, which cannot die, for ideas never die. The breath goes out of a man's body, and it is dead; synods and councils of mighty men are dissolved and scattered; churches and hierarchies decline and crumble; but ideas never die, truth never dies but is immortal. It may for a brief period be hid, but the time will surely come when "truth crushed to earth shall rise again," for "the eternal years of God are hers."

(*The Manifesto* XVII, 9, p. 213) [1887]

59

Christian Communism, No. 4. *Theo. Kaiandri*
. . .
What of the future of the Shaker societies? My opinion is that they have a great future before them, but that to attain to it they must abandon their spiritualism and recover the intense, self-denying religiousness which characterized Ann Lee and her converts.

The Christian religion undoubtedly contemplates the existence of societies of religious celibates, and as originally founded the Shaker societies more nearly realize that New Testament institution than any other societies that I know anything about.

If the Shaker institutions could be rehabilitated after the pattern Ann Lee set, and if the Shaker theology could be replaced in the New Testament simplicity in which Ann Lee established it, the Shaker societies would soon become a great power in the social, industrial, political and religious world.

The weakness of Shakerism lies, I think, in the fact that it has put Ann Lee since her death up into its theology, where she herself would never have consented to be put, and down out of its life and spirit in which she would have delighted to remain. . . .

(*The Manifesto* XVII, 7, p. 166) [1887]

60

[Letter—*Elijah Myrick.*]
. . .
Suggestive is the query, "What of the future of Shakerism?" I am at one with the writer of that splendid article. If a sacred regard and

rigid adherence to first principles had been the rule, "the simplicity in which Ann Lee established them, the Shaker societies would now be a great power in the social, industrial, political and religious world." Personal adoration will never atone for lack of living principles. Improved methods of cultivating the soil will bring an acceptable harvest, while the stars will shine without our praise of prayers.

"Divine things can never die." Compare one hundred years ago with now, and be grateful that the assumed deities have retired from the affairs of men; that the noblest and best are permitted to live and bless this green beautiful earth, that their blood is not required "for Christ's sake."

(The Manifesto XVII, 8, p. 177) [1887]

*   *   *

61

[Untitled Item]

Ann Lee once prophecied that she saw individuals flocking to the standard, of which she was bearer, by hundreds and by thousands! In view of the few representatives of Shaker principles, this sounds oddly enough; but there have been millions flocking to the doors of our theology for many years—The prophecy is more than fulfilled in a very marvelous and encouraging manner.

(The Shaker II, 4, p. 32) [1872]

62

Time, its Records. *Alonzo Hollister.*

. . .

If the spirit of God operates among mankind like wheels within wheels, the center being much smaller and slower in movement than the circumference, may not attract so much attention, though it be the source, both of motion and power to those more external.

THE SHAKERS

People see a small body of Shakers, view their external organization and habits, and, perhaps, think them a strange curiosity—. . . .

(The Shaker I, 10, p. 78) [1871]

63

The Shakers. *Anon.*

. . .

. . . We are, at times, the subjects of a withdrawal of spiritual light;
the present is such a season with the Shakers; but surely as morning
succeeds the night, and spring the winter, so surely do we know an
increasing light is at hand. . . .

. . . *We* are few and ignorant now; by-the-by we shall be the many
and of the most wise on the earth! . . .

(The Shaker II, 1, p. 8) [1872]

64

Resignation. *Oliver C. Hampton.*

. . .

No effort should be spared to shun all unnecessary sufferings both
physiological and psychological, but when this has been faithfully
done, and there still remains a residuum . . . it is wise and prudent to
make a strong effort to pass into the realm of sweet resignation at once,
and there remain in patience and prayer until we have become perfectly passive under the stroke of our affliction. . . .

. . . it being a time of the Church's experience and travel, where
much waiting and great patience are especially in order, let us take
hold of the gift and be daily, nightly, and hourly exercised therein and
pray not only for ourselves but for each other, not only each other—
but for our friends not of our order, not only for our friends but for
our enemies everywhere, for all saints and particularly for all sinners. . . .

(The Shaker Manifesto XV, 2, pp. 27–28) [1885]

65

A Conversation [*Anon.*]

. . .

"The spirit world is a world of causes; thus, of effects." *Mind* is the primal cause of all material existence. Our physical being is in every way subservient to the spirit that animates it; therefore the origin of disease is *spiritual.* It is through the mind that we learn the laws of our physical being; and through ignorance, and the perverted appetites of the mind, these laws are transgressed.

. . .

We must remember that the dawn of only the second of the seven cycles of progress in the Church of the Millennium is opening upon us. . . .

(*Shaker and Shakeress,* Social Gathering, August 19, 1873, p. 4) [1873]

66

Address of Antoinette Doolittle

. . .

Every cycle has its prophets—as guiding stars; and they are the burning candles of the Lord to light the spiritual temple on earth, for the time being. When they have done their work, they will pass away; but the candlesticks will remain, and other lights will be placed in them.

(*The Shaker* II, 6, p. 42) [1872]

BIBLIOGRAPHY

Sources of the Texts and Works Cited

Authorized Rules of the Shaker Church. Mt. Lebanon, N.Y., 1894.

Avery, Giles Bushnell, ed. *Testimonies of the Life, Character, Revelations of Mother Ann Lee, and the Elders with her.* . . . . (Second Edition) Albany, N.Y.: Weed, Parsons & Co., 1888. [Alternate title: *Precepts of Mother Ann Lee and the Elders.*] A revision of Rufus Bishop, *Testimonies &c.*, 1816.

Blinn, Henry Clay. *The Life and Gospel Experience of Mother Ann Lee* (Second Edition) East Canterbury, N.H., 1901. [First Edition: 1882.]

————. *Church Record 1784–1879*, Ms., Canterbury, N.H.; collection of Canterbury Shaker Village.

Brown, Thomas. *An Account of the People Called Shakers: Their Faith, Doctrines, and Traditions.* Troy, N.Y.: Parker and Buss, 1812.

Dowe, Arthur W. *The Day of Judgment as Taught by the Millennial Church (Shakers), With a Few Rays of Light Gathered from Scriptures and Other Sources.* San Francisco: Rembaugh Pub. Co., 1896.

Dunlavy, John. *The Manifesto, or a Declaration of the Doctrine and Practice of the Church of Christ.* New York, N.Y.: Edward O. Jenkins, 1847 (reissue of the original 1818 edition).

Dyer, Joseph. *A Compendious Narrative.* Concord, N.H.: Isaac Hill, 1819.

Elkins, Harvey. *Fifteen Years in the Senior Order of Shakers: A Narration of Facts Concerning that Singular People.* Hanover, N.H.: Dartmouth Press, 1853.

Evans, Frederick W. *Elder Frederick W. Evans.* Pittsfield, Mass., 1893.

Green, Calvin. *Atheism, Deism, Universalism and Fatalism Refuted, &c. . . . A Discourse Delivered in the Meeting House of the United Society at Harvard, Massachusetts, September 19, 1830.* Ms. Sabbathday Lake Society Library.

————. *Biographic Memoir of Calvin Green.* 2 vols. Ms. Sabbathday Lake Society Library. [before 1850]

BIBLIOGRAPHY

————. *Biographical Account of the Life, Character, & Ministry of Father Joseph Meacham, the Primary Leader in Establishing the United Order of the Millennial Church. 1827.* Ms. (copy dated July 15, 1859) Sabbathday Lake Society Library.

————. *Incontestible Position Relative to the Pre-Existence of Christ.* Bound with Letters of Joshua H. Bussell. Ms. Sabbathday Lake Society Library. [ca. 1830?]

————. *Letter to Elder Lorenzo Grosvernor, New Lebanon, April 11, 1852.* Ms. Sabbathday Lake Society Library.

————. *Letter to Joshua H. Bussell, Alfred, Maine. June 29, 1856.* Ms. Sabbathday Lake Society Library.

————. *A Summary View of the Millennial Church, or United Society of Believers, Commonly Called Shakers.* Albany, N.Y.: C. van Benthuysen, 1848 (reissue of the original 1823 edition).

Grosvernor, Roxalana L. *Sayings of Mother Ann and the First Elders Gathered from Different Individuals, at Harvard and Shirley Who Were Eye and Ear Witnesses.* Ms. Sabbathday Lake Society Library (no date, but ca. 1845; a variant Ms., Philadelphia Museum of Fine Arts collection).

Hollister, Alonzo G. *Mission of the Alethian Believers, Called Shakers: The Truth of Eternal Life, Lived Here and Now.* Mt. Lebanon, N.Y., 1899.

————. *Synopsis of Doctrine Taught by Believers in Christ's Second Appearing.* Mt. Lebanon, N.Y., 1893–1902.

Lyon, John. *Considerations of Religious Doctrine.* Enfield, N.H. Ms. Sabbathday Lake Society Library.

McNemar, Richard. *The Kentucky Revival; or, a Short History of the Late Extraordinary Outpouring of the Spirit of God in the Western States of America, &c.* Cincinnati: John W. Browne, Press, 1807.

———— (Pseudonym: E. Wright). *A Review of the Most Important Events Relating to the Rise and Progress of the United Society of Believers in the West; With Sundry Other Documents Connected with the History of the Society. Collected from Various Journals.* Union Village, O.: Union Press, 1831.

The Manifesto. Published by The United Society, vols. I–XXIX, January 1, 1871, to December 1899.

Title variations:

The Shaker (1871–1872) George A. Lomas, editor

Shaker and Shakeress Monthly (1873–1875) Frederick W. Evans and Antoinette Doolittle, editors

The Shaker (1876–1877) George A. Lomas, editor

The Shaker Manifesto (1878–1882) George A. Lomas, editor

The Manifesto (1883–1899) Henry C. Blinn, editor

Meacham, Joseph. *A Concise Statement of the Principles of the Only True Church, According to the Gospel of the Present Appearing of Christ. &c.* Bennington, Vt.: Haswell and Russell, 1790.

BIBLIOGRAPHY

Millennial Praises, Containing a Collection of Gospel Hymns, in Four Parts; *Adapted to the Day of Christ's Second Appearing.* Hancock: J. Talcott, 1813.

Wells, Seth Y. *Testimonies Concerning the Character and Ministry of Mother Ann Lee and the First Witnesses of the Gospel of Christ's Second Appearing; Given by Some Aged Brethren and Sisters of the United Society, Including Sketches of their own Religious Experience. Approved by the Church.* Albany: Packard & Van Benthuysen, 1827.

White, Anna [?]. *Presentday Shakerism.* Mt. Lebanon, N.Y., n.d. [ca. 1895?].

————. *The Motherhood of God.* n.p., 1903.

White, Anna, and Taylor, Leila. *Shakerism, Its Meaning and Message.* Columbus, Ohio: Fred J. Heer, 1904.

Youngs, Benjamin S. *The Testimony of Christ's Second Appearing, Exemplified by the Principles and Practice of the True Church of Christ.* Albany, N.Y.: The United Society, 1856.

Selected Further Readings, Annotated

1. General Bibliography

MacLean, J. P. *A Bibliography of Shaker Literature, with an Introductory Study of the Writings and Publications Pertaining to Ohio Believers.* Columbus, Ohio: Fred J. Heer, 1905. [The first general bibliography of Shaker works and related materials.]

Richmond, M. L. *Shaker Literature: A Bibliography, in Two Volumes. Vol. I, By the Shakers; Vol. II, About the Shakers.* Hancock, Mass.: Shaker Community, Inc., 1977. [A nearly complete bibliography to 1976.]

2. Camisards

Lacy, John. *A Cry From the Desart: or, Testimonials of the Miraculous Things lately come to pass in the Cevennes, Verified upon Oath, and by other Proofs.* London: B. Bragg, 1707. [A translation of François Maximilien Misson, *Theatre sacré des Cévennes,* published during the height of the London excitement over the French Prophets.]

3. General History

Andrews, Edward Deming. *The People Called Shakers.* New York: Oxford University Press, 1953. [The most influential general history; limited in its presentation of theology/spirituality, as Andrews presumes a "classical form" of Shakerism as ca. 1850.]

Desroche, Henri. *The American Shakers; From Neo-Christianity to Presocialism.* Ed. and trans. John K. Savacool. Amherst: University of Massachusetts Press, 1971. [A reading of Shakerism as a social movement, seen from within a European socialist ideological context.]

BIBLIOGRAPHY

Melcher, Marguerite Fellows. *The Shaker Adventure*. Princeton: Princeton University Press, 1941. [A well informed general history with emphasis on the Ohio and Kentucky Societies.]

Robinson, Charles Edson. *A Concise History of the United Society of Believers Called Shakers*. East Canterbury, N.H.: [The Canterbury Society], 1893. [Sympathetic to Shaker thinking in the late nineteenth century; published by the Canterbury Shakers on behalf of The United Society.]

4. Communitarianism

Hinds, William Alfred. *American Communities: Brief Sketches of Economy, Zoar, Bethel, Aurora, Amana, Icaria, the Shakers, Oneida, Wallingford, and the Brotherhood of the New Life*. Oneida, N.Y., 1878. (Rev. ed 1902 and 1908.) [Shakers viewed as part of the American social experiment.]

Nordhoff, Charles. *The Communistic Societies of the United States; from Personal Visits and Observation: Including Detailed Accounts of the Economists, Zoarites, Shakers, the Amana, Oneida, Bethel, Aurora, Icarian, and Other Existing Societies*. New York: Harper & Brothers, 1875. [A detailed presentation of the post–Civil War communities.]

Noyes, John Humphrey. *History of American Socialisms*. Philadelphia: J. B. Lippincott & Co., 1870. [Shakers as part of the American social experiment.]

5. Cultural Studies

Andrews, Edward Deming. *The Community Industries of the Shakers*. New York State Museum Handbook 15. Albany: The University of the State of New York, 1933. [General industrial history.]

———. *The Gift to be Simple: Songs, Dances, and Rituals of the American Shakers*. New York: J. J. Augustin, 1940. [Emphasizes especially the forms developed in the 1837–1847 mystical revival.]

———. *Shaker Furniture: The Craftsmanship of an American Communal Sect*. New Haven: Yale University Press, 1937. [Presentation stresses the 1850's "classical forms."]

———, with Faith Andrews. *Visions of the Heavenly Sphere, A Study in Shaker Religious Art*. Charlottesville: The University Press of Virginia, 1969. [The inspirational drawings of the 1837–1847 mystical revival.]

Patterson, Daniel W. *The Shaker Spiritual*. Princeton: Princeton University Press, 1979. [Excellent and exhaustive study of Shaker worship music and related ritual forms (gesture, sacred dance, etc.).]

Sprigg, June. *By Shaker Hands*. New York: Alfred A. Knopf, 1975. [Wide-ranging presentation of every category of Shaker industry, craftsmanship, and tangible culture; theological/spirituality insight limited to the early nineteenth century as the "classical period."]

355

INDEX TO PREFACE,
INTRODUCTIONS
AND NOTES

INDEX

33, 156, 160; and Shaker decline, 22, 158 n 1

Christ, absent, 6, 7, 9; Anointing-, 211, 213, 305; Body of, 3, 13, 14, 19, 159, 180, 210, 212, 260, 268; and community, 2, 3, 33, 38, 43, 44, 45, 65 n 5, 159, 180, 181, 182, 184, 208, 259, 262, 305; Eternal-, 209, 210, 259; experienced, 1–3, 5, 12–14, 25, 31, 33, 38, 43, 44, 45, 181, 213, 268; "female-," 12, 28, 34, 44, 45 n 1; and gift, 1, 5, 30, 46, 87, 88, 208, 258–261, 306; and glory, 6, 7, 9, 12, 13; God-in-, 2, 5, 88, 211, 258, 305; identity with, 13, 45, 180; -in-us, 1, 5, 12, 13, 30, 88, 305; and Jesus, 212; life in, 1, 7, 87, 159, 208; and Mother Ann, 3, 11–14, 28, 34–35, 37, 43, 44, 45 n 1, 65 n 5, 88, 99 n 8, 207–210, 212; -nature, 14, 31, 156, 159, 211, 258; and perfection, 7, 16, 43–45, 259 n 2; Presence of, 1, 2, 3, 11, 12, 268; Second Coming of, 1–4, 6–15, 28, 31, 33, 34, 37, 38, 43, 44, 45, 88, 180, 212, 305; and sin, 10, 49 n 3; -Spirit, 14, 16, 31, 88, 145–146, 146 n 18, 210, 211, 259, 263, 268; as Truth, 25, 213; and Union, 1, 2, 5, 13, 14, 33, 38, 43, 44, 45, 180, 181, 184, 208, 260, 268, 305, 306; universality of, 25, 45, 46, 213

Christlife, and equality, 157, 208, 209; and Eucharist, 268; experience of, xiii, 4, 25, 87; and gifts, 88, 158, 259–261, 265; living of, 4, 13, 25, 27, 87, 156, 157, 180, 258, 261, 262, 264, 268; and *metanoia*, 156; and perfection, 16; sharing of, 33, 43, 158, 260, 268; as transformation, 30, 156, 208, 259, 264; unfolding of, 209

Christology, 38, 45 n 1, 88, 210–213

Church, as Bride, 212; as Christ, 44–45, 159, 210–213; and community, 28, 44, 180–183, 208, 211; -Order, 181–183, 208, 263, 266; and progression, 23, 87; separateness of, 24; Shaker-, 4, 28, 29, 46, 88,

180–183, 264 n 5, 304, 305; Union of, 24–26, 32, 212, 305, 306; universality of, 24, 26, 45–46

Clinton, Gov., 15

Clough, Elder Henry, 159

Colossians, 1:27, 1; 3:3, 1

Communism, economic, 23, 264; religious, 16, 31, 160; social-, 21, 23, 23 n 18, 31, 264

Community, cf. also Christ, Shaker Societies; and Believers, 4, 16, 43, 181, 208, 260, 264 n 5, 305, 309; call to, 180–181; and celibacy, 33, 158, 160, 181, 209, 209 n 2; and Church, 28, 44, 180–183, 208, 211; of Faith, 5, 26, 87, 159, 182; and gifts, 18, 33, 158, 180, 182, 183, 259, 260, 262, 263, 265, 266, 306; life of, 7, 16, 19, 22, 23, 28, 87, 158, 160, 181, 263, 264 n 5, 266, 303, 308; organization of, 16–18, 160, 208; and *parousia*, 6; of persons, 2, 259, 260, 304–305; and separation, 183, 306; and Shaker Way, 2, 16, 18, 28, 88, 264 n 5, 304–305; and witness, 32, 260; and worship, 19, 33, 260, 275 n 9

Cook, J.B., 39, 39 n 29

1 Corinthians, 7.9, 157; 7:29–31, 7; 12:11, 259; 15:44, 14; 15:51, 7

2 Corinthians, 3:18, 1

Cornelius, 145 n 17

Creation, in Genesis, 115 n 11, 210; New-, 13, 20, 44; "old-," 6; ordering of, 211

Darwin, 155 n 11

De Graw, Elder Hamilton, 211, 308

Dibble, Chauncy, 266

Doolittle, Eldress Antoinette, 160, 182, 305, 309

Dowe, Arthur, 308, 308 n 2

Dunlavy, Elder John, 30 n 22, 38, 44, 45, 69 n 7, 88, 159, 181, 211

Dyer, Joseph, 159

Eades, Elder Hervey, 88, 213, 265

Ecumenism, Alethian-, 25–26; Christian,

INDEX

4, 24–26, 33, 183, 212, 305–306, 308; world, 25–26, 212–213, 305–306, 308

Eleazar, Father, 267

Emery, Simon, 308

Engels, F., 23 n 18

Ephesians, 1:22, 180; 2:19, 17 n 14; 3:16, 263; 3:19, 12 n 10; 4:12, 15–16, 260; 4:13, 259 n 2

Eschatology, 1, 8, 33, 45

Eucharist, and absent Christ, 10, 268; as Real Presence, 10 n 9; and Shakers, 10, 265, 268

Evans, Elder Frederick, 23–24 n 18, 88, 115 n 11, 145–146 n 18, 155 n 19, 160, 182, 211, 212

Experience, of Believers, xiii, 1, 3, 8, 12–13, 18, 23, 31, 33, 37, 43–45, 87, 99 n 8, 207–209, 212, 213; of Christ, 1–3, 5, 12–14, 25, 31, 33, 38, 43, 44, 45, 181, 213, 268; of Christlife, xiii, 4, 25, 87; of Faith, xiv, 31, 37, 44, 45; and Shakers, 8, 33, 38, 46; and Shaker Way, 2–3, 5, 26, 210

Faith, community of, 5, 26, 87, 159, 182; experience of, xiv, 31, 37, 44, 45; as process, 33, 114 n 10, 115 n 11, 309

Frazer, Elder Daniel, 160, 182, 308

Galatians, 3:28, 2

Gifts, cf. also Christ, Christlife, God; backward-, 261; and celibacy, 156, 158, 160; come-up-higher-, 119 n 13, 261, 262, 267, 306; and community, 18, 33, 158, 180, 182, 183, 259, 260, 262, 263, 265, 266, 306; diversity of, 24, 261, 265, 266; ecstatic-, 17, 19, 31, 262, 263, 267; evaluation of, 260–261, 263, 306, 308; -forever, 263, 306; and forms, 29, 33; forward-, 261; and Gospel, 86, 262; inspirational-, 266–267; leading-, 260; and need, 258, 260, 262; and progression, 261–263, 264 n 5, 267, 268, 306, 308; receiving of, 258–259, 263, 265, 266; recognition of, 2, 88, 97 n 7; -for seasons, xiii, 32, 263, 265, 266, 303 n 1, 304, 306; sending of, 26, 32, 265;

and Shaker Way, 2, 4, 20, 26, 32, 304; sharing of, 33, 158, 260, 262, 265, 266, 268; simple-, 261–263, 265, 267; and Spirit, 2, 10, 18, 27, 259–264; travel in, 1, 261–263, 265, 306; Union is-, 260–261; witnessing-, 260, 268; and worship, 88, 260, 263–264, 266–268, 303 n 1

God, as Father-Mother, xiii, 28, 33, 38, 44, 45, 90 n 3–4, 207–213; as Gift, 2, 5, 30, 46, 191 n 4, 258–261, 306; and image, 210; Kingdom of, 6–8; is Love, xiii, 2, 8, 191 n 4, 258; mystery of, 45, 80 n 11, 209, 210; and union, 210, 260

Gospel, Christ of, 8; opening of, 14–16, 23, 86, 306; Path of, xiii; and "relation," 181; travel in, xiv, 33, 86–88, 211, 262, 267, 303; unfolding of, 25

Green, Elder Calvin, 35, 45, 159, 182, 183, 210

Grosvernor, Roxalana, 36 n 25

Hampton, Elder Oliver, 183, 213, 256 n 3, 266, 267, 308

Harmonism, 158

Hebrews, 12:1, 13

Hollister, Elder Alonzo, 25, 38, 160–161, 307

Incarnation, extending-, 209, 211; "new-," 12, 28

Jackson, Eldress Rebecca, 24, 308

Justin Martyr, 306

Kendal, Mother Hannah, 265

Lee, Ann, cf. Mother Ann

Lee, Father William, 14, 15, 17, 18, 99 n 8

Life, cf. also Christlife; "carnal-," 30; of celibacy, 15, 156, 158, 209, 209 n 2; and Christ, 1, 2, 13, 145–146 n 18, 208; common-, 7, 16, 19, 20, 22, 23, 28, 87, 158, 160, 181, 263, 264 n 5, 303, 308; Eternal-, 30, 182, 259; forms of, 21, 28, 86, 158, 208, 303, 303 n 1, 305, 308; and gifts, 2, 87, 97

INDEX

INDEX

INDEX

Mother-, 26; religious, 25–26, 38, 46, 305

Wardley, James, 6, 6 n 7, 8, 10, 159, 212, 303
Wardley, Jane, 6, 6 n 7, 8, 10, 159, 212, 303
"Waymarks," 18, 19, 20, 20 n 15
Webster, Eldress Ruth, 160
Wells, Elder Seth Y., 36 n 25, 37
Wesley, John, 132 n 15
Wesleys, 10 n 9
Wetherbee, William, 160
Whitcher, Elder Benjamin, 159
Whitcher, Eldress Mary, 159
White, Eldress Anna, 2 n 1, 24, 27, 31, 38, 264, 268
Whitman, Walt, 304
Whittaker, Father James, xiv, 4 n 5, 14,
15, 16, 17, 18, 86, 155 n 19, 159, 181, 265, 305
Worship, cf. also Progression; and community, 19, 33, 260, 275 n 9; and dance, 17, 263, 266, 267, 303 n 1; and ecstatic movement, 9, 17, 17 n 14, 263, 267, 273 n 8; and form, 9, 10, 17–20, 264, 265, 267; and gifts, 88, 260, 263–264, 266–268, 303 n 1; and life, 19; and music, 155 n 19; and silence, 9; and songs, 9, 18, 267; and Spirit, 10
Worster, Abijah, 265
Wright, Mother Lucy, 17, 18, 19, 260, 263, 264

Youngs, Elder Benjamin, 6 n 6, 34, 38, 44, 45, 45 n 1, 88, 181, 210, 211, 212, 266

INDEX TO TEXTS

INDEX /

Christ, absence of, 5, 57, 172, 298;
anointed, 223–225, 227, 231–234, 241,
243, 246, 248; blood of, 60, 67, 70,
297–299; body of, 46, 60, 63, 72–76,
79–83, 139, 140, 189, 190, 196, 203,
215, 220, 223, 227, 237, 238, 240–242,
244, 246, 282, 297–301, 332; Church
of, 51, 64, 65, 76–77, 82–84, 129,
133–135, 161, 162, 171–172, 196,
202–203, 223, 224, 232, 236, 238, 246,
249, 285, 298, 313; cross of, 47, 58,
63, 65, 66, 67, 77, 83, 98, 99, 113, 119,
161, 163, 170, 185, 186, 189, 196,
232–234, 239, 243; death of, 68–69,
146, 232, 298, 300; and Father, 66, 73,
81, 82, 83, 93, 98, 144, 146, 150, 162,
220–221, 223, 238, 245–248, 332; as
Father, 147–148, 150, 219, 223, 227,
231; and female, 216, 224–225,
239–240, 243, 248; first appearance
of, 48, 63, 98, 104, 106, 108, 139, 147,
149, 170, 216, 225–227, 232–233, 246,
248, 280, 281; fold of, 311; following
of, 47–49, 52, 63, 67, 69, 75, 98, 109,
147, 149, 150, 161, 166, 176, 196, 199,
217, 233, 245, 246, 298–300, 313, 332;
-in-us, 59, 80, 84, 85, 138, 166, 188,
192, 216, 223, 237, 241, 242, 252; and
Jesus, 136, 142, 147, 150, 168, 170,
198, 201, 216–219, 226, 227, 231,
237–238, 241–243, 245, 246–248, 250,
252, 312, 313; Kingdom of, 53–55,
64, 66, 84, 122, 133, 166, 167, 171,
199, 231, 241, 285, 300, 301, 315, 334;
life of, 187, 243, 250, 313, 316, 317,
324, 325; as mediator, 99, 213, 217,
230, 249, 251; -order, 179, 219, 244,
246; power of, 63, 65; pre-existence
of, 250–252; presence of, 46, 123,
137, 298; promise of, 48, 57, 61, 63,
73, 105, 123, 202, 232, 237, 280, 281,
345; and revelation, 64, 66, 76, 126,
128, 129, 133, 217–219, 221, 228; and
salvation, 47, 57, 62, 68–72, 74, 76,
77, 80, 134, 147, 170, 215, 216, 226,
231; as second Adam, 82, 146, 170,
225; -sphere, 250–252, 257; -Spirit,
47, 49, 53, 55–57, 59, 60, 77, 80–81,
84, 85, 133–136, 138, 140, 142, 146,
152, 170, 175, 188, 191, 192, 195,
202–203, 215–220, 223, 232, 237, 244,
245, 246, 248, 250–251, 318; suffering
of, 67, 69, 146, 232; union with, 60,
73, 83, 140, 146, 163, 165, 189, 229,
242–247; witness of, 188, 240–242,
276, 335; work of, 46, 56, 98, 100,
122–123, 139, 140, 148, 152, 192, 198,
216, 227, 241, 246, 302, 345; and
world, 161–163.

Christ-life, 119, 126, 201, 294, 324

Christ's Second Appearance, to all,
136–137; and Antichrist, 64, 66, 105;
character of, 237–240; and Church,
47, 61, 78, 80, 83, 129, 147, 171, 175,
228, 233, 236, 239–241, 252, 341;
desire for, 51, 53–55, 57; and female,
225; following of, 146–147, 149; and
gospel, 194, 196; and Mother Ann,
48, 57, 80–82, 84, 99, 135–137,
146–152, 176, 198, 226, 228, 229, 232,
240–243, 250; and Resurrection, 112;
and revivals, 185; and salvation, 63,
74, 83, 145, 147, 170, 226, 232, 235;
and Scripture, 106, 133; testifying
to, 58, 107, 270; work of, 99, 108,
129, 133, 139, 148; and worship,
280–281

1 Chronicles, 13:8, 281

Chrysostom, 201

Church, cf. also Faith; anointed, 74, 198,
224, 241, 243; and celibacy, 162–163,
171, 197, 201, 249; ceremonies of,
185, 339; is Christ, 74, 77, 220; is
Christ's body, 46, 60, 72–76, 79–83,
139, 196, 203, 215, 220, 227, 238,
240–242, 301; Christian, 122, 136,
172, 246, 317; and community, 171,
175; divided, 313, 314, 318–319, 322,
325, 330; and equality, 171, 175, 193,
194, 203; false-, 232; and future,
171–172, 206, 334; and gifts, 54, 78,
83, 145, 194, 203, 205, 286;
government of, 194–195, 203–204,
285–286; head of, 59, 78–80, 113, 135,
196, 215, 220, 223, 238, 240, 241, 312,
321; and Holy Spirit, 79, 161; and

363

INDEX

146–147, 194, 242, 312; and creeds, 315, 325, 327; and gospel, 145, 194, 332; and obedience, 66, 78; oneness of, 113, 129, 133–134, 184, 282, 312, 317, 324, 332; and revelation, 105, 141; and Spirit, 133; strengthened, 48, 145; and testimony, 188; travel in, 114

Father, cf. also Christ; anointing of, 73; and Church, 129; and gifts, 105; in us, 244; love of, 143, 189; and perfection, 116; and religion, 106; revealed, 66; and Son, 230–231, 238, 254; union with, 73, 137

Field, Floyd, 329

Fitch, Samuel, 54, 59–60

Frazer, Elder Daniel, 167, 198, 346

Galatians, 3:16, 73; 3:19, 217; 3:27–28, 162; 3:28, 77; 4:4, 231

Genesis, 1:25, 90; 1:28, 93; 3:4–5, 95; 6:9, 117; 17:1, 116

Gideon, 104

Gifts, and Church, 54, 78, 83, 145, 194, 203, 205, 286; diversity of, 279, 282, 284–285, 317; of inspiration, 277, 279; leading-, 246, 268, 272; and progression, 195–196, 272, 275, 295; promised, 63; of prophecy, 48, 65, 121; and Spirit, 48, 53, 57, 62, 63, 73, 79, 145, 194, 268, 282, 320, 338; spiritual-, 65, 295, 296, 343; from Spiritual World, 100

Gillespie, Eldress Mary, 301

God, cf. also Love; anger of, 65, 68, 106; anointed of, 56, 59, 80; attributes of, 214, 219–223, 251, 255, 257, 339; children of, 220, 237, 249, 256, 297; in Christ, 68, 143, 220–221; conceptions of, 144–145, 166, 220, 222, 249, 325; duality of, 254–256, 268, 286; Fatherhood in, 135, 136, 166, 168, 170, 213, 214, 217, 230, 232, 246, 249, 251–256, 268, 288, 311, 316, 331; fear of, 71, 166; image of, 67, 214, 221, 230, 239, 255; Kingdom of, 80, 111, 163, 168, 319, 320, 331; knowledge of, 66, 75, 110, 114, 117,

170, 220–221, 235, 249, 288, 294, 336; law of, 52, 62, 83, 90–92, 102, 130, 163, 169, 333; living-, 144; manifestations of, 59, 118, 170, 215, 229, 237, 296, 329; Motherhood of, 82, 135, 136, 143, 150, 166, 168, 170, 201, 213–215, 217, 230, 232, 246, 247, 249, 251–256, 268, 288, 311, 316, 331; mystery of, 63, 64, 79, 225; Order of, 106, 118; people of, 61, 62, 65, 76, 103, 109, 114, 129, 145, 146, 148, 161, 170, 187, 190, 191, 196, 221, 269, 271, 282; power of, 48, 53, 54, 57, 58, 62, 63, 65, 66, 75, 78, 82, 104, 105, 107, 130, 232, 249, 252, 253, 270, 272, 273, 275, 294, 318, 328, 329; presence of, 55, 93, 185, 187, 188, 334; promises of, 53, 55, 62, 78, 102, 109, 124, 150, 187, 234, 281; revelation of, 48, 56, 64, 65, 68, 76, 101–107, 128, 129, 131, 133, 141, 163, 166, 187, 196, 215, 220–221, 223, 226, 249, 254, 277, 280, 281, 297; separation from, 95–97, 100, 102, 106, 321; is Spirit, 221–223, 251, 255, 311; Testimony of, 102–107; truth of, 64, 65, 119, 125, 127, 131, 134, 191, 326, 327, 341; union with, 85, 91, 94, 97, 100, 136, 192, 205, 327, 330; visions of, 53, 296; will of, 62, 67, 69, 91, 93–104, 107, 117, 123, 130, 139, 188, 215, 232, 251, 279, 280, 284, 299, 311, 323, 327, 331; work of, 47, 53, 56, 57, 66, 75, 105, 107, 113, 117–119, 124, 126, 170, 171, 178, 185, 186, 190, 213–215, 217, 220–221, 228, 234, 241, 244, 247, 269, 271, 279, 293, 297, 332, 334

Godwin, William, 137

Goepper, Elder Leopold, 89

Goethe, 285

Goodale, Cornelius, 184

Goodrich, Dr., 51, 52

Goodrich, Hannah, 164

Gospel, cf. also Obedience; of Christ, 185–186, 194, 317, 319; and Church, 114, 193; freedom of, 192–195; -journey, 142; and law, 130, 146, 148–150; ministering of, 73, 343;

INDEX

INDEX